Mel Bay Presents

The AUTOHARP OWNER'S MANUAL

Everything from Maintaining to Building an Autoharp

Compiled and Edited by Mary Lou Orthey

Design and Illustration by Ivan Stiles

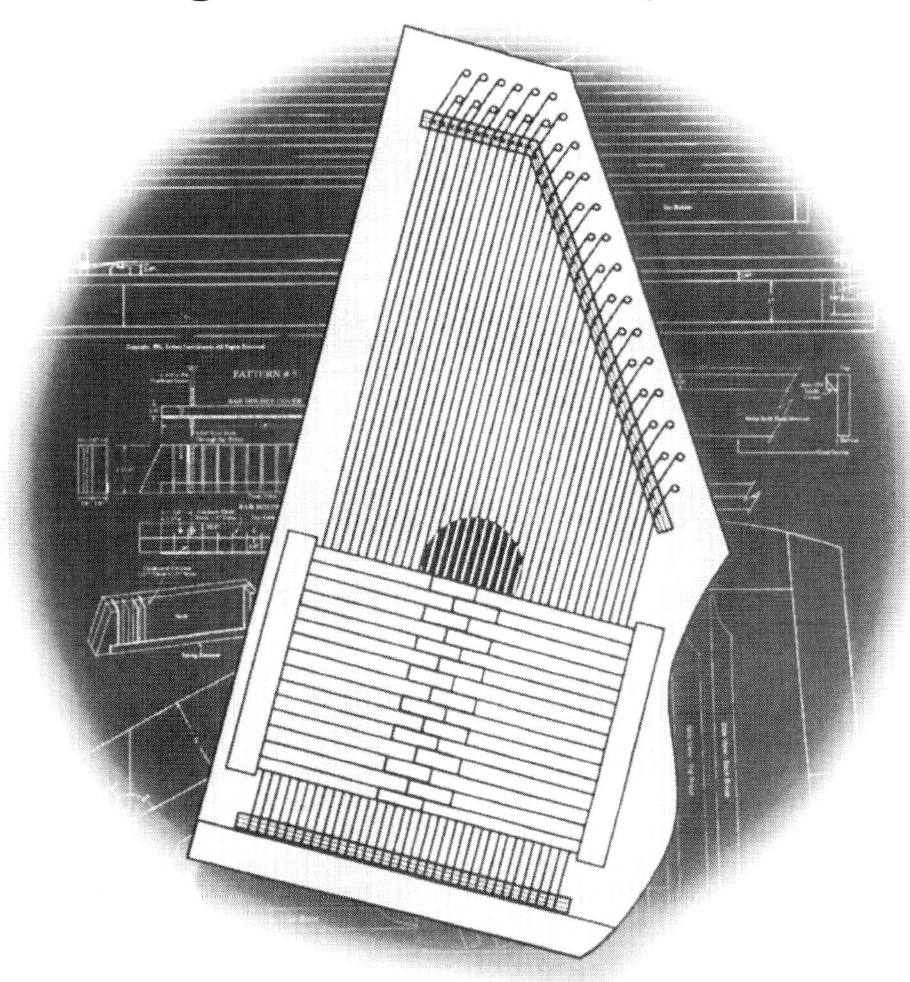

© 2000 BY MEL BAY PUBLICATIONS, INC., PACIFIC, MO 63069.
ALL RIGHTS RESERVED. INTERNATIONAL COPYRIGHT SECURED. B.M.I. MADE AND PRINTED IN U.S.A.
No part of this publication may be reproduced in whole or in part, or stored in a retrieval system, or transmitted in any form or by any means, electronic, mechanical, photocopy, recording, or otherwise, without written permission of the publisher.

Visit us on the Web at www.melbay.com — E-mail us at email@melbay.com

MW00650182

Foreword

This manual was compiled to fill a need for autoharp owners. So many folks live out in the boondocks (musically or geographically speaking) where they play their 'harps behind closed doors for their own amazement. Eventually they may graduate to small performances for their pets – and finally for their family and friends. Somewhere in this process, they will break a string and/or wear down the felts on their chord bars. What then? I've met more than a few souls in my travels who just play without that string, or push so hard on the offending chord bars they develop a sore wrist.

From 1988 through 1997, I published and coedited *Autoharp Quarterly*. In that magazine, my coeditor Ivan Stiles and I addressed maintenance problems along with a myriad of other subjects written especially for the autoharp player. The articles in this book are taken from those nine years of publication. Many have been updated to meet current innovations, problems, and instruments. Several subjects are addressed from varied but equally viable standpoints. (As the ol' banjer-maker said, "There's more 'n one way to skin a cat.")

It is my hope you will find this book to be invaluable in the maintenance and enjoyment of your wonderful and versatile autoharp, which Johann Sebastian Bach must have envisioned when he wrote: *"You only have to hit the right notes at the right time, and the instrument plays itself."*

Acknowledgments

All thanks to Ivan Stiles, who has once again pulled me through a publication with his fine graphics, experienced eye, wisdom, and uncanny patience; to the now publisher/editor of *Autoharp Quarterly*, Mary Ann Johnston; to Neal Walters whose computer wisdom has kept me sane; to Cathy Britell, Alan Mager, Dorothy Wagner, and Byrtis Walter for their proofreading, time, and caring; to the many autoharp teachers who kept after me to do this *now*; to Julie Davis and Alex Usher for their ever-present encouragement; to the contributors – Gregg Averett, Catherine Britell, Chuck Daniels, Carey Dubbert, Mark Fackeldey, Tom Fladmark, George Foss, Lindsay Haisley, John Hollandsworth, Alan Mager, George Orthey, Glen Peterson, Lucille Reilly, Marty Schuman, Ivan Stiles, Bob Taylor, Lyman Taylor, and Steven J. Young who have shared their knowledge with the autoharp community; and to Meg Peterson for her guidance in this effort, and for her manifold autoharp books which helped me come out from behind my own closed doors in the first place.

Mary Lou Orthey
Newport, Pennsylvania
Spring, 2000

To George

The Autoharp Owner's Manual

Alphabetical Listing

The Autoharp Owner's Manual

Listing by Subject Matter

MAINTENANCE

TUNING AND CHORDS

CONVERSIONS

STRING SCHEDULES

ADD-ONS

MECHANICS

PERFORMANCE

HISTORY

Annual Mechanical Tune-up

AQ Volume IX, Number 3

IT S SPRINGTIME!

George Orthey

It's sulphur and molasses time again – with maybe a bit of fiddlehead "salat" thrown in for good measure. Time to dig out of the winter blahs and get your well-played autoharp ready to go for the music season.

Worse than castor oil is the idea of restringing and refelting your 'harp. But these procedures are periodically necessary to keep your 'harp up to top performance. You will find chapters covering these topics in this book.[1] I'll not redo that detail here, but add a few ideas.

The most obvious question is "How do I know it needs new strings and/or felts?"

If you play a lot, I recommend restringing every two years – maybe even every year, if you really give it a workout on a near daily basis. If your strings are just tarnished a bit, a piece of Scotch Brite (a plastic scouring pad) will do a nice job of cleaning up the strings. I personally don't see the need to use this on an everyday basis. Others do. This is up to you. Also, even if the tops of the strings look clean, hook your fingernail under a string and slide it along. See if you peel off a ridge of dirt from the under side of the string. Even worse, your string might have a rough scratchy feel, indicating rust and corrosion. If so, a restringing will do wonders for the sound of your 'harp.

Your felts will tell you when they need replacement. They will tell you in pain, because you have to push so hard to get damping, and they will tell you in play-through (the strings which should be damped play through). Take a look under your chord bars. Gently press down your most common chord. If you can see deep cuts in the felt where it meets the strings, you obviously need refelting or felt repair.

Something I have recently discovered in removing old felt is that you can remove the "stuff" from wooden bars and plastic/metal bars with heat, (yes, and without burning or melting the bar). We know it's easy with an aluminum bar to just put it on a low burner for a minute, heating it, then wiping the felt and "stuff" off the bar. Since wooden or plastic/metal bars can't stand this treatment, I just pull the bulk of the felt off the bar leaving the "stuff" behind. ("Stuff" is the residue left after the felt is removed. It's made up of a thin amount of adhering felt, a layer of two-sided sticky tape, and a layer of glue.) Put a flat piece of metal on top of a low-heat burner, and let it heat the metal plate *just* to the point where it steams off a drop of water. Touch the "stuff" side of the bar to this plate for a couple of seconds, and quickly scrape the melted layer off the bar. This leaves a clean surface except for a very thin layer of the old contact glue. This layer will help the new felt stick firmly in place. Just touch the bar to the metal long enough to melt the "stuff" without heating the bar itself.

If you only have one or two bars to clean off, just stick with the tried and true method of tediously scraping the residue off with a knife edge or chisel.

You may find a felt that has a low spot, or maybe a soft spot, which lets the unwanted strings play through. Find the area of play-through and tease the felt up so it makes good contact with the strings. Use the old hat pin or ice pick to repeatedly jab holes in the side of the felt.

When you get the spot puffed up to where it's giving you a straight felt with even damping, stabilize the area by putting some glue into the side of the felt. Silicone glue is best because it remains flexible. I've also done this with Elmer's Glue. Just don't get the glue up onto the top surface of the felt. Let this set up and dry (eight hours) before you use the bar.

Another option for quick repairs of a badly worn bar felt is to silicone it. You don't have to take the felt off. Put a layer of DAP 100% Silicone Sealant or similar Silicone glue on the face of the felt being sure the deep string cuts are completely filled. Place the bar firmly onto a piece of wax paper – felt-side down – on a perfectly flat surface (do *not* rock the bar) and let the glue set up over night. The next day, remove the wax paper and trim away the excess silicone. You again have a straight, flat felt surface.

Siliconing felts is great, if you don't mind the silicone "squick" and "sprong" sounds. To alleviate these sounds for the fussy players, I put a good dusting of chalk line powder on the bars right after removing the wax paper. This helps reduce the squickiness and sprongimess considerably. (Try those two words in your next Scrabble game!) With a layer of silicone rubber on it, a bar will last at least five to ten times as long as the original felt.

Occasionally, one may find two bars slightly too close to each other. If the felts stick out from the side of one or two of those bars, they will hang up at that point, going up and down together. The glue layer is the worst offender here. This can usually be trimmed back even with the bar, using a sharp razor blade, and cutting carefully along the offending side of the bar.

On hand-crafted 'harps that have the bars on combs made out of Delrin, the "teeth" of the Delrin comb may actually be slightly bent away from each other, separating the bars. Give the comb tooth a good push in the direction you want the offending bar to go. The Delrin will not break. But *don't* try it with an Oscar Schmidt extruded plastic comb. These will not bend, and most certainly will break. The Delrin comb teeth will stay in place once you get them where you want them.

Back to strings. After you put new strings on your 'harp, be sure you level the string bed.

If your autoharp has fine tuners, be sure they are all level, if the fine tuner is in fact your dead-pin end bridge. For hand-crafted 'harps where there is a bridge in front of the fine tuners, it is not necessary to level the fine tuners, except for the esthetics of appearance.

To check for level string bed, lay a good straight edge across the string bed. Without pressing the straight edge down more than enough to keep it in place, lightly play each string. You'll no doubt find areas in which you have strings that play loud and clear. If the strings are perfectly level, they should, each and every one, buzz or rattle against your straight edge. With an uneven bed, the rattlers are high, and the clear-playing strings are low. Most often the worst offenders are the very large wound strings, which stand above the string bed because of their large diameter, and the largest non-wound strings in the middle C area. There isn't a whole lot you can do with the big wound bass strings except to lower the bridge or string stop point for the lowest three or four strings. The large stiff non-wound strings are easy to correct once you understand why they stick up above the rest of the string bed. Here's a cross-section of a dead pin bridge as on a model A-type 'harp:

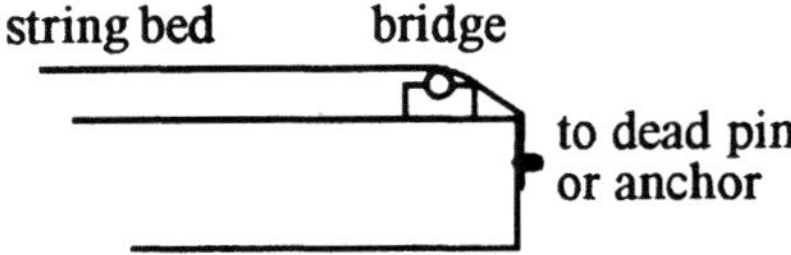

Small diameter wires bend easily over the bridge, and go straight from the bridge out across the string bed. Large stiff wires resist bending over the bridge, so we see the wire coming off the bridge substantially above the string bed:

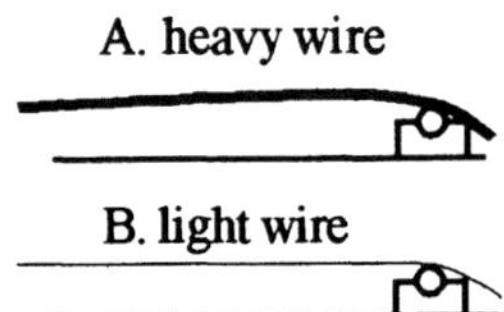

The wire arches up over the bridge, then out onto the string bed (A) above the level of the thin wires of the upper octave and small wound strings. The larger core wire of the low bass strings also contributes to this high string level effect along with their larger diameter. The net result will usually be substantial play-through of the smaller wound strings.

So how do we get this all straight? We can't very well raise the low strings, but we can lower the high ones. Simply by taking advantage of the problem itself, which is a very stiff large diameter wire at the bridge. Just simply, with the 'harp fully up to tune, bend the offending high wires down across the bridge:

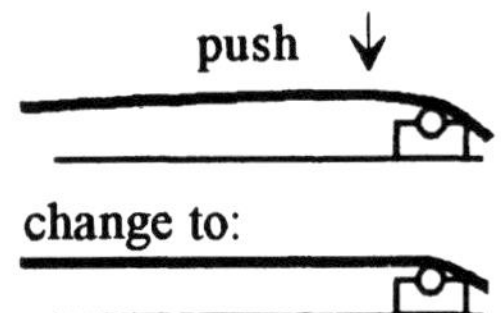

Push down firmly on the wire just in front of the bridge which will force a conforming bend over the bridge. Once this bend is present, the wire will stay down in that position because of its large stiff nature. The greatest down push is needed at the lowest large non-wound strings with diminishing amount of bend needed on up through the middle octave. The smaller strings will lie flat on their own. Some correction of the lowest bass strings (1F, 2G, 3C) which all have larger stiffer core wire can be achieved by giving these strings a downward bend over the bridge, also.

This problem is present but to a lesser degree in the fine tuners/anchor bar system of Oscar Schmidt because of the large radius of the stop as compared to the small bridge rod. It will, however, still have some of the same effect of giving play-through of the small wound strings and may need leveling to a lesser degree.

On at least some hand made 'harps, the correction for the very large bass strings is built in by lowering the bridge under the several largest wound strings.

All of this of course assumes a level 'harp body and bridge system. A badly warped or bent out of shape 'harp will require major surgery, and then only if the instrument is worth it.

If you are restringing and not refelting, which is most likely the case, you should be sure that the new strings are exactly in the same place as the old ones. At the tuning pin end of the string, they will be exactly where the old ones were, but at the dead pin/fine tuner end, the strings may be as much as 1/16" out of place horizontally. When you put the strings on, before you tune it up, try a slightly worn bar in place and see if the strings are lined up with the grooves of the bar felt. If they are not, loosen the string and align it; then tighten it up again. This way, the new strings will be pre-seated in the chord bar felt and you won't have a break-in period of zips and sizzles.

Last but not least, tune it up as soon as you restring it. Don't leave it in a random tuning. Tune it again the next day.

Now it's time to fix a mess of dandelion and poke greens – or collard greens and bacon, so we can be sweet and healthy – just like our 'harps! ❖

[1] For a complete and detailed rundown of restringing and refelting, see "Restringing The Autoharp" p. 23 and "Refelting And Siliconing Chord Bars" p. 7.

Chord Bar Arrangements

AQ Volume V, Number 4; Volume VI, Numbers 1, 2

HOW TO STRIKE A FAMILIAR CHORD

George Orthey

My purpose here is not to show you the "best way" or the "only way" to place your chord bars on your instrument. The aim here is to show you some of the many ways you can arrange the bars for your specific comfort and convenience. You choose. I will also explain the rationale (to the best of my ability – a few defy explanation) for each method.

A Bit Of History

One question I often get is, "Where or how did anyone decide the 15-bar-good-old-standby-sold-by-the-millions Oscar Schmidt was a good chord bar arrangement?" Well, to that light, let's take a brief history trip through the evolution of chord bar placement. (Note: All the chord bar arrangements are described as you look at the 'harp in your lap, long bass side toward you.)

In Karl Gütter's old original Chord Zither, (which we now believe Charles Zimmermann chose to copy rather than manufacture the very complicated autoharp of his own invention),[1] a simple C Major scale was used. The chord bars were laid out like this:

IV / F   V⁷ / G⁷   I / C

By adding a B♭ note, (A♯), to the scale, the key of F was added:

B♭   C⁷   F   G⁷   C

Later, players wanted a few other stray chords, so the next three chords were added on the end like so:

Gᵐ   A⁷   Dᵐ   B♭   C⁷   F   G⁷   C

A mechanical genius came on the scene and decided more chords could be added by placing the buttons on the 'harp in two tiers. So the standard twelve bar setup was added to the foray:

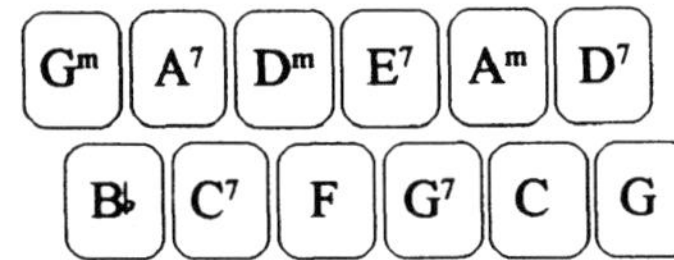

Segments of the chord bar arrangement from the previous setups were meticulously kept intact, and new chords were tacked on without any uniform systematic logic. The final stage (affront) was then to add:

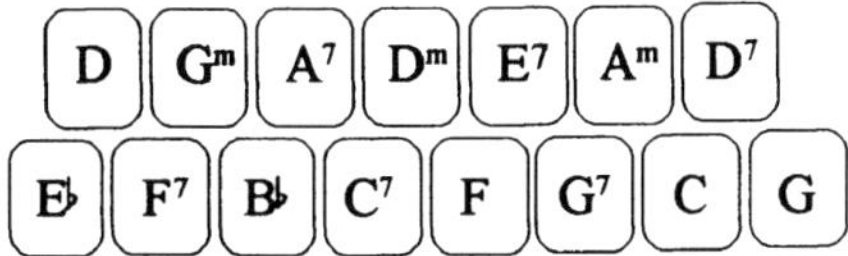

This innovation not only added the key of B♭, which was good, but it also, as an added bonus, enabled people with the hand span of Michael Jordan to play in the key of D!

The 21-bar arrangement followed with the chord bars in a logical systemic layout. The chord bar setup was essentially now the same for each key:

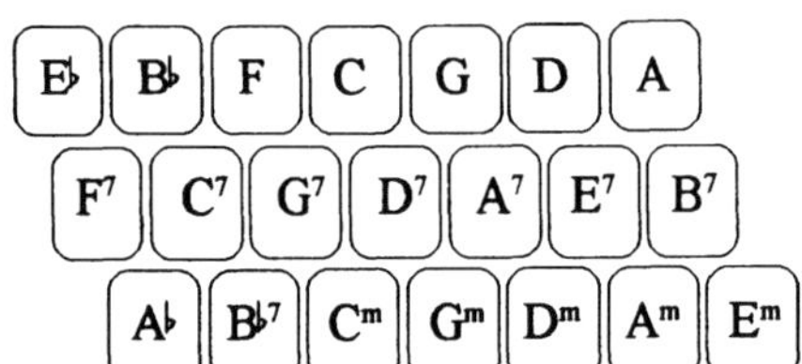

Because autoharp playing becomes ever more exacting and demanding, history continues to move its hand rapidly across the evolution of this instrument. In the interest of the players who use my 'harps, I've taken the standard arrangements many steps further. Let me show you a few very simple, minor variances that are widely accepted by today's players.

In most chromatic 'harps, unless otherwise specified, I remove the A♭ and $B\flat^7$ from the bottom tier, move all the minors over, and add B^m and $F\sharp^m$. And so, the bottom tier of the 21-bar 'harp would then be:

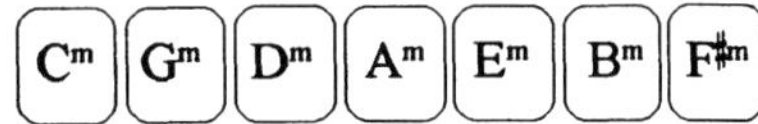

This places the relative minor directly below the major and removes the seldom-used inconsistent key of E♭.

Another simple variant of this standard layout desired by "old-time" music players, is to add a key of E. This is done by changing the $F\sharp^m$ to an E chord. Thus:

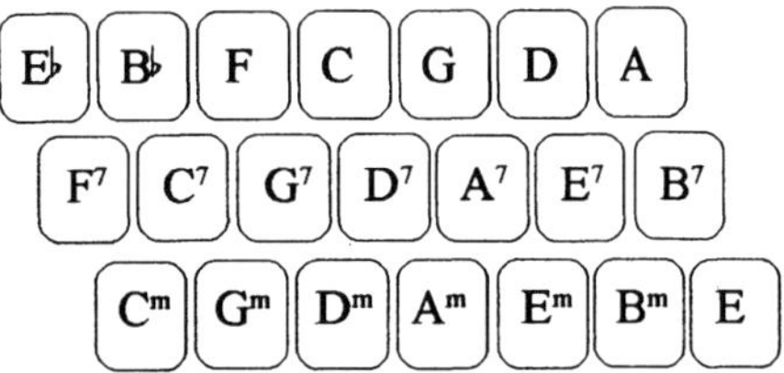

Let's also now bring in two other common standard chord bar setups – the Oscar Schmidt Festival and the Wildwood Flower 'harps.

First, look at the Festival 3-key diatonic in the keys of F, C, G:

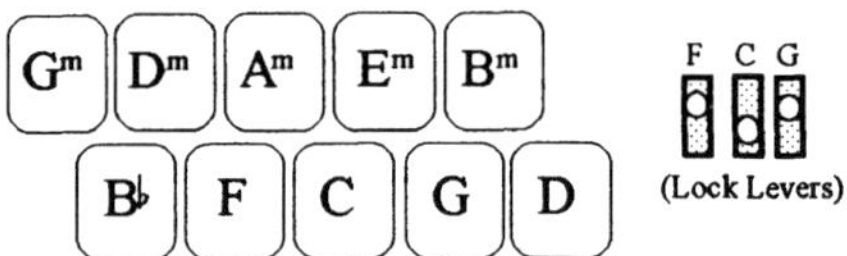

– and the Festival in the keys of G, D, A:

Notice that the Festival 'harps lack the seventh chords in their original configuration. Some players cut the sevenths in themselves. If you do this, you must use the lock levers to play in the keys of C and G, or D and A, depending on which 'harp you have.

Second, the Wildwood Flower single key (key of D) diatonic 'harp takes a leaf from the original Gütter/Zimmermann 'harp. The major chord setup is the old IV, V^7, I with the three relative minors above them:

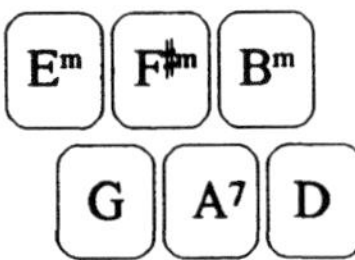

So we have four commercially made 'harps – the 15-bar, the 21-bar, the Festival, and the Wildwood Flower. Bar setups are inconsistent one from another, thus driving many serious performers out of their minds. One solution is to develop a logical, uniform chord bar arrangement to apply to all. Another is to play only one 'harp.

Today's Players

Most serious performers do want to play more than one autoharp for various reasons, and have developed chord bar arrangements that are consistent, logical, and comfortable. We'll take a look at several of these arrangements, both chromatic and diatonic. When possible, I'll comment on why the player picked his particular bar setup. Note the chord bar patterns shown aren't to full scale size as found on the 'harp. Make a full-sized diagram of the chord bar arrangement you want to try on a piece of paper and tape it over your bars. Now try the hand comfort, fingering, and chord bar accessibility.

My Variation of the 21-Bar 'Harp

In the first part of this chapter, I described two variations that are frequently desired on the 21-bar chromatic 'harp. I change the lower tier of bars of this 'harp from:

A♭ B♭^{7} C^m G^m D^m A^m E^m

to:

C^m G^m D^m A^m E^m B^m F♯^{m}

If you would want the key of E, make the end bar an E Major rather than F♯^{m}. Another alternative to get a key of E diatonic scale only is to add an Orthey Bar[2] for the key of E, which will change the already existing E^7 to E Major without sacrificing the F♯^{m} chord.

If you want to shift your chromatic 'harp in the circle of fifths, for example – if you want to play in the keys of E, B, and F♯, and if you don't care about B♭, F, and C, see Figure 1 in the next column.

Figure 1:

E♭ B♭ F \ C G D A \ E B F♯
F^7 C^7 G^7 \ D^7 A^7 E^7 B^7 \ F♯^{7} C♯^{7} G♯^{7}
C^m G^m D^m \ A^m E^m B^m F♯^{m} \ C♯^{m} G♯^{m} D♯^{m}
Take these three off. Add these three.

Figure 2:

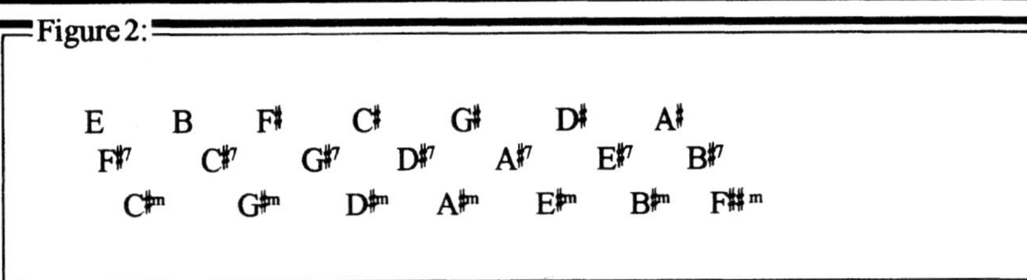

Similarly, you can move your chord bars anywhere you want on the Circle of Fifths.[3] For the harper who wants everything, move one 'harp to the "back side" of the Circle. See Figure 2 above.

After you've perused Figure 2, you may say " E♯? B♯? F♯♯? *Whoa*!" – (You know them better as F, C, and G.)

You've now come full circle. So, armed with two autoharps at the next festival, you can play in every key! Your "back side 'harp" will drive the jammers nuts!

The Gospel According to Bryan Bowers

– has to do with sweet tuning, fullness of sound, room to play, and *hand comfort*. His preference can mainly be used for single key diatonics. However, it is adaptable and logical for multiple key or chromatic autoharps.

Here's his single key (D) diatonic setup:

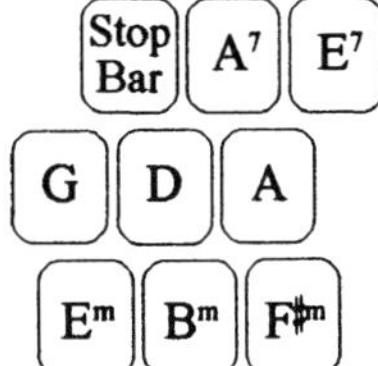

Bryan plays bars G, D, and A with fingers number one, two, and three. He shifts up with finger number three to play the A^7. He plays the partial key of A with the same hand position over one space. The relative minor is played by moving the same finger from the major down to the minor. The Stop Bar mostly fills a space, but he uses it occasionally to stop all of the strings.

Bryan's gospel extended to a full 21-chord setup would be:

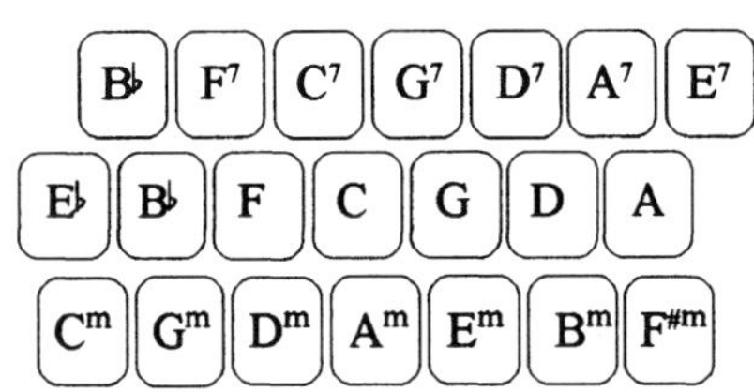

This can be done completely on a 21-bar open chord bar system, like the ChromAharp and most luthier 'harps. The cover of the Oscar Schmidt would prevent the E^7 chord in this configuration. A variant of this would be to move the sevenths all to the left one position. This results in a very tight triangle of chords for each key:

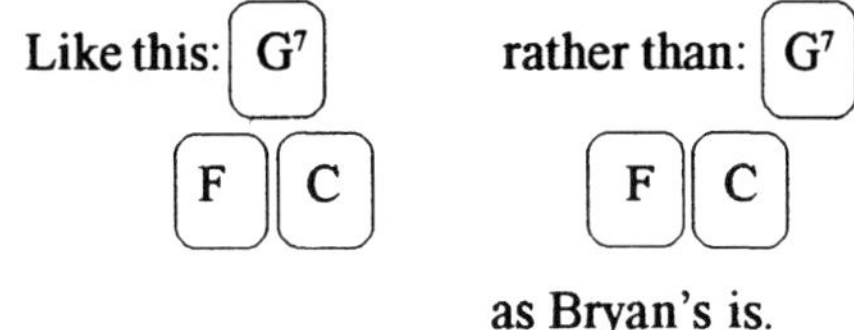

as Bryan's is.

Great Minds Stomp Down the Same Furrow

John Hollandsworth and my wife, Mary Lou, learned to play on a 15-bar autoharp. They, each not aware of the other, wanted 21 bars, and independently came up with the exact same solution. With some imagination, they arrived at a consistent restructuring by taking a 15-bar segment as the standard for the entire setup:

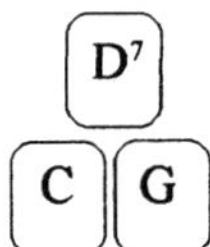

By repeating this configuration across the bottom two rows in the sequence of the Circle of Fifths, the desired range of keys was obtained. Now all keys can be played like the key of G on the 15-bar 'harp. The minors are logically placed in the top row above their relative majors.

The resulting chord bar arrangement used by Mary Lou is:

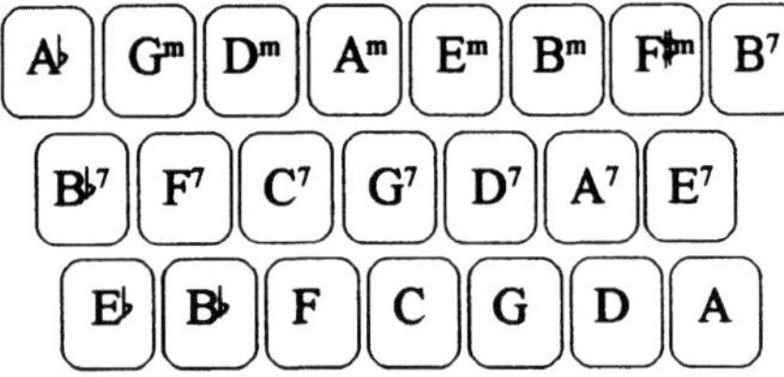

You will notice her 'harp has twenty-two bars. The inconsistent A♭ and B^7 have been added to the top row.

John's 'harp is similar, except it has twenty-one bars, with no B^7 chord.

"Oh, C♯ is a Wonderful Key!" – Mike Fenton

One of Mike's many autoharps is his C♯ 'harp. He loves its tuning.

Mike also likes the diminished 7th chords.[4] He sort of turns Oscar's pattern upside down with the relationship of majors to sevens similar to Bryan's. And Mike likes the diminished 7th chords, a common item on the want list of many chromatic players. (John and Mary Lou have now added diminished 7ths to their 'harps as well.) Mike's setup is:

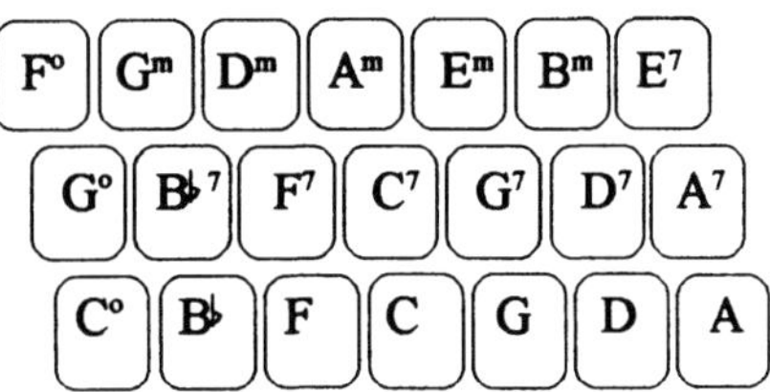

This 'harp only plays in five keys. The E added variant of the modified standard Oscar layout (mentioned earlier in this article) plays in seven keys.

Mike's single key 'harps have evolved over a period of time. He uses unusual chords, like suspended fourths. One example of his most common and recent chord bar arrangement is in the key of C:

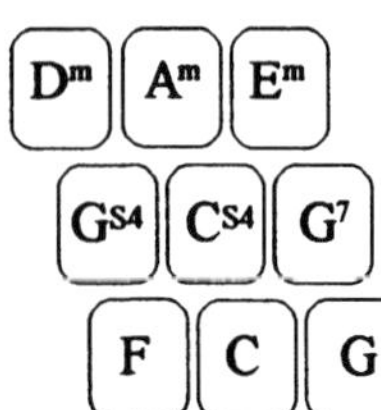

and his single key system is consistent with his 21-bar 'harp.

Drew Smith

Drew, a great thumb lead man, I believe played an old 15-bar 'harp, and liked the two-tier configuration. He plays, for the most part, only one autoharp – a chromatic one. His main requirement of the 'harp is to be able to play in as many keys as possible. His 'harp has twenty-two narrow bars. It has the greatest range of keys of any I know:

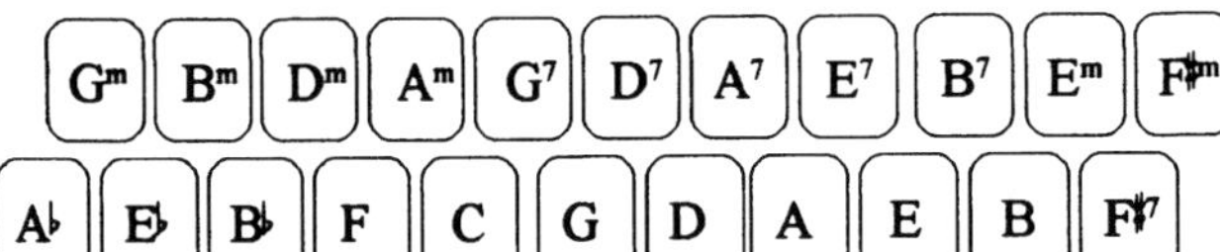

This system uses the same finger pattern for the three chords of each key, being similar to Bryan Bower's pattern. However, with only two tiers of chord bars the group is closer together. This system requires customized chord bars, and cannot be done as a variant of the OSI 21-bar system. This arrangement plays in nine keys, (E♭, B♭, F, C, G, D, A, E, B), giving a full octave range. The only major drawbacks I see are that it requires custom bars, the relative minors are not all near their majors, and the chord bars are quite close together.

Martha Kiker

Martha Kiker is a very fine all-around instrumentalist. I have used her chord bar arrangement not only for the Annabelles (one of the old-time bands in which she plays), but also now for all three-key diatonic 'harps I make where the future owner needs help with bar placement.

Martha's main concern was "I play a 21-bar standard autoharp. Why can't I have my three-key diatonic 'harp as a segment of my 21-bar setup, so I don't have to learn a new pattern?"

Sooo…if you take the GDA segment from my standard 21-bar 'harp:

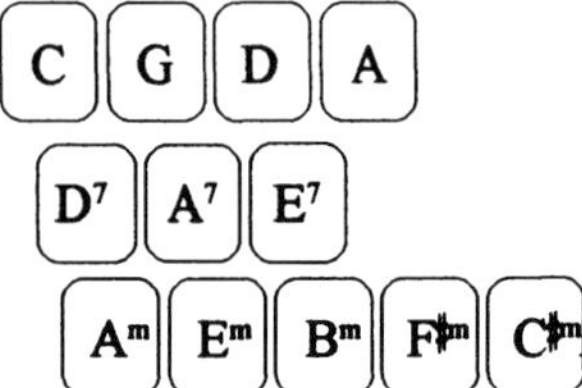

Consider the above, and move the C♯m up next to the E^7. Add the three lock bars for the three keys of G, D, and A. You will then have:

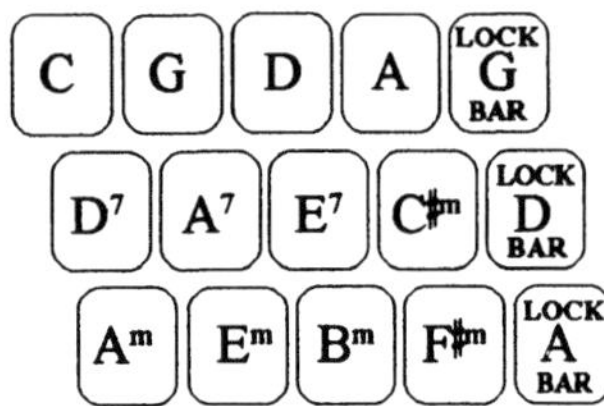

Because there are lock bars involved, a cover is needed. A 15-bar cover for this setup can be made by cutting off an OSI 21-bar black plastic cover to the 15-bar width. With a bit of doctoring around, you can make it fit.

Ivan Stiles

The first revision of the single key diatonic was done with Ivan to incorporate the three major and three minor chords, and to add a partial seventh chord of the next key to extend the single key 'harp to perform in two keys …almost. Thus the 1 7/8 key 'harp[5] was born:

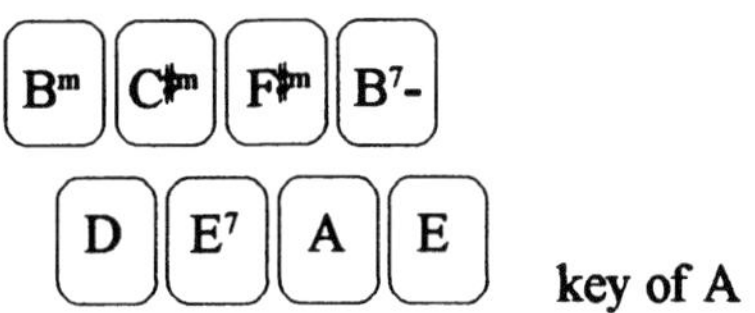

key of A

In this 'harp, the B^7 does not have the third, but is a three-note chord of the one, five, seven notes. The B^7 chord normally has the notes B, D♯, F♮, and A. In the B^7-, the D♯ is missing. It makes a good chord and almost doubles the capability of the single key 'harp.

The setup of the ever-popular D 'harp would be:

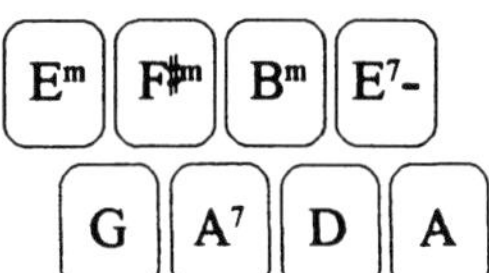

Janette Carter

Janette always played a 15-bar autoharp:

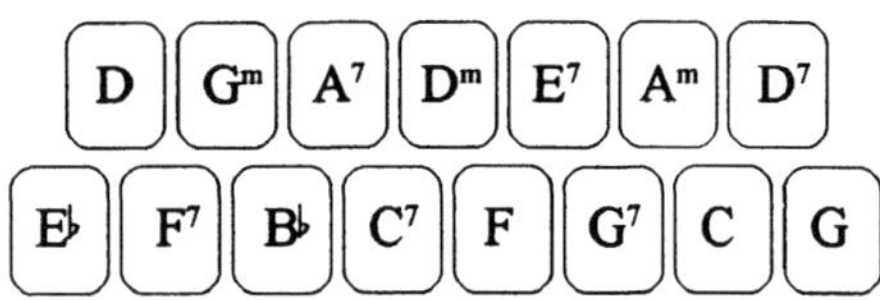

…but she loved the sound of the key of D on her autoharp.

Janette, however, doesn't even

come close to Michael Jordan for hand-spread. I said to her, "How often do you use the G^m chord?" And she said, "Well, hardly ever." Thus:

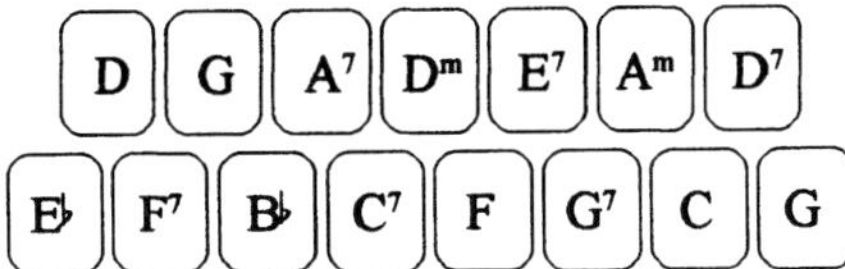

Make note of an often overlooked concept here. Do you have any chords you never play? If you do, you want to replace them with something you would use. The price of a chord bar change is a $2 piece of felt.

Joe (Kilby Snow) Riggs, and probably Kilby himself

We won't get into the upside-down and backwards part of this subject. Joe's (and Kilby's) 'harp is set up as a simple four-key C, G, D, A 'harp:

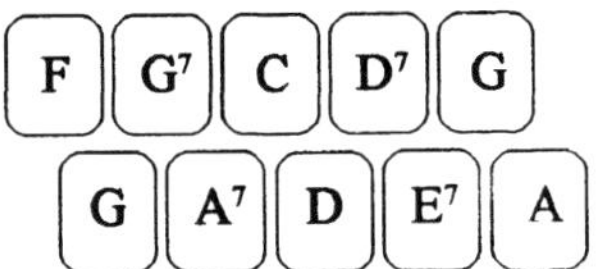

Note that the A♯ and D♯ notes are not needed in these chords. Kilby and Mike Seeger used/use them in their drag notes.

However in Joe's 'harp, the extra strings were used to gain some doubles. He made his E^7 chord an E^7-. (As discussed in the Ivan Stiles diatonic setup, the third is omitted in this chord.) Joe took out two D♯, three A♯, and two G♯ notes, plus he added a 37th string to the 'harp. Thus, he had eight extra strings to enhance the sound and range of the instrument. Joe's 'harp uses these extra strings to get a low D, and go up to a C♯ D at the top, and has five paired strings.

Lindsay Haisley

In Lindsay's book, you should have at least one autoharp with 150 bars, with a very nice chord bar arrangement for that two-key 'harp, as well. Here's Lindsay's setup for this instrument. You'll note that it contains only 18 bars, thus adding extra playing room. This 'harp has flip-open chord bar holders, thus giving him the ability to interchange chords:

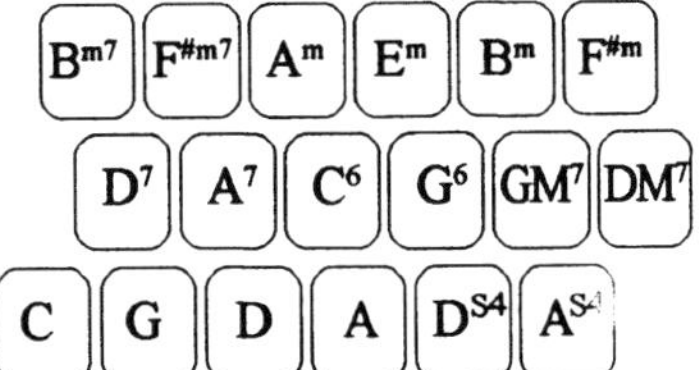

Don't worry if you don't understand this – I don't either. I'm not sure if anyone understands it – but Lindsay does, and that's all that counts. I do know however, from hearing him play, that nobody has any questions except "How does he do that?"

Addendum: September 1999

Nancy Carlisle

I have just built a 'harp with a chord bar setup I've not run across before:

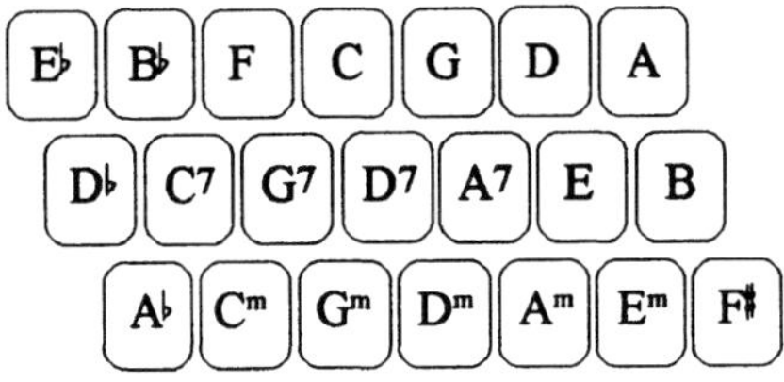

Although, in my opinion, the minors are placed a bit illogically, Nancy uses this setup, and can play in all 12 major keys! She has given up many of the sevenths and some minors, and a few chords have only six or seven notes playing. But it's one to try if you want to be able to play in *all* of the major keys. With these chords, you have it! ❖

Find Alan Mager's preference in chord bar setups for diatonics in "Chromatic To Diatonic Conversion" p.69, and Carey Dubbert's chord bar setup for diatonics in "Clean Melody Picking The Easy Way" p.66.

[1] See "The True History Of The Autoharp" p.125.
[2] The Orthey Bar is an add-on bar to turn a chromatic 'harp into a single key instrument.
[3] See "Questions And Answers" p.122 for information concerning the Circle of Fifths.
[4] See "Explanation And Use Of Diminished 7th Chords" p.49.
[5] See "Converting Your Autoharp To A 1⅞ Key Diatonic" p.60.

Refelting And Siliconing Chord Bars

AQ Volume IV, Number 4

FELT BAD ABOUT YOUR DAMPED 'HARP?

George Orthey

"How often should I refelt my 'harp bars?" is a question I get a lot in workshops. "How often" is mainly a factor of "how hard" and "how much" you play. I have an 1890s Dolgeville 'harp that plays reasonably well with its original felts. On the other hand, I have seen Laurie Sky and Judie Pagter wear felts halfway to the bars in six months.

Signs of needing new felts are: having to push the bars too hard; a fuzzy "zip" sound made by some damped strings when you push the bar down; the damped strings still make a faint fuzzy note with the bar down. This wear is most evident in the mid-range of the instrument, where you do most of your playing.

If you still need some help deciding, check one of your most-used chord bars. Push down gently on the bar while looking through underneath where the felt meets the strings. If you see sharp, peaked notches (like a knife cut) cut into the felt by the damped strings, it's time to refelt.

It is not necessary to refelt all the bars. Just do the ones that show significant wear. Felts used to replace worn bars should be like the other felts still on the 'harp. If they are not, you may find an unacceptable difference in action and touch.

Another question I hear frequently – "How about silicone glue?" There is no question that heavily siliconed bar felt is almost indestructible. (If you're going to use silicone on your felts, it's best to put it on after you have the felt on the bars, and before you notch them.)

The big "however" with silicone is the *squick!* and *sprong!* you get from the bars going on and off the string bed. Bryan Bowers puts it on like he is caulking seams in his fishing boat. Ivan Stiles' teeth split and his hair stands on end at the first *squick!* without even getting to the *sprong!*, which inevitably follows. However, some folks silicone their bars. So, here's the procedure:

Siliconing The Felts

If you plan to refelt your bars and choose to silicone them, it's easiest to do this before notching the bars. If you have worn, uneven felts already in use on your 'harp, siliconing is an option for correcting these problems without refelting. At any rate, the procedure is essentially the same in either case. The main difference is a lot more fussy trimming of the silicone on bars which are already notched.

A few things you need to do this:

1. Silicone rubber glue/caulking. I prefer the clear rather than color, finding it more durable and less noticeable. I recommend DAP 100% Silicone Sealant which is readily available at hardware, building supply, and automotive stores.

2. A piece of waxed paper to put under the siliconed bars while the silicone dries.

3. Chalk dust. This can be purchased from most hardware and building supply stores.

4. A perfectly flat surface so your bar face will come out perfectly flat. I use the machined table tops of my tools, such as a table saw. You can usually find a perfectly flat spot on your kitchen counter. Check it carefully with a good straight edge.

So here's how: Using a skill not unlike putting toothpaste on a toothbrush, squeeze a bead of glue along the felted face of the bar covering it from one end to the other. On a cut bar felt, don't fill the notches. Place the siliconed bar face down on the waxed paper which is on your flat surface. Placing your index finger of each hand (two of them, assuming you have just two hands) about two inches apart near the center of the bar, and press it down *firmly. Do not rock the bar end to end,* and be sure the bar is perfectly vertical – not slanted – on the flat surface. Take your fingers off without disturbing the bar. Do the same with each bar. Leave them alone, undisturbed overnight.

The waxed paper can then be peeled off the siliconed bar, leaving a shiny, thin layer of pliable silicone rubber. The maker of the glue says it lasts at least ten to twenty years. That's if you don't play your 'harp. Even so, the siliconed felt will out-last plain felt by at least five times, in my experience.

When you remove the waxed paper, you must trim the excess silicone that squeezed out from under the bar, so the silicone only remains on the face of the bar which normally dampens the strings.

The major drawbacks of *squick!* and *sprong!* can be reduced considerably by coating the newly siliconed face of the bar with chalk dust as soon as possible after removing the waxed paper. Put a sprinkling of the chalk dust on a sheet of newspaper and smack the siliconed face of the bar down smartly on it. Then brush away the excess from the bar. Just enough remains to greatly reduce the stickiness of the surface. The dust comes in red and blue, so you can have your artistic choice.

The stickiness of the bars naturally diminishes with time, so when the chalk eventually wears off, the bars are no longer sticky.

Another twist of this procedure used by some, is to silicone the bars right on the 'harp's string bed. This compensates for string beds that aren't perfectly level, and also results in reduced play-through of the heavy bass strings. (There will be a slight contouring of the silicone to the shape and positions of the strings.)

You will need to remove the bar covers and springs (leave the combs and bar guides in place) so the bars will sit down on the string bed. *Place waxed paper on top of your strings!*

Silicone your bars as above, placing them on the waxed paper-covered strings exactly in the correct position. You'll need to place a weight on top of the bars to hold them in place while the silicone dries. It's best to do every other bar one night, and the other odd bars a second night. This is a somewhat Draconian solution and is only needed in real problem 'harps, but it does work in my hands.

Squicks! and *sprongs!* notwithstanding, (your decision), I'll now try to guide you through the delicate subject of improving your damped 'harp by refelting those bars.

Before Removing The Bars

1. Write down the order of the chord bars so you can get them all back in the right place when you're done with the felting process.
2. Before removing the bars from the combs in the 21-bar 'harp, check to see that the chords are marked on the bars. They are usually marked on the side or bottom near the "round hole" end of the bar. If they are not marked, do so with a glass writing pen or other fine point pen (*not wax pencil or ball-point pen*). Use a pen that does not wipe off after it dries.

Before Removing Old Bar Felt

1. Place each bar back on the 'harp in its proper location one at a time. With the same pen used above, mark a line on the side of the bar directly above each string that is open. This line will be your reference for cutting the new felt.

Remove Bar Felts From A 15-bar 'Harp

1. I prefer here to straighten the bars. These bars in most cases are slightly curved, so that when placed against a straight edge, the ends of the bar do not touch the straight edge. This discrepancy can be corrected now, if you wish. (If you don't want to be so fussy, stop here and go on to #2 under this subtitle.)

To straighten these bars, tear off the old felt leaving the residue that sticks to the bar in place. Very gently sand the face of the bar using a long strip of sand paper on a flat surface (use a belt sander if you have one). Don't rock the bar back and forth. Keep it flat. You will find that the residue comes off the mid-portion of the bar, but not the ends. Stop when the mid-portion is cleaned down to base shiny metal. If you check the bar with a straight edge now, it should be flat from end to end. Coat the prepared surface of the straightened bars with contact cement. Make sure that the areas where the old felt base remains near the ends of the bar have been coated well. Let this coating dry completely, and apply the felt as described below.

2. If you don't want to straighten the bars, just remove all of the old felt and felt base by scraping it with the edge of a stout knife or chisel. Note that the felt base is a piece of cellophane tape much like two-sided Scotch tape. All of this plastic tape strip should be removed.

Removing Bar Felts From A 21-bar 'Harp

1. On ChromAharp-type instruments, where the bars are metal and plastic, the felt and felt base should be scraped off as above. On OSI 21-bar and Festival 'harps, where the bars are entirely aluminum, the bars can be heated. The felt strip glue is a hot melt glue. Heat the bars hotter than you can touch, but not red hot. When these bars are heated on a very low stove burner, the felt and felt base can be scraped off easily. The easiest way to handle a hot bar is to hold it at one end with a pair of needle-nosed pliers. Note: if you get the bars hot enough that the glue on them starts to smoke, they're too hot.

Applying Bar Felts

1. Felt sizes: 21-bar and Festival 'harp bars are normally 1/4" wide by 3/16" thick. 15-bar instrument bars are 5/16" wide by 1/4" thick. All felt strips come backed with pressure-sensitive glue, which is covered with a strip of waxed paper.
2. Remove the waxed paper. Be sure not to remove the felt base cellophane film!
3. On a 21-bar style chord bar, carefully align the felt with the bar at the "U" end, just short of the "U."

Lay the felt along the bar, keeping it aligned on each side until you reach the other end. The felt will be longer than the bar. After it is in place, cut off the long end of the felt strip, about 1/4" onto the bar.

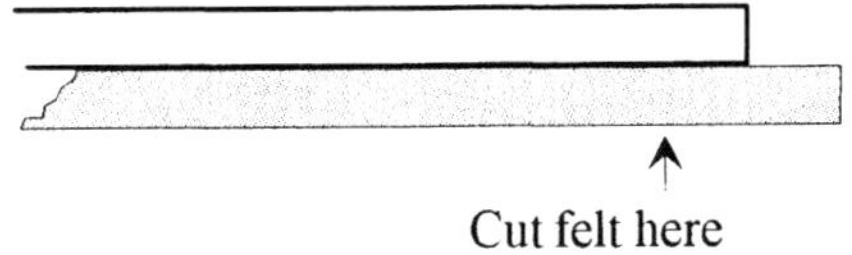

Firmly press the felt in place so the sticky face is solidly attached to the bar.

On a 15-bar style chord bar, the felt should be aligned with the end of the chord bar. Lay the felt along the bar, keeping it aligned on each side until you reach the other end. Trim any excess off the end so that the bar and felt strip are of equal length.

Notching The Bar Felts

1. The marks you made on the bars earlier should be clearly present. Draw a straight line down onto the felt from those lines on the side of the bar.

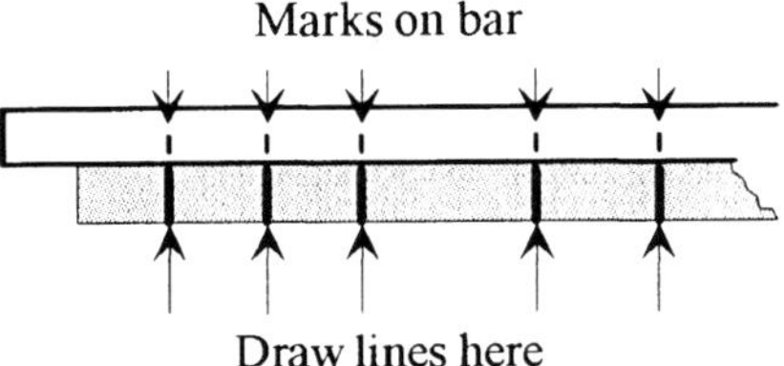

2. Now we cut the felts. An extremely sharp knife is needed here. I use an old straight razor that I keep honed and stropped shaving-sharp. Single-edge commercial razor blades will also work. The edge should be sharp enough so you don't need to saw back and forth to cut.

Make an inverted "V" cut at each mark on the felt. Since the lines on the bars were placed exactly over the strings on your 'harp, the cuts you will make on the new felts can be relatively narrow (1/8" to 3/16" wide). Better to cut them a bit narrow than too wide.

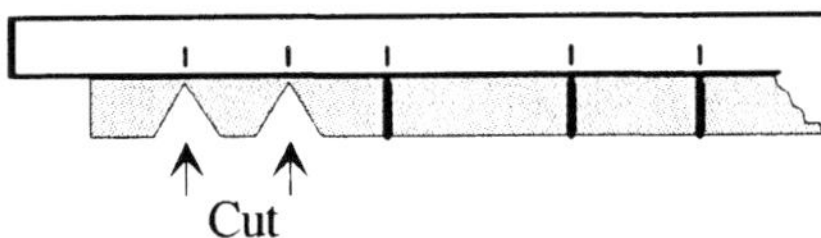

3. Now put the bar in place on your 'harp and check to see that each "player" string is clear of the felt. If a notch is too narrow, trim off a bit more felt. If the notch is too wide, glue a notch piece back in with silicone glue, making sure it is just flush with the face of the bar felt. Recut this notch in a few hours after the glue is set.
4. Put your damped autoharp back together. Enjoy! (I felt good helping you with this. I hope you felt better, too!) ❖

For more discussion concerning felting and siliconing chord bars, see "Annual Mechanical Tune-up" p. 1.

Improving The Action Of Chord Bars

AQ Volume IV, Numbers 1, 2

BARS -WHERE THE ACTION IS

George Orthey

Action is the ease, smoothness, and travel distance of autoharp chord bars when they are depressed. Ideally, the bar action should be quick, easy, smooth, and silent. Speed of play and minimum hand and arm fatigue are the principal benefits of good action.

When correcting the action of the bars, one should keep in mind that noise reduction is a very desirable side effect.

Our objectives in action adjustment will be: (1) to reduce bar travel to the minimum without interfering with the strings; (2) to minimize spring pressure (resistance) needed to return the bar to its resting position; (3) to eliminate any source of friction, catching, or irregular travel of the bars.

The Open Bar-Type Autoharp

First, we'll consider the open bar 'harp (e.g. the 15-bar instrument).

If the action of this type of instrument is too low so the resting bars interfere with the free vibration of the strings, simply put a shim under the base of the bar holders. I prefer to use a thin layer of silicone glue and a layer of double thick felt. To some degree, you can adjust the bar height by how tight you make the screws holding the bar holders in place. The felt between the bar holders and 'harp body also damps the conduction of noise from the bar holder to the body of the 'harp.

More often however, too high is the problem. Ideal chord bar height for most people playing with picks is the thickness of a new 50 cent piece at the bass end, and close enough that a thin sheet of cardboard will just slide between bar felt and strings at the treble end. Usually the bass end is close to correct, and if necessary can be shimmed down with squares of felt cloth 1/4" x 1/4" placed on top of the bar end under the bar holder cover. Glue the squares in place with a bit of silicone glue between them and the bar holder cover. Don't glue them to the bar. They will surely get knocked loose and fall out.

To put them in, put a small dab of silicone glue on one side of the felt square, (just a bit of glue about the size of a pin head is all that is needed), depress the bar, and slide it in on top of the bar under the bar cover with the glue side up. I use tweezers to put the square in place. Place it out of sight. When you let the bar up, it holds the felt in place until the glue dries.

A wonderful side effect to this procedure, as with most things that improve action, is that it also removes a major source of bar noise.

If you have a lot of "fuzzies" on your bar felts, get your felts cleaned up by singeing them, but don't set them on fire! Just singe the fuzzies off the damping face of the bar felts. I use quick sweeps with a propane torch. The felts will look a bit brown. Take your finger and wipe off the brown "bitzels." This procedure will keep the fuzzies down, and the bar action as well. Speaking of "down," the smell of burned chicken feathers during the singeing is a bit much.

With the treble end bar holders, we usually find a great excess of bar travel. This is because the bar holders are the same at the bass and treble ends. The string bed face itself is lower at the treble end and the bar clearance can be set closer at this end. Therefore, usually considerable lowering of the bars is needed at the treble end.

If the action is just a bit too high here, shim the bars down with a layer or two of felt squares as described for the bass end.

If the clearance is very high and you are a brave person, first decide how much you need to lower the bars, (usually 1/16" to 1/8"), still leaving proper bar clearance from the strings. Then remove the bar holder covers, bars, springs, etc. Remove the treble bar holder. You are going to saw the top face off the bar holder. Don't grub it up! I use a skip-tooth blade on the band saw. (It's not as rare as a saber tooth tiger in the tar pits.) You are, of course, just sawing off the amount you decided was necessary to lower your bars to where they should be.

Smooth up the top surface of the bar holder with 80-100 grit sand paper. Lay the sand paper flat, and slide the bar holder top across it. Check the screw holes in the top of the bar holder to see if they are deep enough for the bar holder cover screws. If not, you may have to drill them deeper. Put it back together and check your clearance. Still a bit too high? Shim it down.

Whoops! Cut it too short? Shim up under the bar holder. With up or down felt shimming, an absolutely exact action can be obtained.

Now we'll establish proper spring return and reduce excess spring action. Remove the bar holder covers. With all the springs and bars in place, observe where the bars stand. Normally, you will find the bars sticking out well above the bar holders (as much as 1/4"). All of this excess above the bar holder is excess spring action. Ideally, the bars should all be about 1/16" to 1/8" above the bar holders. This position will give good return, hold the bars firmly in place, and will have reduced spring pressure to fight. If the excess above the bar holder is small, (less than 1/8"), trim off some felt between the bar and the spring to lower the bar.

If the excess is great, cut off the spring – a little bit at a time. Cut off only one end of the spring, since this spoils the nice flat spring end. After it is cut to the right length, you need to square up the cut end a bit, using needle nose pliers or a hemostat. Even though the spring's end is not perfect, it can be set in some silicone glue to hold it in place vertically, with the good flat original end up against the chord bar.

Now be sure that all bars work freely – no rubs or catches. A piece of fine sand paper will smooth up rough corners on bar ends.

Do your 12- or 15-bar 'harp chord bars have end play causing clicking when playing? Cut a strip of plastic from a plastic cottage cheese tub. Slip it in place between the end of the bar and the bar holder. Then put the bar holder cap back on. – Real loose? Put one or more at each end. Make it the same height and width as the face of the bar holder that the bar end rides against. If you want it there permanently, put a dab of silicone glue on the face that goes against the bar end holder.

Are your 12- or 15-bar 'harp chord bars loose between plastic and metal? Make a strip of cloth 1/2 by 3". Put a stripe of silicone glue on it and stuff it in the hole in the end of the bar.

It should be noted that if your 'harp has a substantial bow to it, the action at one end of the chord set may be substantially different from that at the other end. Compensate this by shimming under only one end of the bass chord bar holder so the action is uniform. This shimming should set the chord bar uniform in relationship to the strings – not to the body of the instrument.

When it's together, you should have fast, smooth, easy, short action.

The Covered Bar-Type Autoharp

On to a new bar. Get out your Oscar 21, and hum a few verses of "How Dry I Am."

The open bar discussed and enjoyed in the first part of this chapter was simple and easy. With OSI plastic covers, it's harder. (Cover charge?) Noise suppression is again closely related to action correction.

The way these 'harps are set up, the chord buttons hold the bar position downward and the springs hold them up in whatever slap-dash position they may take. The lower tier buttons (minors) usually hold the bars close at the base and way off the strings at the treble and the upper tiers (majors) are just the reverse. In almost all cases there is over all 1/8" to 1/4" travel of the button to get contact. Someone once told me "The sounds of the chord bars remind me of a construction company setting up for business on a Monday morning."

The first thing we must do is to get the chord bars to lie in the proper position essentially independent of the chord buttons. This position relative to the string bed is exactly the same as described for open bar 'harps. (Note: if you don't know the chord bar arrangement, write it down before you take it apart. Also, when you take the chord bars off, be sure they have identification on them. Mark them so you can easily get them back in the right place.)

Take your cover off and remove all the buttons. Lay the buttons in order on a flat pan, making it easier to get them back in place.

You'll notice on the inside of your cover, there is a hollow from end to end of the cover. This hollow needs to be filled in so the area above and below the chord button area is flat.

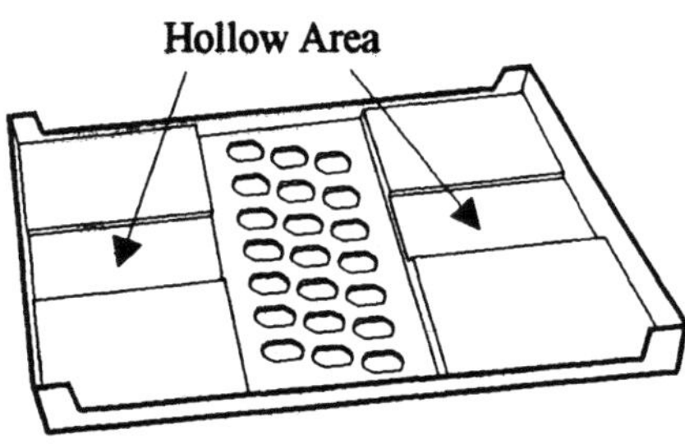

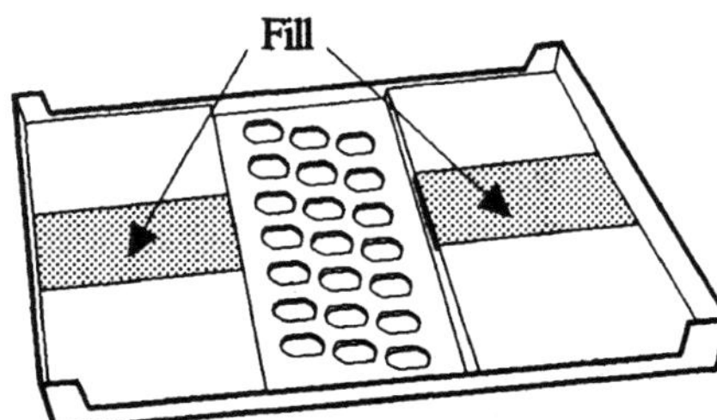

Put silicone glue in the hollow areas to make them level with the adjacent area. Now lay a sheet of wax paper on the silicone glue and a flat square of wood on top of that. When the glue sets up by the next day, you will have these two areas essentially flat:

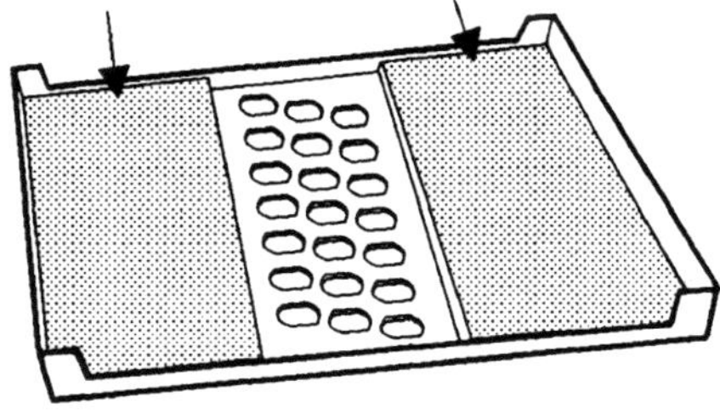

Remove the wood blocks and waxed paper. By trial and error based on a good guess, place two strips of bar felt across the under side of the cover as shown.

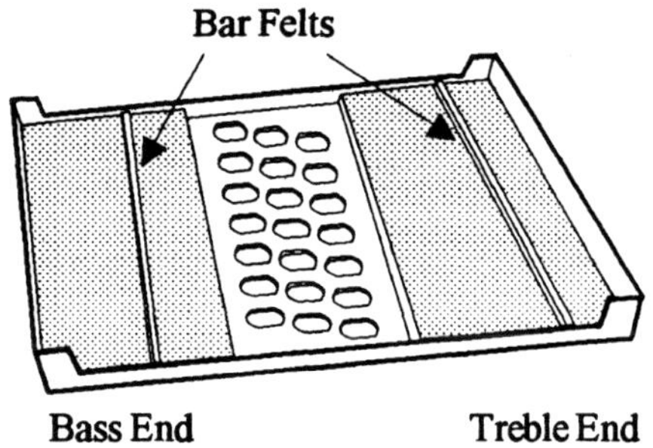

Now you understand why we had to make that area flat. We need to have this bar felt lie flat across. I use the self adhesive on the felt to keep it in place. Don't press it tightly. Just put it in place enough that it will stay, but can be removed. Put the cover in place without the buttons, just the bars on the 'harp. Look through under the cover to see the set of bars. Since the cover slopes closer to the bars at the ends, the bar height can be adjusted by how close to the ends of the cover you set the strips of felt. Move the felt if necessary to the locations that give you the right bar height above the strings at each end. When you find the exact spot for the felts to give you correct clearance, press them in place firmly.

When you put the buttons back in place, you will find there is a good bit of play between the buttons and the bars/cover. This must be corrected by build up of the button base and/or bar groove.

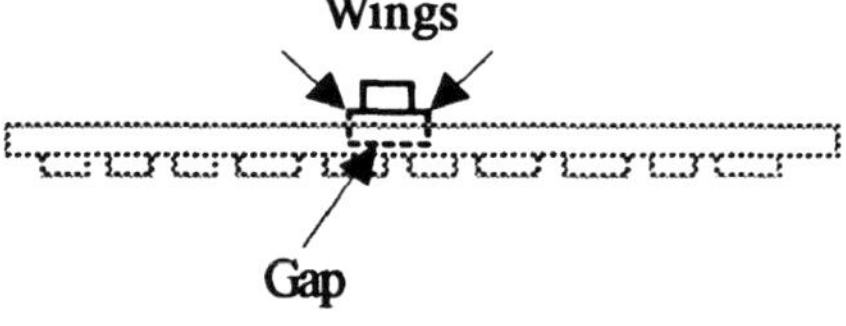

This gap must be reduced. Buildup in this gap should be slightly cushioned so it won't rattle, and sufficient in thickness to bring the button up so the "wings" just bear on the padding under the cover.

I start the buildup by gluing a narrow strip of double thick felt to the bottom edge of the button base.

To do this, put a layer of contact cement

on the bottom edge of the button. Then touch it while still wet to a 1/8" x 1" strip of felt. This sticks the felt on without saturating and hardening it with glue.

To determine the amount of additional buildup needed, put it all together and check the bar clearance again to be sure it's all right. Press each bar down with its button and let it up gently so the button comes up, but still sits in the bottom of the bar groove. With a fine point felt tip pen, make a mark on the side of the button even with the face of the cover. Now grip the button and raise it so the wings just bear against the under side of the cover. Make another mark on the side of the button. The distance between these two marks is the amount of fill you still need between the button base and the bottom of the bar groove. Using strips of cardboard, wood veneer, or paper match body, build up a layer in the bottom of the bar groove equal to the correction determined by the two pen marks you made on the side of the button. The correction should be about the same for each button in the same tier. The correction will be slightly more in the tier toward the treble than in the tier of minors toward the bass because of the slope of the chord bar.

You should also note here that if your 'harp has a bow so that the action is different at one side of the chord bar set than at the other, a correction will be necessary to make the action uniform on all the bars. This correction can be done in either of two ways. First, you can remove the cover and chord bars, and the screw through the chord bar bass end comb nearest the middle of the 'harp.

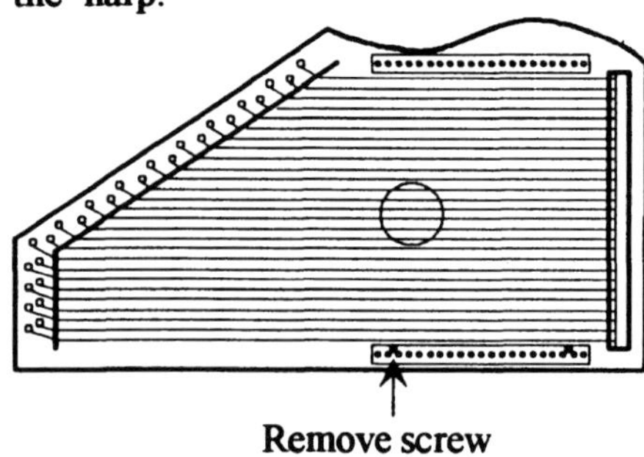

Remove screw

Place a shim under the comb and metal clip to raise the comb so it is parallel to the bass string.

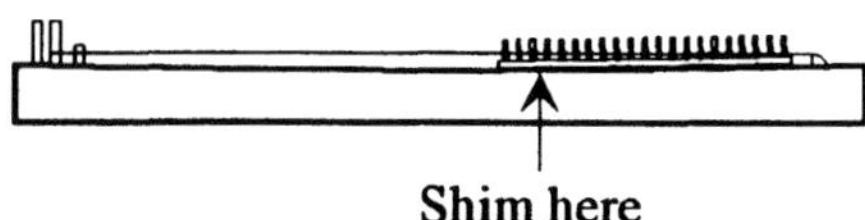

Shim here

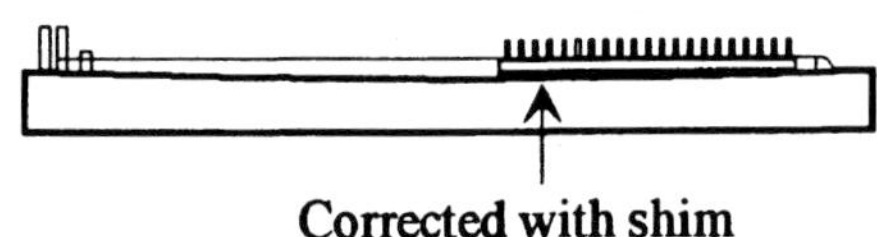

Corrected with shim

Then reassemble. This should correct the action variance.

A second way you can make the correction is to change the hole in the cover so the cover alone, not the comb, is raised at that same corner.

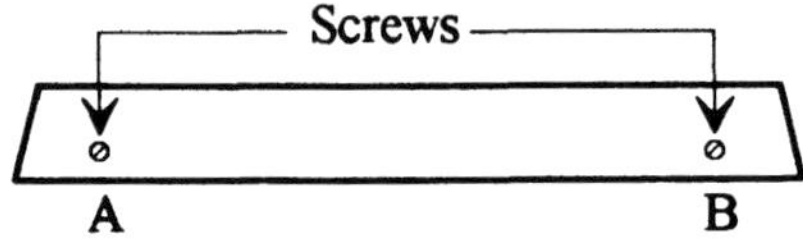

Just take A and make the hole in the cover a slot rather than a hole.

Make the slot extend downward from the original hole. Raise this corner of the cover up until the cover is exactly on a plane with the strings. The cover will sit like this:

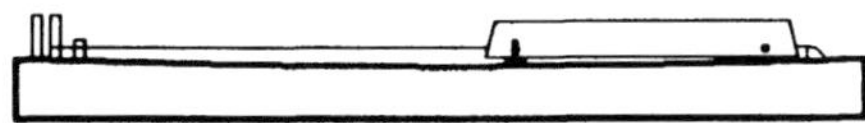

It is normally not necessary to make any correction at the treble end since there is no significant bow to the 'harp body up there on the short edge. You will note that with all this muxing about, we have not only shortened and made the action uniform, but we have also added felt between chord bars and cover, and between buttons and bars. The result being not only excellent action, but a noise reduction of the construction company to some thumping and mumbling of workers down under the cover.

Until recently, I have not as a rule found it necessary to make changes in the springs or chord bars to improve action or noise. The bar and comb system was inherently quiet and smooth once the cover and bar travel corrections are made. However, now I find it necessary to reduce the spring height. The current generation of Oscar Schmidt 'harps uses a higher, much stiffer spring, making the action very hard. Many of the new 21-bar 'harps also have the bass end comb mislocated so the springs jam in the chord bar ends.[1]

One additional correction that is more noise related than action related is replacing the under-cover foam cushion with silicone glue and double thick felt. Eight years ago when I routinely used the OSI 21-bar kit on my new 'harps, I always replaced the foam pad with felt. It's simply quieter, and more durable.

Remove all of the foam pad and its adhesive from the inside of the bar cover. Lightly sand the flat area that you will cover (same area you removed the foam pad from). Use a medium to coarse sand paper – just enough to rough the surface. Cut a piece of double thick felt cloth large enough to cover this area. Put a wet coat of silicone glue on one face of the felt. Place the piece (glue face down, of course) onto the inside of the cover. Smooth it in place so it is glued firmly with no air pockets between the felt and plastic. Allow it to set up over night.

Now the tedious part – cutting the holes through the silicone and felt: I now use a tool steel die made for this purpose to cut out the felt and silicone in the perfect button shape with one smack. Before I had a die, I used a small curved chisel and small straight chisel to cut the felt out. Wood carving or leather working tools work well for this. Careful work with an X-acto knife and small cuticle scissors will do too. Anyway, the object is to cut the hole in the felt and silicone slightly smaller than the hole through the plastic cover.

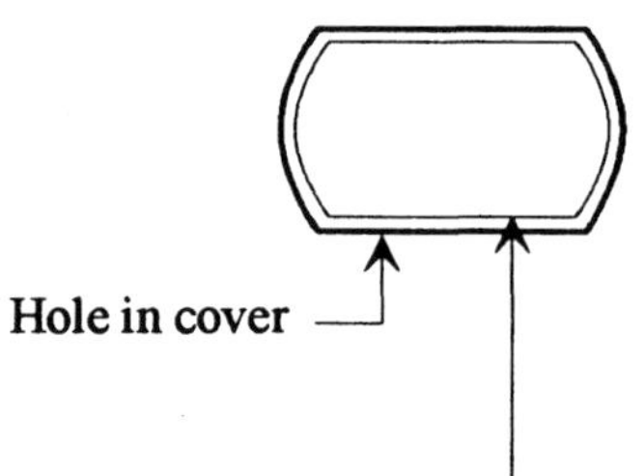

This allows the chord button to ride only against felt and silicone and it is absolutely silent. Place the cover over a piece of wood so you cut through the hole, through the felt, against the block of wood. This will prevent you from tearing the felt away from the back of your cover while giving you good clean cuts through the felt.[2]

Now you've done away with the heavy machinery of the construction company. You've seen the bright lights, heard the loud noises. Relax. Enjoy. All your bars are quiet.

Silicone glue – Although I preferred

the original formula GE Silicone Glue, it's no longer available. The new Silicone II Clear glue works about the same. As near as I can tell, the Silicone Glue "Household Glue" (at the top it says "100% Silicone Rubber Sealant") is the original glue newly packaged, and is the same as the original. I definitely prefer the clear over white or brown colored Silicone. The glue is available at most hardware stores.

Double thickness felt cloth is a specific term. Standard felt cloth available at any major dry goods store is either single or double thickness. ❖

[1] To correct these problems, see "New Comb Adjustment"p.13.

[2] For another approach to chord bar travel, read "Correcting Chord Bar Action"p.14 for a unique and permanent fix.

New Comb Adjustment

AQ Volume VIII, Number 2

A FEW MORE BARS BUT NOT MUCH ACTION

George Orthey

If you're contemplating trading in your old 15-bar 'harp for a brand new 21-bar variety, here's some sound advice you'll probably be needing.

While doing some maintenance work on several OSI 21-bar 'harps, I noticed an annoying and consistently present problem. On these instruments, the chord bars are sometimes hard to push and sometimes even jam at the bass end. If you think you have this phenomenon, remove the chord bar cover and check it out.

The bass end of the chord bars in some newer 21-bar 'harps are like this:

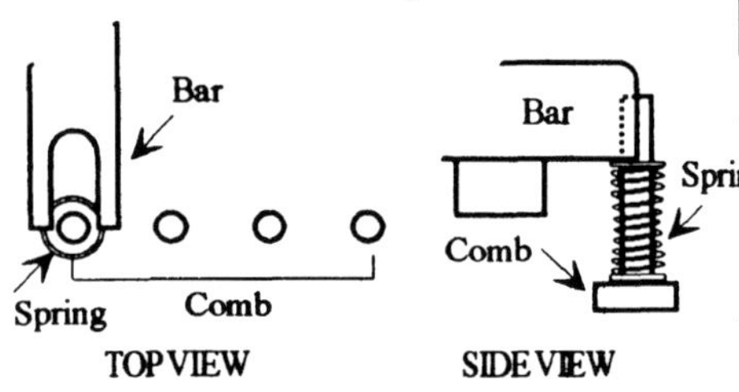

Since the comb and springs that lift the bars are not properly located under the end of the bar, the springs sometimes slip by the end of the bar and jam.

The bass end of the chord bars should look like this:

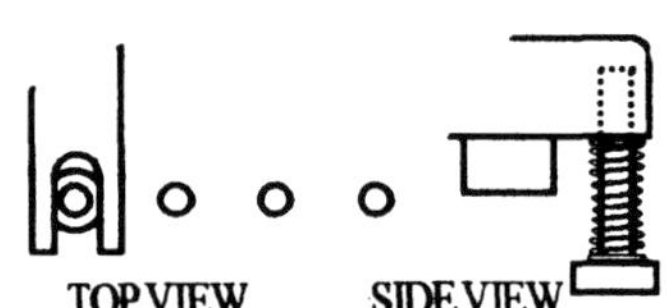

The comb should be set well into the slots in the bass ends of the bars so the springs sit firmly under the bars.

The problem is very easy to correct. Simply take the screws out of the comb base and drill new holes for the screws so that the comb will sit under the bars as it should.

When you take the comb off, you'll find two or three (depending on the number of screws through the comb) holes in the 'harp body. Just drill a hole the same size approximately 3/32 to 1/8 inch closer to the sound board like so:

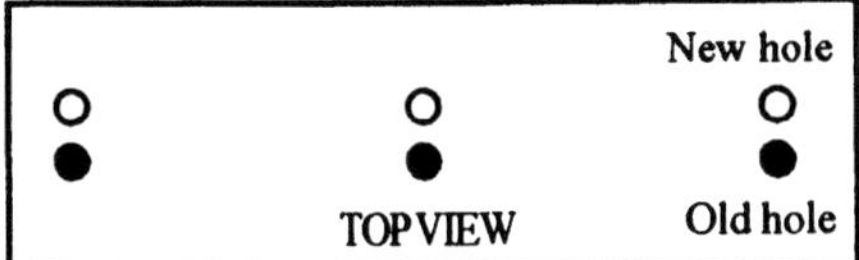

Then reinstall the comb.

You may need to drill new holes in the metal clips that go under the comb. The clips are used to attach the chord bar cover in place. They are self-evident when you take the cover off. They sit under and alongside the comb like so:

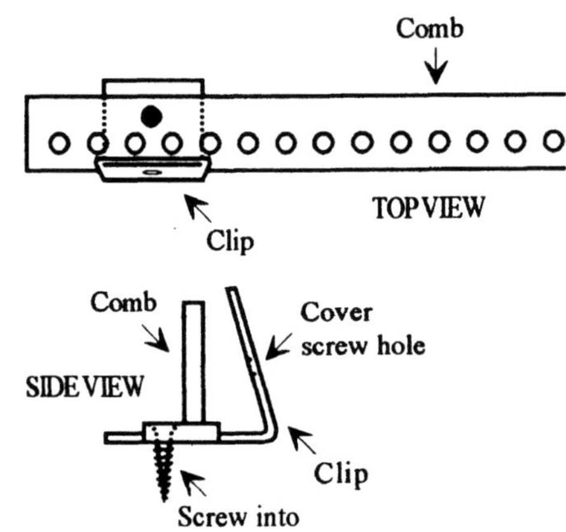

You must correct the right screw hole in the metal clip. Drill the new hole through the clip alongside the existing hole for the screw that goes through the comb and clip into the 'harp body:

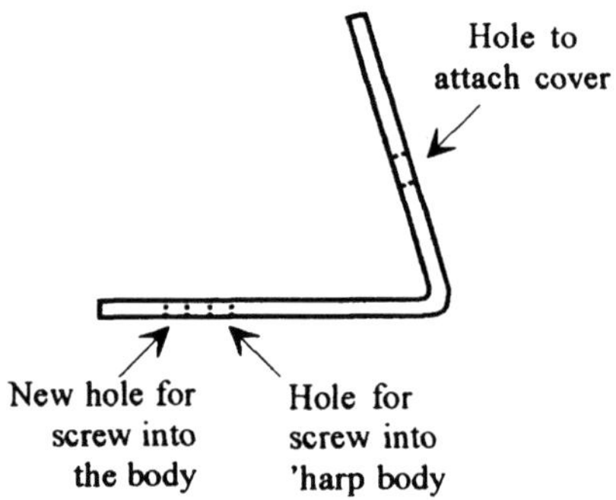

Drilling this new hole in effect will leave the metal clip in the same place it was before you moved the comb closer to the sound board.

CAUTION!

When you drill this new hole in the metal clip, hold the clip with a pair of vice grips, not with your fingers!

Now put it all back together. With the combs moved under the bass end of the chord bars, put the screws through the comb, through the new holes in the metal clips and into the new holes in the 'harp body. Put the bars and cover back in place and your "hangovers" are gone! The bars are open again! ❖

AQ Volume VIII, Number 1

WHAT UNCLE OSCAR LEFT OUT

Chuck Daniels

Correcting Chord Bar Action

For some time, I have worked on making Oscar Schmidt 'harps more playable by doing various things to the actions with the goal of quieting down the 21-chord button noise and lowering the chord bars closer to the string bed. I've done many 'harps using padding to achieve this, with pleasing results, but always felt there had to be a way to control and adjust the action independently of using the plastic cover with its irregular surface.

I have devised a system and installed it on many 'harps with everyone being extremely pleased with the change in the playability of the 'harps. The basic idea is to use a metal strip to hold the end of each chord bar down at the proper height from the strings. These strips are screwed down on each end through the chord bar holder into the 'harp body, allowing for precise and separate adjustments at all four corners of the bars.

The strips are made from 1/2"x 1/8" aluminum bars covered with thin felt. For these strips to fit under the cover, I had to cut a recess in each end of each chord bar for the hold-down strip to fit:

Something else I usually do is reduce the pressure of the springs by cutting off about 1/3 of the height. Since the chord bar is closer to the strings, you can use a shorter spring. If you suffer any finger or joint problems, this makes the instrument easier to play with less pain and strain.

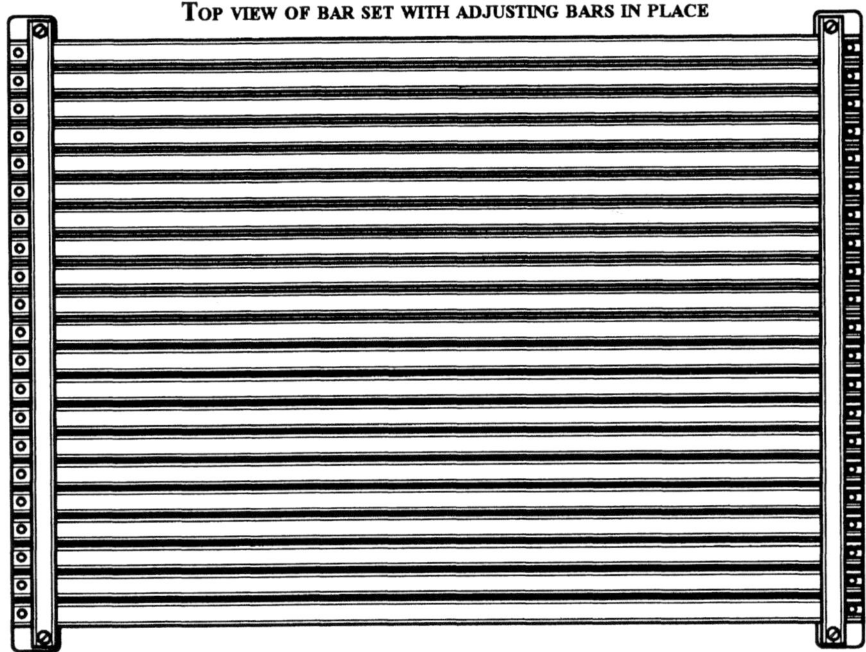

With the action now finished, I punch out a new pad for the button area inside the cover using Molefoam (as in foot pads). This eliminates the clatter of the buttons against the cover. If the button is too low for your liking, you can put a small piece of leather shoe lace inside the chord bar to raise the button up a bit.

This "fine-tune" bar adjustment system has been tried by several well-known autoharp players who felt that the action has as good and tight a feel as they had seen. As one Winfield winner put it, "It feels like a real musical instrument; not a toy."

If you want to try this, you'll need a belt sander and a metal band saw. ❖

For more information concerning the correcting of chord bars, read "Improving The Action Of Chord Bars" p.9 and "Dealing With The Mechanical Noise Of Chord Bars" p.15.

Dealing With The Mechanical Noise Of Chord Bars

AQ Volume II, Number 3

LISTEN TO THE JINGLE, THE RUMBLE, AND THE ROAR

George Orthey

This sound, while playing your 'harp can be purely and simply the strings you want damped so they make no sound. Well, they aren't, so they do –

You need to hold the bars down to make chords. But this makes your finger tips black and blue. Improper felting, an uneven string bed, bent bars, uneven felt height, incorrect fine tuner tightening, and harmonics can all be part of your problem. We'll attack these culprits one at a time.

The bars should move smoothly and easily when pressed down. The action of the bars should be low enough to make damping quick and easy. The setting of bar action is a whole different kettle of fish in itself, and will be addressed fully in another article in this book.[1]

Let's get the felts right. Take the bars off and look at them. If the felts are worn or falling off or otherwise unsatisfactory, refelting is essential. If they are just loose, particularly the ones which dampen just one string, a bit of silicone glue will do wonders. Fill a shoulder of glue on either side of the offending felt to firm it up so it won't rock. This is particularly a problem on the seventh chords where there are a lot of single dampened strings.

Check the surface of the bars. Is it straight and even? While you have those bars out, lay a good straight edge lightly across the face of the felts. If some touch and some don't, the short ones will give poor damping.

If the individual bar is arched, the ends won't touch the strings at all. No matter how hard you push the middle, it just bends worse and rumbles worse – particularly in the bass. Many 15-bar autoharp bars are like this to varying degrees. Proper refelting or siliconing will correct these uneven felt problems.

I prefer refelting because I feel there is better damping with good felt that has not been siliconed. When refelting the arched 15 bar 'harp bars, take the felt off by just tearing it off. This will leave quite a bit of old felt and glue still on the bar. Don't take this off the ends of the bar. Just take it off the middle. The buildup left on the ends of the arched bar will compensate for that arch. This effect can be done perfectly with a long flat file or a belt sander. You will need to put a layer of contact cement on the face of the bar particularly where the old felt is left on to prepare it to make good contact with the pressure sensitive glue of the new felt.[2]

A word about felt here – felt should be firm enough not to wiggle around and wear rapidly, but not so hard that you have to break a finger pushing bars down. Felts should have a slight sponginess when you squeeze them.

Placing the bars too close to the end of the strings, particularly the bass strings, will also cause rumbling. If the bars are moved down toward the bottom end of the 'harp, the first one or two bars will dampen very poorly, no matter how hard you push down. If you must move the bars all the way down, make sure the end chords are ones you don't use much. Be careful when you move the bars that you are not placing them dead center over the harmonic line (the 1/3 node bell line) on the bass. This will give you sounds you don't want.

You will notice that rumble is worse in a 21-bar chromatic 'harp. Narrow felts, bars near the dead pin end of the strings, and the dampening of many strings all contribute to this problem. Some chords only sound eight of the thirty-six strings. This makes one "player" string for every four "thumpers" on a full strum. The more accurately you play your 21-bar 'harp, therefore, the less the roar.

A single-key diatonic will have the bars ideally placed away from the dead pin bridge. On this 'harp, 15-bar type bars with wider felts dampen better, and you have fourteen to twenty strings playing in each chord. This makes the "players" to "thumpers" ratio about one to one. The "players" will drown out the "thumpers," and the roar will be lessened appreciably.

Sound quality and responsive ness of the instrument also are contributors to this problem. If the "player" strings have poor quality, the "thumpers" come to the fore. In a good, full 'harp, the "players" will make the "thumpers" less noticeable.

If you have fine tuners on your 'harp, they may be the cause of uneven damping. If a cam is allowed to ride up too high, it will raise that one string above the others, thus causing poor damping of the adjacent strings. To get rid of and/or avoid this, tighten the cams down all the way. Back up two to four turns, and tune the 'harp with a wrench on the tuning pins. Now the fine tuners are set, and can be used for fine tuning. This resetting of the fine tuners needs to be done whenever they get uneven enough to cause irregularity in the string bed.[3]

Now the problem of harmonics – what are they? They are the overtones. As a string vibrates, it moves as a whole, giving the fundamental note played.

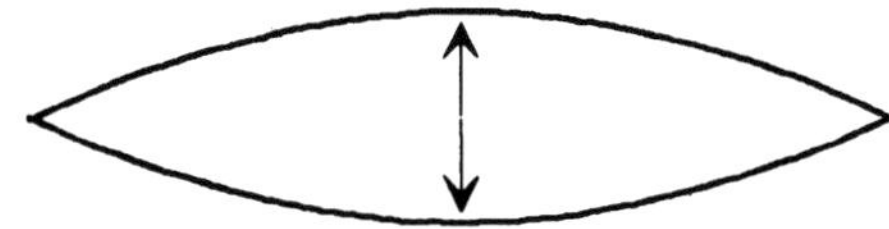

The string also vibrates the half node an octave up.

This is the bad one you hear in the upper strings when the felts are situated over the middle of the strings. Visualize that if a bar dampens a string exactly at the midpoint of the string,

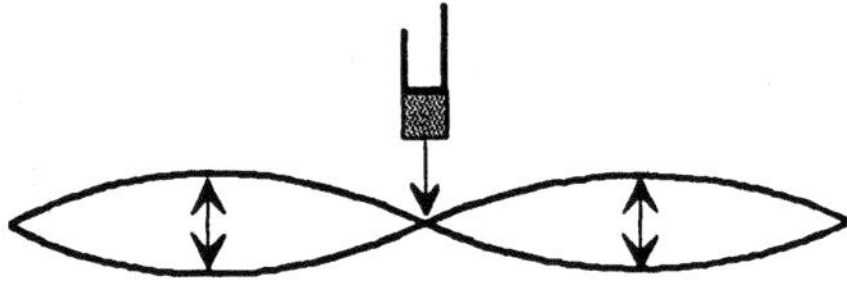

(where it doesn't move anyway), absolutely no damping occurs, and the string rings like a bell.

Speaking of bells, you might have noticed those beauties in the high register of the chords made by the bars nearest to your ear on a 21-bar 'harp.

To thicken the plot, let it be known that there are also third nodes – and fourth nodes, – and so on. The higher they go, the weaker they become.

Don't wish them away. If these nodes did not ring, autoharps would be dead-dull-flat-poor! The overtones give richness and fullness to all stringed instruments.

In approaching the unwanted overtones problem, we must be aware that these particular harmonics are the strong 1/2 node tones at the treble end and 1/3 node tones in the bass of the 'harp. These points on the strings must be found if we are going to avoid them.

While you have those chord bars off the 'harp, find a pencil with a good eraser and cut the eraser to a wedge. Place the point of the wedge lightly on a string at about 1/2 (or at the 1/3 point, depending whether you are working in the treble or the bass) point of the string length. Pluck the string while you move the eraser lightly along the string, immediately lifting the eraser off the string after you pluck it. When you find that point at which the bell is clear and ringing, mark it with a small felt tip pen. Do this for all of the treble strings at the 1/2 node, and all the bass strings at the 1/3 node. You now have marked the "bell line" of your 'harp. The line will look approximately like this:

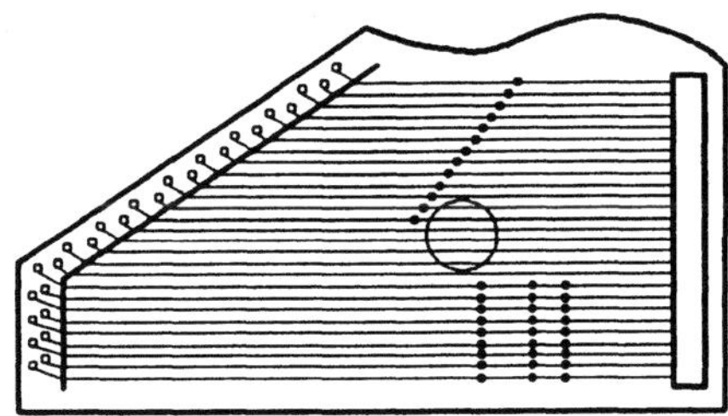

This line now becomes a guide. Try to keep as many felts from damping the strings right over this bell line as possible. If you have one bar, this is easy. If you have ten bars of the 15-bar type, or fifteen bars of the 21-bar type, easy. But that's not what we have. With the above narrower bar sets, keep the whole set just to the right of the bell line.

With a regular 15-bar or 21-bar 'harp, you must cross the bell lines. Now we get to messing about with the bars. If a bell point is between bars rather than directly under the felt, if a bar crosses the bell line on a string that plays, or if the felt is simply away from the bell line, the bell will be reduced or not occur at all. Of course, getting one bar off the bell may put two others onto bells. You have to move the whole set, not just one bar.

How do you do all this moving around? Remove the combs on the 21-bar 'harp, or the bar holders on the 15-bar 'harp. Put a strip of two-sided Scotch tape on the back of the combs or bar holders. Move them around, stick them down and try new positions. Don't do drilling until you figure out where you are going with your bars.

The 21-bar set is the most difficult to change. Moving it around gradually left to right and back again over about a 1/2 inch range keeping them vertical, (that is square to the strings), is about all you can do. Some harmonics are entirely unavoidable. Try to keep them on the bars you use the least.

The 15-bar set allows more monkeying around because they can be skewed left or right. The bass bell line can be avoided somewhat independently from the treble bell line. Simply put the bass bell line exactly between two bars, not under them. These bars are wider and obviously allow less bell to sound because of better dampening.

When you find your best fit, put the bars permanently in that position on the 'harp.[4]

Keep in mind the jingle, the rumble, and the roar will never altogether disappear from the autoharp. The tick-tack, scritch-scratch of the dampened strings is part of autoharp music, as are the bells of the harmonics. This is your rhythm section – your built-in accompaniment and will always be there to some degree. However, good felts, avoiding "bell lines," straight bars, and evenly adjusted fine tuners should keep it from stealing all of your thunder. ❖

[1] See "Improving The Action Of Chord Bars" p.9.
[2] For more about felting, read "Refelting And Siliconing Chord Bars" p.7.
[3] The subject of fine tuners can also be a noisy one. Read "Fine Tuners – How They Work" p.17.
[4] Read more about this subject in "Harmonics" p.35.

Fine Tuners – How They Work

AQ Volume VIII, Number 1

TUNIN' FINE, SURE AS YOU'RE BORN

George Orthey

Fine tuners are the next best thing since Gütter invented the autoharp. Unfortunately, not everyone knows how to use them properly. And some folks shy away from them altogether, still using the old familiar wrench and tuning pegs.

The fine tuners are marvelous devices that not only allow exact and simple tuning capability, but save unnecessary wear on the tuning pin holes.

The fine tuner system consists of an anchor bar and 36 individual cams and cap screws, one for each string on the instrument. On autoharps equipped with 37 strings, the fine tuners are best placed on the top 36 strings, since the high short strings are most problematical to tune to an exact note. First, let's understand –

How They Work

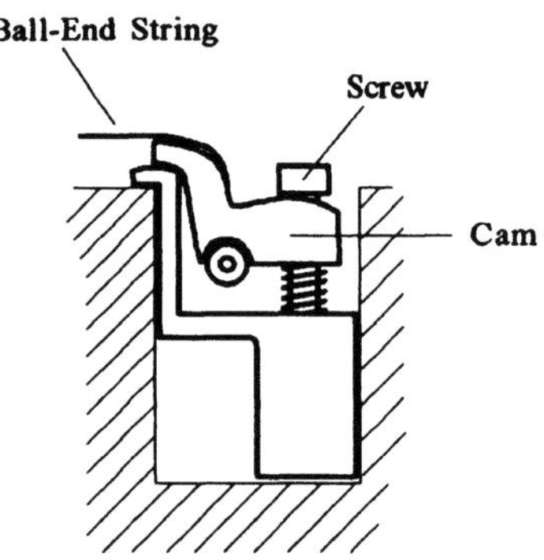

When the screw through the cam is tightened, the cam tips back, putting tension on the string. So the tighter the screw, the higher the note. There is, of course, a limit to how far the screw can be tightened. It should never be forced beyond its limit. When a cam has reached bottom, it should be backed up about three or four full turns, and the string brought up to pitch with the regular tuning pin.

Some Dos And Don'ts With Fine Tuners

1. Do use them.
2. Do *tune up* to pitch. If a note is sharp, let it *down below* the pitch you desire. *Then* bring it up to the exact pitch. If you let it down to pitch, it will tend to settle a bit flat.
3. Don't tune up with the wrench on the tuning pin, then let down on the fine tuner. This causes the fine tuners to gradually creep up. The cams will ride up out of the position and make your string bed uneven.
4. Do keep the cams down where they are within four turns of being bottomed out. The cams will stay even and the strings will come off the leading edge of the cams, reducing the chance of string buzzing.
5. Do be very careful if you have the old silver-colored aluminum anchor bar and cams. The metal is soft, and the threads can strip easily.

In The Beginning

I normally tune a new autoharp immediately after stringing, using the wrench and tuning pins. Then I continue to tune it every time it needs tuning for about one or two weeks with the tuning pins. After that, I use only the fine tuners. When some of the fine tuners start reaching bottom, I level all the fine tuners to the correct even level position. Then tune up the strings with the tuning wrench. Now I go back to just using fine tuners again. Using this procedure, I normally only have to level the fine tuners and tune with the wrench about once a year.

A Word About Washers

Washers are sometimes used with fine tuners under the head of the cap screws. Unfortunately, some fine tuner sets have been made with small lock washers rather than flat washers. *Lock washers should never be used under any circumstance.* They make the fine tuner work in an irregular manner, and may cause serious wear and damage to the fine tuner. Flat washers, when available, will reduce wear and make the tuner work more smoothly and will reduce friction. Washers of any kind are not absolutely necessary, and the fine tuners will work well without them.

Changing A String

Changing a string with fine tuners is a little more work than with an anchor bar or dead pins. Unwind the tuning pin approximately three to four turns and remove the string from the tuning pin. Then unscrew the cap screw in the fine tuner until it comes out of the anchor bar. Lift out the cam and screw and remove the broken wire. Replace it with a new wire. Oscar Schmidt directions tell you to clip the tail off the winding at the ball end of the string. But don't. Clip the tail off only on the middle octave large non-wound strings, and also maybe the lowest three wound strings, so they will seat up in the cam. All remaining small wire strings in the top octave and small core wire strings in the bass octave should just have the tail bent over to lie alongside the windings.[1]

I have met people who are scared to death of the fine tuners and refuse to use them. I have seen instances where the chord bars will not damp properly because the string bed is so uneven. An unnamed performer I know had loosened the screws to the point where they were almost out of their seats. All these problems can be avoided by following these few simple steps. ❖

If you have fine tuners on the other strings, but don't have one for that high, top string, read "Tuning High Strings Without Fine Tuners" p.18.

[1] See "Restringing The Autoharp" p.23.

Tuning High Strings Without Fine Tuners

AQ Volume II, Number 4
HIGH STRUNG
George Orthey

Do you have fits getting those top strings exactly in tune – particularly the top pairs on the diatonic 'harp? A few years ago I figured out a solution – and it works!

An inexpensive simple way to fine tune these top strings is to put a fine-thread machine screw alongside the string between the tuning pin and the post or bridge. A machine screw does not have a point like a wood screw, but it will screw into a hole just a bit smaller than the screw itself. Try it on a scrap of wood to be sure you get the right size drill.

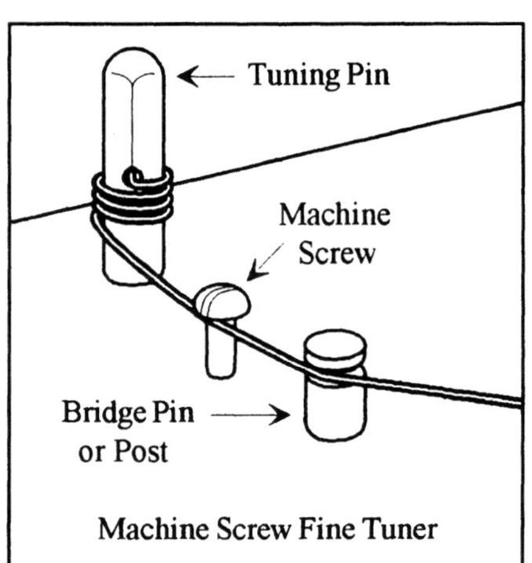

Machine Screw Fine Tuner

As you tighten the machine screw down, it will press against the string giving you a very sensitive fine tuning without interfering with the regular tuning pin action. Tightening the screw raises the pitch of the string; loosening it lowers the pitch. If you polish the under side of the screw head where it bears against the string, it will work even smoother. (I mount mine in a drill chuck, spin it and polish it with a fine sand paper.) Coat it with a very thin layer of oil or grease where the screw and string touch.

Note: There is a very short range of adjustment with which this will work. Remember, it's a "fine tuner." ❖

Loose Tuning Pins

AQ Volume I, Number 3

LOOSE TUNING PINS

George Orthey

Original tuning pin holes for zither pins found in everything from $30,000 harpsichords to Made-in-Hong Kong door chime souvenirs, are drilled at 3/16 inch.[1] The zither pins are supposed to be about 12/1000 inch larger. Converting this to decimal, 3/16 becomes .187 inch, and the pins should be .198 to .200 inch. In truth, the pins vary from .185 to over .200 in routinely available commercial pins. Any replacement pins you use should be at least .196 diameter. (If you are not mechanically inclined, don't get excited about all of this technical minutia. Take this article to a handy friend, who will be glad to know these facts before drilling into your 'harp.) Keep in mind that the pins are like a very finely threaded screw. Turned clockwise they go deeper, and turned counter-clockwise they come out.

If a single pin in an instrument is "soft" loose, simply replacing it with a larger standard pin may do the job.

Pin tightener available from someone who does piano repairing may tighten slightly loose pins. Pin tightener is a liquid that causes permanent swelling of the wood. A drop at the base of the pin, allowed to soak in overnight, will tighten it.

If the pins are set shallow in the pin block, setting the pins deeper may improve tightness, but some caution needs to be exercised here. Remove a few pins and check the pin hole depth. It may be as little as 3/8" to 1/2". If this is the case, you are in luck and with some careful work, you can do wonders.

As noted earlier, the standard pin drill (3/16") is .187 in diameter. If you drill the holes with this, it'll just make it worse.

The next smaller standard drill is 11/64" or .015 less. That's too small. So now what? Thanks to machinists who must do very exact work, drill bits are made in .002" intervals. So, visit your local machine shop folks, explain how desperately you need their help, play them a tune, throw yourself on the floor and kick and scream if you must, but get them to sell you a drill bit about .180" diameter. Using this drill, increase the depth of the hole to about 1" deep. Caution! Don't drill through the back of your 'harp! (An easy way to be sure of drill depth is to wrap a piece of masking tape around the drill bit 1" from the tip. You are 1" deep when the tape reaches the surface of the 'harp.) The drilling is best done on a drill press to be exact – always just one clean motion, in and out. Do not reenter with the drill, or you will ream the pin hole. When drilling this deeper hole, start with the drill turned off. Lower the drill into the hole until it touches bottom, then turn the drill on and drill to the desired depth. Bring the drill out all in one smooth continuous motion. Turn the drill off, and go on to the next hole and repeat the procedure.

Now turn your pins in about 1/4" deeper than they were before. To use this method, the pins must have originally been set quite high thus allowing the 1/4" deeper position without bringing the string windings on the pin too low.

A method I particularly like is shimming the pin hole. This procedure will only work if the pin hole depth is 1" or more. If the depth is less than one inch, drill the hole deeper as described above.

Cut strips of hardwood veneer 1/8" wide by about 2" long. Put a very small amount of "yellow" glue on one face of the strip and stand it in the back of the pin hole. Be sure the glued surface of the strip is facing the pin hole wall, not the pin. Drive the tuning pin gently into the hole. The pin should go in, and the wood strip should stand still.

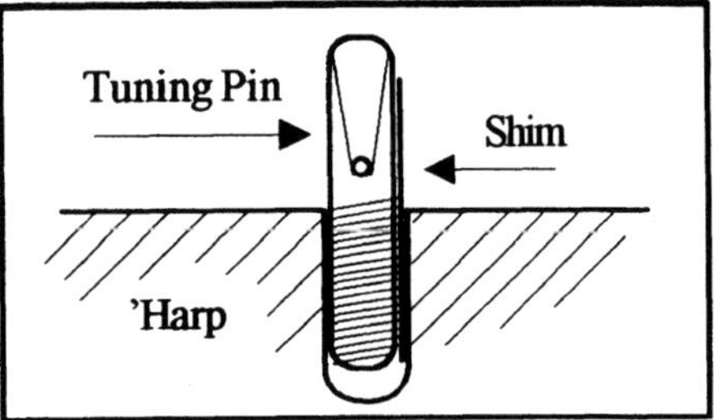

After setting the pin about 1/4" deep into the 'harp, use your tuning wrench to turn the pin slowly to its normal depth. The strip should not turn with the pin. When the pin is in place, cut the excess shim at the surface of the 'harp.[2] The next day your 'harp will be ready for restringing. Don't forget to back the pin out one full turn for every 5/8" of wire you intend to wrap around the pin. Usually three to four turns are just right. String length often varies. If excess string length is present, cut the string off so that you have about two inches of wire to wind on the tuning pin. If you do this, you can forget how many turns were on the pin originally.

Check your 'harp before taking the strings off to see how many turns you have on your pins. (Aargh! Now he tells me!) If the pins are still too loose, you can repeat the shimming.

A quick and easy way to shim a loose pin is to put a strip of fine sand paper in the hole with the sand side away from the pin. Use a strip long enough to go from the bottom to the top of the hole, extending out the top just a bit. Tap the pin in gently about 1/4" and turn it slowly in to the proper depth.

Plugging and re-drilling can also be used for very loose pins. A metric hardwood dowel 1/2 cm in diameter works perfectly. Use a very thin coat of yellow glue on the sides of the pin hole, and also a very thin coat on the sides of the plug. Insert the plug. You must wait at least 24 hours before re-drilling. I prefer waiting a week. Re-drill the hole using an under-size machinist drill about .180" diameter. Do not create a shallow pin hole. Make the depth an absolute minimum of 3/4". The ideal depth is about 1".

There are also commercially available oversize (.215") zither pins. They have some real drawbacks in my hands in that they are not as well-finished as standard pins, and are so much larger that it is difficult to get a tuning wrench onto the pins. They do work, and are quick and easy to use in a low-value 'harp where simple functional integrity is the main issue.

Materials Needed
And Where To Find Them

Undersized drill bits: Machine shop, machinist, or machinist supply
Yellow glue: (Elmer's Craftsmen, Franklin Titebond) Any hardware store
Tuning pins: Any hammered dulcimer, autoharp, zither, or psaltery maker; piano supply house; Oscar Schmidt Int'l.
Veneer: Major lumber yards; Constantine's, 2050 Eastchester Road, Bronx, NY 10461; Craftsman Wood Service, Chicago, IL
Micrometer (For measuring pin sizes): Car repair shop; machine shop
Dowel - Lumberyard
1/2 cm Hardwood dowel - No known source in the United States. ❖

[1] Not all sources show such extreme variance in size. Good quality sources provide pins .198 diameter, plus or minus .001. They are known to be available from Schaff Piano Supply and American Piano Supply companies.

[2] The shim can also be glued in the pin hole before putting the tuning pin in place. Position the shim with glue on one side as described. Then turn a #9 1 1/2– 2" screw into the hole along side the shim. This holds the shim in place while the glue dries – at least over night. Then remove the screw and drive the pin in as described.

Replacing Uneven Bridge Pins (Oscar Schmidt Model B)

AQ Volume VIII, Number 3
REPLACING UNEVEN BRIDGE PINS
Bob Taylor

I have had the (mixed) pleasure of fixing uneven bridge pins on OSI "B" model 'harps, and would like to offer a few suggestions to those of you who could use a few pointers on this subject:

1. Have a supply of spare pins on hand before attempting to raise or lower pins – it's easy to deform the string groove and increase string breakage.

2. Pull the low pins up with vice grips padded with leather, or a drill press chuck. If all else fails, I use a small modified claw hammer, with a wellpadded caul, pivoting over the frame area only!

3. If using new pins, check that the string groove is the same distance from the pin top – file or shim as needed in the next step.

4. It is much easier to seat the pins level with their neighbors with a small arbor press, or even in a large vise with one large steel jaw and one well-padded jaw, than to hammer the pins in. Try to cover three or four pins on each side of the pin to be set. One pin will go in easily; when the neighboring pins are reached, the press will stop.

5. If repinning the whole 'harp, or a large section, make a "stop" for the press. I use ¼" plexiglass and several layers of thin felt. This sheet is drilled to accommodate the pins and is laid on the 'harp's face. It stops the press a uniform distance above the 'harp's top. This is how OSI sets the pins – or did prior to 1984. They are not bottomed out in their holes, but are pressed in through a spacer.

I believe that the bridge pins and metal anchor (or fine tuners) at the bottom end account for most of the difference in sound between the "A" and "B" OSIs. In the "A" model, the string vibrations are transmitted through several mediums to the frame: the metal or plastic bridge saddle, the wooden bridge, and the 'harp top. This produces the complicated, edgy, slightly percussive attack typical of the model "A," compared to the more organ-like, instant attack of the "B," with its direct string-pin-frame connection. I think the mass of the pins gives the "B" slightly more sustain and sweetness, at the expense of volume and "punch." Both sounds have their fans.

Finally, the OSI "B" was designed and in production before the Zagar gang drill. Originally, the silk screen used for the note names and logo also contained dots where the holes were to be located, and workers sat at drill presses drilling 72 holes in each 'harp body – what an exacting, boring job! On early "B"s you can see the irregularity in the rows of pins, especially when the drillers had too much coffee. The Zagar was subsequently designed and built, and was a blessing! ❖

When Your Guide Pins And Your Finger Picks Collide

AQ Volume VIII, Number 4

KEEP YOUR PICKS - AND YOUR COOL

George Orthey

Do you play a Model "A" type 'harp, an Oscar Schmidt Model "A," a ChromAharp, or any of the several handmade 'harps that have a bridge with small guide pins on the bridge? If so, you may have trouble with the hole in the face of your finger-pick catching on those pins. This causes your picks to fly, no matter how tightly you clamp them on your fingers. (Ever hear Bryan Bower's story about one of his picks flying off and landing in a woman's cleavage? The woman was sitting in the front row...)

Well, let me tell you Little Roy Lewis is one smart little rascal! He figured out that a strip of small plastic tubing put on those guide pins lets his picks glide noiselessly and smoothly over the pins and bridge.

He uses some "clear plastic tubing," so I went to a medical supply place and bought an oxygen supply kit – the kind that goes from the bottle to the nose. It's made out of clear plastic tubing a bit less than ¼" diameter. This generally costs less than a dollar, and has close to 10 feet of tubing in it.

I cut a piece about 4" long – (maybe you would want more, if you play all up and down near the bridge). I lay the piece of tubing alongside the bridge.

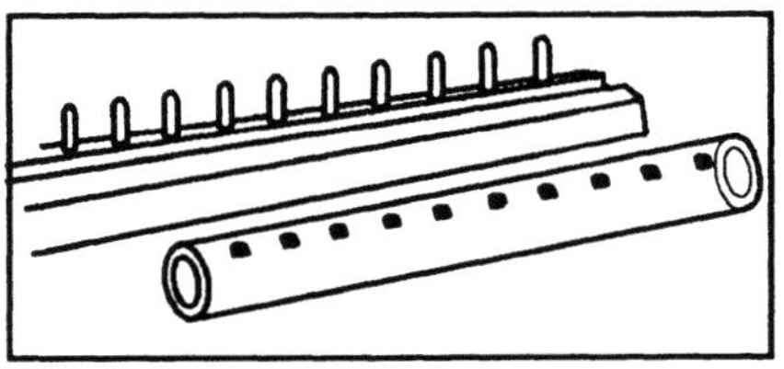

Using a glass writing pen or other fine-tip marker that will write on the plastic, I make a small tick mark on the tube next to each guide pin.

Then using a small drill bit 1/16" or 3/32", I drill a hole through one side of the tubing, making a series of holes halfway through the tube that coincide with the guide positions, as they have been marked on the tubing.

Now I put the tube in place on top of the guide pins and press the newly made holes down over the pins.

The tube sits down on the bridge.

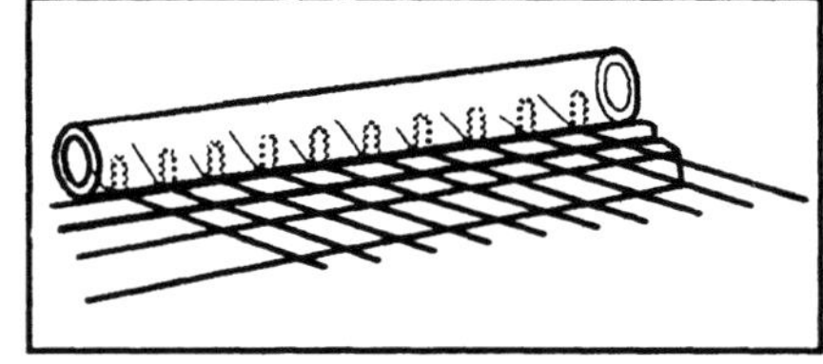

It doesn't interfere with the strings or the tuning, and lets the picks glide across the bridge and guide pins, without catching! Thanks, Little Roy! ❖

Restringing The Autoharp

AQ Volume V, Number 3

STRING ALONG WITH ME

George Orthey

It never ceases to amaze me to see autoharp players from novice to pro, who, if not terrified by the thought of refelting and restringing, at least break out into a cold sweat. Hands become Ripley Records with five thumbs each. I'm here to tell you that these jobs are tedious, yes – life-threatening, no.

We'll try to alleviate some of those "shakes" by walking you through the complete procedure you should follow when restringing a 'harp.

When do you restring? When your 'harp needs it. The time varies greatly. For you who rarely play, never touch strings with sweaty, sticky fingers and store it in perfect humidity and temperature, string replacement could be every ten years – maybe never. (Who cares? You've no doubt forgotten where you stored it, anyway.) On the other hand, for my "demo" 'harps, (really my wife's), played by every french-fry-crunching would-be-Bowers that comes along, (bare-fingered, yet), the strings last (almost fall off by) one season. I've never seen a seriously played 'harp with strings more than two years old that won't show a great sound improvement with a new set of strings.[1]

Locate and buy a set of strings to fit your 'harp. Do this before you tear it apart. You don't find autoharp strings at the corner grocery.

There are Model A and Model B Oscar Schmidt International (OSI) strings. Model A strings go on the old black box-type 'harps that have bridges. The string loop ends go to small posts on the dead-pin end. There is a dead-pin end cover that must be removed to get at these. Model B strings go on the newer OSI 'harps that have guide posts at the tuning pin end and an anchor bar, or fine tuners at the dead pin end.

All ChromAharps are Model A-type 'harps. OSI Model A strings made before January 1993 have an eyelet (ferrule) that's too small to fit on the ChromAharp's large dead pins. New Model A strings made after that date have the eyelet removed. These will fit the ChromAharps, a great change for those owners, since ChromAharp strings are hard to find. If you must use an older Model A string, remove the eyelet or make a noose in the dead pin end of the string to accommodate the large dead pins.

There are also LaBella Model A and Model B strings available. The Model As will fit both ChromAharp and OSI Model A 'harps, and the Model Bs will fit the OSI Model B 'harps.

Some luthier 'harps are OSI-compatible for strings. However, many handmade 'harps with fine tuners require Model A Special strings[2] for best performance. Ask your luthier about this.

Zither wire that is used on psalteries and hammered dulcimers is also a suitable substitute for smooth wire (not wound) strings. Use approximately the same diameter wire for replacement. Make the wire long enough, that when placed in position on the deadpin end, it will extend about two inches beyond the tuning pin. This will give you about four winds on the pin when the string is tuned up. You'll also need to put a ferrule in the end loop for OSI fine tuner or anchor bar.

Clean up your act. Before we take the strings off and get started, now's a good time to remind you that when you have the 'harp apart, you can do a thorough cleanup of the instrument. It's also a time to do other maintenance and repair as well. Check for loose pins as you remove the strings. Make a note of which ones are loose, and shim the holes before restringing.[3]

You also may notice on some 'harps with the anchor bar or fine tuners that the anchor bar or fine tuner bar tends to ride up out of the body rather than remain well-seated down in the body. This will only get worse with time, so fix it now.

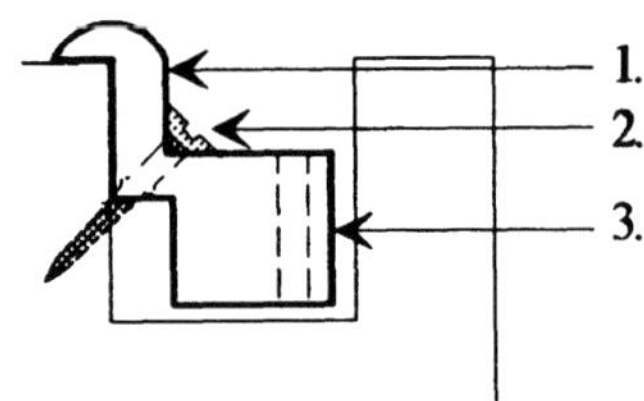

Fine Tuner Base Bar

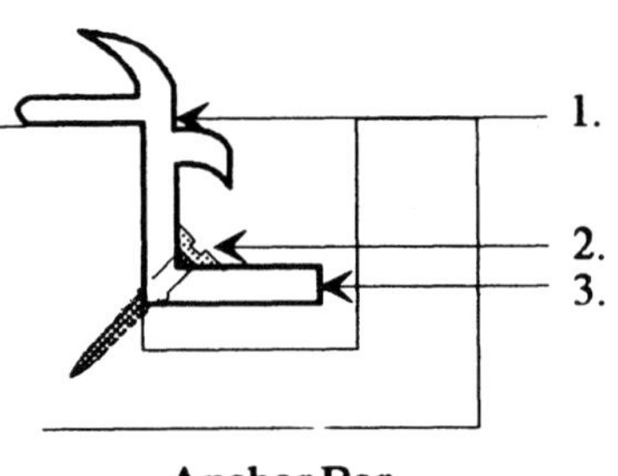

Anchor Bar

Be sure the anchor bar/fine tuner base bar will seat tightly down on the face of the 'harp at this point (1). Remove the bar and drill a 1/8" hole through the bar as indicated in the drawing (2) at three or four points equally spaced along the bar. Note OSI has already done this on the newer sets of fine tuner bars, so if you are putting in a set of fine tuners (this is the time to do it) to replace the old anchor bar, you may find there are predrilled holes. When drilling the holes in an old bar, I slightly countersink these holes to give added clearance above the screw head. Place the bar back in the 'harp body, well-seated at (1), and drill a 3/32" pilot hole through the hole in the anchor bar and into the 'harp body as illustrated. Do not drill clear through the back. Just drill about 3/4" deep. Use a 3/4" #4 flat-head screw. Put some candle wax or soap on the screw. It will turn in easier. When the screws pull tight, they will lock the bar firmly down in place so there will be no more ride-up. If there is a space behind the bar here (3), take one or more layers of thin wood veneer or hard paper like manila folder and shim this space full.

Note: Lightly mark the exact position of the anchor bar before removing it so that it can be returned to the exact same position. If the anchor bar is being replaced by a fine tuner system, the base bar of the fine tuners should go in the same position. This is necessary so that the string bed will be in the exact position after restringing as it was before.

Restringing Your 'Harp

One string or 37, the procedure is the same. We'll do one string, then later advance to the whole 'harp.

(A) Remove the string. Back the tuning pin out, unwinding the string from the pin until the string pulls straight out of the hole in the tuning pin. This will set the pin so it will return to its original correct height when the new string is installed. This unwinding is accomplished easiest for a broken string by grasping the end of the piece of wire left on the pin with a pair of hemostats or needle-nose pliers while unwinding the pin. Note: the pins are threaded. They rise about 1/4" every three to four pin turns. If the string is no longer wound on the pin, unwind the pin three and one-half to four turns. When the new string is put in place, 2 1/2" of wire will wind on the pin to bring it exactly back to its rightful position.

Remove the string at the deadpin end. If you have an A Model-type 'harp, you will need to remove the dead-pin cover and slip the string eyelet off the dead pin. In a B Model with an anchor bar, you may find the string wedged. Wiggle it, push it down, back, and out of the anchor bar. If you have fine tuners, completely remove the screw and cam from the fine tuner base bar. Grasp the string eyelet and pull the string out of the cam.

String replacement Prepare the replacement string eyelet end for remounting.

For Model A 'harps, do not clip the winding tail (3). When the eyelet (1) is placed over the dead-pin, the winding tail (3) should point toward the bass strings of the 'harp. Now the last wind before the tail lies under the string at (2) not across the top of the string. This will make the string settle and hold tune much quicker.

3. 2. 1.

If you have a Model B 'harp with an anchor bar (not fine tuners), slip the ball and winding under the anchor bar with the standing wire seated in the full depth of the slot in the anchor bar. Don't clip the tail. The position of the tail and ball make no difference. They will settle in place when the string pulls tight.

With fine tuners, properly seating the string and ball in the fine tuner cam is essential to obtaining a no-slip string that settles and holds tune after two or three tunings. **NO MATTER WHAT THE FINE TUNER DIRECTIONS SAY, DO NOT CLIP THE TAIL OFF THE WOUND BASS AND TOP OCTAVE STRINGS.** Clip the tails as closely as you can only on the very stiff middle octave strings.

Now with a bass or top octave string, bend the tail back alongside the windings as illustrated.

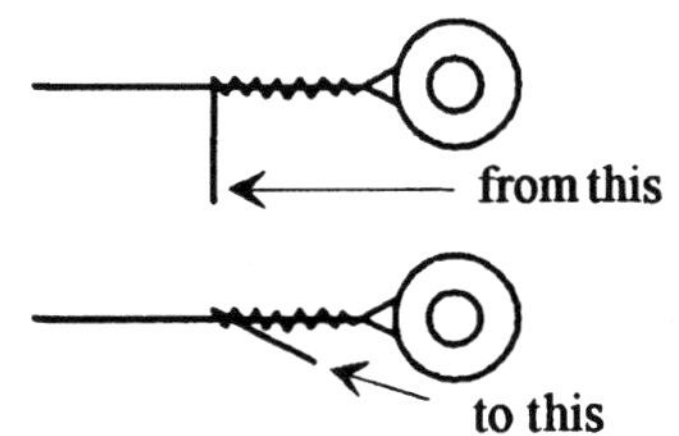

The windings and tail seat up into the fine tuner cam like this:

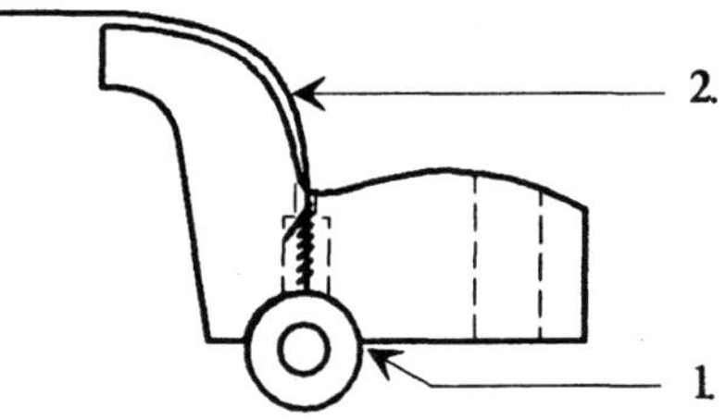

The ball should sit in the curved seat in the bottom of the cam (1). Align the ball with the seat. Bend the string at (2) in the direction the string will lie when properly in place and tuned. This bend will cause the ball to properly align when you pull the string tight after the fine tuner cam is in place.

For the mid-octave strings, clip the tail as close to the standing wire as you can:

This will still leave a stiff, sharp point on this very short tail. When this string pulls up into the cam seating the ball, this sharp end will catch and the string will not unwind. If you clipped the tail on the thinner bass and treble strings, the tail would simply unwind as you tighten the string. It would not settle and hold.

Before you put the fine tuner cam back in place, make a loop with the string, holding each end and slide the loop through under the bars. If you just poke the straight end of the wire through under the bars, it will get amazingly tangled with the adjacent strings. Grab the loop when it comes through and keep it above the strings, releasing the tuning pin end of the string and guiding it to the tuning pin. Put the tip of the string through its tuning pin and clamp your hemostat on the tip of the string so it can't come back out of the tuning pin. Place the cam in position on the fine tuner base bar. Check to see that the ball is seated and the standing wire is properly aligned. Turn the fine tuner screw all the way down. You will back it up a bit later, but until then it keeps the string and ball properly seated while you wind the string on the tuning pin. Be careful about sliding the string around under the chord bars, particularly the very hard wires. They can easily damage the bar felts or tear them loose. You can protect against this by placing a piece of manila folder paper between the strings and the chord bars.

Some new fine tuner sets include small washers. Check carefully to see if they are lock washers or flat washers. Do not — repeat — *do not* use lock washers! If you do, you'll ruin your fine tuners, and they will function in a very erratic manner. Washers are not necessary. Flat washers make fine tuners work smoother. Throw the lock washers away. I also have found that a small drop of graphite lock oil in the threads of the machine screws make the fine tuners work much easier.[4]

Now you are ready to wind up the string on the tuning pin. I don't like the sharp points of the wires sticking out the other side of the tuning pins, so I make a small loop in the end of the string and put the sharp point back in the tuning pin.

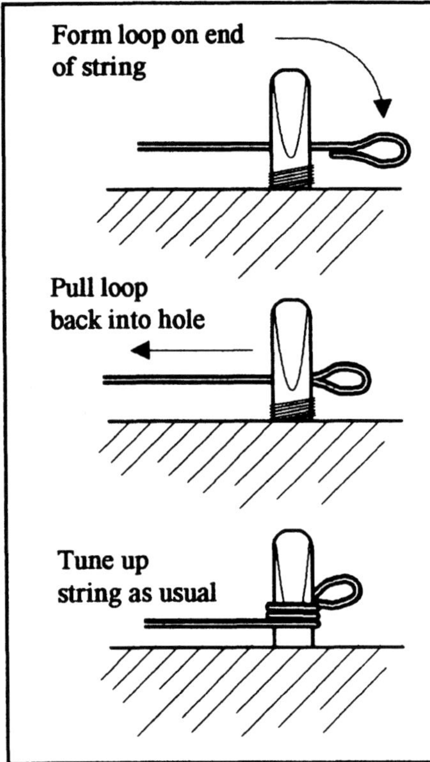

Turn the tuning pin, winding the string onto the pin so it makes a nice clean spiral on the pin. Do not let the wire cross itself.

If you have a Model B type 'harp with guide posts rather than a bridge, the string should come across the guide pin essentially level to the tuning pin. Make a closed, tight coil.

If yours is a Model A type 'harp with bridges, the string should come across the bridge and angle down toward the face of the 'harp. Make an open spiral winding. The pins on these 'harps are usually slanted to facilitate this. This gives a firm downward pressure of the string on the bridge. Without this strong down-pressure, you will lose brightness, and may have unwanted "buzzy" sounding strings.

Before pulling the string tight, be sure it is in place, the ball end is well-situated in the anchor bar or on the dead-pin, and the string is not tangled in the bar felts. Pull the string up to tune. Back off the fine tuner screw to level the cam if you have fine tuners. Now tune the string several times using the tuning pin only.

– **And so on.** We are finally back to restringing the whole 'harp. No more sidetracks. As I said, single string replacement will simply be repeated 36 times. One major difference here is that it makes life much easier if you remove the entire chord bar mechanism first. Don't do it on your backyard picnic table. It's murder finding those little springs in the grass. I suggest doing it on a white sheet. It makes little parts easy to find. Keep track of the pieces so you get it all back together later. It's not a bad time to glue the springs in place in the bar holder or on the combs using silicone glue.

Tension mounts. Before you remove the old strings. Make note of any pins that are noticeably too high or too low. Measure how much the discrepancy is compared to the other pins. Write this down. Now release the tension about one turn on all A notes, then all the B notes, all the C notes, etc. This will release the tension uniformly across the 'harp and prevent the unequal stress of starting at one end and going straight through in order. As I mentioned before, notice loose, soft pins.

Now start from the bottom and remove the strings. Draw the middle of the string up as you turn the tuning pin until the string is fully unwound. Now pull the string out of the pin. It may be necessary to clip the tip off the string on the very stiff mid-octave strings to get it to come out of the pin. Then, as described for a single string, remove each one from its anchor bar/dead-pin/fine tuner.

If you don't want to take all the strings off and clean your 'harp up, you can take the fully tuned 'harp and remove the strings one at a time, replacing and rough tuning the new string before going on to the next. This is simply repeating the single string process thirty six times. Be sure to rough tune each string as you put it on to maintain equal tension on all parts of the 'harp.

Now back to a complete "de-tuning." With all the strings off, do whatever cleanup, pin tightening, fine tuner installation/fixation needed.

If you had a tuning pin that was at an incorrect height in your 'harp, you can now adjust it to its proper height. If it was too low by, say, $^1/_8$", raise it $^1/_8$" now, or if it was too high, lower it by that much now. Turn the pin counterclockwise to raise it, clockwise to lower it.

Keep in mind correctly positioned pins in this stringless state may not be uniform in height even though they'll be correct when retuned. This is due to the variance in the standard string length.

With idealized strings on custom 'harps, the tuning pins will in general, all be essentially level when detuned. Strings should have excess length trimmed off so that about $2^1/_2$" of wire will wind on the tuning pin. The pins are backed out 3 - 4 turns from the normal tuned position when the strings are removed. This will accommodate the $2^1/_2$" of wire, and the pin should return to the normal correct level when tuned up.

The process of restringing is simply one at a time, like putting single strings in place. You don't have the chord bars to work around, though. Remember to bend the tails in the bass wound strings and in the top octave strings. Clip the tails in the mid-octave for fine tuners. Don't clip the tails on anchor bar or Model A-type 'harps with dead-pins.

Put the strings on, pulled to light tension. Carefully check for seating and correct positioning of the strings. They should be equally spaced coming off the dead pin bridge or fine tuners. Check the fine tuners to see that they are all essentially level.

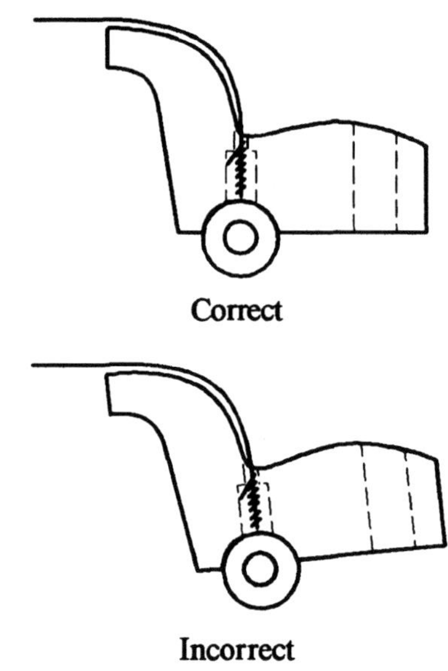

Correct

Incorrect

If, when this is all in place, a tuning pin is obviously too high or too low, you can remove the string, correct the pin, and then put the string back on. I would not fool with this for minor corrections so long as the pins are tight and it all works OK.

Ready to tune up? Do the reverse of the "de-tuning." Tune up all the A notes, all the B notes, all the C notes, etc. till all is rough tuned. Now I use a stiff thumb pick and strum across the strings hard. The vibration and firm strum on the strings will settle them.

Once you have started pulling the strings up, don't leave it half-tuned or all out of tune. Tune it all. Tune it correctly, settle it, and retune. If you allow a 'harp to sit randomly out of tune, it will take forever to hold tune when you get around to it. A string is like a lost cat. It keeps trying to go back home. If you tune your 'harp correctly right away, it should hold its pitch within a few days. For the first few days, tune it using the tuning pins to get the stretch out. After that, use the fine tuners if you have them.

Put your bars back. Enjoy!

Tools, Materials, and Cost

1. A set of properly matched strings for your model 'harp – ($45.00 OSI set)
2. Philips screw driver
3. Hemostats or needle-nose pliers
4. Wire cutter
5. Fine tuner set – ($139.00 OSI set) ❖

Restringing is also discussed in "String Problems"p.27.

[1] Find more symptoms of tired strings and a quick fix for tarnish in "Annual Mechanical Tune-up"p.1.

[2] See "String Designation Chart for Diatonic Autoharps"p.62 for updated information concerning manufactured string sets.

[3] See "Loose Tuning Pins"p.19.

[4] See "Questions And Answers"p.122 for this procedure.

String Problems

AQ Volume I, Number 4

STRINGS THAT GO SPRONG

George F. Orthey

Tuning problems are not at all unique to the autoharp. Every stringed instrument owner is blessed with the tuning dilemma to some degree. However, with the autoharp, we are talking at least 36 strings here, which makes us lovers of this instrument just a little more interested in the tuning subject than, say, the three- or four-stringed Appalachian dulcimer player.

Good physical condition of the 'harp is basic to its staying in tune. If your autoharp is warping, coming apart at the seams, or has loose pins, you have headaches. If the 'harp won't stay in shape or the tuning pins won't hold, all else is lost.

Restringing a 'harp, either one string or a whole set, must be done properly. Each string should be firmly seated at the ball end so that no further slippage will occur after the 'harp is tuned. This is easiest to do by tuning the string up above its intended pitch, repeatedly plucking the string and observing it to drift steadily flat. Keep tuning it up till it doesn't drift flat and holds steady at a note one half step above its intended note. Pull the brass-wound bass strings and the middle octave of non-wound strings up 1 or 2 notes high till they stabilize. Do this with each string as you put it on. But, don't leave it there. Tune it down below its intended pitch. If you are just doing one replacement string, bring it up to pitch. If you are doing a whole replacement set, leave it tuned low and go on to the next string. After the strings are all on, tune all the As, then all the A♯s, all the Bs, etc., so you load the 'harp evenly.

Do all your stringing and tuning in one sitting. Don't ever let a randomly tuned 'harp sit for any length of time – even overnight. A piano tuner's nightmare is a randomly pitched piano. It can be carefully retuned many times and still it will wander aimlessly. These are all issues of string "memory."

A 'harp in poor tune cannot be tuned today for performance tomorrow. It must be brought to pitch, allowed to stabilize, then retuned as near as possible to the time of performance. It's still likely to drift out of tune as you play it.

The once-tuned string, like a lost cat, has a burning desire to try to go back home.

A 'harp that is changed from chromatic to diatonic tuning where a few strings are changed 1/2 step flat or sharp will result in some strings staying in tune and some going out. Again, like the lost cat, the ones you dragged away from their home will try to stray back.

This can be minimized by overdoing it the first time. Tune it up or down an extra one half step. Leave it overnight. Then tune it right. Be careful of the smallest wound and the top small smooth wire strings. If you are tuning up, they can't be pulled up too much without the risk of breaking the string.

Avoid too much winding on the pins.[1] Standard replacement strings are made to wrap about four turns around the pins. If you are using hammered dulcimer wire or guitar wire for a replacement, a string length about 2 to 3" beyond the pin will give you four to five winds. Too much winding, overlapping, and uneven coils on the pins will increase the chance of slippage and therefore, should be avoided.

For the new player, I would like to put a word in here about replacing a broken string. So many people have asked me, "When replacing a string, how do I know when I have wound a string enough times on the pin? How far into the 'harp should I turn the pin?" I tell them to remember to back up the tuning pin as many revolutions (counterclockwise) as the string is wrapped on the pin. Then remove the old wire. Put the new string through the hole about one-quarter inch past the hole, bend over the end, and turn the pin clockwise the same number of turns. Better yet, use the method I developed years ago. After pulling the string through the hole, double the end over about one quarter of an inch with needle-nosed pliers or a hemostat. Then, carefully guide the loop back into the hole before rewinding. This technique helps keep the string from pulling back through the hole while tightening, and you won't have those string ends stabbing your fingers or pulling the threads of your clothing. When tuned, the string should come tight with the pin back where you started.[2]

Don't ever pick up your 'harp by the tuning pins — especially the high treble pins. Just the weight of the 'harp alone will be enough to move the pins enough to knock those strings out of tune.

So why does a perfect, well-strung, solid 'harp like yours still lose its tuning on the bed post overnight? Or more frustrating yet, between the 2 p.m. tuning and the 3 p.m. autoharp contest?

String drift on the bridge after tuning can be a cause: You pluck string #1 gently, then turn it up to pitch. Then the next, (#2 string), you get too high, so you pluck it gently and turn it down to pitch. The first time you strum the 'harp firmly, the #1 string will drift sharp, the #2 string, flat. To avoid this, tune all strings up to pitch while plucking the string firmly and repeatedly. The string will settle at its proper pitch now, not later.

If you are a very gentle tuner and gentle player and have not properly seated your strings, avoid asking Drew Smith or Mike Fenton to show you a few licks with their strong thumb leads on your 'harp. If you don't heed this advice, you will have to re-seat your strings and tune up – again. This time using a firm steady plucking on each string.

String age is a very controversial subject. Some say replace strings when you break them. This results in strings that vary from one hour to ten years old on the same 'harp. Others say restring periodically, as the strings will go "dead" and will be hard to keep in tune. My experience shows both to be correct. For those who play gently, clean their instruments meticulously, store them in cases, and treat them generally like the crown jewels, breakage rarely occurs and frequent replacement of strings is not necessary. For those people who "ride 'em hard and put 'em away wet," annual replacement is a must for both sound quality and tuneability.

Last and probably by far the most frustrating problem in the fine tuning of 36 strings is The Constant and Unpredictable Ravages of Weather. Temperature gives rapid and short-term change; humidity, long-term change. Unfortunately, different string diameters, tensions, and some wound- vs. unwound-string effects cause strings to go sharp or flat independently. The shorter, higher-pitched, and tighter a string, the more it is affected by the weather. Temperature gives rapid and short term change; humidity, long term change.

Having weathered 32 years of craft and music shows in all seasons, I have made the following discovery: if an instrument is tuned at say – 2 p.m. on a sunny afternoon, no matter how bad it sounds the next morning in the middle of a cloudburst, later that day, when the sun is shining again, it will be miraculously back in good tune!

Anything that can be done to stabilize the instrument's environment will help to reduce the problem. Tune it in a temperature/humidity controlled environment similar to where you will be playing. Keep it in a case and protect the case from extreme heat and cold. If a sudden summer hail storm appears and the temperature drops 30 degrees as you stand waiting your turn to compete in a contest, you can always hope it keeps up long enough that the sound of the hail on the tin roof will drown out your out-of-tune 'harp. And, you can rest assured that the poor soul who is at that moment competing on stage is hearing his 'harp slowly go mad. There are no favorites played in this game. ❖

[1] Updated information is found in "Restringing The Autoharp" p.23. Standard strings often have excess length and will need to be cut off so that 2" of wire will wind on the tuning pin.

[2] See illustration of this procedure in "Restringing the Autoharp" p.23.

Adding The 37th String

AQ Volume IX, Number 1

BRINGING THE 37TH STRING BACK TO LIFE

Dr. Victor Frankenharp
(aka George Orthey)

In the early part of this century, my instrument of choice, the autoharp, had 37 strings. Ah, I remember well playing lovely tunes for my faithful friend Igor while he gathered monster parts from here and there. We enjoyed these pastoral scenes immensely – Igor with his shovel, me with my Oscar Schmidt 'harp. Those were the nights!

Regrettably, those memorable times ended abruptly. After my Monster paid a friendly, get-acquainted visit to the local village, the ungrateful inhabitants torched our castle. My beautiful autoharp was cremated! I was harpbroken.

Igor's collection was lost as well, but it was easily refurbished. However, he found his gatherings dull without my hauntingly beautiful music, and complained bitterly. I, too, was uncommonly morose. Thus, one fine rainy evening, I sent Igor down to the village to collect a replacement for my beloved 'harp. But to my horror, the replacement did not come up to the standards of my fried friend. Müller's "Pray for the Dead" lacked that old pizazz. "Crossing the Bar" was awash. Even Walton's "Death" just didn't have that "git up and git." Why? Oscar Schmidt had buried the 37th string – the high D zinger was missing! I immediately called for my master scavenger-assistant. With Igor's parts and my know-how, we created a most satisfying 37-string autoharp!

In this article, I will share my secrets which will enable you to stitch together create your own masterpiece. Take care to follow my formula. Otherwise, your creation could turn into a monstrous nightmare.

It Begins

Oscar Schmidt didn't redesign the body and chord bars to eliminate the 37th string's space when they laid it to rest. The space is still there. The "Wildwood Flower" would be a lot more satisfying with a C♮ and D at the top, since it is a D diatonic instrument. Any 'harp often played in G or D would benefit from a D zinger. Lyman Taylor suggested dropping a note in the bass and retuning the instrument to get a D zinger at the top of the 'harp. This could cause some string-length problems. So, since the space is still there, why not bring that 37th string back to life?

To accomplish this, you must install a tuning pin (see #1 in the illustration below), a dead pin (#4), and a guide post or bridge stop (#2 and #3) for each end of the string.

Equipment Needed

1. Drill – preferably a drill press
2. 3/16" New sharp drill bit
3. 3/32" Drill bit (Model "B" 'harps only)
4. 5/64" Drill bit (Model "A" 'harps only)
5. Guide pin (Model "B" 'harps only)
6. #6 Round head steel screw 1" long (Model "B" 'harps only)
7. One tuning pin
8. Model "A" #36 C string or 2' piece #5 or #6 music wire
9. Two 4d finishing nails (Model "A" 'harps only) (d = penny)

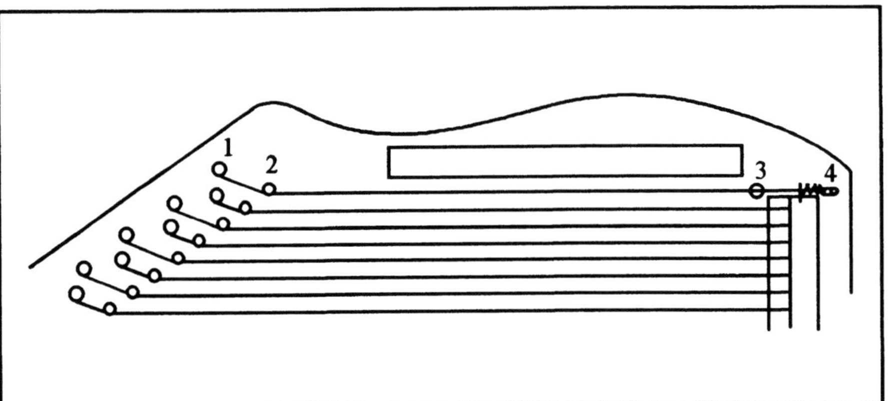

The existing top string (C string) is 8 1/4"-8 1/2" long. It can be tuned up to a C♮, but will suffer breakage in some cases if tuned up to D.

By installing a guide pin at #2 on the same line as the other guide pins, you will reduce the string length of the new top string to 7 3/4" or less which can easily be tuned up to D.

The bridges can be extended up on the ChromAharp and Oscar Schmidt Model "A" types enough to accommodate the extra string. If you do this, it would be best to replace the bridge rod with a piece long enough to extend under the new string.

Scavenging For Parts

All except the tuning pin, guide pin and string can be found in a good hardware store. The other parts can be collected from an Oscar Schmidt dealer or autoharp or hammered dulcimer makers. Even I, Dr. Victor Frankenharp, usually have an extra auto-cadaver with serviceable parts. (I can bribe Igor out of a part or two with a rousing 'harp rendition of "Day Is Dying," his favorite.)

The Procedure

Carefully mark the position of the new guide pin and tuning pin so each is in the same relative position as the existing pins, just one step up. Using the 3/16" drill, set up so you will drill a hole approximately 3/4" deep. Don't drill through the back! (I once slipped while altering my monster's neck. He complains constantly about the keg bungs I used to plug up the holes. He is very vain.) Drill the hole in one clean motion. Don't reenter the hole with the drill, because you will ream it.

Put the guide pin in its hole and tap it in until the string groove is at the same exact height as the existing strings. If this pin fits loosely, put a bit of glue on the side walls of the hole.

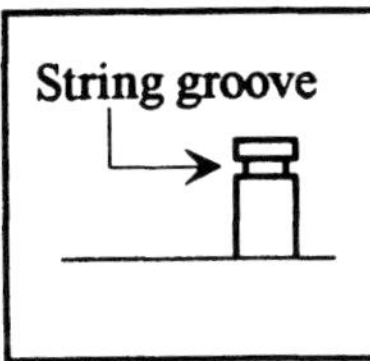

At the dead pin end of the string, (anchor bar fine tuner end – see point #3 on illustration below), find a spot exactly 1/4" above the top string. Drill a 3/32" hole on a slight angle away from the vibrating string bed.

Be sure you drill this into solid wood which is clear of the chord bar assembly.

When you turn the screw (at position #3) into the 'harp, the groove in the top of the screw should end up in line with the string. And the screw should be turned into the 'harp to a depth that the string will lie at the same height as the existing strings.

Last, put the dead pin/anchor pin

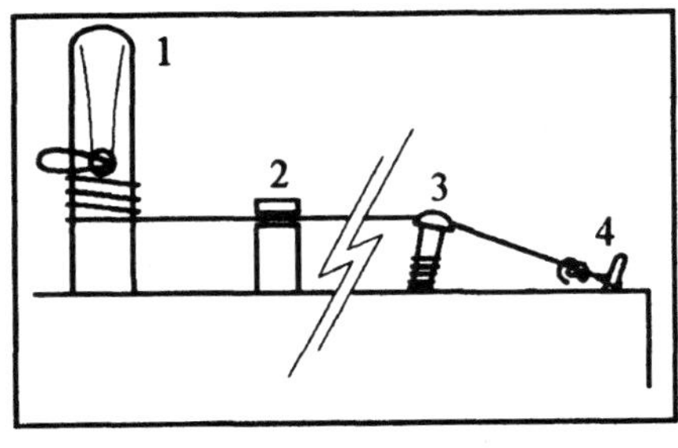

(at #4 position) either through the metal cover found behind the anchor bar slot, or just beyond the edge of that metal cover. Be sure the hole is drilled on a slant away from the direction of the string pull so the loop end won't slip off the pin, and to repeat, be sure it is into solid wood. Also, be sure a tail is left on the loop end of the string to prevent it from unwinding.

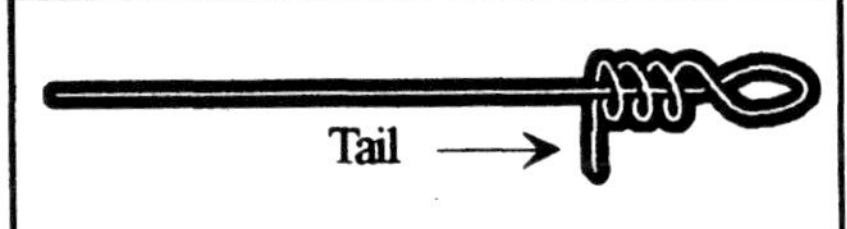

If you have a Model "A"-type 'harp, you won't need the guide pin (#2) or dead pin end screw (#3). You simply extend these bridges up if necessary. Drill for a dead pin down over the end of the 'harp – and for a bridge guide pin like the existing pins just 1/4" up from the last pin on the 'harp. I use #6 bridge pins. You can make one out of a 4d finishing nail.

In any case, a #36 C Model "A" string or a similar piece of .014 wire can now be put into place. Cut off excess wire so that about 2 ½" of wire will be wound on the tuning pin. Drive the tuning pin into the hole so it reaches the same height as the existing tuning pins. (The timid can turn it in with a tuning wrench.) Back it out four full turns. Insert the tip of the wire through the hole in the tuning pin. Bend a little loop in the

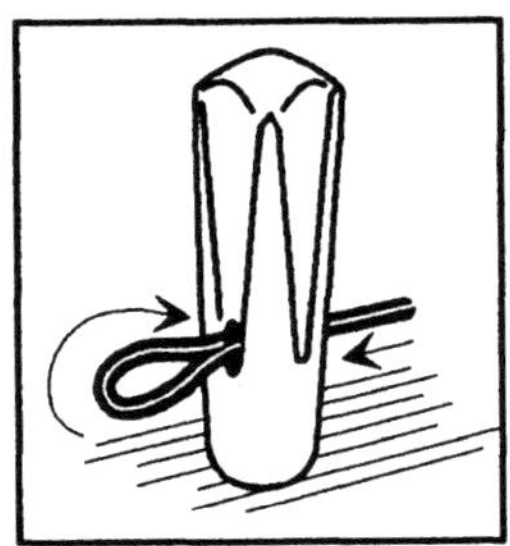

end and pull end back into hole. Then turn the pin until the string comes tight. The tuning pin should be at the same height as the other pins when the string comes up to tune. Keep the string as level as you can off the guide pin to the tuning pin on your "B" Model 'harp:

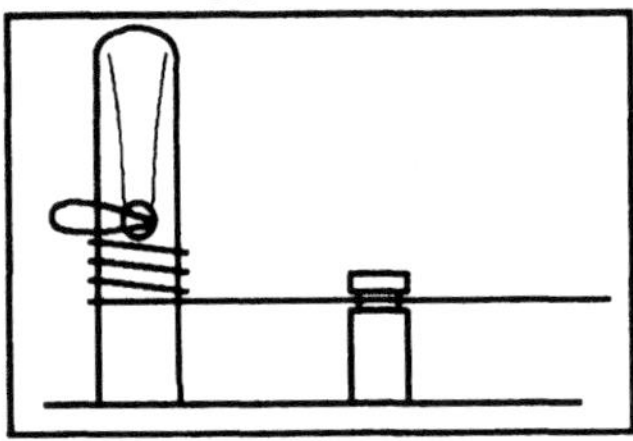

If you have bridges, (Model "A" style), be sure the string winds on the pin close to the sound board as shown here.

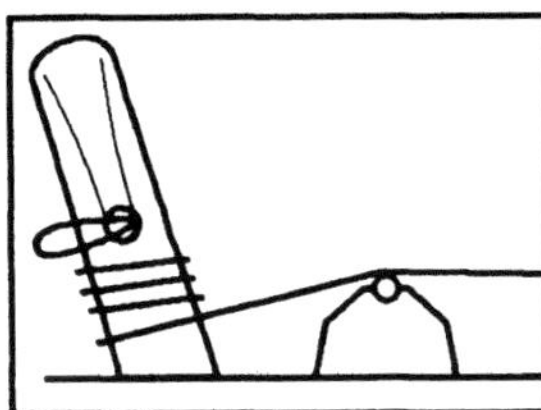

Now for your "Wildwood Flowers," where this change is almost a "must," change the tuning of the top strings as shown in the chart below:

String:	31	32	33	34	35	36	37
Tune From:	F♯	G	G	A	A	B	–
To:	F♯	G	A	A	B	C♯	D

For instruments other than a D diatonic autoharp on which you have installed this string, simply tune that string up to a high D.

Isn't that much better? Ending on a D tonic zinger is so very satisfying. It reminds me of the time Frau Müller and Igor…but that's another story. ❖

Strings – Their Ideal Sizes And Lengths

AQ Volume II, Number 2

"STEINWAY GRANDE AUTOHARPE"

– And Why It Just Ain't So

George Orthey

Why is an autoharp just an autoharp – and a piano just a piano? And who sez, anyway?

Most everyone has had the experience of tuning a string too high, with the final result being a resounding BANG! This breaking point may be found the hard way with time and costs of string replacement, or it can be predicted with great accuracy – using the pencil and paper method.

First, let's get rid of the mistaken idea that if a string breaks before you get it up to pitch, you can just replace it with a smaller string – then it'll tune up OK. A given length of string, (non wound), will break at the exact same note regardless of the string diameter. This is a fact well known to the old harpsichord makers, but one that is still intuitively doubted by the novice. So, why use different diameter strings? To reduce the tension necessary to pull the higher strings to pitch.

Thirty-two years ago, while working on experimental psalteries and hammered dulcimers with my friend, Howie Mitchell, we decided that this string "fact" must be re-proven. I guess we broke a few hundred pieces of wire only to find out that those rascals knew what they were talking about. We found that a 40" vibrating length of musical wire, like that used on autoharps and hammered dulcimers, will break when you pull it up to near middle C.

This then relates to the octaves. **By taking 1/2 and 1/4 of 40", you can determine the break lengths of the first and second octaves above middle C.** Another way to put this: middle C (autoharp string #12), cannot exceed 40" in length; the next C above middle C (autoharp string #24), cannot exceed 20" in length; and the highest C (autoharp string #36), cannot exceed 10" in length. (The numbering system used here is based on the Oscar Schmidt standard string numbering.)

We have only gone higher than middle C so far in this discussion. **As you go up the scale, each octave requires a string length of one half the previous octave string length. Similarly, as you go down the scale, each octave requires a string length of twice the previous octave string length.** Therefore, the C below middle C should theoretically be 80" in length. To compensate for this, wound strings are used. The lower the string, the less effective this compensation. The low D on the Oscar Schmidt Wildwood Flower™ tuning should be 8 to 9 feet long. It has been shortened to 20". This stretches the limits of "correctability."

The above break length numbers are all maximum theoretical lengths. In reality, due to bending over bridges, around pins, and such, one cannot normally get away with more than 90 to 95% of break length. This friction and bending factor affects thinner wire a bit less than heavier wire, thus giving the slightly false impression that by going to a thinner wire, one can tune a string to a higher note.

It is also generally stated by the old harpsichord makers that a string at less than 50% of its break length becomes dull and thumpy, while a string of more than 85% of its break length sounds thin and thready, making the kind of sound that causes you to lean your head away lest you get belted in the ear by a breaking wire.

Thinking about all this in regards to the autoharp: #12C is 19-20" long right at 50% of break length and #36C is at 8-9" long near its extreme tension. If you use a smooth wire below middle C, like the old A model 'harps, #10A♯ and #11B strings will be as dull as dishwater. Using windings on the wire will correct this to a great extent.

The strings from middle C up through about the middle of the top octave of the autoharp are the strings that are actually at 50 to 80% of break length – the ideal. Think about it. Where is the forte of the 'harp? Certainly not in the low bass, where huge corrections have been made with windings – nor at the top, where we have stretched things to the limit. The mid-range of the 'harp may also be slightly enhanced because of its position on the sound board. This is unavoidable.

'Twould be nice to have a "Steinway Grande Autoharpe." With the clear, bell-like tones of a concert harp at the high end, and the dark, full boom of a timpani at the other.

The autoharp's size, shape, and the convenience of optimum playing room all demand bending the ideal. Also for the convenience of transportation, an autoharp is not a piano, and that's OK with me – Mary Lou takes at least three of them with us wherever we go.

Addendum: September 1999

by John Hollandsworth and George Orthey

Wound strings, unlike smooth wire strings, do not fit the calculated break length values easily determined by mathematical formula, one over the twelfth root of two (.943875) times any known break length. This will give you the break length of the sequence of half-step notes. (For example, .943875 times 40" would give you the break length of C♯.)

The use of windings allows a shorter wire length to be tuned to a much lower note, and in general, the larger the winding (overall diameter) of the string, the lower it can be tuned.

The purpose of this set of measurements was to determine, using a standard autoharp string set, what range of notes a given string can effectively produce, what notes of good quality it will produce, and at what note will a given string break.

We used the standard OSI designations of wound strings, 1F - 12C, and also the added LB string in the Model A special sets used on many handmade 'harps.

Our method was to use a fully strung and tuned autoharp so the quality of the notes in their working environment could be evaluated.

Each wound bass string was in turn tuned down to a slack state, then gradually tuned up until a weak but definable note was reached. The string was then tuned up 1/2 step at a time with empirical evaluation of the quality of the notes produced. The eventual break of the string established an upper extreme limit. After breaking each string, it was replaced by a new string which was tuned to its proper note before repeating the procedure on the next higher string. We started from LB and proceeded up through 1F to 12C.

The string set used was a standard set produced by American Winding Company, and measurements were taken to ascertain it was the same as OSI Model A, OSI Model B, and Orthey Special Model A string sets.

The Evaluation Chart

The *starting note* on the Evaluation Chart was the lowest note that was clearly definable, and measurable with an electronic tuner.

The *low acceptable tone* notes below the ideal good tone showed diminished volume and resonance compared to the ideal. They also were noticeably slack under the thumb pick.

The ideal *good tone* notes showed essentially equal quality, resonance, and clarity. They would be the string/note combinations of choice for nonstandard bass octave tunings commonly found on diatonic 'harps.

The *poor high tone* notes were characterized as having very tight thumb pick resistance coupled with a thin, hard, thready sound of diminished volume.

It is interesting to notice the closeness of the smaller wound strings' ideal notes to their break notes compared to the break notes of the larger wound strings. ❖

Editor's note: John Hollandsworth is a Mountain Laurel Autoharp Champion.

EVALUATION OF WOUND STRINGS FROM LB TO 12C

Designated String Note	Starting Note	Low Acceptable Tone	Good Tone	Poor High Tone	Break Note
LB	C	C-D	E-G	G♯-A	A♯
1F	D	E	F-A	A♯-C♯	D
2G	F	F♯	G-B	C♯-D	E
3C	F♯	G-A	A♯-D♯	E-F	F♯
4D	B	C-C♯	D-E	F-F♯	G
5E	C	C♯	D-F	F♯-G♯	A
6F	C	C♯-D	D♯-F♯	G	G♯
7F	C♯	D	D♯-G	G♯	A
8G	D	D♯-E	F-G♯	A	A♯
9A	D♯	E-F	F♯-A♯	B-C	C♯
10A♯	E	F-F♯	G-B	C	C♯
11B	E	F-G	G♯-C	C♯	D
12C	G	G♯-A	A♯-D	D♯	E

The starting note to the break note range incorporates notes found within a one octave range centered on the designated string note.

DESCRIPTION OF WOUND STRINGS FROM LB TO 12C

Designated String Note	Core Size	Description	Overall Diameter
LB	.022	3 layer brass wind	.100
1F	.022	2 layer brass wind	.085
2G	.022	2 layer brass wind	.073
3C	.022	2 layer brass wind	.069
4D	.020	single brass wind	.052
5E	.020	single brass wind	.050
6F	.018	single brass wind	.047
7F	.018	single brass wind	.045
8G	.018	single brass wind	.042
9A	.018	single brass wind	.038
10A	.018	single brass wind	.036
11B	.018	single brass wind	.034
12C	.018	single brass wind	.030

String Substitution

AQ Volume VI, Number 4

WHEN YOUR G-STRING BREAKS

George Orthey

The first, best, and least stressful place to find a replacement string is in your 'harp case. Carry a full replacement set at all times. Draw a single replacement from that set and replace it at your leisure. If your replacement set has a string or two missing, you can always get away with using the next numbered string down – i.e., if you need a 24C string you can use the 23B string as a replacement. The string may be a bit too long. If it is, cut it off so you have 2½" of string wound on the tuning pin. This is not a waste of a whole set of strings. You should restring every 1–3 years. Use this set to restring, then buy a new set for spares. Nonetheless, most people don't – so now what? You are ready to trounce Tom Schroeder, Les Gustafson-Zook, et al. next week in a contest, and you have broken your 8G and 28D strings.

The first thing you need to know is the size of the strings you have broken. The chart at the end of this article is for standard Oscar Schmidt Model B strings. These values are essentially the same for Model A strings except 10A#, 11B, and 12C of the Model A sets are non-wound .028 diameter wire. The diameter values for wound strings are more or less .002 (two thousandths).

The chart shows the Model B strings and their size. The zither wire (small music wire) is readily available from most music supply houses and is used by hammered dulcimer makers and harpsichord makers.

For smooth wire strings, save the ball out of the end of the broken string and reset it in the end of the new piece of zither wire.

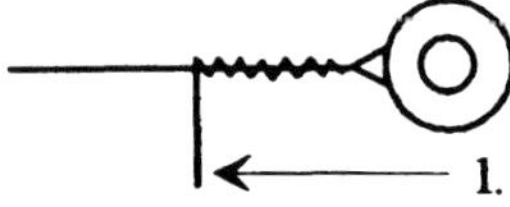

Leave the tail on the "wound around" wire (1). It will help stabilize the winding as the ball seats in the anchor bar or fine tuners. With fine tuners it helps if you bend the tail back (2) along the windings.

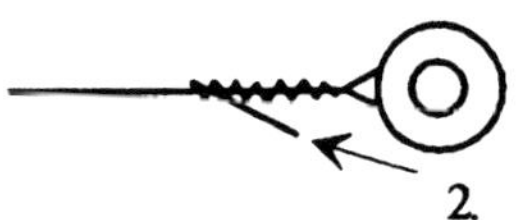

It helps to have a small pair of needle-nosed pliers or hemostats to hold the ball while twisting the wire for the loop end.

When you place the string in position on the 'harp be sure to cut the length so that you have about 2½" of wire to wind on the tuning pin.[1]

Guitar wire in standard custom gauge strings is available in diameters of less than .014 up to .024.

You will find the windings at the ball end are not the same as we use on autoharps, so I normally remove the end, save the ball, and reset it as described above. The string diameters are marked right on the envelopes. I had no problem at Galax last year finding .012, .017, and .020 guitar strings that would substitute for most of the upper and middle octave. .024, .026, and .028 will be the most difficult to find. Do not be afraid to use wire that is ± .004 (four thousandths) from what you actually want for temporary replacement. In this regard, a 2nd guitar string (normally .017 ±.002) will replace anything from 22A# to 36C in an emergency.

Now we get to the real headache for non-standard string sources – and that is the wound strings of the bass octave. I strongly suggest going back to "Rule 1." Carry a spare set of strings. It's the only surefire way to find a good replacement string that will fit your autoharp properly.

The major problem is that the windings of the standard 'harp are only on the vibrating length of core wire and do not (should not) extend around guide posts, over bridges, into anchor pins or fine tuners, and onto tuning pins. The ends of the standard wound autoharp strings are managed like the smooth wire non-wound strings since they are not covered by windings. Standard wound guitar wire, though, has windings from the ball to the very end of the wire.

Tuning pins will accept wound strings up to .048 wire through the hole. Fine tuners will accept wound strings up to .050 and will allow the ball to seat OK.

The anchor bar on Oscar Schmidt Model B and C 'harps will not accommodate any wound string above .030 and therefore prevents use of any wound guitar string without modifications.

And so – for Model A 'harps from 6F up, you can substitute a guitar string of proper size. For Model B and C 'harps with fine tuners from 6F up, you can substitute a guitar string of proper size.

Keep in mind, for both of these, the windings will extend across bridges or around guide pins and the windings may loosen and get buzzy soon. The windings will also raise these strings above the level of the string bed causing less effective string damping.

If you must substitute a string of larger diameter or any wound string in an anchor bar, you will need to remove the windings from the string at each end. This can be done using an anvil and a small ballpeen hammer. Tap the winding starting about 3" from the end of the wire, slightly flattening the wire for about ½". Then continue to hammer a bit harder on the rest of the winding out to the end of the wire. The winding wire,

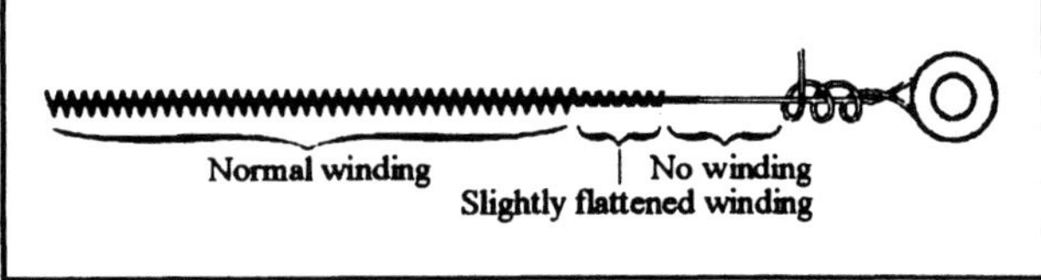

being softer than the core wire, will break loose and come off. Leave the slightly flattened winding in place on the first ½" where you started. You now have a wound wire with the core wire only at one end. Put a ball in the end of the wire about 1-¼" from the end of the winding. (See preceding illustration.)

On the heavier wound wire, you will need to remove the windings similarly from the tuning pin end of the wire. Place the string in position from the fine tuner or anchor bar across the 'harp and mark where you want the slightly flattened winding (about 1" short of the guide post). Then, remove the wire from the 'harp and hammer the windings as described above. Cut the wire off about 2" beyond the tuning pin and you will now have a reasonable facsimile of an original autoharp string.

Same rule applies for guitar wire size:

Guitar String Sizes
For 'Harp String Substitutions

Third wound guitar .... .028±.004
Substitute for 11B or 12C

Fourth wound guitar .... .034±.004
Substitute for 9A to 12C

Fifth wound guitar .... .046±.004
Substitute for 5E to 8G

Sixth wound guitar .... .056±.004
Substitute for 1F to 4D

You see that finding a substitute among commonly available guitar strings or zither wire is easiest for the smaller wound and non-wound strings. Fortunately, it's most commonly the smaller strings that break.

What about the interchangeability of Model A and B strings? You can do this, but they are not exactly the same.

1. The Model Bs are shorter than the model As. So, for an A string on a B 'harp, cut the string length to 2½" beyond the tuning pin before winding it up on the tuning pin. For Bs on an A 'harp, use a smooth wire from one or two positions below. It will be longer and fit OK. In the bass, you just put up with one or two turns on the pin.

2. The ferrule in the eyelet of the B strings will not go over the dead pin on the A 'harp. You have to remove it. Tedious, yes; impossible, no.

3. The windings are not located in the same position on the core wire. The windings will lie on the bridge, touch the guide posts, etc. It will work OK as a temporary substitute.

Hopefully, this article concerning the bare essentials of string substitution has convinced you to go back to paragraph one and get a spare set of strings. Its better to be safe than sorry when your G-string breaks!

The String Substitution chart on the right is based on the standard tuning of a chromatic 'harp. ❖

Also read "Strings – Their Ideal Sizes And Lengths" p.31.

[1] See "Restringing The Autoharp" p.23.

String Substitution
For Standard Chromatic Autoharps

String	Diameter	Standard Zither Wire
36C	.014	#5
35B	.014	#5
34A#	.016	#6
33A	.016	#6
32G#	.016	#6
31G	.016	#6
30F#	.018	#7
29F	.018	#7
28E	.018	#7
27D#	.018	#7
26D	.020	#8
25C#	.020	#8
24C	.022	#9
23B	.022	#9
22A#	.022	#9
21A	.024	#10
20G#	.024	#10
19G	.024	#10
18F#	.024	#10
17F	.026	#11
16E	.026	#11
15D#	.026	#11
14D	.028	#11½
13C#	.028	#11½
12C	.030	↑
11B	.034	
10A#	.036	
9A	.038	
8G	.042	
7F#	.046	Wound
6F	.048	
5E	.052	
4D	.052	
3C	.064	
2G	.074	
1F	.088	↓

Harmonics

AQ Volume II, Number 4

WOLVES IN THE ATTIC

George Orthey

Do you hear eerie, howling sounds in the background when you play your 'harp? When you pluck the strings in the extreme upper register of your 'harp, do you sometimes hear high-pitched, wavering sounds, like a pack of wolves baying at the moon?

Bryan Bowers is the first person I know to identify this phenomenon. He calls the noise "Wolf Sounds."

Wolves seem to lurk in various places in the autoharp. They can, however, always be found in the attic (upper register). Since these howlings are harmonic vibrations of very short strings, or harmonics of the played strings, they are principally discordant to the high-pitched strings of the 'harp.

So far, I have located four major dens in the 'harp. First and foremost to all autoharps, wolves are found between the bridge or guide posts and the tuning pins. They can be reduced or eliminated by using Bryan's wolf tamer. He places a piece of black, uncut bar felt under the strings in this gap. The felt should be very firm, and fit tightly so that the strings are solidly damped in that gap. I use 5/16 by 5/16" firm felt similar to bar felt. This felt can be obtained from a piano repair person.

Then there is a wolf who lives back in the cave inside the 'harp in the metal tie rod or brace. If such a rod is not incorporated into the frame, it can ring like a harmonic bell. If the wolf is in there, and the bar is under great tension, he will howl a monotone note when you thump or play your 'harp. Only the most sensitive ear has found him, and so, except to that ear, he is of minor significance. Most 'harps do not have such a tie rod.

The third wolf lives in the basement, and howls a much higher discordant harmonic to the wound strings. This is one that Bob Lewis located and defined. This wolf lurks around strings with windings that end far from the bridge or guide pin. If the gap between windings and the end of the vibrating string exceeds 1/2 to 3/4 of an inch, the wailing of this creature can make it nearly impossible to reach a perfectly desired pitch. He is always discordant. Using model A strings on a model B 'harp, or vise-versa, and/or using a mis-manufactured string, are usually the worst offenders for harboring this wolf. The problem can be minimized by changing the offending string. If you want to accurately eliminate the basement wolf, you could find the sometimes elusive custom wound strings. But they're usually not necessary.

Another attic wolf recently located, is on my Orthey autoharp. It is in the "V" between the bridges at the treble end of the 'harp below the chord bars. When plucked, the top three to five strings have wavering harmonic sounds that are just discordant enough to present a problem when trying to tune them properly. By placing Bryan's wolf tamer felt under these strings, one can reduce the sounds. They can be eliminated entirely by placing a suppressor bar on top of these strings to press them down slightly in this gap. The bar is a piece of about 1/4 by 1/4 inch wood or plastic, long enough to fit over the top of the highest four or five strings. It can be held in place by two or three screws through the bar into the sound board. 3/4 inch by #4 screws work best for me. Just pull the screws tight enough to push the strings down slightly, but not tight enough to interfere with the tuning. (This suppressor bar does reduce the wolf, but it adds a friction problem when fine tuners are present on the 'harp.)

Probably all 'harps harbor wolves to some extent. Some more – and louder – than others.

Some folks may not mind the wolves in their attics or basements enough to eliminate them. These folks are purists. When they sing and play "Bury Me Not On the Lone Prairie," they mean every word of the song. The wolves in their 'harps howl like coyotes, and if they howl loudly enough, no one will stay around to jam with them. Discordant wolf wailings are not socially acceptable if they make the 'harp sound out of tune. And so, around these folks when they want to jam, definitely, "– the wind blows free –" ❖

Find more information concerning harmonics in "Dealing With The Mechanical Noise Of Chord Bars"p. 15, "Harmonics – What Are They?"p.36 and "Harmonics – Remedies"p.38.

Harmonics – What Are They?

AQ Volume VII, Number 1

'HARPMONICS

George Orthey

***'harpmonics**: 1. the partials or overtones of a fundamental tone on an autoharp. 2. (used with a plural v.) the flutelike tones of the strings of an autoharp made to vibrate so as to produce overtones. 3. (used with unprintable adj.) the dissident, obnoxious, ringing notes in an otherwise respectable chord; "What is that noise? #!*?@! wolf-tones."*

The overtones of the playing strings of an autoharp, as with any stringed instrument, add fullness and quality to the sound of that instrument. Under certain circumstances, a damped string may sound discordant overtones, which we call harmonics. Here, we deal with understanding this occurrence and the treatment of these unwanted sounds.[1]

First, let's review a few basics of harmonics: When you play an open string, all of these partials (the consecutive, equal parts of a string) will form as in Figure A.

Figure A

String Action	Segment Playing	Note Playing	Node Linear Chart
 bridge — bridge	Whole	Fundamental 3C, e.g.	Bridges
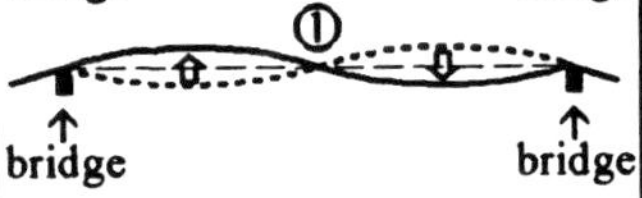 ① bridge — bridge	1/2	First Harmonic 12C (Middle C)	Bridges &①
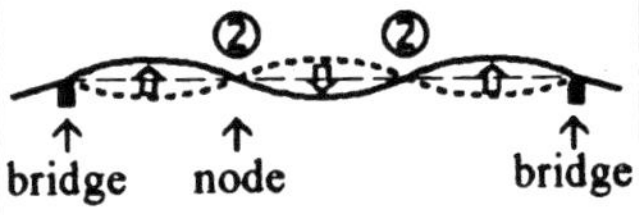 ② ② bridge node bridge	1/3	Second Harmonic 19G	Bridges &②
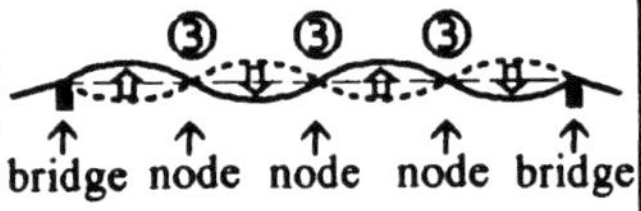 ③ ③ ③ bridge node node node bridge	1/4	Third Harmonic 24C	Bridges &③

The example designation of 3C, 12C, etc. is based on standard OSI string numbering and position on the autoharp.

If you are into mathematics, you can also see that the first harmonic node, mid-point node, would also be a node of the 1/4, 1/6, and 1/8 segmented strings. Thus also playing 24C, 31G, and 36C.

In Reference To Figure A

The fundamental and first harmonic (the octave), are usually the loudest. Other harmonics that make notes within the range of the 'harp plus one octave higher can also be substantial and annoying. There are many harmonics: 1/4, 1/5, 1/6, 1/7, etc. that make very high notes, way above the 'harp range. These are trivial to most players, and unheard by the listener.

At the point marked "node" for a particular harmonic, the string stands perfectly still, even though it is sounding a clear, bell-like note. Herein lies the crux of harmonic problems on the autoharp. If the damper bar "damps" a string exactly over a node where the string doesn't vibrate anyway, that harmonic will play loud and clear regardless of how firmly the damper is pressed. This harmonic sound will even be enhanced to the ear by the fact that the other harmonics and, of course, the fundamental of that string are damped out.

The half node ① harmonic is the loudest and busiest since it plays not only the half, but also the quarter and one-sixth harmonic. All of these even numbered fractions will form a node at the half-point of the string. On the string bed chart (Figure B), you can see by the location on line ① that these are the very loud harmonics that play in the upper octave of a chromatic autoharp.

These particular harmonics are unavoidable and keep many players from using the E♭ and B♭ keys. These can be avoided if you can be satisfied with a narrow set of chord bars as you would find on a diatonic 'harp.

The next harmonic, the 1/3 node ②, is the great little ringer that plays throughout the entire range of the chromatic 'harp. Even worse, it forms an almost vertical line in the bass, resulting in one or more chord bars that play near or on the harmonic line through the entire bass octave. This harmonic line plays the 1/3 and 1/6 node of the strings.

Now we come upon another interesting attribute of harmonics. When a harmonic is dividing the string into three or more parts and the string is touched by a damper on one node, there's another node exposed in your area of play. If you strike a string midway between nodes, the relative harmonic plays loudly. If you strike a string exactly over the node of a harmonic, that harmonic is greatly reduced, and is almost unheard. If you look at line ② across the playing area of the 'harp (Figure B), it roughly forms an arc up through the bass, then diagonally up through the middle and upper octaves. If your thumb sweep follows the node line, this harmonic will be minimized. If you play out toward the tuning pins, or close to the chord bars, you will be playing between the nodes, and therefore will maximize the loudness of the harmonic. This harmonic is mainly noticed in the B♭, F, and C keys on a standard 21-bar 'harp.

Now let's consider the 1/4 harmonic node line ③. The nodes form for this harmonic on the 1/2 node line ①, and 1/4 node lines ③. For this harmonic, play a bit farther out on the strings on the line, or closer to the chord bars on the 1/2 node line ①. This harmonic mainly affects the keys of G, D, and A on a standard 21-bar 'harp.

For the folks who like to play way up near the tuning pins, please take note that this will be between nodes for every harmonic on the 'harp. It is close to the principal node (bridge) for the fundamental vibration of the string. This gives a "chingy" high-pitched sound on the playing strings because of its accent of harmonics over fundamental string vibration. It also, unfortunately, plays loud and clear every "damped" undesirable harmonic possible on the 'harp.

The "awfulest" for harmonics are the old "play below the bars" 'harps. The chord bars sat across all the harmonic lines from top to bottom, and the strings were played close to the bridge, putting maximum accent on the partial/harmonic notes.

Ideal avoidance of harmonics can be best achieved in the diatonic 'harps with a very narrow chord bar set placed off the 1/2 ① and 1/3 ② node lines. You can then play in the area of the 1/4 ③ node line in the upper octave, and thus avoid all significant harmonic lines.

In Reference to Figure B

If you really want to visualize all of this, take the chord bars off your 'harp and find and mark the harmonic node lines on the strings with a magic marker. (Use a magic marker that won't per-

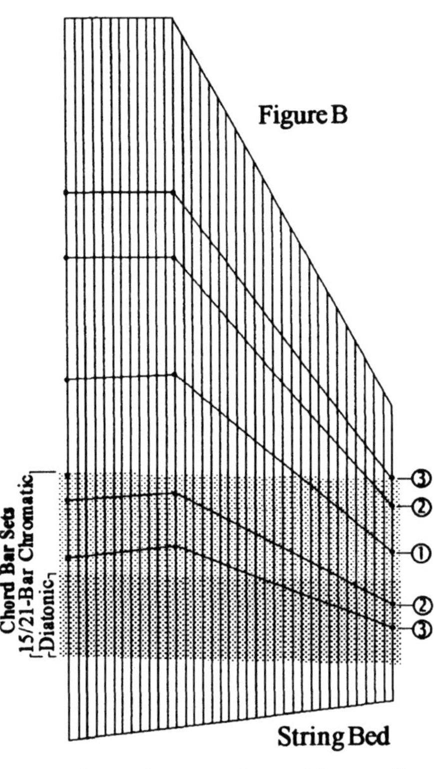

manently mark your strings. Almost all markers will wipe off with a cloth or Scotch Brite.) The approximate location of the lines can be found by measuring 1/2, 1/3, and 1/4 the distance from bridge to bridge. (Note: I use the term "bridge" to define any string end stop, be it fine tuner, guide pin, anchor bar, or an actual bridge.) You only need locate the points at each end of a straight bridge section. That is for standard autoharp or Chromaharp at 1F, 13 C♯, and 36 C string positions. Then connect these points with straight lines.

If you just want to do one harmonic, I suggest you do the 1/3 ② line. This will clearly demonstrate the harmonic caused by the bar damping at a node and also the ability to reduce the harmonic by playing close to the other node. If you want to put all three line sets ①, ②, and ③, I suggest you use different color magic markers for each line group.

If you take a blank uncut felted bar, it will give you an excellent demonstration of the harmonics. Place the bar in each consecutive chord position, and pluck the strings slowly from bottom to top. You will hear thud, thud, thud, etc. As you cross a harmonic node line, you will hear loud and clear the bell-like "ding" of the harmonics. On the loudest of the ding strings of the 1/3 node harmonic, pluck the string next to the chord bar, and continue to pluck, moving gradually across to the tuning pin. You will notice that the harmonics will sound the loudest between the nodes, and diminish to almost nothing when plucked directly over the undamped node. Do this for each chord bar position, and visualize the whole picture of where the harmonics are and where you need to play to reduce them. This will show you as nothing else will the importance of playing on the node line. ❖

Read "Harmonics" p.33 for more information on this subject.

[1] Many mechanical tricks have been attempted to minimize the loudness of the harmonics. This is discussed in "Harmonics – Remedies" p.38.

Harmonics – Remedies

AQ Volume VII, Number 2

'HARPMONICS WHAT TO DO ABOUT THEM

George Orthey
and Stephen J. Young

***George:** These are some thoughts of mine and others on the management of 'harpmonics. Particularly noteworthy is a complete and remarkably excellent method for removal of autoharp harmonics by Winfield champion, Stephen J. Young. I believe there are mechanical and psychological hurdles that should be understood and hopefully overcome to at least partially alleviate this problem.*

We'll tackle the mechanical considerations first. I have tried several methods of altering the felt at the point where it engages a string node to enhance or improve its damping effectiveness. First, I simply add a layer of felt cloth using a thin layer of silicone glue to hold it in place directly over the offending string. (See # 1 on Figure A below.)

Lastly, try teasing the felt up by pricking the side with a sharp point like a hat pin or small ice pick. (Ask your grandmother "What's a hat pin?") This causes the felt to rise up in a bump at that point. Then stabilize the felt by rubbing a thin layer of silicone glue into the *sides* of the felt. (See 4 on Figure A). Again, be sure to let the glue harden before playing.

Since all of the above make the felt slightly thicker at that point, you will require somewhat greater bar pressure to get clean damping of the other strings.

As an aside, if you have "play-through" (or incomplete damping of strings) throughout your string bed, do not confuse this with harmonics. Check for worn felts and/or an uneven string-bed. Harmonics will only be at the exact points where the bars cross 1/2, 1/3, 1/4 etc. nodes.[1] If the offending sounds do not occur at these specific points, they're not harmonics.

The following are unabridged dissertations by Steve Young concerning the subject of harmonics on the autoharp. In his cover letter, Steve points out that a significant amount of woodworking and mechanical skills are required to install and maintain his dampers. However, in my opinion, his procedures would completely eliminate the harmonics where they could be fitted on a diatonic autoharp.

Figure A

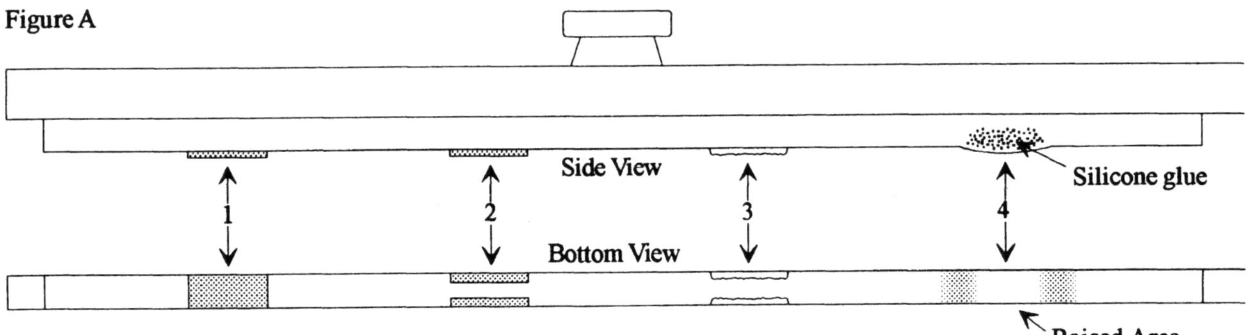

Secondly, I have added a thin strip of felt cloth near each edge of the bar felt where it engages the offending string, thus getting two-point damping. (See 2 on Figure A). I found this to be the most effective, but tedious, and the little pieces tend to fall off.

The third choice is similar to the second choice above, but rather than adding felt strips, put a small ridge of silicone glue on the face of the bar felt near each edge. (See 3. on Figure A). Be sure to let it harden thoroughly (at least 24 hours) before playing.

Steve: December 1991

Displaced Damping
To Eliminate Overtones

Bell or *chime* tones occur on damped strings when the damping felt lies near one of the string vibration node points. Although the fundamental vibration is effectively damped, some of the overtones can come through unchecked. Nearly always these overtones are not notes of the chord being generated and the interference with the chord is quite disconcerting. Figure B shows an arrangement I use on the wooden chord bars of my Mary Lou Signature model Orthey 'harp to reduce some of the bell tone problems. The method is to displace or extend the damping point the width of a chord bar up or down the string with an out-rigger mounted on the bottom of the bar. The generation of bell tones is sensitive to the damping point. If the string is damped even only 1/4" away from the node, the bell tone is significantly reduced. My outriggers are 1/2" long, 1/4" wide, and 1/16" thick. They are glued in place flush with the bottom of the chord bar in a 1/4" wide by 1/16" deep groove routed into the bottom of the chord bar (Bar #1 in Figure B on the next page).

This technique requires that there be a chord bar on one side or the other of the offending bar that doesn't damp the string. The notch in the felt of this

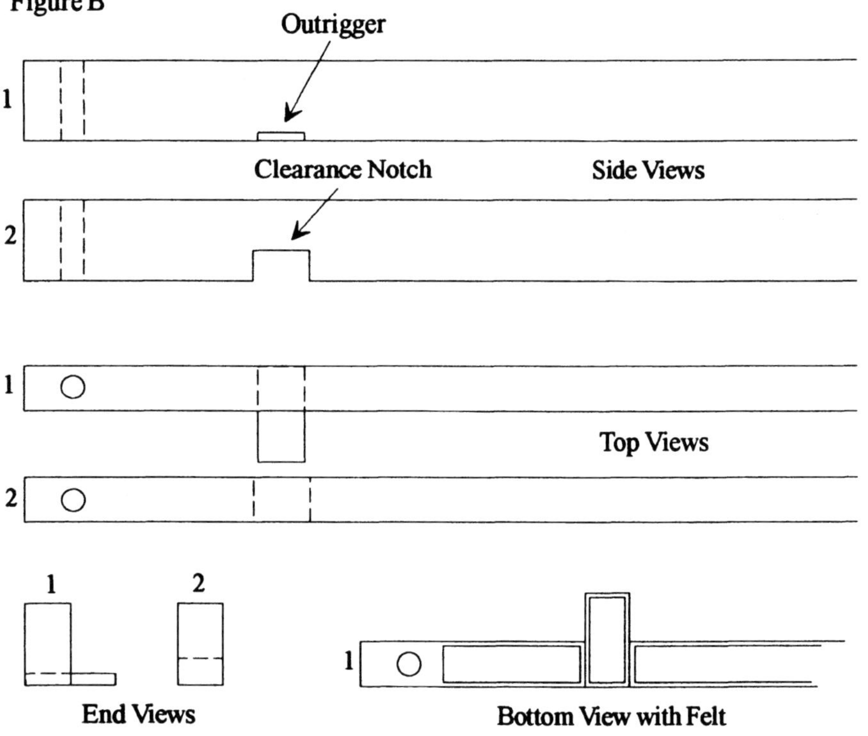

adjacent bar will be the new damping spot. Test to see that damping at this new point improves the situation. It may be that the initial damping point is a little off the node and the new point is closer. If the chord bar on either side could be used, test to see which is the better (or make an outrigger that uses both). The adjacent chord bar will have to be notched on its underside so that when it is pressed, it does not interfere with the outrigger (Bar #2 in Figure B). The depth of the notch must be a little more than the sum of the outrigger thickness and the chord bar travel (the distance the chord bar must be pushed from its resting position to engage the top of the strings). The chord bars must be strong enough to sustain this notch without weakening substantially. My outrigger thickness is 1/16". The travel is about 5/64", so I made the notch about 5/32" deep. This is about 1/3 the thickness of the 7/16" high chord bars used on this instrument. So far, I have not noticed any weakening of the notched bars. I would be leery of using this technique on wooden chord bars less that 7/16" in height without some kind of reinforcement. For clearance, the width of the notch should be a bit wider than the width of the outrigger. I used 5/16".

I expect this technique won't work on Oscar Schmidt B- or C-model aluminum chord bars without much modification.

Under-String Damping
To Eliminate Overtones
December 1991

On my Mary Lou Signature model autoharp by George Orthey, the C-chord bar damps the high B (#34), C♯ (#36), and D (#37) strings very near their 1/2 length node points (bell line). The overtones from these strings are so strong that the top end of the chord is essentially useless. To provide better damping on these strings, I devised the mechanism shown in Figure C. It is a 1" x 2" lever made of 1/16" plywood and mounted under the strings with one end of the lever lined up with the C-chord bar. When the C-chord bar is pressed, a push rod, mounted on the underside of the bar and between strings 35 and 36, rocks the lever and forces felt up onto the strings from beneath and at a point well away from the node line. The lever is spring loaded so that it returns to its original position when the bar is released. The push rod is always in contact with the lever so no felt is needed to eliminate clatter. The rod length must be adjusted so that the felts on the far end of the lever contact the strings from below just as the felts on the chord bar contact the strings from above. Most of the details of the mechanism are noted in Figure C. This design can be modified as necessary to handle individual situations. The lever should be mounted so that the top is about midway between the soundboard and the strings. On my instrument, the strings are mounted almost 3/8" above the soundboard. On a standard OS instrument, the distance is more like 1/4". The height of the lever

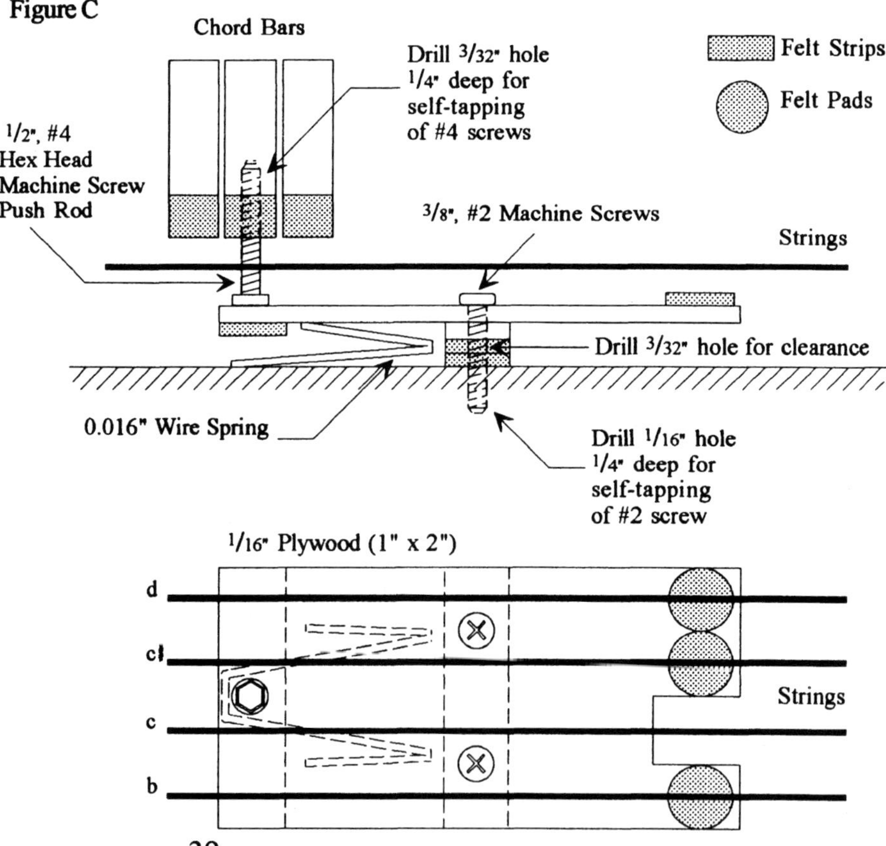

can be adjusted either by using a thicker wood strip for the fulcrum or by adding strips of single-thickness, adhesive-backed felt. The mounting screws should be left loose enough that the lever can move freely. The spring was made from a used 0.016 autoharp string, and is held in place by a bead of glue. It should not be so strong that it adds appreciably to the force needed to press the chord bar. This mechanism can be used only very near the edge of the soundboard. If used in a more active region, some damping of the soundboard occurs. More importantly, the sound of the damped strings is transmitted directly to the soundboard through the fulcrum and is amplified into a disconcerting *clank*.

Comparison Of Autoharp Bridge Designs

February 1992

The bridge designs on the Liberty and Mary Lou Signature model autoharps by George Orthey are significantly different from conventional designs in the high treble region of the instrument. For the last few strings, the tuning-pin bridge is cocked upward. A corresponding jog in the anchor bridge maintains the required string vibration lengths in this region. A comparison between the Mary Lou Signature design and the conventional design of a Goose Acres instrument by Peter Smakula is shown in Figure D. Both instruments are 37-string models. The tuning-pin bridge on the Orthey instrument changes slope between strings 30 and 31. The slope of the anchor bridge changes between strings 24 and 25.

I expect George introduced this design to provide more playing room on the high strings. On Figure D, schematics of 15-slot chord-bar assemblies are superimposed at positions I use for the two instruments. (The bar spacing is 9/32".) Positioning on the Smakula instrument was dictated by requiring *adequate* damping on all strings for the last chord bar in the assembly (closest to the anchor end) while still maintaining adequate playing room on the high strings. The distance from the last bar to the anchor end is about 3/4" at the highest string and 1 1/4" at the first bass string. The assembly on the Orthey instrument is positioned about the same if measured from the bass tuning-pin bridge. The consequences of the modified design are clearly evident. The distance from the last bar to the anchor bridge is increased by about 1/2" for most of the strings. Damping on the last bar is improved from merely adequate to very good. For many of the higher strings, the distance is decreased substantially, but these shorter strings can be damped at smaller distances and still achieve good damping. The significant improvement is a 3/4" increase in playing room on the high strings.

A further consequence of the design modification is a reconfiguration of the relationship between chord bars and bell lines. The 1/2-, 1/3-, and 1/4-length bell lines are shown on Figure D. With the Orthey design, the influence of the 1/2 bell line has been decreased from conflict with five chord bars to only two or three. The influence of the 1/3 bell line, on the other hand, has been increased substantially since it now lies directly under the first chord bar throughout the entire wound string course. (As set up by George, the chord-bar assembly was mounted 1/4" closer to the anchor end. Then, the first chord bar just missed this bell line. But, this position provided unacceptable damping on the high strings of the last chord bar.) The influence of the 1/4 bell line is about the same for either design.

Taking all these considerations into account, especially the increased playing room, it would seem that George's modification represents a significant improvement in autoharp design.

A second conclusion that can be drawn is that even 15 chord bars is still too many for an autoharp. Even with George's design, 13 is the maximum. The first two bars should be eliminated. Then there is no problem at all with the 1/2- and 1/3-bell lines. This limitation is quite consistent with the requirements for a two-key diatonic instrument. Here we need two lock bars and ten chord bars

Figure D

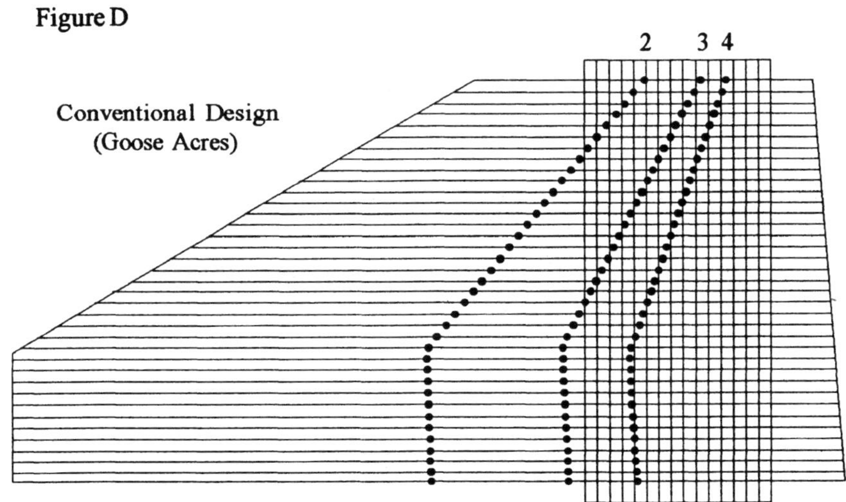

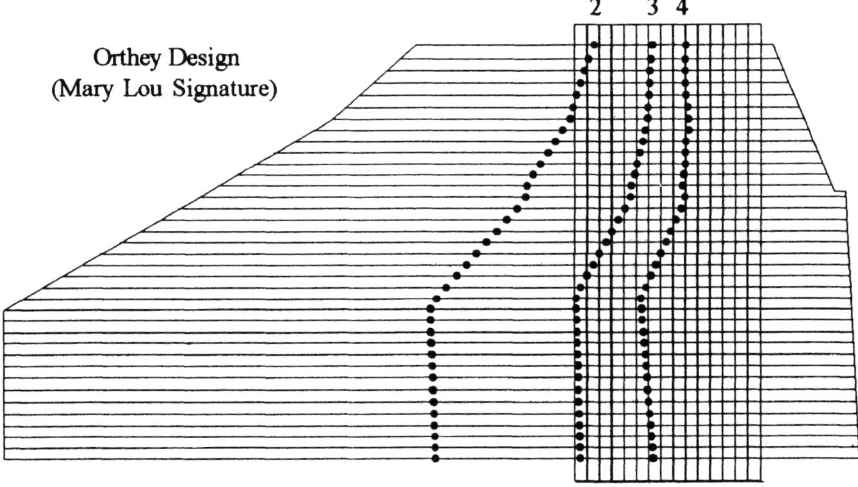

(*e.g.* for a C/G instrument; F, C, G, D, G7, D7, Dm, Am, Em, Bm) for a total of 12 bars. These would fit nicely into George's design with the advantage of even more playing room or a little more space between the last bar and anchor bridge.

The outrigger idea works really well. The under-string damping idea doesn't work quite so well. Here are two other techniques I use that are easy to implement:

1. Put dominant 7th and diminished chords at the bell lines. These chords are relatively busy (having four notes in them) and tend to hide the bell tones better than the three-note majors and minors.
2. If there's an overtone problem on a *new wound string*, do nothing for a few weeks. These tend to diminish as the string ages.

George: Steve has added a lot of information on the mechanics of physically fixing 'harpmonics. I would like to make some comments on the psychological aspects of this subject.

If you listen to the harmonics and allow them to become a serious irritant, they become dominant in your thought and become self-enhancing. The harmonic sounds, thumps of non-playing strings, slight *squick* as the bars engage the strings, and all other annoying but inherent sounds of the autoharp are predominantly prominent to the player. They are generally less noticeable and in many cases nonexistent to the audience enjoying your music. I have found that allowing a person (whose playing you enjoy) to play your 'harp for you from 15 feet away may change your whole concept of sound enjoyment and acceptability of your instrument. Try it and then as you play, think about what your listener hears, concentrate on that and enjoy the good things of your 'harp.

Mark Fackeldey says: "Learn to love 'em! Hammered dulcimers have their sustained ring. Hurdy-gurdys have their buzz. Didgeridoos are all abuzz. Mongolian singers have their overtones. Brass-strung Irish harps have their harmonics. So do autoharps. I love it all. Bagpipes? Banjos? Each has characteristic sounds. If you don't like harmonics, the autoharp is the wrong axe for you. Thanks for the info, though – we can use it to bring out more of those charming harmonics."

I hope we've helped you alleviate some of your problems. With further development of your playing accuracy/techniques, and with some mechanical and psychological adjustments, you can keep the wolf from your door – at least hopefully keep it from howling right in your ear. ❖

Editor's note: Steve Young is an International Autoharp Champion.

[1] See Figure A in "Harmonics – What Are They?" p.36.

Tuning and Temperament

AQ Volume II, Number 4

THE WELL-TEMPERED AUTOHARP

Mary Lou Orthey

If you took piano lessons as a child, you will surely remember a little ditty entitled "The Well-Tempered Clavichord." I wondered what that meant. Sounded pleasant, "well-tempered." But clavichords, I thought, were bones. Maybe the song was about a happy bone? At that point, I had mastered tunes about a weasel, a cockroach, and a waltzing fairy. So why not a bone?

Many moons later, I now know what a clavichord is, and have an understanding of "tempered." (Will wonders never cease?) In this article, different temperaments will be discussed as they apply to the tuning of another multi-stringed instrument, the autoharp.

Pitch is that attribute of a sound determined by the frequency of vibrations of sound waves. When an autoharp player tunes his instrument, he/she adjusts each string so that it will vibrate a specified number of times a second. The pitch we hear when we pluck a string is due to a blend of various frequencies. An autoharp string, as with any other stringed instrument's individual string, emits several frequencies at the same time. The lowest frequency, (fundamental frequency), is produced by the string vibrating as a whole. The higher frequencies, (harmonics, or overtones), are produced by the string vibrating in parts. A string vibrates as a whole, and in halves, 3rds, 4ths, 5ths, etc., at the same time. If we pluck the C below middle C on our 'harp, it will also sound middle C (half, or 2nd harmonic of the fundamental); it will sound G above middle C (3rd harmonic); it will sound the C above middle C (4th harmonic); the E above that C (5th harmonic), etc. Overtones are whole-number multiples of the fundamental frequency of a string, and theoretically go on ad infinitum. Low strings, therefore, have a very faint fundamental tone compared to the multitudinous dominant overtones, which makes tuning difficult. These strings can be tuned easier by tuning their harmonics to fundamental tones in an upper register. Heavy strings, like the lowest C on the piano, vibrate only 32.7 times a second. The thinnest strings that produce the highest C on the piano vibrate more than 4,000 times per second.

The notes we are familiar with today did not always have the same pitch. Handel tuned the A above middle C to 422.5 vibrations per second. Our concert pitch today places the same A at 440 vibrations per second.

Length and tension of a string determine the pitch or tone that string will make when it is plucked. Tuning your autoharp, as in tuning any stringed instrument, is simply regulating the tension of each string to provide the required pitch sound of that particular string. The length of the string is predetermined by the construction of the instrument. This, of course, determines the absolute limit to which the string can be tuned.

> "Temperament in music is a system of adjustment of the intervals between the tones of an instrument of fixed intonation. It may be pure temperament, in which the intervals are set exactly according to theory, or equal temperament, as in a piano, in which the pitch of the tones is slightly adjusted to make them suitable for all keys."
>
> – *Webster's New World Dictionary*

In tuning the autoharp, as the piano, one must slightly adjust the pitch of tones to make it suitable for playing in all keys. There are several different ways serious 'harp players approach this subject. This article is meant to help us understand the methods used by a few of these folks who strive for the tunings, or temperaments, which sound best to their ears.

The following charts are copied exactly from the tuning of four autoharp personalities – two nationally-known teachers/performers; a luthier; and the world's most famous autoharp performer.

Cast of Characters

Bryan Bowers: one of the best-known autoharp players in the world. He plays predominately single-key autoharps, which he sweet-tunes, but was playing two- and three-key instruments for a time. Bryan's multi-key charts show his preference for the tuning of those particular 'harps.

Ivan Stiles: a nationally known autoharp performer and teacher, Ivan is the 1991 International Autoharp Champion. He is also cofounder of *Autoharp Quarterly* and was *AQ*'s coeditor from 1988 until 1997.

Charles Whitmer: a music teacher in the public school system in Spring, Texas. He is a nationally known autoharp teacher who travels all over the country teaching the fine points of autoharp playing. Charles is especially known as an excellent teacher of beginner students.

George Orthey: a maker of autoharps who has worked closely with Charles Whitmer and Ivan Stiles to find the best tuning possible for autoharps in all keys. He has extended Charles' system to include numerical values for the full range of the instrument.

Charles Whitmer

STRING	AUTOHARP CHROMATIC CENTS	AUTOHARP G-D-A CENTS	AUTOHARP F-C CENTS
C	+7	+7	+5
B	-3	-3	-8
A#	+7	—	+7
A	+3	+3	-3
G#	-13	-11	—
G	+6	+6	+3
F#	-10	-9	—
F	+7	—	+6
E	+1	+1	-7
D#	0	—	—
D	+5	+5	+1
C#	-11	-11	—
Mid. C	+7	+7	+5

Charles tunes his upper octaves by tuner, and tunes his bass by ear to obtain proper pitch in the lower wound strings.

George Orthey

CHROMATIC, C, G, D, E, A, and G-D-A AUTOHARPS	
STRING	CENTS
C	+13
B	0
A#	+9
A	+6
G#	-10
G	+9
F#	-7
F	+9
E	+3
D#	+2
D	+7
C#	-9
C	+9
B	-3
A#	+7
A	+3
G#	-13
G	+6
F#	-10
F	+7
E	+1
D#	0
D	+5
C#	-11
Mid. C	+7
B	-4
A#	+5
A	0
G	+2
F#	-16
F	0
E	-6
D	-3
C	-3
G	-26
F	-30

This is a full-scale variant of Charles Whitmer's tuning, developed by Charles, Ivan Stiles, and George Orthey. It is particularly acceptable on chromatic, G-D-A, and D 'harps.

This tuning was also found by Bryan Bowers to be acceptably close to his "by-ear" sweet tuning for his A-E autoharp.

Bryan Bowers

AUTOHARP D-A-E	
STRING	CENTS
E	+12
D#	+8
D*	+13
C#*	-16
B*	+3
A	+8
G#	-13
G	+4
F#	+8
E	0
D#	-1
D	+2
C#	-15
B	-2
A	+7
G#	-17
G	0
F#	-2
E	-3
D#	-15
D	+3
Mid. C#	-12
B	0
A	0
G#	-19
G	-5
F#	-11
E	-9
D	-9
B	-28
A	-23
G	-29
E	-33

Chart = 33 strings. Three strings in this 'harp are doubled.

AUTOHARP F-C	
STRING	CENTS
C	+13
B	+13
A#	+24
A	-1
G	+5
F	+12
E	-5
D	+7
C	+6
B	-2
A#	+15
A	-1
G	+4
F	+9
E	-10
D	+3
Mid. C	0
B	-11
A#	+5
A	-5
G	0
F	+4
E	-10
D	-5
C	-10
A#	-5
G	-15
F	-24

Chart = 28 strings. Eight strings in this 'harp are doubled.

Bryan's D-A-E 'harp and the F-C 'harp were first tuned by George Orthey according to his extension of Charles' tuning. Bryan then took the 'harps and adjusted the tuning to his ear. The above two charts are the result of that effort. The * after the top E, D#, D, C#, and B strings on the D-A-E chart shows that the bridges were adjusted to accommodate these higher notes. The pitch of these strings cannot be reached on a standard autoharp.

AUTOHARP G	
STRING	CENTS
D	+1
C	+7
B	0
A	-7
G	+6
F#	-11
E	-11
D	+4
C	+2
B	-15
A	-11
G	0
F#	-16
E	-18
D	+1
Mid. C	0
B	-11
A	-12
G	+7
F#	-9
E	-13
D	+2
A	-22
G	-13

Chart = 24 strings. Twelve strings in this 'harp are doubled.

The G 'harp tuning chart above is taken exactly from Bryan's sweet-tuned single-key 'harp. This 'harp was pulled two half steps higher than average. The bass was strung with guitar strings. These factors would likely alter the stress factor. With normal autoharp strings, it would be expected that the bass would be tuned somewhat flatter than indicated. The only wound pair of strings was G below Middle C. The remaining pairs were in the middle octave and the lower portion of the top octave.

Equal Or Even Temperament

Most electronic tuners are set up to give equal (or even) temperament tuning (tone pitches adjusted slightly for playing in all keys). Many 'harp players simply turn on their tuners and go "straight across the board," as the tuner dictates. Drew Smith uses this tuning exclusively. He plays with Roger Sprung and the Progressive Bluegrass Band, and must be able to play with all instruments in all keys.

Just, Or Sweet Tuning

Believe it or not, folks, A♯ and B♭ are not exactly the same note! (And, to make matters worse, D♯ is not really exactly E♭, and so on.) There are different intervals between the notes A, A♯, and B than there are between the notes A, B♭, and B, e.g. This is where temperament, or shading, comes to the fore. Fixed instruments like pianos; fretted instruments such as guitars; brass and woodwinds – must have this shading built in to make the two notes (e.g. A♯ and B♭) the same pitch, because these instruments are meant to be played with other instruments *in all keys*. Temperament is built in when placing the frets on the fret board; in the length of the tubing on a horn; when tuning the piano, etc. People, if blessed with good pitch sense, when singing or when playing fretless instruments, shade or temper these subtle differences. What they are doing is bending the tones to fit the key they are using. This is instant sweet tuning.

Because true just or sweet tuning can only be achieved in one-key instruments, it is used mainly by single players who perform on stage by themselves. Bryan Bowers is known for his many diatonic 'harps, and his sweet tunings of these 'harps. See his Key of G sweet tuning.

Mean-Tone Tuning

Mean-tone tuning is the middle ground between the sweet and the equal tunings, and can be used in 2-, 3-, or 4-key 'harps. The pitches are changed from the equal tunings, but not to the extent that they are changed in the single key sweet tunings. A 'harp in this tuning will be sweeter than an equal tempered one, and will sound good by itself. However, if the player wants to jam with other instruments, he/she must be aware of the fact that the 'harp may not sound in perfect tune with others in all keys. In a mean-tone tempered 'harp set up to play in 4 keys, – e.g. A, D, G, C, – the player can expect to be in tune with other instruments in D and G, but could notice in the Keys of A and C, the 'harp may sound a little "out of key" in a few chords.

Charles, Bryan, and Ivan use this tuning with their multi-key 'harps set up to play diatonically with or without lock bars. (Find Charles' G-D-A and F-C tunings, Bryan's D-A-E and F-C tunings, and George's C-G-D-A-E tuning charts.)

Stretch, And A Few Loose Ends

What this all amounts to, then, is the refinement of what piano tuners call "stretch." As the pitch of the instrument goes up from middle C, the intervals between the notes are tuned to become ever so slightly larger, making the pitch sound a bit sharper as the scale progresses upward. Going down the scale from middle C, the intervals are tuned to become comparatively larger between the notes, and the pitch becomes flatter as the scale progresses downward. Some stretch is necessary to make the instrument sound in tune. It is needed, particularly in the bass in the heavy, wound strings. To sound "right," the bass of the 'harp is tuned progressively flat. For example, the low D on a Wildwood Flower is tuned 40 cents flat to sound *just right*. Note in the sweet tuning charts that the tunings run *flat in the bass* and *sharp in the treble* for that reason.

The preceding chromatic tuning charts are mean-tone tunings close to equal temperament, but still sweet enough to make a difference in the sound of the 'harp.

This is in no way a comprehensive study of temperament. It is meant to help us understand tunings a bit better – without losing our tempers in the process. ❖

Construction Of The Musical Scale

AQ Volume V, Number IV

AND YOU THOUGHT PYTHAGORAS JUST DID TRIANGLES!

Lindsay Haisley

In the beginning, music was first a voice – or voices together, singing. When music demanded more, the drum was there, as was anything struck, stroked, slapped, or tapped, which makes a sound. These sounds produced rhythmically became music. Some of these drums had voices of their own, producing tones both high and low, imitating human voices, or inspiring human voices to imitation. Homo sapiens, ever inventive creatures, developed ever more complex instruments, using not only skins on logs, but vibrating columns of air and strings of sinew or gut stretched tight over just about any object with a little bit of resonance to it. Long ago, these early musical experiments with hollow bones, conch shells, hunting bows, hollow branches and the like, developed into the three great classes of percussion instruments, the wind instruments, and the stringed instruments.

Singers (at least those with a musical ear) noticed very long ago that when two notes are sung, plucked, or blown together, some combinations of notes, which we call intervals, sound better than others. This is called *consonance*. Anyone who has ever played an out-of-tune autoharp (and who among us hasn't?) is familiar with what consonance is not!

People in different cultures created their music around sets of musical intervals which were consonant to their ears, either involving or opposing this consonance with intent. A set of notes related by such consonant intervals is called a *scale*.

The music-makers and the music-listeners did fine for millennia. But "inquiring minds want to know" and there were always people asking why some intervals were consonant and others not. When these folks started to look into the matter, things started to get complicated. One of the first to investigate this question was the Greek scholar, Pythagoras, famous for his triangles. Pythagoras took a string and stretched it tight over a couple of supports so it could vibrate. He made a third support which he could move back and forth under the string so that it could be divided into two vibrating sections, each with the same tension. This instrument is called a *monochord*. Pythagoras made the interesting observation that when the two parts of the string on his monochord vibrated with notes whose interval sounded consonant, the ratio of the lengths of the two sections was 1:1, 1:2, 2:3, or 3:4. Today we know these ratios as unison, octave, fifth, and fourth intervals. (These nice, neat numeric relationships pleased the numerologists of Pythagoras' day, as they have numerologists ever since. Numerologists, believing that numbers have magical powers, are always excited to observe numeric relationships in things which everyone else knows are magic, such as music.)

Unlike Pythagoras, we now know that, given the same tension, the frequency of vibration of a string is inversely proportional to its length. This means, for instance, that if the two parts of the string on a monochord sound an interval of an octave (i.e. have a length ratio of 1:2), then the frequencies of the two notes will be in the ratio of 2:1. Since frequencies are a basic property of musical notes (and vibrating strings of equal tension are not) let us proceed using the frequencies of notes as their defining "physical" characteristic. The first important thing we can conclude from this is that a musical interval is defined by the *ratio of*, not the *difference between*, the frequencies of two notes. This is important. A string vibrating 40 times a second sounds a note an octave above one vibrating 20 times a second. Similarly, a string vibrating 4,000 times a second plays the octave above one vibrating 2,000 times a second.

So how can we use Pythagoras' simple consonant ratios to define the notes of a full scale? We start with any note, go up an octave, and we've got the ends marked out. Notes with a frequency of $4/3$ and $3/2$ times the frequency of our starting note give us the fourth and fifth notes of our scale, respectively.

Let's look at these notes in relation to a C scale. We have:

Note:	C	F	G	C
Ratio:	1:1	4:3	3:2	2:1

If we go a fifth up from our fifth note and then down an octave, we get the second note of the scale. Doing the math, we get $3/2$ times $3/2$ times $1/2$, or $9/8$ times the frequency of C. This will be our D note on our C scale. Going up a fifth from this note gives us a note whose frequency is $9/8$ times $3/2$, or $27/19$ths of the frequency of our starting C. This is the "A" note of our scale. These are the notes of what is called the pentatonic scale, one of the oldest of scales and one which has cropped up spontaneously in cultures all over the world. Already, however, we can see that the ratios of the notes are getting bigger. We sense the numerologists standing in the shadows, grinning and sharpening their pencils!

Let's ignore them for the moment and go on to develop the ratio of notes in a full major scale as we know it today. A fourth interval below the A is E, $81/64$ths the frequency of our starting C. A fifth above that is B, $243/128$ths the frequency of C. The numerologists are salivating, but we've made it all the way to defining a full diatonic scale. The frequencies of our notes, relative to our starting C are:

Note:	C	D	E	F	G	A	B	C
Ratio:	1:1	9:8	81:64	4:3	3:2	27:16	243:128	2:1

This scale has been around for a long time, and is known as the *Pythagorean scale*.

If this discussion so far appears to you to be a numerological conspiracy, you may be right. Please bear with me a bit further though, since we're going to come back to earth directly and relate this to autoharps, believe it or not. Let's look for a moment at the intervals between adjacent notes of our Pythagorean scale. We observe that the intervals between adjacent notes which we know as "whole steps," (all except E to F and B to C), have a frequency ratio of 9:8. Similarly, those intervals known as "half steps" (E to F and B to C) have a ratio of 256:243. Remember this number! Now let's start to fill in the notes comprising a *chromatic* scale containing all sharps and flats. A fourth down from B is F♯. This note bears a ratio relationship to our starting C note of 729:512. If we figure the interval between F and F♯, we note that this half step may be expressed by the ratio 2187.2048. *Stop right here!* The numerologists have come in and raised a Texas-sized ruckus and we are in *Big Trouble*! How can a scale have two different sizes of half steps? This is obviously going to cause problems if we want to tune an instrument to our C scale with an F♯ thrown in for good luck and then decide to play in G, in which the F♯ is part of the diatonic scale.

Things get even more complicated if we try to add more notes to our chromatic scale in this fashion. If we decide to tune, say, an autoharp by starting with the Fs, then tuning the Cs (a fifth up from the Fs), then the Gs, the Ds, and so on by fifth intervals, we'll eventually end up at E♯, technically the same as an F. If we compute the ratio between this E♯ and the F with which it is supposedly identical, we find that the notes are *not* the same, but different by the interval 531441:524288! (The numerologists think they have died and gone to heaven!) This interval actually has a name. It's called the *Pythagorean comma*. (And you thought Pythagoras just did triangles!) Anyone who has ever tired to tune an autoharp by ear by listening to fifth intervals has probably encountered this problem. You can hear the fifths quite nicely by listening to the consonance of each interval, but when you get back around to where you started, you'll find the last fifth interval is *off* in a big way! You can, of course, get around this by tuning each fifth interval just a little bit narrow, but that doesn't gain you any points with the numerologists.

As long as music and instruments were simple, all of this was just so many numbers; however, with the development of the pipe organ and more complex polyphonic music, precise tuning became an important subject. A variety of scales was proposed to overcome the limitations of the Pythagorean system of perfect fifths, but all these scales had problems. Pipe organs still had certain intervals, such as the fifth between G♯ and E♭, which were known as *wolf intervals*, and were never to be played by caring organists, nor written by caring composers. I leave it to your imagination to fill in the details. The most useful compromise using fractional intervals is a scale known as the *one-quarter comma scale*, which actually works quite well for diatonic instruments (including autoharps) as long as they can be confined to playing in one or two keys.

By Johann Sebastian Bach's time, music had become quite complex. Most music was polyphonic, often with many modulations and key changes within a single piece. The use of accidentals (notes not in a diatonic scale) was common. Some other way of defining the notes in a scale was needed.

Mathematics had also come a long way since the days of Pythagoras and the ancient numerologists. Using math tools somewhat more advanced than fraction arithmetic, it became possible to define a scale in which *all* the intervals are equally imperfect. This allowed the wolf intervals to be broken up into a lot of little wolf puppy intervals spread out over the entire scale – all equally out of tune, but none so much so as to be objectionable. How is this done? With a little thought, one may see that it is impossible to define such a scale using fractions, so let's forget consonant intervals for a moment and take a stab at the problem from another perspective. For a start, let's assume that our chromatic scale should consist of 12 equal musical intervals. We need a number representing a halftone interval by which we can obtain the frequency of any note, if we know the frequency of the note just below it. Taking our C scale again, we can obtain the frequency of C♯ by multiplying the frequency of C by our halftone interval. If we keep going on up the scale this way, we eventually get to the C note an octave above our starting point which we know for sure must have a frequency of twice our starting C. The problem boils down to the question, "What number, multiplied by itself 12 times, equals 2?" If you made it through junior high math, you'll recognize that the answer is the 12th root of 2, approximately 1.05946. If we arrange a chromatic scale so that each note has a frequency of $2^{1/12}$, we will come out 12 notes later an octave above where we started, and will have developed the scale known as the *tempered scale*. All intervals in this scale are equally "out of tune." J. S. Bach was a great proponent of the tempered scale, and wrote a series of pieces for the well-tempered clavichord, which firmly established the tempered scale in modern music.

Our ears still long, however, for the purity of the older scales with their absolutely consonant intervals. Perfect fifths still sound sweeter than tempered fifths. This is why some of us who play diatonic 'harps prefer to use one of the older scales in which the intervals are "sweetened."[1]

All of our electronic chromatic tuners are tuned by their makers to a tempered scale. The meters on these tuners are graduated in units called "cents." A cent is one hundredth of a half tone interval. Anyone so inclined can grind through the math on a pocket calculator and determine the differences in cents between the notes of a tempered scale and those of any of the older, fraction-based scales. ❖

[1] See "Tuning And Temperament" p.42.

AQ Volume VII, Number 3

NOW THAT'S PROGRESS

Dr. George Foss

Chord Progression

Chord:
Three or more tones sounded simultaneously…
(*Harvard Dictionary of Music*)

Progress:
Movement toward a goal…
(*American Heritage Dictionary*)

Chord Progression…
A sequence of chords within a key leading to a point of repose or cadence…(*George Foss*)

In learning most musical instruments (violin, flute, trumpet, etc.) we are concerned with the melodic progression from one single tone to the next. However, in a few instruments (piano, guitar, and especially autoharp) we must consider the movement of full chords from one to the next. Even if we are primarily interested in the tune or melody line, we must also consider the full chords which contain the individual melody tones. This idiosyncrasy of the autoharp makes an understanding of the principles of chord progression very important for the autoharp performer or student.

First, let us review briefly the basic chords found in every Major key. See Figure A.

Figure A

In the Key of C Major

I II III IV V (V^7) VI VII*

CM dm em FM GM (G^7) am b°

In Any Major Key	Chord Quality	In the Key of C Major
I The TONIC	Major	**C Major (CM)**
II The SUPER-TONIC	minor	**d minor (dm)**
III The MEDIANT	minor	**e minor (em)**
IV The SUB-DOMINANT	Major	**F Major (FM)**
V The DOMINANT chord	Major	**G Major (GM)**
V^7 The DOMINANT SEVENTH	combination of all tones found in the Major Dominant (V) chord and the diminished Leading-tone (VII) chord	**G dom. 7th (G^7)**
VI The SUB-MEDIANT	minor	**a minor (am)**
VII* The LEADING TONE	diminished	**b dim (b°)**

* Diminished quality chords are not found on standard autoharps

Simply to move randomly from one chord in a key to other chords in the same key will not necessarily produce a *chord progression*. A true *chord progression* creates a classic pattern:

Repose—Tension—Resolution

To help us understand (and to recreate) the nature of chord progression, let us divide the chords of a Major key into four classes:

3rd Class chords (III and VI) are the most static chords with the least inherent tension and sense of movement;

2nd Class chords (II and IV) are intermediate chords with some quality for movement but still distant from Tonic;

1st Class chords (V and V^7, also VII) are the chords of greatest tension demanding further motion, usually directly towards…

TONIC chord, the point of resolution and the chord within every key which produces the ultimate repose.

Figure B lays out the various classes of chords in graphic fashion. If the chord classifications are followed from left to right, a chord progression is achieved. If we move in the opposite direction (even temporarily) a *retrogression* results.

Figure B

3rd Class Chords	2nd Class Chords	1st Class Chords	TONIC
III (em) Mediant	II (dm) Super-tonic	V (GM) Dominant	
VI (am) Sub-mediant	IV (FM) Sub-dominant	V^7 (G^7) Dominant Seventh	I (CM) TONIC
		VII (b°) Leading-tone	

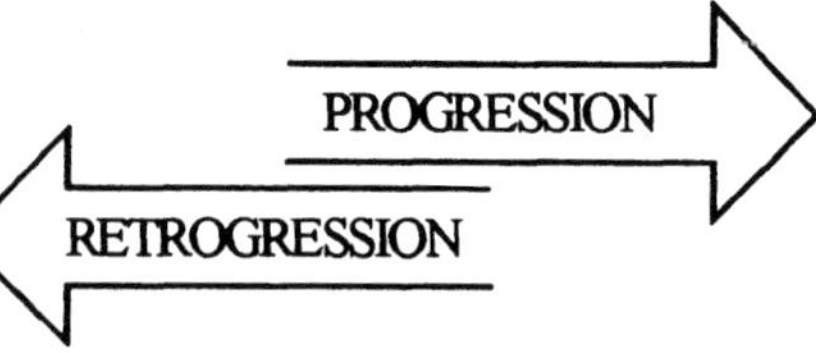

Below are a few observations about chord progressions to consider when choosing the chords for your harmonizations.

1. Progressions to Tonic reinforce the

sense of Tonic or key feeling.
2. Retrogressions tend to weaken the sense of Tonic or key feeling.
3. A chord progression may begin with the Tonic chord or a chord from any of the other chord classifications.
4. A Tonic chord may be inserted at any point in a progression without disturbing the sense of chord progression.
5. Any chord in a progression may be repeated consecutively without disturbing the sense of chord progression.
6. A chord classification may be omitted or skipped within a progression. This is termed *elision*.

Here are some graphic representations of various chord progressions:

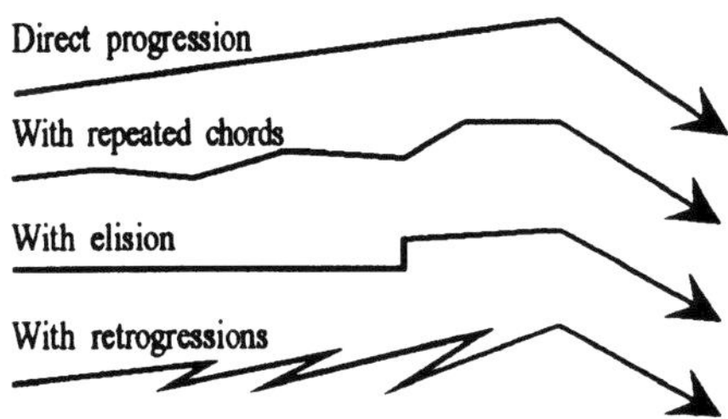

A chord progression usually equates to a musical phrase ending with a pause point or *cadence*. This length of musical "stuff" represents the same amount as a line of a poem. Therefore, in a song, a line of the lyric ending with a comma or period is matched directly by a melodic phrase ending with a pause or cadence. If this melodic phrase is harmonized, we have a chord progression.

If we always play from printed sheet music, we do not need to worry with the details of chord progression. That has already been done by the composer or arranger and we can simply follow directions. If, on the other hand, we are harmonizing a tune we know only by ear or if we have only the printed melody line, then we must accurately and effectively choose our chord progressions. This process is much like planning a motor trip. We have various options and desired results to consider. We can opt for the fastest and most economical route by heading directly to the nearest Interstate and follow the I-network to our final destination. Or we may choose the route of greatest scenic beauty with points of interest and diversion. Unfortunately, many autoharp players travel entirely on the Interstate network I to IV to V^7 to I. It's direct, it's fast, it's easy to follow, you can't get lost, and it's boring if it is the only route taken phrase after phrase after phrase. By using the chart of chord classifications we can choose alternate routes for variety and a myriad of other subtle effects; side roads III or VI, route II instead of IV, or highway V instead of the congested traffic on V^7.

The nature and tempo of a tune are of great importance to the types of progressions needed and to the style of harmonization which is appropriate. Quick dance or fiddle tunes have short phrases with frequently simple melodic lines. These require equally short and direct chord progressions; I – V – I or I – IV – I – V – I. Slow tunes with longer phrases and frequently sentimental lyrics beg for a more colorful and less direct treatment. Remember that the I, IV, and V(V^7) chords are all of Major quality and their exclusive use, especially in slow pieces, becomes extremely colorless.

Each musical phrase usually ends in one of the following patterns called a *cadence*:

V or V^7 to I	This most common pattern is called an *Authentic cadence.*
Phrase ending on V	This pattern usually occurs at the midpoint in a melody and is called a *half-cadence*.
IV to I	This elision pattern at the final cadence is called the *plagel* or *"Amen" cadence.*
V or V^7 to VI	This surprise ending is called a *deceptive cadence.*

Autoharpists frequently speak of *sustain*. The quality called sustain can be affected by the quality of workmanship in the basic instrument and in the chord-bar mechanism. It is also affected by the quickness and smoothness of co-ordination of the player in changing from one chord button to another. It can also be enhanced greatly by a consideration of *common tones*. In music theory, common tones are tones shared between two consecutive chords in a progression. For example, when we move from the I chord (c-e-g) to the IV chord (f-a-c) the tone "c" is a common tone. When we play these chords on the autoharp, no matter how slowly or ill-coordinated, the tone "c" rings through the shift and enhances that quality we call sustain. Play the following progressions with the common tones give in the parenthesis:

I (eg) III – IV – V (g) I

I (ce) VI (ac) IV (f) V^7 (g) I

The second progression has more common tones and a noticeable increase in "sustain."

With your autoharp in hand (or on lap) begin on the I (Tonic) chord and travel across the classification chart many times, each time slightly changing your route. Continue doing this with the insertion of Tonic chords at various points in your progressions. Try some progressions with elisions, skipping from VI to V^7 or from IV to I. Experiment with repeating chords within the progression, I – VI – IV – IV – V – I or I – II – I – V – V – I. Also try lateral moves from one chord to another within the same classification, I – III – VI – IV – II – V – V^7 – I. Then do it all again in each of the keys you find yourself using frequently. This experimentation will not only familiarize you with many different chord progression patterns, but hearing some of these new progressions may inspire in you an original piece. ❖

Explanation And Use Of Diminished 7th Chords

AQ Volume II, Number 4

USING DIMINISHED CHORDS ON THE AUTOHARP

Lindsay Haisley

Several people have asked me to explain the use of diminished chords on the autoharp. In this article I'll give you a broad understanding of these very powerful chords and how to make and use them.

What are diminished chords? We see them frequently in music indicated by the superscript " ° " symbol. Technically, a diminished chord consists of three notes separated *by minor third intervals*. If we add a fourth note yet another minor third up we have what is actually called a *diminished seventh chord.* Adding one more minor third interval brings us to the note an octave above where we started. To be totally accurate then, diminished chords on the autoharp are actually diminished seventh chords, however at this point I shall pull out my folk license and refer to all such chords in this article as diminished chords or simply "dim" chords.

To understand this musically, take your autoharp and carefully pluck every *3rd* string going up the 'harp starting at or above the lower A (below this note the scale is incomplete). You will be playing the notes of a diminished chord. Most other chords consist of intervals which vary in size as you go up the notes of the chord. This makes one note, called the *root*, special in every chord. This is the note on which we start the sequence of unequal intervals which defines the chord. Thus, a G Major chord is defined starting on a G note. The next note is a B, a *major* third up, followed by a D, a *minor* third above the B and finally another G, a *fourth* interval above the D. Because the intervals in a diminished chord are all the same, any note in it can be the root note. A C° is the same as a D♯°, an F♯°, and an A°, at least as far as the autoharp is concerned. Each diminished chord bar on your 'harp can thus be thought of as producing four diminished chords. Three diminished chord bars will yield chords in all 12 keys, a welcome economy on an instrument where each chord added usually means that another must be removed.

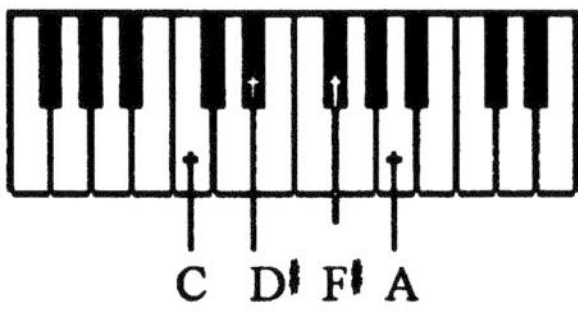

I call my three diminished chords C, G and D (C, C♯ and D would do as well). The notes in these chords are:

CHORD	NOTES IN CHORD
C°	C D♯ F♯ A
G°	G A♯ C♯ E
D°	D F G♯ B

Let's turn now to the subject of how to use diminished chords. Chords are familiar landmarks to our musical senses. We've all been conditioned since childhood to hear them in certain sequences and patterns, well ingrained in our brains. Each chord calls to mind other chords related to it in our mental musical patterns and either encourages, allows, or discourages changes to each other chord, depending on their relative positions in these patterns. For example, play a G^7 on your 'harp. Like the old story about dropping one shoe, one's musical ear cries out for what we call "resolution" to the C chord. A seventh chord always wants to resolve to the chord a 5th interval below (or 4th interval above) it. Thus G^7 resolves to C, D^7 resolves to G, etc. If we resolve a D^7 to a G and make the G a 7th as well, the ear is satisfied with the first resolution but wants to hear a further resolution of the G^7 to a C. One can keep going in a logical sequence this way, and many songs such as "Five Foot Two," "Sweet Georgia Brown," and "Salty Dog Rag" make use of this "Circle of Fifths" progression.

Each diminished chord allows or encourages musical movement in *several* directions. Using a diminished chord is like standing on a concrete hilltop on a skateboard – it's easy to go in any direction, as long as it's down. This makes it an ideal chord to place between other chords to enhance the change between them. C Major to D minor is an "allowed" change. C Major to C♯° to D minor has a lot more musical excitement. In general, the use of diminished chords in this fashion gives music a much more fluid feeling.

Like any other chords, diminished chords can be used to give a flavor to a piece of music. Consider the first line to "Somewhere Over the Rainbow." If you're playing the piece in C, the word "birds" in "bluebirds fly" is a C°. The syllables "town" and "Beth" in "O Little Town of Bethlehem" (key of C) are C° and C♯° respectively. The latter is, in fact part of the C, C♯°, D minor transition mentioned before.

Diminished chords come into their own on the 'harp when one starts using them for picking melodies. Just as they can be used as transition chords between diatonic chords, they can also be used to pick out notes between the notes in a diatonic scale, allowing you to take full advantage of the chromatic nature of your instrument. Consider the usual way of picking a scale on the 'harp. To play a C scale we might proceed as follows:

NOTE	→	C	D	E	F	G	A	B	C
CHORD	→	C	G	C	F	C	F	G	C
(or)	→	C	G^7	C	G^7	G	F	G^7	C
(or)	→	F	E^7	Am		etc...			

All of these ways of picking a C scale sound good in the proper context. Missing from this, however, are all the sharp and flat notes, called *accidentals*, between the diatonic scale notes. They are there on the instrument and in many pieces of music, but the traditional autoharp chords are awkward or unusable to isolate them for melody picking. If you have diminished chords on your instrument, you can play a full chromatic scale in C as follows:

NOTE →	C	C♯	D	D♯	E	F	F♯	G	G♯	A	A♯	B
CHORD →	C	G°	G	C°	C	F	C°	C	D°	F	G°	G

This, on the face of it, is really remarkable. What is even more amazing is that a great many pieces of music which use lots of accidentals are very comfortable with diminished chords behind these notes. Take for example the song, "Glow Worm." The first line of the chorus, and the chords which go with it in the key of C are:

NOTES	A	G	F♯	G	G♯	A
WORDS	Glow	little	glow	worm,	glim-	mer
CHORDS	F	C	C°	C	D°	Dm

When you play it with these chords it sounds instantly familiar!

If you start working with pop music from the first half of this century you will encounter this situation a lot. Songs which were previously un-playable on the autoharp fall right into place using dim chords. Listen to my *(Auto)Harps Alive!!* album and you will hear dim chords all over the place!

If you want to put diminished chords on your autoharp here are some suggestions. First, if you really want to learn to use these chords you should have or get a 21-chord autoharp. The limitations of the 12- and 15-chord systems are too severe to take full advantage of a chromatic autoharp. You can not, of course, put dim chords on a diatonic autoharp. The notes just aren't there. A stock Oscar Schmidt 21-chord 'harp comes equip- ped with chords to play in E♭, B♭, F, C, G, D and A. The keys of E♭ and B♭ are not fully supported on the instrument and besides, if you hang out with string players rather than brass players, you'll be playing mostly in C, G, D, A and wishing you could play in E. This, therefore, is what I recommend for OSI 'harp players. Remove from your 'harp the chords A♭, E♭, B♭7 and C minor and make for yourself the three diminished chords and an E Major. On OSI 'harp 21-chord systems the chord buttons can slide in the bars, allowing them to be positioned anywhere in the chord set. If your 'harp isn't an OSI 'harp and comes with different chords, or with the buttons permanently attached to the bars, you will probably want to work with the maker to get things set up the way you want them.

I have the chords on my OSI chromatic 'harps arranged as follows:

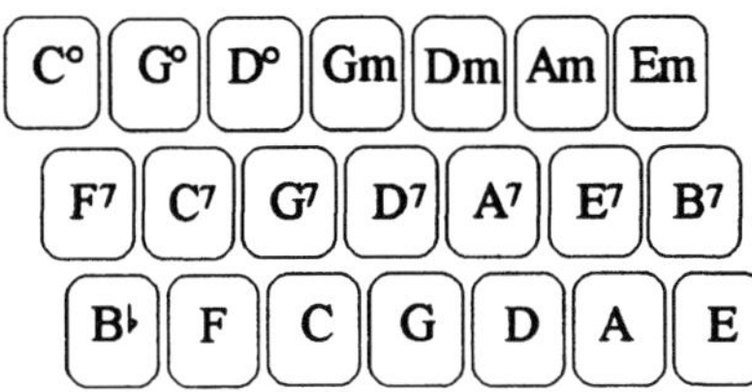

This arrangement works quite well for me. The dim chords are mainly thumb chords, and standard 1-4-5 patterns fall right into place beneath the fingers for both major and minor modes. In major modes, the frequently played tonic chord (the chord bearing the name of the key of the piece) is usually under my strong middle finger. I have easy access in minor modes to the 4 minor and 5 chords and also to the 7th of the key major (e.g. D7 in the Key of D minor). The latter is used a lot in minor-keyed folk music. ❖

For a short discussion of diminished chords, see "Questions And Answers – Diminished Chords" p.122.

AQ Volume VI, Number 3

FLOATING PENTATONICS

Ancient Principles for the 21st Century Autoharp

Marty Schuman

Floating Pentatonics

According to reputable archeologists, the earliest autoharps were tuned to a diatonic scale, i.e. do, re, mi, etc. They were designed to be played in one key. Later, the chromatic scale with all the sharps and flats became standard. This allowed the autoharp to be played in several keys.

In more modern times, artists, most notably Bryan Bowers, have reintroduced the diatonic scale autoharp. Though limited to one key, it is maximized for that key. This is achieved by changing the strings not needed from the chromatic scale to a doubling of some strings in the diatonic scale. In addition, the entire instrument is tuned to itself through a "just" tuning, as contrasted to equal tempered. The effect is a more powerful, yet sweeter sounding autoharp.[1]

Diatonic Stringing
C C D D E F F G G A A B C

Chromatic Stringing
C C♯ D D♯ E F F♯ G G♯ A A♯ B C

In recent years, Dr. George Foss (aka Captain Pentatonic) has been an enthusiastic advocate of the pentatonic autoharp. The pentatonic scale dates back to ancient China and consists of the 1, 2, 3, 5, and 6 of any diatonic scale. For example, the diatonic C scale: C, D, E, F, G, A, B becomes C, D, E G, A in its pentatonic form. With an autoharp set up in a five-note scale, more strings are available to double and an even "sweeter" tuning is possible. Pentatonic 'harps are exceptional for playing "mountain modal" tunes e.g. "Little Maggie," "Little Birdie," "Little Sadie," "Pretty Polly," etc. One drawback – a pentatonic autoharp is pretty well limited to those kinds of tunes, and in one key at that.

If one plays across all the strings of a chromatic 'harp the resulting cacophony is quite offensive to the ear. A much more acceptable sound results when all the strings of a diatonic autoharp are sounded. However, the sound of all the strings of a pentatonic 'harp is – purely celestial! That is because all the strings are in a universally-accepted total harmony – like a fine wind chime.

"Open" playing refers to the technique applied to the diatonic 'harp whereby one refrains from depressing any chord bar at certain times. Beautiful flowing "fills" are achieved in this manner. Ron Wall is the pioneer of this technique. Mark Fackeldey is exceptional at applying intricate open runs between the melody lines. And, Mike Fenton of England first took open playing and applied it to his thumb lead style for fast fiddle tunes.

When you use the open style technique, accuracy in hitting the "proper" string becomes important. Even so, at times the 4th and 7th note of the diatonic scale will come through and not be harmonious with the rest of the notes. The human ear generally forgives these "off tones" and integrates them with the whole. It is my understanding that dogs have such sensitive hearing that the sound of the 4th and 7th note coming through has at times led them to turn against their masters.

Over the past few years I have developed a system of incorporating pentatonic scales on the diatonic autoharp. This allows one to play strictly pentatonic (e.g. "mountain modal") tunes in three keys on a single-key diatonic 'harp. But most astounding is a principle I call *Floating Pentatonics.* Instead of playing melody on a diatonic 'harp and the open parts on that diatonic scale, one plays the melody diatonically and open parts on the chord's corresponding pentatonic scale.

Diatonic/Diatonic (open) becomes *Diatonic/Pentatonic (open).* The effect is a fluid melody line with no offensive tones. Wrong notes are automatically eliminated. Subtle chord shadings are possible as well as "hammer on" and other effects. Floating pentatonics can be applied to any diatonic tune; slow or fast, traditional or modern. Floating pentatonics is compatible with all styles of playing, including strum, pinch, thumb lead, flat picking, and cross picking.

To try floating pentatonics, you need not totally alter your autoharp. You will need to start with a single-key diatonic 'harp with a three-tiered chord bar mechanism. Tools needed include crowbar and sledgehammer.

Pentatonic scales can be viewed as chords, in which case they take on the designation 6+9 (added to the 1, 3, and 5). Using a D 'harp for demonstration purposes you will need to cut the following chord bars:

D_{6+9}	D	E	F♯	A	B
A_{6+9}	A	B	C♯	E	F♯
G_{6+9}	G	A	B	D	E

Placement of these chord bars in relationship with their "straight" counterparts (D, A, G) is critical. This is because in floating pentatonics both chords are depressed simultaneously with two fingers of the left hand. After much experimentation I have found the following layout of the basic chords most conducive to rapid chord changes.

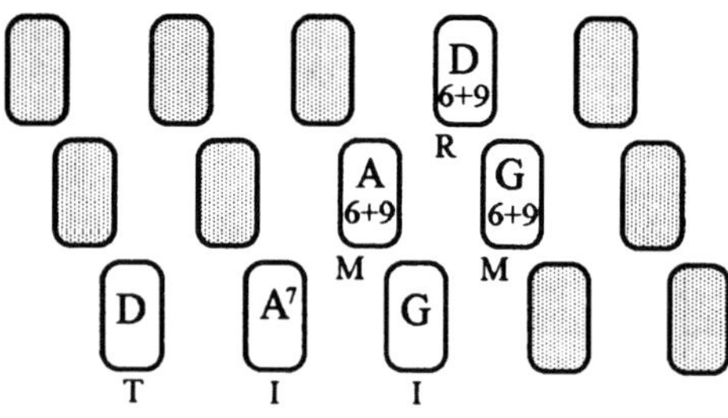

Left-hand Fingering:
T - Thumb; I - Index; M - Middle; R - Ring

This layout is basic. Other chords (grayed buttons) are omitted in this article for purposes of simplification.

For playing a strictly pentatonic or "modal" tune, one depresses one of the pentatonic chords and keeps it down the entire time. Lock bars are neither necessary nor desirable. Depress other chords as needed while keeping the pentatonic chord down.

Example

Little Birdie

D modal

D6+9 ➲ entire tune

```
                        A7
Lit - tle bird - ie, lit - tle bird - ie

      A7       A7
Come and sing me your song.

                       A7
What a short time to be here

        A7  A7
And a long time to be gone.
```

The A^7 chord is just used where designated, not sustained.

To play the same tune in G modal, simply depress the G6+9 the entire tune and use the D chord as appropriate.

To apply Floating Pentatonics one must depress the chords in pairs, i.e.

D	+	D6+9
A^7	+	A6+9
G	+	G6+9

On the open part of open playing, lift up on the straight chord while keeping its pentatonic counterpart depressed. This is not difficult if your chord bars are in the position described earlier and you use the proper fingering. In time, this "home position" becomes natural.

Example

Wildwood Flower

```
D6+9 G6+9 D6+9        D6+9
D    G    D     D6+9  D           A7
I  will  twine, I  will  min - gle

D6+9  A6+9        A6+9     D6+9
D     A7    A6+9  A7       D
My    ra  -  ven  black    hair.
```

Repeat chords from Line 1
With the ros - es so red and

Repeat chords from Line 2
The lil - lies so fair.

```
D6+9                     D6+9
D                  D6+9  D
And, the myr - tle so   green

    G6+9          D6+9
    G             D
Of an em - er - ald hue
```

Repeat chords from Line 1
The pale am - a - ni - ta

Repeat chords from Line 2
And is - lip so blue.

Although there are not many applications in these two examples, you will find that fiddle tunes have many more uses for Floating Pentatonics.

In summary: Floating Pentatonics is the practice of playing any diatonic tune against constantly shifting pentatonic scales. Get in tune with the past and future – think *Floating Pentatonics*! ❖

[1] See "Tuning and Temperament" p.42.

New Chords For The Autoharp

AQ Volume VI, Number 4

ALL THAT JAZZ

Lindsay Haisley

Back when I was in college I began doing some fairly serious photography for our school publications. One of the "principles of nature" that I quickly learned was what I might call the Law of Trade-offs, or "You don't get something without giving something else up." In the case of photography, the trade-off is between film speed, available light, and shutter speed. Less light means longer exposures or faster film. Faster film means poorer image quality. If you want to have it all, you need to buy a more expensive camera – yet another aspect of the Law of Trade-offs. It was thus no great shock when I encountered the Law of Trade-offs in music. The autoharp is probably as good an example of this law as one will find anywhere.

Many 'harpists have struggled with the chord limitations of even a 21-chord harp – part of the trade-off for having such a nice, light instrument with so many strings on it. If you need all possible chords at all times, you buy a piano, but you can't carry a piano to a folk festival![1] Add more bars, and you need smaller fingers and because the bars are smaller you have worse problems with harmonics. Keep the bars the same size and you have to increase the size of the chord bar holders, making it harder to reach all the strings. If you want to have your cake and eat it too you will need a bigger, more expensive 'harp, etc. For people who are terminally frustrated with the limitations of 21 chords, replacing one's standard chord bar holders with "flip-top" holders is relatively painless and involves a rather different trade-off. Such chord bar holders, available from a variety of makers, allow one to flip open the retainers holding the chord bars at each side of one's 'harp and swap out any or all of the chord bars therein in a matter of seconds. Oscar Schmidt's 21-chord covered chord bar arrangement is not particularly conducive to this sort of thing; however, OS 12- and 15-chord arrangements lend themselves readily to this kind of setup. Custom-made autoharps can be ordered with flip-open chord holders.

Such an arrangement allows one to have a nearly infinite selection of chords assuming (yet another trade-off) that one has the will and stamina to carry around a nearly infinite selection of chord bars. The major trade-off, of course, is that at any particular time one still has only as many chord bars on one's harp as one has chord bar positions. Changing chords in the middle of a song (or even between songs during a performance) can be an excessive hassle even with the simplest of setups. While this is an obstacle for performance, it is far less so for recording. Because modern recording need not be done in real-time, one has the option to stop, change chords and take up again where one left off, even in the middle of a song.

I had the pleasure of collaborating with Jim Hudson on an autoharp and hammered dulcimer album of American standards on which we used this technique on nearly every song. Many of the beautiful tunes that we recorded such as "Stardust" and "Autumn Leaves" make use of a wide variety of subtle chord changes far beyond the conventional range of the autoharp. Because every song was unique in its musical needs, and because we had a limited supply of chord bars, I resorted to custom-cutting most of the required chords on a song by song basis. At the end of each day of work, I found myself sitting in the middle of piles of chord bars and surrounded by felt fragments littering Jim's nice studio carpet. Jim would lock the studio door each day at this point and not let me out until I had cleaned up the mess! Everything worked out just fine.

From the point of view of a traditional 'harp or hammered dulcimer player, the first big leap required for the songs we recorded was the extension of our standard chord set around the circle of fifths. This means that if we were working on a song such as "Any Time" in the key of C, we needed the chords of E^7 and A^7 as well as the more standard chords. This is, of course, to be expected, and if one has a standard 21-chord harp one can usually cover an adequate segment of the circle of 5ths in keys such as C, G, and F. The next step involved the use of diminished 7th chords, which I've written about at some length.[2] Diminished 7th chords allow one to expand chordal accompaniment to cover fully chromatic melodies and are required for many songs from the musical tradition in which we were working. I keep a set of diminished 7th chords on my 'harp for this purpose as part of my standard chord set. Beyond this point things started to get interesting. Probably the next most common chord was a 6th chord, made by adding the 6th note of the scale to a standard major chord. For instance, a CM chord contains the notes C, E, and G. Adding an A to this triad produces a C^6, a very useful chord. Some songs also required a minor 7th chord which conveniently works out to be identical to a 6th of the relative major chord. An $Amin^7$, for instance, consists of the notes A, C, E, and G – identical to the notes in a C^6. Although a major 6th and it's relative minor 7th were usually not required in the same song, this did reduce the number of chord bars required for the project.

To put a handle on this for everyone who relates to music better than to numbers, imagine the word "leaves" in the first phrase of the song "Autumn Leaves." If you can hear it in your mind, you'll hear a minor chord based on the second note of the scale. This is actually a minor 7th. The same chord occurs on the word "wonder" in the first phrase of the chorus of "Stardust." Another chord which one encounters frequently is the major 7th chord. This is a very distinctive chord to hear and play, but very confusing to talk or write about since it's easily confused with the (straight) 7th chord, also built on a major chord. The 7th of GM, for instance, is written G^7 and consists of a G, B, D and F. This is the G^7 found on the autoharp and familiar to everyone. If we use an F# instead of an F in this chord we have a chord of a different color. This is the *major* 7th, conventionally written GM^7 or $G^{7}+$. The major 7th can be a very subtle chord and frequently occurs in sequences of chords which we might call "chord melodies," as opposed to single note melodies.

Many popular tunes, especially those which have orchestral accompaniments, use such chord melodies at the ends of phrases or as a counterpoint to a vocal melody. Such pieces have a rich and complex harmonic structure and frequently have two, three, or even four chord changes per measure of music. A good example of such a piece would be "I Left My Heart in San Francisco." The word "heart" at the beginning of the chorus is written in some arrangements as a major 7th. Autoharp players frequently fudge such chords as minor and major 7ths by playing a straight minor or major – a useful compromise since these chords will almost always sound OK in this context, even if a bit of the richness of the music is lost.

A variety of other chords occur frequently enough to deserve mention. A 9th chord is made by taking a 7th chord and playing the second (aka the 9th) note of the scale at the top end instead of the tonic. For instance, a C^7 might contain the notes C, E, G, and B♭ with a C on top for good measure. A C^9 would consist of a C, E, G, and B♭ with a D (no C!) on top. The sound is quite different, and as the discerning 'harpist will already have realized, involves a bit of a compromise on the 'harp. The chord is, of course, based on the note C, however we are leaving out the Cs altogether above a certain point in order to create the distinctive 9th chord sound. A good compromise is to substitute Ds for Cs in the top one or two octaves of the 'harp and leave the lower octaves at a straight C.

One will likewise encounter suspended and augmented chords frequently enough to put them in the catalog. A suspended chord substitutes the 4th note of a major scale for the 3rd normally found in a major chord. An augmented chord substitutes the sharp of the 5th note of the scale for the 5th normally found in a major chord.

Numbers, as I've said, are very hard to hear. In order to appreciate these chords they must be played and heard. What I'm going to do here is give you a homework assignment. The notes to 4 special chords are listed in the chart following. Those of you who want to pursue this subject further should get hold of four blank chord bars and some felt. If you don't have these chords already on your harp, cut them and put them on in any positions that feel comfortable. When you place your chords on your harp, be sure that you leave on the chords C, or G^7, and F which work quite harmoniously with these new chords.

Chord	Notes			
CM^7	C	E	G	B
C^6	C	E	G	A
C#dim	C#	E	G	B♭
Dm^7	D	F	A	C

Play with the chords for a while and become familiar with how they sound. See if you can find some familiar tunes which sound good with this particular combination of chords. ❖

[1] See "Strings – Their Ideal Sizes And Lengths"p.31.

[2] See "Explanation And Use Of Diminished 7th Chords"p.49.

More New Chords For The Autoharp

AQ Volume VII, Number 3

BEYOND BASICS, CHORDWISE

Lindsay Haisley

This is an absolutely beastly chapter about an absolutely fascinating topic. All of us have played the old standard folk tunes with three chords for about as long as we've played the autoharp. Most of us at one time or another, have had either the ambition or desire to go beyond the simple traditional chord arrangements in our playing. We often lack the experience or knowledge to know what works and doesn't work in developing our own chord arrangements for the songs we know and like. The ability to work creatively with chords is, like most musical skills, part intuition and part acquired skill. A good part of developing creative arrangements is confidence in the validity of our intuition in this regard, and a good part is just plain old fashioned musical learning, listening, imitating, mixing and matching, and other skills which we all use to keep growing artistically. To develop the skills necessary for working creatively with chords, many folks need to meet and best several common beasts.

The First Beast

This beast, often known as the *Beast of Doubt*, asks, in so many words, "Did you make that arrangement up, or is that the way it's really played?" We often lack confidence in the validity of our "play." So many of us have had to grow up and take life and it's pleasures with the seriousness of adults. "Playing is, after all, for children," says the Beast of Doubt. Overcoming this beast can be somewhat scary, and it may take a while to realize that this beast really has no teeth. He growls and threatens from within us as we diverge from the beaten musical path, but is powerless to hurt us.

The Second Beast

This beast, known as the *Beast of the Experts*, is actually a cousin to the first beast. He says, "The way you're playing that song is nice, but it's not the way Uncle Jeb and the Pie Ridge Waffle Stompers play it." Now you've been listening to Uncle Jeb for years, and you think the Pie Ridge boys are the cat's pajamas, and who are you, after all, to play a song differently when Uncle Jeb and the boys have "nailed it to the wall." This beast can be a little harder to overcome, since he rears his head in group situations whenever someone says, "That's not the way that song goes." Now it's always risky business to take a song everyone knows, and rewrite it to your particular liking. One must realize, however, that "standard" arrangements are often just agreements about chords, words, melody, etc. so that people can play together harmoniously. Observing standard arrangements in group musical situations is a form of courtesy and one often finds that courtesy given is courtesy returned, and can build the basis for collective exploration of new musical ideas. One has the most fun playing with people who are open to new musical ideas and interpretations – and if it's not fun, it's not going to be good music. Playing with friends who like your musical style, and whose style you appreciate as well, easily leaves this beast behind. Diverging from and improvising on standard chord arrangements can even be a way to emphasize their simplicity and beauty. One may return again and again to a traditional arrangement in a song with flights of fun and fancy in between making clear the solid ground on which the piece stands.

The Third Beast

The third beast is known as the *Beast of Inexperience*, and is actually a blood brother to the second beast. Uncle Jeb and his confectionery crew have been playing for years and years, and know chords that you didn't even know existed until you heard them from up on Pie Ridge. Everything you make up sounds like lite syrup compared to their rich and sugary harmonies. "Why bother?" says this beast. "You'll never be that good." Now this beast takes some work to overcome, and this is where the fun comes in. Uncle Jeb didn't get where he got by not bothering. He absolutely loves to play, and has experimented with all kinds of chords and chord combinations in every piece he plays. He may be well ahead of you in this department, but we're really not running any races here, and there's no time like the present to start your own exploration of ways to enrich your autoharp music with new and different harmonies. This beast never really goes away, but you'll find that he'll always retreat before you every time you make an advance.

Onward Through The Fog

What I'm going to give you here is a road map to the edge of uncharted territory. Beyond this, you'll have to keep going on your own. Think of your 'harp, if you will, as a musical off-road vehicle (or an all-terrain beast tamer). Once you've followed the discussion in this chapter, you may well want to put it aside and come up with your own map based on your own preferences.

Let's consider, for starters, the conventional way in which we select chords for your basic three-chord song with no notes except those on the major scale. We can draw a chord chart for the melody chords as follows. I'm referencing everything to the key of C, however the same general discussion applies to any key with appropriate transitions. G$^{(7)}$ means either G or G^{7}.

We're sticking with "stock" chords here, so let's proceed by applying this

Note	C	D	E	F	G	A	B	C
Chord	C	G(7)	C	F	C	F	G(7)	C
Alternate Chord	F	–	–	G^7	G	–	–	C

chart to a bit of a "stock" song such as "Oh, Susanna." I've placed the melody chords below the words.

Oh I come from Al - a - bam - a
C GC   C   C F C   C

with a ban - jo on my knee
C GC C G C G

Just to break the mold for the sake of watching the Jell-O spill, let's construct an arbitrary chord scheme based on chords which are rooted on the notes of the scale. This chord scheme looks as follows. The chord based on the note of B is a diminished chord (sans the 7th) which we'll ignore for the moment since there's no B in our sample phrase.

Note	C	D	E	F	G	A	B	C
Chord	C	Dm	Em	F	G	Am	??	C

We have a few new chords in here, obviously, and are well away at this point from a three-chord scheme. Using this chord scheme to play *Oh Susanna* is rather surreal.

Oh I come from Al - a - bam - a
C DmEm G   G Am G   Em

with a ban - jo on my knee
C Dm Em Em Dm C Dm

The phrase, played this way, sounds as if it doesn't really belong anywhere. Although the notes are from the C scale, we've lost the sense of the piece being grounded in a key. On the other hand, the introduction of minor chords here shows promise. Let's consider how we might modify this chord scheme to give it more of a sense of having a home. The introduction of minor chords provides us with a place to go here. For every major key with its major chords there is a corresponding minor key, known as the relative minor of the major key with its own set of minor chords but using the same set of notes as its relative major. A relative minor key is always two notes down (actually a minor third interval) from its major cousin. In the case of C, the relative minor is A minor. The chord set which works with a minor key certainly has a sense of home, being almost as strong in our cultural musical genes as the major mode. Let's look at the chords which we might use to play the same notes in an A minor scale.

Note	A	B	C	D	E	F	G	A
Chord	Am	Em	Am	Dm	Am	Dm	Em	Am
Alternate Chord	Dm	–	–	–	Em	–	–	Dm

We now have three possible sets of chords for the notes of the C scale, each with some sort of consistency, albeit the second has something of the consistency of thumb tack pudding. We could easily continue this process as long as our musical sandbox has sand in it and, in fact, could attach an entire set of chords to each note of the C scale. However, we're not exploring all the possibilities here, only trying to point out where a few of them lie. As a principle of exploration, let's decide that comfort is to be our guide in making something new, since comfort is something which can be understood by everyone. For comfort's sake, let's say that we're going to start and end the phrase with the chords familiar to us from the traditional arrangement of the tune. Let's also limit our chord focus for the moment to notes which fall on the beat, these being the ones which are close to the harmony chords which go along with melody as we're familiar with it (the syllables "come," "Al," "bam," etc.)

We have the armory and mobility now to begin a quest to vanquish the third beast. We can mix and match from our chord sequences and see what we come up with. A common chord motion at the beginning of a phrase is from the major chord to its relative minor, in this case from C to Am. If the word "Come" is on a C chord, can we get to an A minor for the "Al" in Alabama? On the autoharp, it doesn't quite fit, but let's see if we can get there in a roundabout way. "Al" falls on a G. A G chord here does not really take us anywhere (try playing it and see). Since we're exploring minors, let's look at the relative minor chord scheme. We see that a G note can use an E minor chord which is a move in the right direction. "Bam" could still be an E minor chord, but we're trying to get to A minor here, so let's fall back down to a C chord, dropping finally to the A minor chord on "with." The "ban" syllable in banjo falls on an E note. We played a C chord on "bam" so lets play an E minor chord here to keep things moving. To complete the phrase, we can easily put a D minor on the "on," and conclude the phrase with the traditional G chord on "knee." What manner of mischief have we created? Let's stop and take stock.

Oh I come from Al - a - bam - a
C   Em   C

with a ban - jo on my knee
Am Em   Dm G

This definitely has comfort. The feeling of the phrase flows nicely between major and minor modes on which chord sets we've drawn here. We haven't used any thumb tack pudding here, so let's see what happens if we fill in the rest of the notes using our second scheme.

Oh I come from Al - a - bam - a
C DmC G EmAm C Em

with a ban - jo on my knee
AmDmEm Em DmC G

This is definitely interesting, but needs a bit of polish to make it feel good all around. We've put an A minor from our tacky chord set on the first "a" in Alabama. We've not used an F chord in here yet, and that will fit nicely here. That will save the A minor for "with." The final result...

Oh I come from Al - a - bam - a
C DmC G Em F C Em

with a ban - jo on my knee
AmDm Em Em DmC G

I hope you've been playing along with this. If so, you have doubtless heard the third beast howling with disappointment. You can work on this phrase further, simplifying it if you like, keeping in mind that what we've uncovered here is the nice flow between the major and minor modes. By the time you're done, the third beast will be nowhere in sight. There are other ways to approach the same process. Consider the differences between major and minor chords. Each major chord in a major mode has one or two minor chords which differ from it by only one note. Often these minors can be substituted for the similar major with interesting results. A D minor, for instance, can often be used in place of an F (still in the key of C) and an A minor for a C chord. Sometimes simple substitutions such as these will work and sometimes they won't. There are no fixed rules. One finds that creative chord sequences in a song have a natural flow to them much like the melody. There's no formula for composing a masterpiece, but we know when we hear something strong, whether we hear it from another or make it up ourselves. Listening sincerely for that sense of "rightness" in our music and in that of others – the inner smile, is the magic to banish the first beast.

What of the second beast? Well you can bet that Uncle Jeb has picked a lot of thumb tack pudding over the years. It took him a long time to get to where he could hear really good musical lines and chords in his head, and his trail is littered with thumb tacks – and beasts! They just stand there scratching their heads and tapping their feet. Uncle Jeb more or less ignores them, which is, in the long run, what it takes to get where you're going. ❖

OCTOBER • 1991 VOLUME FOUR • NUMBER ONE FIVE • DOLLARS

AUTOHARP QUARTERLY®

THE • MAGAZINE • DEDICATED • TO • THE • AUTOHARP • ENTHUSIAST

IN THIS ISSUE

BARS -- WHERE THE ACTION IS

BUILD YOUR OWN AUTOHARP
Fourth In A Four-Part Series

RECORDING WITH THE AUTOHARP

INTERACTION
A Lesson With Fran Stallings

COPYRIGHTS AND COPYWRONGS

130 AUTOHARPERS SET WORLD RECORD

The Turn-Around Chord

AQ Volume VI, Number 2

THE TURN-AROUND CHORD

Dr. George Foss

What is a "turnaround" chord? It is a pivotal chord used to modulate temporarily from the basic (tonic) key of a piece to the 'dominant' key. This modulation, or key change, from the tonic key to the key a fifth higher is the most common modulation found in music. The "turnaround" chord is always a Major quality chord (or a Dominant-seventh quality chord).

Confusion about the "turnaround" chord results from the fact it is called different names by various kinds of musicians. So, let us review these briefly:

The music theory teacher calls it the Secondary Dominant (or Secondary Dominant-Seventh) since it is literally the dominant (or dominant-seventh) of the Dominant key in a piece. A less formal term frequently used by music theory students is V of V (or V^7 of V).

The music student working out problems of harmonic analysis may use the descriptive term, $II^{\#4}$ (or $II^{7\#4}$) since it is the chord based on the second degree (II) of the key and is altered by raising the fourth degree to create a Major (or dominant-seventh) quality chord. This alteration of a tone (#4) in the basic key portends a shift to another key.

Folk and traditional musicians coined the colorful term, "turnaround" chord, I suppose, because it turns the piece 'around' from the tonic key to the dominant key.

Other traditional musicians, especially autoharp players call it the "extra chord" since it is a chord outside the usual chords found in any one key and on autoharps (especially diatonic 'harps) requires an 'extra' chord bar.

Any piece or arrangement longer than a few minutes can benefit greatly from modulation, no matter how briefly, to another key. The "turnaround" chord facilitates a smooth shift to the dominant key and adds the ingredients of variety and freshness to what would otherwise be sameness or stale quality in a single unchanging key.

Let us look at some segments of familiar tunes which commonly employ "turnaround" chords and tonic-dominant modulations. The most familiar "turnaround" chord is virtually demanded by the melody of the opening phrase of "The Star-Spangled Banner." The raised fourth degree (#4) of the scale occurs in the melody on the syllable <u>ly</u> in ear-<u>ly</u> of 'dawn's early light.' This raised fourth degree followed by a cadence on the dominant tone is a perfect spot for a "turnaround" chord, and a brief modulation to the dominant key.

Other tunes which do not have the raised fourth degree in the melody also use "turnaround" chords to provide shifts to the dominant key. Here is the opening phrase of "A Mighty Fortress Is Our God" with the word *our* being a perfect place for a "turnaround" chord.

The modulation to the dominant key can occur within a phrase and is not limited to cadences at phrase endings. For example, here is the opening phrase of "All Through The Night."

The middle section of "Dixie" is frequently harmonized with a "turnaround" chord and an extremely brief shift to the dominant key.

Two further examples of "turnaround" chords can be found in the inner phrases of the familiar Christmas carols, "Hark! The Herald Angels Sing" and "O Come All Ye Faithful."

Once the "turnaround" chord has shifted the harmony into the new key, the duration of the modulation can vary greatly. In some cases (like "Dixie" above) the key shift can be very brief. Sometimes the harmony can remain in the dominant key for an entire phrase or even an extended section of the piece before returning to the tonic key. Regardless of the duration of the key shift, these modulations impart a freshness and heightened interest to an arrangement.

Remember the "turnaround" chord performs as a dominant chord (or a dominant-seventh chord) in the *upcoming* key and should be followed immediately by the tonic chord (I) of the new key (the V chord of the original key).

Below is a chart giving the *tonic/dominant* relationships which can be found on the various autoharps commercially available. Also given are the "turnaround" chords and their spellings.

TONIC/DOMINANT RELATIONSHIPS

Key of Piece TONIC KEY	TURNAROUND CHORDS $II^{\#4}$	$(II^{7\#4})$	Spelling	To New Key DOMINANT KEY
E♭ Major	F Maj.	(F7)	f a c (e♭)	B♭ Major
B♭ Major	C Maj.	(C7)	c e g (b♭)	F Major
F Major	G Maj.	(G7)	g b d (f)	C Major
C Major	D Maj.	(D7)	d f# a (c)	G Major
G Major	A Maj.	(A7)	a c# e (g)	D Major
D Major	E Maj.*	(E7)	e g# b (d)	A Major
A Major	B Maj.*	(B7)	b d# f# (a)	E Major *

* Chords not usually found on standard chromatic 'harps

Players of diatonic 'harps can also avail themselves of the "turnaround" chord in the key of their instrument if they have that "extra" chord bar available. However since the "turnaround" chord has a chromatically altered ('outside the key') tone, we must use an incomplete dominant-seventh chord as our "turnaround." As long as the altered (#4) tone is not found in the melody (as it is in "The Star Spangled Banner") the incomplete dominant-seventh type of "turnaround" chord is quite effective. Here is a listing of some common diatonic 'harp keys and a spelling of the incomplete "turnaround" chords.

Key of 'Harp	Incomplete $II^{7\#4}$	Dominant Key
F Major	g – d f	C Major
C Major	d – a c	G Major
G Major	a – e g	D Major
D Major	e – b d	A Major
A Major	b – f# a	E Major

I hope that this explanation of the secondary dominant (or secondary dominant-seventh), V (or V^7) of V, $II_{\#4}$ (or $II^7_{\#4}$), "turnaround" chord and "extra chord" will help you in making more varied and interesting arrangements or help you locate those 'nice' harmonies you hear in some favorite pieces but just can't locate on your 'harp. The "turnaround" chord can be a helpful and versatile friend in making better music. Remember the lines from the Shaker hymn tune, "Simple Gifts:"

To turn, turn becomes our delight, For in turning, turning we come 'round right. ❖

Converting Your Autoharp Into A 1⅞ Key Diatonic

AQ Volume I, Number 1

TAKE MI OUT IS THE BALL GAME

George Orthey

Just got a new 'harp? Why not convert your old one into a 1⅞ key diatonic? ⅞? Yes! That extra bit enables you to use a 1-key diatonic scale with ⅞th of another key, allowing you to play a break in a fiddle tune, or just play along in a different key.[1] All of the notes of the primary key are present on the diatonic 'harp, so only one of the notes of the second key is missing. Therefore, the 1⅞th key 'harp. You'd for example, in a D diatonic 'harp have ⅞th of the key of A, also. So your 'harp would be set up with the following bars: F♯m, Em, Bm, E7 (partial), G, A7, D, A. The G, A7, and D with their respective minors make up the standard key of D. The A, E7, and D make up the key of A, minus the third in the E7 chord. In selecting two keys for a 'harp, remember they must be an adjacent pair in the series (Circle of Fifths): E♭, B♭, F, C, G, D, A, E. (These are the series of fifth interval chords). The second key is always immediately to the right of the primary key in this series. For example, if you want your primary key of the 'harp to be A, the ⅞th key must be E.

Nitty Gritty Mechanics Of Changing Your Sow's Ear Into A Silk Purse

There are two components of this exercise. *First, determine the notes of the scale you need. Then retune the notes which are not needed in that scale.*

This can be done quick and dirty by simply taking the key, for example, A, and determining the notes you need for your diatonic scale: A, B, C♯, D, E, F♯, G♯. The key of A has three sharps. Now tune the strings of the unnecessary notes up or down, generally ½ step up if the 'harp body is in good condition. Thus, starting at the bottom notes of the harp, in the key of A, you would retune the standard strings: F, G, C, D, E, F, F♯, G, A, A♯, B, C, C♯, etc. to F♯, G♯, C♯, D, E, F♯, F♯, G♯, A, B, B, C♯, C♯, etc., continuing all the way to the top strings of course, ending on the very high C♯. This quick and dirty method does not make the most balanced sound quality, however. But it does work, and no string replacements must be made. Also, only a few of the tuning pin note markings must be changed.

If you are into changing some strings and you have your handy-dandy marker (Pilot SC or other glass marking pen) in tow, go for a better balance.[2]

You will notice certain requirements/characteristics in the diatonic tunings:

1. Usually the lowest note of the 'harp is the tonic of any one of the three principal major chords: e.g., on an A 'harp, D, A, and E are the principal chords. I would use a low D and E particularly with the oversized strings available today.
2. The lowest six notes are the tonics of the six principal chords.
3. The note at the break of the bridge (the 14th string from the bottom) is the D right above middle C, or very near it.
4. The top note of the 'harp cannot exceed the D two notes above the standard top C.

String replacement requirements you will need:

1. The strings above #14 (D) can be used without changing their size (wire gage).
2. Notes in the bass, strings #1-12, can be changed from standard tuning considerably by using larger or smaller wound strings.
3. The bottom bass string (F on a standard 'harp) cannot be tuned more than three notes lower.

Keep these guidelines in mind. Remember if you "tune up" too much, you will get excess stress and maybe string breakage. And, too, you may behold the wonders of an instant folding 'harp. On the other hand, if you "tune down" too much, particularly in the lower mid-portion of the 'harp, the sound will be dead.

The second major project in the "sow's ear to silk purse" transformation is to felt and notch a set of eight bars and mount them on the 'harp.

You must have standard 12- or 15-bar holders. Refelt eight bars. Place them in the lower eight slots. Some folks may be very neat and cut out the unwanted segment of the holder. This will require cutting off the bar holder cap also to a proper length and drilling a new hole in the cap and in the 'harp body to fix this holder in place. After cutting, glue the bar holder back together with plastic cement used for model building. If you're not handy, don't worry about all this cutting and drilling. It's not necessary to reach the last inning of this ball game.

After you have refelted those eight bars, the chords can be marked and cut. To do this, simply list the eight chords you will use in order with notes that play in each chord listed. Place the bars in their respective slots one at a time, marking a small dot on the side of the felt above each string that plays in that chord. Using a very sharp knife or razor blade, cut a V or U in the felt so that the dot you marked is exactly in the center of the piece you cut out. Using this method, you will line up the notches precisely with the strings you want to sound. Secure the bars in the holder. By now the strings you have replaced or retuned have gone out of tune again, so tune it up and give it a strum. You'll be amazed at the full grand sound you will get out of that old friend. ❖

Read "Converting Your Autoharp Into A 1⅞ Key – Or A Multi-Key Diatonic" p.61. Also see "Chromatic To Diatonic Conversion" p.69. Ivan Stiles' 1⅞ diatonic chord bar setup is found in "Chord Bar Arrangements" p.3.

[1] For a discussion concerning the choice of diatonic keys, see "Questions And Answers" p.122.

[2] See "The String Designation Chart" p.62.

Converting Your Autoharp Into A 1⁷/₈ Key – Or A Multi-Key Diatonic

AQ Volume VI, Number 3

SAME OLD BALL GAME WITH A BRAND NEW MI

George Orthey

This is a sequel/update of information I wrote in the article, "Take Mi Out is the Ball Game."[1] Since that time, in making numerous diatonic autoharps, I have found that even the most trivial changes of notes in the bass or which strings are to be paired will significantly alter the character and quality of the sound of the 'harp. Simply tuning all the sharps to naturals in the key of C, for example, gives a diatonic scale 'harp, but it will not be well-balanced, and the pairs won't all be where you want them.

There are certain basic principles that one should observe in designing a diatonic tuning for the autoharp. The actual notes of each diatonic scale are simple basic information. How you place them on the 'harp will greatly affect the sound of the instrument. You will find that on the single-key diatonic, it is easier to get a good fit than on the two- and three-key instruments. On the multiple key 'harp, you have fewer *extra* strings, you have more bass notes that you'll need, and fewer optional strings to pair.

The designation of lower, middle, and upper or top octave is standard to the ubiquitous Oscar Schmidt Autoharps and string sets. Standard OSI string numbering from #1 at the bass to #36 or #37 at the treble end is used throughout the article.

Basic Rules Of Thumb For Tuning The Diatonic 'Harp

1. You can't tune the top note on a standard 'harp above C♯ (top of upper octave).

2. You can't tune the top part of the upper octave up more than one or two notes without it getting thin, thready, even "breaky."

3. If you can come up with a tuning that raises the mid octave by one or two whole notes, particularly in the lower half of the octave, (they are the largest non-wound strings), it will greatly improve the sound of the middle octave where the melody is most usually played. This is done by adding pairs higher up in the mid to lower top octaves (usually in the area of G to about A), and having fewer strings in the bass octave. This in effect moves higher pitched strings to lower positions, making the notes brighter, louder, and more piercing in nature.

4. The mid octave, particularly the lower part, should *never* be tuned down.

5. In the bass, the lowest notes should be the tonics of the principal chord; in a G-D-A 'harp, the principal chords are C, G, D, A, and E. Therefore, the first five strings on the bottom of the 'harp should be tuned to the tonics of those chords: E, G, A, C, and D. (You could make a low D the first string below E, but you'd have to give up a note you want somewhere else.) Then continue with the diatonic scale of the 'harp through the upper bass notes.

6. All paired notes should be contained within the area in which you play melody, mid octave up through the lower half of the top octave.

7. On a single-key diatonic, a full octave should be paired from tonic to tonic of the key in the range described in (6.) above.

8. On a multi-key diatonic where a full octave cannot be paired, show preference to principal notes, that is, tonic, fifth, third, and fourth.

9. Use a string one size larger in the bass. Use a 1F string for F♯or G; use a 2G string for A, A♯, B, C; use a 3 C for D, etc. This will put added burden on a 'harp. Be sure your 'harp can stand this added stress.

WARNING!

Any tuning that raises the pitch of any significant number of strings to higher notes will increase the stress on the 'harp body. You do this at your own risk. If your 'harp is not in good condition, don't!

10. Always try to end the top of the 'harp on the tonic or fifth of the key. In the very popular G-D-A range, there is a great advantage to having a shorter 37th string that can be tuned up to D. I routinely do this in reworking OSI's Wildwood Flower 'harps. Standard configuration of these instruments ends on B, (a nothing note) at the top. I delete the top octave double G and add C♯, and a D as the very top notes.

11. Do not cut the chord bar felt for any 3rd or 7th in the lowest eight notes. The harmonics of these notes are discordant to the notes in the body of the 'harp. End of the "thumb" rules.

For the low notes, F and below at the bass, I use larger, custom made strings. 1F strings will work, but they lack the real boom in the bass.

Models A and B strings are not generally interchangeable. (There are exceptions, if you know what you're doing.) ❖

To learn about string limitations, see "Strings – Their Ideal Sizes and Lengths" p.31.
See the "String Designation Chart" p.62 for string schedules, including 18 separate tuning and string formulas for three-, two-, and one-key autoharps.
For a discussion concerning the choice of diatonic keys, see "Questions And Answers – Chromatic VS. Diatonic Decision" p.122.
For more information concerning conversion, read "Chromatic To Diatonic Conversion" p.69.

[1] See "Converting Your Autoharp Into A 1⁷/₈ Key Diatonic" p.60.

String Designation Chart For Diatonic Autoharps

AQ Volume VI, Number 3

STRING DESIGNATION CHART

George Orthey

Using The Chart

1. The string designation chart is set up in this book so the pages can be copied for placement under the strings of your autoharp. The lines are 1/4" apart.

2. One note on each tuning is designated with an asterisk (*). This note should be deleted if you have a 36-string autoharp. All the strings and notes above the deleted string/note should be moved down one position.

3. There are now three standard manufactured string sets:

Model A – these have a loop end and are used on old Model A Oscar Schmidt 'harps, ChromAharps, and some handmade 'harps without fine tuners. Prior to 1997 they were made with string 1F – 9A wound and 10 A♯ – 36C non-wound. Since 1997, they have been made 1F – 12C wound and are similar in diameter to the Model B strings.

Model B – these have a ball end to be compatible with the anchor bar or fine tuners, and are used for Oscar Schmidt Model B and C 'harps.

Model A Special – these 37- string sets have a ball end to be compatible with fine tuners. The added string is a low bass (LB). The remaining strings are labeled 1F – 36C. Strings LB and 1F – 12C are wound strings. The LB is larger in diameter than the 1F. These string sets are standard for Fackeldey, Fladmark, and Orthey 'harps with fine tuners.

Be sure to check with your autoharp maker if you have any question as to what string sets you should be using.

4. In general, I use the designated string or the next larger (lower) string for the wound strings on the bass. That is, LB for low D, E, F; 1F for G; 2G for C; 3C for D, etc. In general, I do not move these up more than one full step. This may result in a slightly increased burden on the instrument. However, this should be no problem for a 'harp in good structural condition.

5. In the diatonic 'harps, because of the great variance from standard chromatic 'harps, you will notice some added or deleted strings. The stringing on the chart is idealized and can be modified to better fit the standard set without seriously altering the sound. For example, in the F, C, G autoharp, you will notice that 2 #2G and 2 #11B strings are suggested, and the 1 #6F and 1 #12C are deleted. This will still work OK using a straight set of LB and 1F – 36C for a 37-string 'harp or 1F – 36C for a 36-string 'harp.

6. The LB strings in this chart are relative newcomers to the standard autoharp string community. These strings are larger in diameter to enhance the bass, particularly for notes below the standard low 1F string. The LB strings are good for low D and E notes on diatonic autoharps. In any case, a 1F string can be substituted for the LB string in this chart, if an LB string is not available. The 1F string is .083 inch diameter. The LB string manufactured for the Model A Special sets are .102 inch diameter.

There are no commercially available LB strings for the OSI and ChromAharp autoharps. If the ball is removed from the standard Model A Special LB string, it will fit the Model A OSI and ChromAharp autoharps. For experienced 'harp string mechanics, the Model A Special LB ball can be reset 1/2 inch closer to the windings, and the string will then fit a standard OSI Model B instrument.

Non-standard strings including the extra large bass can be obtained from custom string makers for any 'harp.

7. String sets can be purchased through any OSI dealer for the standard Models A and B sets. Single strings are more of a problem, and are more likely to be available from an autoharp luthier. The Model A Special strings are available through the luthiers using these sets on their instruments.

Note: "The String Designation Chart" p.62 is set up so you can place a page under the strings of your autoharp. The lines designate the location of the strings on the instrument. You can tune, using this chart as a template. ❖

STRING DESIGNATION CHART FOR DIATONIC AUTOHARPS

Octave Designations ⇩	KEYS⇨		F-C-G		G-D-A		F-C		G-D		F		C		G		D		A	
	Standard Tuning		Note	String	Note	String	Note	String	Note	String	Note	String	Note	String	Note	String	Note	String	Note	String
	37	D*	C	36	D*	36	C	36	D*	36	C	36	C	36	D	36	D*	36	D*	36
	36	C	B	35	C#	35	B	35	C#	36	A#	35	B	35	C	35	C#	36	C#	36
	35	B	A#	34	C	34	A#	34	C	35	A	34	A*	34	B	34	B	35	B	35
	34	A#	A	33	B	33	A	33	B	34	G	33	A	34	A	33	A	34	A	34
	33	A	G	32	A	32	G	32	A	33	F	32	G	33	G	32	A	33	A	33
	32	G#	F#	31	G#	31	G	31	G	32	F	31	G	32	G	31	G	32	G#	32
	31	G	F	30	G	30	F	30	G	31	E	30	F	31	F#	30	G	31	F#	31
Upper Octave	30	F#	F	29	G	29	F	29	F#	30	E	29	F	30	F#	29	F#	30	F#	30
	29	F	E	28	F#	28	E	28	F#	29	D	28	E	29	E	28	E	29	E	29
	28	E	E	27	E	27	E	27	E	28	D	27	E	28	E	27	D	28	E	28
	27	D#	D	26	E	26	D	26	E	27	C	26	D	27	D	26	D	27	D	27
	26	D	D	25	D	25	D	25	D	26	C	25	D	26	D	25	C#	26	D	26
	25	C#	C	24	D	24	C	24	D	25	A#	24	C	25	C	24	C#	25	C#	25
	24	C	B	23	C#	23	C	23	C#	24	A#	23	C	24	C	23	B	24	C#	24
	23	B	A#	22	C	22	B	22	C	23	A	22	B	23	B	22	B	23	B	23
	22	A#	A	21	B	21	A#*	21	B	22	A	21	B	22	B	21	A	22	B	22
	21	A	A	20	B	20	A#	21	B	21	G	20	A	21	A	20	A	21	A	21
	20	G#	G	19	A	19	A	20	A	20	G	19	A	20	A	19	G	20	A	20
	19	G	G	18	A	18	A	19	A	19	F	18	G	19	G	18	G	19	G#	19
Middle Octave	18	F#	F#	17	G#	17	G	18	G	18	F	17	G	18	G	17	F#	18	G#	18
	17	F	F	16	G	16	G	17	G	17	E	16	F	17	F#	16	F#	17	F#	17
	16	E	E	15	F#	15	F	16	F#	16	E	15	F	16	F#	15	E	16	F#	16
	15	D#	D	14	E	14	F	15	E	15	D	14	E	15	E*	14	E	15	E	15
	14	D	D	13	D	13	E	14	D	14	D	13	E	14	E	14	D	14	E	14
	13	C#	C	11	C#	12	D	13	D	13	C	12	D	13	D	13	D	13	D	13
	12	C	C	11	C	11	C	11	C#	12	C	11	D	13	D	13	C#	12	C#	12
	11	B	B	10	B	10	B	10	C	11	A#*	10	C	11	C	11	B	10	B	10
	10	A#	A#	9	A	9	A#	9	B	10	A#	9	C	10	B	10	A	8	A	9
	9	A	A	8	G#	8	A	8	A	8	A	8	B	9	A	8	G	7	G#	8
	8	G	G	7	G	7	G	7	G	7	G	7	A	8	G	7	F#	6	F#	6
Lower Octave	7	F#	F	5	F#	6	F	6	F#	6	F	5	G	7	F#	6	E	4	E	4
	6	F	E	4	E	4	E	5	E	4	E	4	F	5	E	4	D	3	D	3
	5	E	D	3	D	3	D	4	D	3	D	3	E	4	D	3	B	2	C#	3
	4	D	C	2	C	2	C	3	C	2	C	2	D	3	C	2	A	2	B	2
	3	C	A#*	2	A	1	A#	2	A	1	A#	2	C	2	A	1	G	1	A	1
	2	G	G	1	G	1	G	1	G	1	G	1	G	1	G	1	E	LB	E	LB
	1	F	F	LB	E	LB	F	LB	D	LB	F	LB	F	LB	D	LB	D	LB	D	LB

NOTE: If you have the optional 37th string on your 'harp, include all notes as listed. If you have only 36 strings, eliminate the notes with an asterisk (*) and move all other strings above those notes down one position. The LB string is a larger, custom-made string available from Orthey Instruments and Fladmark Woodworks. Type A strings fit Model A 'harps. Type B strings fit all other 'harps

Octave Designations ⇩	KEYS⇨		E		B♭-F-C		C-G-D		B♭-F		C-G		A-E		E-B		B♭		B	
	Standard Tuning		Note	String	Note	String	Note	String	Note	String	Note	String	Note	String	Note	String	Note	String	Note	String
	37	D*	B*	36	D*	36	D*	36	C	36	C	36	B*	36	B	36	A#	36	B*	36
	36	C	B	36	C	36	C	35	C	35	B	35	B	36	A#	35	A#	35	B	35
	35	B	A	35	B	35	B	34	A#	34	A	34	A	35	A	34	A*	34	A#	34
	34	A#	A	34	A#	34	A*	33	A#	33	G*	33	A	34	G#	33	A	33	G#	33
	33	A	G#	33	A	33	A	32	A	32	G	33	G#	33	F#	32	G	32	F#	32
	32	G#	G#	32	G	32	G	31	G	31	F#	32	G#	32	F#	31	G	31	F#	31
	31	G	F#	31	G	31	F#	30	F	30	F	31	F#	31	E	30	F	30	E	30
Upper Octave	30	F#	F#	30	F	30	F	29	F	29	F	30	F#	30	E	29	F	29	E	29
	29	F	E	29	E	29	E	28	E	28	E	29	E	29	D#*	28	D#	28	D#	28
	28	E	E	28	D#	28	D	27	D#	27	D	28	E	28	D#	27	D#	27	D#	27
	27	D#	D#	27	D	27	D	26	D*	26	D	27	D#	27	C#	26	D	26	C#	26
	26	D	D#	26	D	26	C#	25	D	26	C	26	D#	26	C#	25	D	25	C#	25
	25	C#	C#	25	C	25	C	24	C	25	C	25	D	25	B	24	C	24	B	24
	24	C	C#	24	C	24	C	23	C	24	B	24	D	24	B	23	C	23	B	23
	23	B	B	23	B	23	B	22	A#	23	B	23	C#	23	A#	22	A#	22	A#	22
	22	A#	B	22	A#	22	A	21	A#	22	A	22	C#	22	A	21	A#	21	A#	21
	21	A	A	21	A#	21	A	20	A	21	A	21	B	21	A	20	A	20	G#	20
	20	G#	A	20	A	20	G	19	A	20	G	20	B	20	G#	19	A	19	G#	19
	19	G	G#	19	A	19	G	18	G	19	G	19	A	19	G#	18	G	18	F#	18
Middle Octave	18	F#	G#	18	G	18	F#	17	G	18	F#	18	A	18	F#	17	G	17	F#	17
	17	F	F#	17	G	17	F	16	F	17	F	17	G#	17	F#	16	F	16	E	16
	16	E	F#	16	F	16	E	15	F	16	E	16	F#	16	E	15	F	15	E	15
	15	D#	E	15	F	15	E	14	E	15	E	15	E	15	E	14	D#	14	D#	14
	14	D	E	14	E	14	D#	13	D#	14	D	14	E	14	D#	13	D#	13	D#	13
	13	C#	D#	13	D#	13	C#	12	D	13	D	13	D#	13	C#	12	D	13	C#	12
	12	C	C#	12	D	13	C	11	C	11	C	11	D	13	B	11	C	11	C#	12
	11	B	B	11	C	11	B	10	A#	10	C	11	C♮	12	A#	10	A#	10	B	11
	10	A#	B	10	B	10	A	8	A#	9	B	9	B	10	A	9	A#	9	B	10
	9	A	A	9	A#	9	G	7	A	8	A	8	A	9	G	8	A	8	A#	9
	8	G	A	9	A	8	F#	6	G	7	G	7	G#	8	F#	6	G	7	G#	8
Lower Octave	7	F#	G#	8	G	7	F	5	F	6	F#	6	F#	6	E	5	F	5	F#	6
	6	F	F#	6	F	5	E	4	E	5	F	5	E	4	D#	4	D#	4	E	5
	5	E	E	4	D#	4	D	3	D#	4	E	4	D	3	C#	3	D	3	D#	4
	4	D	C#	3	C	3	C	2	D	3	D	3	B	2	B	2	C	2	C#	3
	3	C	B	2	A#	2	A	2	C	2	C	2	A	1	A	2	A#	2	B	2
	2	G	A	1	G	1	G	1	A#	1	G	1	E	LB	F#	1	F	LB	F#	1
	1	F	E	LB	F	LB	F	LB	F	LB	F	LB	D	LB	E	LB	D#	LB	E	LB

NOTE: If you have the optional 37th string on your 'harp, include all notes as listed. If you have only 36 strings, eliminate the notes with an asterisk (*) and move all other strings above those notes down one position. The LB string is a larger, custom-made string available from Orthey Instruments and Fladmark Woodworks. Type A strings fit Model A 'harps. Type B strings fit all other 'harps.

The Diatonic Tryout

AQ Volume III, Number IV

THE DIATONIC TRYOUT

Ivan Stiles

What Is A Diatonic Scale?

Very simply, a diatonic scale is that familiar musical scale which we all know as do, re, mi, fa, sol, la, ti, do.

How does this differ from a chromatic scale? A diatonic scale has seven tones in a pattern of whole steps and half steps as opposed to the chromatic scale which has twelve tones in half steps. Look at a piano keyboard. Find middle C, and the C above it. In this "octave," you will count 8 white keys. This is the diatonic scale. If you include the 5 black keys, you are now counting the number of notes on a chromatic scale. Thirteen.

What Are The Advantages Of A Diatonic Autoharp?

There are two advantages inherent in the diatonic autoharp. The first advantage has to do with the sound of the instrument. Without all the notes necessary to play a chromatic scale, the standard autoharp has twelve strings that can be retuned to match strings next to them. These are referred to as "double tuned" strings. Double tuned strings add greater volume and depth to the sound of the 'harp. Also, bar position can reduce harmonics.

The second advantage of a diatonically-tuned 'harp is the ability to perform a technique called "open chording." Since, on a diatonic instrument, all the discordant notes have been eliminated from the scale, it is no longer necessary to depress a chord bar each time you want to pinch or pluck a melody note. Look at the following comparison chart between playing a simple scale on a chromatic 'harp and playing the same scale on a diatonic 'harp. (For simplicity, all of my references and examples will deal with the key of G.) On a chromatic 'harp, a chord bar must be depressed for each melody note achieved in the scale. On a diatonic 'harp, a chord bar need only be depressed for the G, B, D, F#, and G notes. This requires only two chord changes to play the scale. The A, C, and E notes are pinched or plucked without depressing a chord bar.

Playing the Scale on a Chromatic Autoharp

Note:	G	A	B	C	D	E	F#	G
Chord:	G	D7	G	D7	G	C	D7	G

Playing the Scale on a Diatonic Autoharp

Note:	G	A	B	C	D	E	F#	G
Chord:	G	O	G	O	D	O	D	G

"O" = Open chord. Release the chord bar and pinch or pluck the desired note. Practice until you can do this cleanly.

Are The Chords Limited?

The chords are only limited by the notes available in the diatonic scale. The key of G has seven notes to use: G, A, B, C, D, E, and F#. The following are many of the chords available in G.

Major (1-3-5):
G — g, b, d
C — c, e, g
D — d. f#, a

minor (1-3♭-5):
Am — a, c, e
Bm — b, d, f#
Em — e, g, b

minor 7th (1-3♭-5-7♭):
Am7 — a, c, e, g (C6)
Bm7 — b, d, f#, a (D6)
Em7 — e, g, b, d (G6)

dominant 7th (1-3-5-7♭):
D7 — d, f#, a, c
A7(part) — a, e, g

Major 7th (1-3-5-7):
GM7 — g, b, d, f#
CM7 — c, e, g, b

suspended 4th (1-4-5):
Gsus4 — g, c, d (C2)
Dsus4 — d, g, a (G2)

diminished (1-3♭-5♭):
F#dim — f#, a, c

The Temporary Tryout

It's time to take the diatonic plunge – the easy, temporary way! On your standard chromatic autoharp, retune all the sharps *except* F# one half step *down*. All C#s become C, D#s become D, G#s become G, and A#s become A. Now tune all the F strings one half step *up* to F#.

This "tryout" won't give you the increased volume and sustain evident on a true diatonic autoharp, but you'll be able to practice the open-chord technique of melody picking.[1] ❖

Editor's note: Ivan Stiles is an International Autoharp Champion.

[1] See "Questions And Answers"p.122 for more information concerning your chromatic versus diatonic decision.

Clean Melody Picking The Easy Way

AQ Volume VIII, Number 1

DUBBERT S ANTI-MUSH BARS

Carey Dubbert

Editor's Note: As you know, the autoharp is based entirely on chords and all melody notes are derived by using different chords for each note. In contrast, a piano allows one to play a continuous chord with one hand while playing a melody "over" that chord with the other hand. Up until now, it hasn't been possible to achieve the same effect on the autoharp – that is, not until Carey Dubbert and his special bars. Carey is a Winfield Champion hammered dulcimist, and the 1999 Mountain Laurel Autoharp Champion.

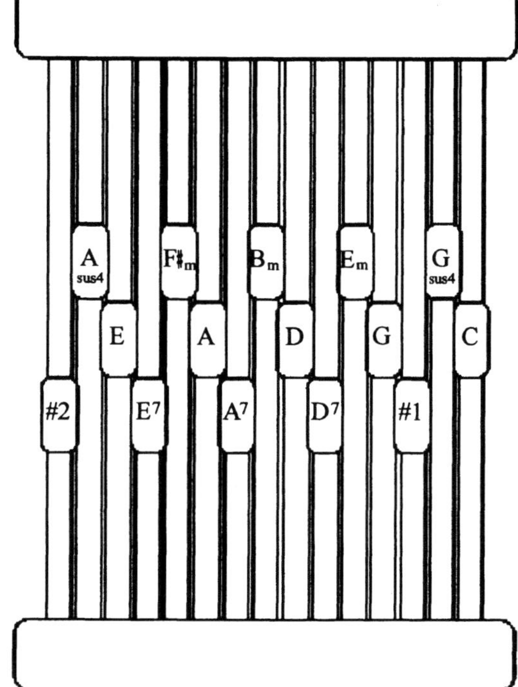

The two special chord bars explained here provide a compromise between changing chords whenever needed to provide a given melody note and using open chording so as not to have to change the chord to provide a given melody note. With the first method, the chord structure of the piece is altered, and the chords usually progress much faster than would be called for by the piece. This can tend to sound choppy and fatigue the ear. The second method allows keeping the chord progression that may be called for by the piece and still have the ability to play melody notes outside the current chord.

The two special bars are best placed at the top and bottom of the 'harp where the thumb (oh yes, it really can move) and the little finger can most easily press the bars. Here is a diagram of how my autoharps are laid out.

The following illustration is my D autoharp (with a compromised A and G). The special bars (#1 and #2 in the diagram) target one specific key and work as a pair in that key. My thumb presses the #1 bar and my little finger presses the #2 bar. In the adjacent keys (up a fifth (G) and down a fifth (A)), one of the special bars will be applicable and the other occasionally. The bars are cut such that one bar accounts for every other note in the key selected, and the other bar allows for the other (also every other) notes in the selected key. Pressed at the same time, all notes would be damped in the upper couple of octaves. The above "every other note" does not apply for the entire bar. The bottom octave has all the felt cut out on both bars allowing the bass strings to vibrate and sustain. It is this bass sustain which makes the two special bars be effective. A chord is strummed or picked with a standard chord bar which includes notes in the lower octave of the 'harp (although other notes may well be sustained). Then, after letting up on the original bar, melody notes can be picked cleanly going back and forth on the two special bars without altering the basic sustaining chord.

So here's how it goes. For example, my 'harp is set up for the key of D as the primary key. My thumb bar is open up to C♯ and then lets every other note in the key of D ring. These are: E, G, B, D, F♯, A, and C♯. The little finger bar has all notes open up to B (about the 10th or 11th string) and then every other note again. These are: D, F♯, A, C♯, E, G, B, and D). If I strum a D Major chord, the notes are D, F♯, and A. If I should want to pick any of the other notes, I may do so by letting up on the D Major chord bar and depressing one or the other of the special bars. The D Major chord will still be sounding while I pick the desired melody note. Any time a melody note falls in the D Major chord, I can again depress the D bar and strum the whole or part of the chord to keep it going. In this manner the melody really

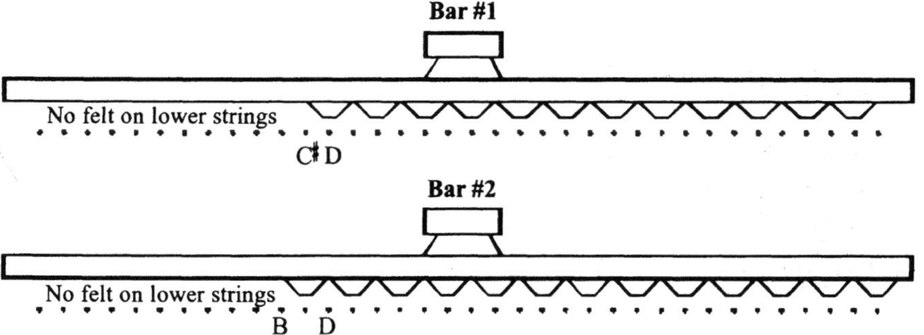

Alternating felt cutouts should reflect your own 'harps stringing to allow for double-tuned strings where applicable.

can come from the chord progression and not the other way around.

On any other autoharp, I would lay it out the same in that the #1 bar would damp out the tonic note about nine to eleven strings (this could be varied to anything you might want) and would begin its "every-othering" there, and the #2 bar would damp out the seventh of the primary key of the autoharp and let the tonic ring and begin its "every-othering" there. With this setup, all autoharps work the same and nearly all fingerings are the same.

The primary limitation is that I cannot strum the chord (such as an important downbeat) and play a note out of the chord at the same time. Color chords such as (in the Key of D) an A^{sus4} or a G^{sus4} or an Em^7 can solve most of these occurrences.

All in all, this is a rather simple means towards very clean melody picking without sounding choppy and without requiring all the accuracy of open chording. ❖

Breaking In A New Autoharp With Sound

AQ Volume VII, Number 4
DO DO THAT VOODOO
George Orthey

I must preface these remarks with the widely unknown fact that I turn into a werewolf on certain nights and can do voodoo on a moment's notice. Therefore, I feel fully capable of occasionally dabbling in witchcraft.

Most wooden instruments have a "new" sound when they come out of the egg. Call that sound harsh, raw, hard, – whatever you want. It'll take at least six months of strong, regular playing to teach it to sing. But, it will take longer than that to reach its full sound potential. The more you play, the more the sound's refined. Somewhere in my dark memory, I recall a warlock telling me "Play music to it. Teach it to sing!" I have for some time now placed new, stiff instruments in front of a boom box. Using a tape of wide range which includes autoharp and bass, I bring the volume up to the point where the resonant vibrations can actually be felt in the back of the instrument. There the youngster sits, usually for several nights or a full weekend, just soaking in the "vibes." I am always careful to stand the instrument so the movement of the back is not restricted. I also believe it is only fully effective on a fully strung, in tune instrument. After all, you want it to sing on key.

I have consulted with guitar building gurus and spirits from Martin Guitar, who agree it certainly can do no harm, and even believe (off the record, of course) there is something logical about it!

Be it witchcraft, wishful thinking, karma, or unproven scientific fact, the result is a crash (bad choice of words) program that equals several month's playing – all in a few days! A sweeter, more mellow, fuller sounding instrument emerges from the smoke of the boom box! ❖

AQ Volume VIII, Number 4

MAKING NEW FRIENDS OF OLD 'HARPS

Alan Mager

Chromatic To Diatonic Conversion

In 1985, I heard Bryan Bowers play for the first time and found that my old interest in the autoharp (I hadn't played one in 15 years) was instantly rekindled. I went home that night with Bryan's record, *The View From Home*. I played it the next morning, then headed for a local music store and bought a new Oscar Schmidt 21-chord 'harp. My goal was to learn to play "Blackberry Blossom" just the way Bryan does.

After a few months, I could play the tune perfectly, but it didn't sound anywhere near as sweet and exciting as Bryan's playing. Then I heard Bryan play in person again, and after the concert I cornered him backstage and asked him why his 'harp sounded so much better than mine. It was then that the world of diatonic instruments, and all its attendant wonders, began to unfold before me.

Soon thereafter, I located a nice secondhand autoharp and did my first diatonic conversion. I was quite pleased with the results, but it took several more conversion projects and lots of talking with others about the process before I felt I had a real grasp of the necessary principles. Now, I'm often asked for advice on 'harp modifications by other players, and the most frequently asked questions concern what chords to use for particular diatonic setups. It is that issue that I will address here.

General Considerations

Most often, the 'harps that end up being converted to diatonics are old 12- and 15-chord Oscar Schmidts that folks pick up at yard sales, flea markets, pawn shops, or from Aunt Millie's attic. So with this in mind, I'm going to focus on chord selection and arrangement for one- and two-key diatonics using 12 or 15 chord bars.

My first suggestion is to arrange your chord bars in three rows; one each for the majors, minors, and sevenths. This makes the most sense with multi-key 'harps, because you can switch from key to key and retain the exact same fingering pattern for all the primary chords in each key. I suggest using the same arrangement even on single-key 'harps. If you do, then your fingering patterns will be the same whether you're playing your one-key diatonic or your seven-key chromatic.

But wait a minute, that old 12- or 15-bar 'harp you're going to convert has the bars arranged in two rows and the chord bar buttons are glued on tight. Don't despair; this is easier to fix than you might think. Here's what you do:

1. *Remove the buttons.* Wrap a piece of cloth or leather around the sides of the chord bar button, then grip the button firmly with pliers, give it a lateral twist, and it will pop off the surface of the chord bar quite cleanly. Parallel jaw pliers work best for this operation. If you don't have these, use pliers with the largest, flattest jaw surfaces you can find.
2. *Clean up the bars.* With a utility knife, slice off any pieces of chord bar button that remain glued to the top of the bar. Then with a power sander, sand down the top surface of the bar to remove all traces of where the button was attached. Sand down the entire top of the bar to give it a nice matte finish.
3. *Glue the buttons back on.* Now arrange the buttons in three rows with as little space as possible between the rows (see Figure 1), and glue them back onto the bars with Super Glue (or a Super Glue clone). For a really clean look, sand the chord names off the buttons before glueing them back onto the bars, or you can buy blank replacement buttons from any Oscar Schmidt dealer.

Figure 1

The next step is to decide in what key(s) you want your new 'harp to play. There are lots of considerations, and you need to think this out carefully before you make your final choice. I strongly suggest getting George Foss' book *Going Diatonic*. It has a wealth of information on the subject of autoharp conversion,[1] including some very well-thought-out string schedules for diatonic 'harps in various keys.[2] The process of deciding whether to make a one- or two-key diatonic and which key(s) to choose could easily be the subject of another chapter (or perhaps a small book). To get back to the subject of chord selection, we'll bypass this process and look at two possible 'harp setups, a two-key diatonic in the keys of G and D and a one-key 'harp in G.

Two-Key Diatonic

For the keys of G and D you must have the following ten chords: C, G, D, A, Am, Em, Bm, F♯m, D^7, and A^7. (Some will argue that the 7ths aren't truly essential. They would be right, but I can't imagine a 'harp without 7ths, so we won't even entertain that possibility here.)

If you have a 12-bar assembly, you will have only two bars left over to play with after you put on the ten chords listed above. You could do any number of things with these two bars, but my suggestion is to add the E^7 and GM^7 chords.

The E^7 is the II^7 chord in the key of D and is quite useful. On the two-key G/D 'harp, however, this chord will be missing one note (the G♯). This missing note gives the chord a somewhat strange, hollow sound, but I find its usefulness is far outweighed by its somewhat unusual sound. (The II^7 chord is rarely held very long anyway, so this will greatly minimize the odd sound.)

The GM^7 is the G Major 7th chord which contains the notes G, B, D, and F♯ rather than the G, B, D, and F of the G^7 chord. In many cases, GM^7 will make a very satisfactory substitute for G^7 and will give you a reasonable substitute for the impossible-to-make I^7 chord in the key of G.

Figure 2

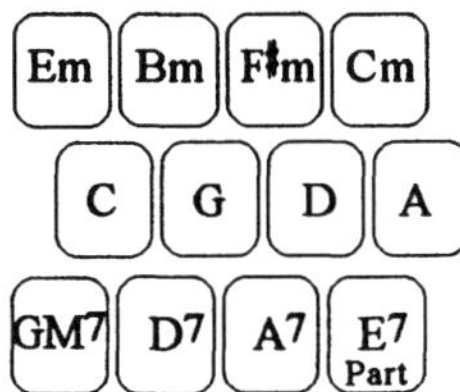

Figure 2 shows how I would set up a G/D 'harp with 12 chord bars. If I had 15 bars to work with, I would use the setup shown in Figure 3, adding some interesting "color chords" which would be quite useful in the chosen keys.

Figure 3

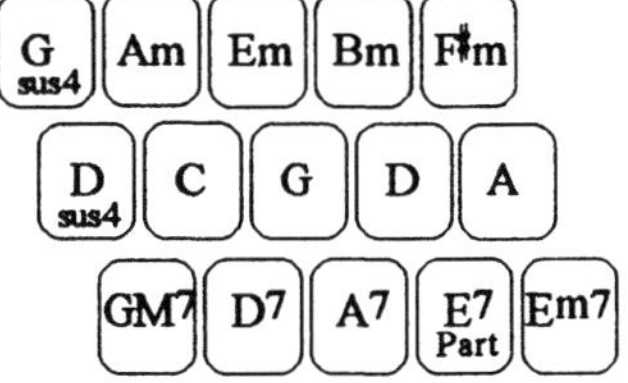

All the possibilities are far too numerous to mention, but my choice would be to add two suspended 4ths, Gsus4 (G, C, D) and Dsus4 (D, G, A) along with a minor 7th, Em^7 (E, G, B, D) which turns out to be the same chord as G^6. The placement of these final three chords is arbitrary, but the placement of the other 12 makes musical sense, and I would recommend sticking with my proposed arrangement for those 12 chords.

Another consideration with a two-key diatonic is, you may want to include two lock bars so that you can lock out the non-diatonic note in each scale. Of course, to do that you'd have to give up two of your original 12 or 15 chords. In the 12-chord configuration, that would leave you with only the ten essential chords, and in the 15-bar arrangement you'd have only three extras (my choices would be E^7, GM^7 and Gsus4).

One-Key Diatonic

We could also set up a single key diatonic 'harp using 12 or 15 chord bars. That seems like a lot of chords, doesn't it? Let me assure you that it's not. My standard setup for a one-key instrument uses 15 bars.

In our example, we'll use the key of G. There are seven chords that are essential for a one-key 'harp, which in the key of G are G, C, D, Am, Em, Bm, and D^7. This means that we can add five extra chords to our 12-chord setup and eight extra ones to the 15-chord 'harp. Now we can really have some fun with the color chords.

My suggestions for additional chords, listed in the order of their usefulness are: A^7 (partial), GM^7, Gsus4, Dsus4, Em^7 (G^6), Am^7 (C^6), CM^7, and E^7 (partial). My suggested arrangements for the chord bars are shown in Figures 4 and 5. In these arrangements, the placement of the seven essential chords as well as the A^7, E^7, and GM^7 makes sense from a musical standpoint. (The chords follow in a progression around the circle of fifths.) The placement of the rest of the chords is arbitrary and could be changed to suit the individual player.

Figure 4

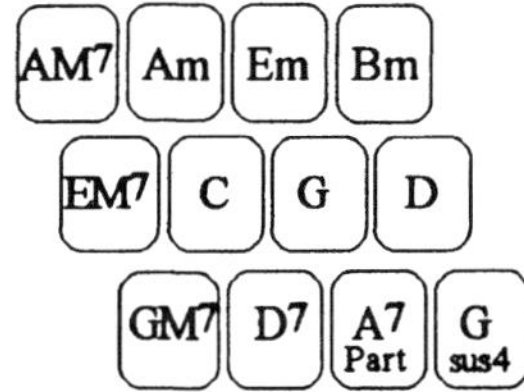

Figure 5

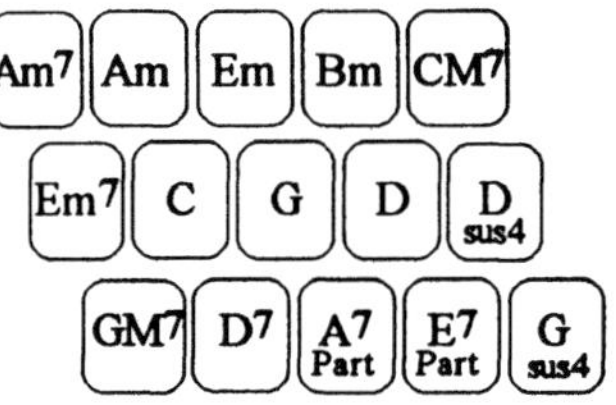

Of course, there are many other chords you could create for a single-key 'harp. You might even consider adding a lock bar to lock out the C and F♯ notes which would leave you with a pentatonic scale. This isn't as far out as it sounds. I have two 'harps set up this way, and I find it a lot of fun to "noodle" in the pentatonic scale. (You could actually make two other pentatonic scales out of the G scale, but let's not get too crazy here.)

Parting Words

With a little care and planning, old 12- and 15-chord autoharps can be converted into very respectable one- and two-key diatonic instruments and be given new life. Every instrument so converted becomes unique, as the imagination and needs of the intended player are built into it. Hearing the results of 'harp conversions has long been a source of fun and fascination for me. Come join the fun! ❖

For more choices of chord bar arrangements, see "Chord Bar Arrangements" p.3. For a discussion concerning the choice of diatonic keys, see "Questions And Answers – Chromatic VS. Diatonic Decision" p.122.

[1] For more information concerning conversion, read "Converting Your Autoharp To A 1^7/$_8$ Key Diatonic" p.60 and "Converting Your Autoharp To A 1^7/$_8$ Key Diatonic – Or A Multi-Key Diatonic" p.61.

[2] See the "String Designation Chart" p.62 for 18 diatonic string schedules.

AQ Volume IX, Number 2
OPTIMIZING THE CHROMATIC 'HARP
Alan Mager

Optimal String Schedules and Chord Selection For The Chromatic 'Harp

I don't know exactly when it happened, but sometime a few years back I suddenly realized how to set up a chromatic autoharp so that all the chords on it sounded good. It's not as if this were divine revelation. The idea was hatched after years of monkeying around with chromatic 'harps trying to make them sound better.

The Problem

As every autoharp player has discovered, certain chords on "standard" chromatic 'harps sound awful. On Oscar Schmidts and ChromAharps fresh from the factory, the "flat" chords, such as B♭, E♭, A♭, and their respective sevenths make the sweet little autoharp sound nastier than a bagpipe.

For a long time, I tinkered with different tunings, tried repositioning the chord bars to avoid harmonics, and did other things to try to make these chords sound better. Nothing really worked. Then the simple truth hit me: The reason these chords sound bad is because they have few, if any, strings sounding in the lower third of the 'harp. Check it out and you'll see what I mean. The best sounding chords have a nice, full bass with several strings ringing in the low end. The horrible sounding chords have nothing going on in the bass.

This problem exists because the lower ten strings encompass a range of about an octave and a half, or about 18 notes on the chromatic scale. Accordingly, about eight notes have to be left out. That's nearly half of what "should" be there. The result is that no given string schedule can provide a suitable bass for all chords.

The Solution

Once I understood the problem, the solution became obvious: To get good sounding "flat" chords, I would have to have a second chromatic autoharp that

Figure 1

STRING SCHEDULES FOR 4-KEY CHROMATIC AUTOHARPS

B♭-F-C-G				G-D-A-E			
36 Strings		**37 Strings**		**36 Strings**		**37 Strings**	
String No.	Note	String No.	Note	String No.	Note	String No.	Note
1	F	1	F	1	G	1	G
2	G	2	G	2	A	2	A
3	A#	3	A#	3	B	3	B
4	C	4	C	4	C	4	C
5	D	5	D	5	D	5	D
6	E	6	D#	6	E	6	E
7	F	7	E	7	F#	7	F#
8	G	8	F	8	G	8	G
9	A	9	G	9	A	9	A
10	A#	10	A	10	B	10	B
11	B	11	A#	11	C	11	C
12	C	12	B	12	C#	12	C#
13	C#	13	C	13	D	13	D
14	D	14	C#	14	D#	14	D#
15	D#	15	D	15	E	15	E
16	E	16	D#	16	F	16	F
17	F	17	E	17	F#	17	F#
18	F#	18	F	18	G	18	G
19	G	19	F#	19	G#	19	G#
20	G#	20	G	20	A	20	A
21	A	21	G#	21	A#	21	A#
22	A#	22	A	22	B	22	B
23	B	23	A#	23	C	23	C
24	C	24	B	24	C#	24	C#
25	C#	25	C	25	D	25	D
26	D	26	C#	26	D#	26	D#
27	D#	27	D	27	E	27	E
28	E	28	D#	28	F	28	F
29	F	29	E	29	F#	29	F#
30	F#	30	F	30	G	30	G
31	G	31	F#	31	G#	31	G#
32	G#	32	G	32	A	32	A
33	A	33	G#	33	A#	33	A#
34	A#	34	A	34	B	34	B
35	B	35	A#	35	C	35	C
36	C	36	B	36	D	36	C#
		37	C			37	D

had more of the notes contained in those chords in the bass.

I played with this concept for some time and finally came up with a system that works for me. I now work with two 21-chord chromatic autoharps. Each can play only in four major keys. One has the keys of B♭, F, C and G, and the other plays in G, D, A and E. Figure 1 shows 36-string and 37-string schedules for these two setups, and Figure 2 shows the chord selection for each 'harp. If you examine the notes available in the bass portion of the 'harp, you will see that all major and most minor chords have a reasonable number of bass notes present.

For the B♭-F-C-G 'harp, F seems to be the optimum key. It clearly sounds the best, and the string schedule is most in line with the F scale. This is true for the key of D on the G-D-A-E 'harp. The keys of B♭ and C are good, solid-sounding keys on the F 'harp as are the keys of G and A on the D 'harp. The key of G on the F 'harp and the key of E on the D 'harp are a little weak but still quite serviceable. I find it quite convenient having the key of G on both 'harps, because it is the key perhaps most frequently called for in jam sessions.

Figure 2

CHORD SELECTION FOR 4-KEY CHROMATIC AUTOHARPS

B♭-F-C-G			G-D-A-E		
Majors:	E♭	(D♯, G, A♯)	Majors:	C	(C, E, G)
	B♭	(A♯, D, F)		G	(G, B, D)
	F	(F, A, C)		D	(D, F♯, A)
	C	(C, E, G)		A	(A, C♯, E)
	G	(G, B, D)		E	(E, G♯, B)
Minors:	Cm	(C, D♯, G)	Minors:	Am	(A, C, E)
	Gm	(G, A♯, D)		Em	(E, G, B)
	Dm	(D, F, A)		Bm	(B, D, F♯)
	Am	(A, C, E)		F♯m	(F♯, A, C♯)
	Em	(E, G, B)		C♯m	(C♯, E, G♯)
Sevenths:	$B^{\flat 7}$	(A♯, D, F, G♯)	Sevenths:	G^7	(G, B, D, F)
	F^7	(F, A, C, D♯)		D^7	(D, F♯, A, C)
	C^7	(C, E, G, A♯)		A^7	(A, C♯, E, G)
	G^7	(G, B, D, F)		E^7	(E, G♯, B, D)
	D^7	(D, F♯, A, C)		B^7	(B, D♯, F♯, A)
	A^7	(A, C♯, E, G)		$F\sharp^7$	(F♯, A♯, C♯, E)
	E^7	(E, G♯, B, D)		$C\sharp^7$	(C♯, F, G♯, B)
Others:	C^{o7}	(C, D♯, F♯, A)	Others:	C^{o7}	(C, D♯, F♯, A)
	G^{o7}	(C♯, E, G, A♯)		G^{o7}	(C♯, E, G, A♯)
	D^{o7}	(D, F, G♯, B)		D^{o7}	(D, F, G♯, B)
	F+	(F, A, C♯)		D+	(D, F♯, A♯)

Fine Tuning the Solution

It isn't enough just to have an ample selection of bass notes available for each chord. You must be selective in which notes are used. Just because something is possible doesn't mean that it's desirable. If you cut notches in your felts for all bass notes available in all chords, you will end up with some bad-sounding chords. Here are my guidelines for notching felts in the bass portion of the 'harp:

1. The lowest note that sounds in any chord should be a 1st or 5th, never a 3rd or 7th. For example, in a C^7 chord (which contains the notes C, E, G, B♭), the lowest string sounding should be C (the first note of the scale of C) or G (the 5th). If you allow E (the 3rd) or B♭ (the flatted 7th) to be the lowest note, the chord will sound as if it has a wrong note in it. (Trust me or try it yourself.) I make an exception to this rule when cutting felts for diminished 7th and augmented chords. These chords are composed of equal intervals and really have no beginning or end, so it doesn't, matter which note sounds at the bottom.

2. Don't cut a notch for a 3rd or a 7th that occurs in the first 6 or 8 strings even if there is a 1st or 5th below it. To my ear, this just sets up too much vibration in the bottom end of the 'harp and creates an unpleasant "muddy" sound.

3. In the first 6 or 8 strings, don't cut notches for two strings that are adjacent to each other, even if they're a 1st and a 5th. Again this just muddies up the sound.

Preferences

If this system of using two 4-key chromatic 'harps makes sense to you, do a little thinking about your personal playing preferences. You may opt for a chord selection that's a little different from mine. Of course, what you'll surely find is that there are always trade-offs and you can never come up with the totally perfect setup. We certainly couldn't achieve perfection with the 7-key "standard" Oscar Schmidt 'harp, and I can't get there even with a 4-key 'harp. Here are some of my reasons why:

1. Sevenths. In my opinion, you can never have enough 7ths on a chromatic autoharp, but I've settled for the seven most useful ones and left it at that.

2. Diminished Sevenths.[1] Gotta have 'em! I can't imagine a chromatic autoharp without them. Of course, they take up space so something else has to go.

3. Minors. This is where my setups suffer the most. I use minors less than majors, 7ths, and diminished 7ths, so when something has to go for lack of space on my 'harps, its going to be minors. You'll notice that on the B♭-F-C-G 'harp I don't have the B minor for the key of G, and on the G-D-A-E 'harp, the G♯ minor for the key of E is missing. I've got the full complement of minors for the key of G on the G-D-A-E 'harp, so I do make up some lost ground there. If you play a lot of music in minor keys, or just like spicing up your arrangements with minor chords, you may want to have more minor chords and give up something else.

4. Augmenteds. I wouldn't really classify augmented chords as "must-have" items, but I got hooked on them several years ago in a Mike Fenton workshop and I find them useful enough to keep one on each of my chromatic 'harps. (There are four different augmented chords, but I can't justify giving up three other chords to get them all.) On

the B♭-F-C-G 'harp I gave up D Major in favor of F augmented (F+), and on the G-D-A-E 'harp I replaced B major with D+. Now this somewhat limits my ability to play in G and E on those two 'harps respectively, but I decided it was more important to have the augmented chords. As I said, there are always trade-offs.

Finally

Be careful of stretching things so far that you end up revisiting the original problem. If you were to keep the D and B Major chords that I replaced with the augmenteds, you'd quickly discover that you could play in the key of D on the B♭-F-C-G 'harp and in B on the other one. If you do this, you're heading back toward the "standard" chromatic setup and its inherent problems that we're trying to avoid. Don't go there! These two keys will sound weak, and you'll begin to wonder why we've come this far only to slip back. Besides, when was the last time anyone in a jam session called for the key of B? ❖

Editor's note: Alan Mager is an International Autoharp Champion.

[1] Diminished seventh is the proper term for what some folks commonly call a "diminished chord." Read more about diminished 7th chords in "Explanation And Use Of Diminished 7th Chords"p.49.

The Jazz-Style Autoharp

AQ Volume IV, Number 3
THE JAZZ-STYLE AUTOHARP
Lyman Taylor

Major credit and thanks go to Marty Schuman who for years entertained and delighted us all playing jazz on his very special diatonic autoharp.[1] *As does Dr. George Foss, (author of* Going Diatonic*), Marty altered the conventional diatonic autoharp by using "delete-note" chord bars. Marty also modified conventional playing by sometimes pushing two or three chord bars at once and by so-doing expanded the number of playable chords. I have merely taken these basic principles, already proven by these "pioneers," and applied them to the 21- bar (chromatic) 'harp. Now the jazz idiom can be made cheaply and easily available to all autoharpists.*

Thanks also to George Orthey who is the source of all wisdom on refelting chord bars.

Have you ever wished you could play jazz chords on your autoharp? Play swing? Blues? Rock and Roll? It can be done! And it's a lot easier than you think. All it takes is a 21-bar chromatic autoharp, a set of blank chord bar felts, a sharp blade, a little work, and a willingness to push two chord bars at once. If you follow the steps outlined below on your 21- bar 'harp, you will be able to play thirty three full chords; five major chords, four minor chords, five major sixth chords (which are also the five relative minor seventh chords), seven dominant seventh chords, three major seventh chords, one augmented chord, and three diminished seventh chords (which are actually twelve). This gives a capability for playing jazz chords in two major keys (F and C) and two minor keys (Dm and Am), while still playing most of the "standard" chords you now play on your 'harp. From the standard Oscar Schmidt 21 chord bar arrangement, you will lose four chords (A♭, E♭, Cm, B^7) but you will gain seventeen new ones ($B\flat^6/Gm^7$, F^6/Dm^7, C^6/Am^7, G^6/Em^7, D^6/Bm^7, $C+$, FM^7, CM^7, $B\flat M^7$, C^{o7}, $C\sharp^{o7}$, D^{o7}... plus another nine, if you choose to count all the diminished seventh chords individually).

The chord bar arrangement is as follows:

Branch –
Gm = $B\flat^6$ + -F
Dm = F^6 + -C
Fork –
Am = FM^7 + -F
Em = CM^7 + -C

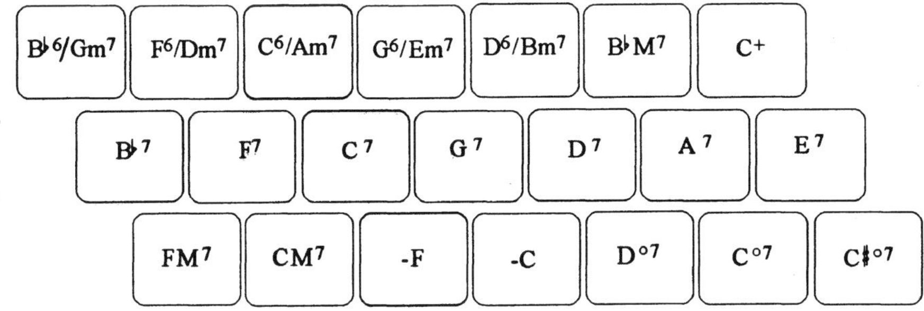

Note 1: Major sixth chords contain the same four notes as the minor seventh chords of their relative minor key (e.g.: C^6 = C, E, G, A; Am^7 = A, C, E, G). The only difference is the bottom/beginning note of the chord (i.e., begin the C^6 chord strum on C and the Am^7 chord strum on A for the final note of the song, or any other time if you want to be "picky." Sound-wise, it often doesn't matter much where you begin your strum). The five minor seventh chords are often acceptable substitutes for major 9th chords discussed later.

Note 2: The diminished seventh chord bars are placed in this order to make playing easier because the D^{o7} (F^{o7}) is usually played with the Key of F, and C^{o7} is most often played in the Key of C.

Pushing The Buttons

One-button chords are: B^6/Gm^7, F^6/Dm^7, C^6/Am^7, G^6/Em^7, D^6/Bm^7, $B\flat^7$, F^7, C^7, G^7, D^7, A^7, E^7, FM^7, CM^7, $B\flat M^7$, C+, D^{o7}, C^{o7}, $C\sharp^{o7}$.

Two-button chords are: **Barre** –
B♭ = $B\flat^6$ + $B\flat^7$
F = F^6 + F^7
C = C^6 + C^7
G = G^6 + G^7
D = D^6 + D^7

Delete-Note Buttons

-F or -C "wipe out" that single note from certain four note chords to produce certain other three note chords, as indicated earlier.

Chording Techniques

Playing one-button chords is the same as on the standard 21-bar chromatic autoharp. Techniques for playing two-button chords can be easily mastered. There are five new techniques to be learned.

The Barre: Barring is done with the thumb. (On occasion you may find it more convenient to barre with a flat finger or two fingertips.) Lay the thumb flat across the 6th and 7th chord buttons of the same letter; depress both equally and a bit hard.

The Arch: To play the 6th chord only, place your thumb in the barre position; then, straighten it, arching it upward; if necessary, tilt it backward slightly to lift the tip of the thumb off the 7th chord bar button.

The Bridge: To play the 7th chord only, place your thumb in the barre position, then, bend it (just like an arched bridge) enough to "clear" the 6th chord bar button, pushing down on the 7th chord bar button down with the tip of your thumb.

The Branch: Depress the prescribed 6th chord button with the tip of your thumb while simultaneously depressing the prescribed "delete" button with a finger.

The Fork: Depress the prescribed major seventh chord button with one finger while simultaneously depressing the prescribed "delete" button with another; normally the index and middle fingers will be used.

Customizing Your Chromatic 'Harp

If you have only one 21-bar 'harp and you follow the plan outlined previously, the conversion will mean the loss of the four chords noted: A♭, E♭, Cm, and B^7. Other chords of your choice may be inserted in place of the C$^+$ or elsewhere.

If you sing soprano or tenor, or play only instrumental solos and/or play with a string band, you may prefer to customize your 'harp to play in the keys of G and D Major, (plus Am and Em), rather than in the keys F and C Major (plus Dm and Am).

These are all value judgments which you will need to make before you begin to create your Jazz-Style 'Harp. Of course, if you have more than one 'harp, that will make your decisions easier. Having two 'harps is really recommended, (one for "standard" music, and one for "jazz"), since on the Jazz-Style 'harp, *all* straight major and minor chords are two-button chords.

If you plan to make a G-D Jazz-Style 'Harp, you may want to cut and arrange your chord bars in the following manner:

Felting Your Jazz-Style 'Harp

Remove the old chord bar felts and refelt the chords you have chosen.[2]

For the F-C 'harp, felts should be cut to allow the following strings to sound:

Chord					
B♭^{6}/Gm^7	=	B♭(A♯)	D	F	G*
F^6/Dm^7	=	F	A	C	D*
C^6/Am^7	=	C	E	G	A
G^6/Em^7	=	G	B	D	E
D^6/Bm^7	=	D	F♯	A	B
B♭M^7	=	B♭(A♯)	D	F	A*
C$^+$	=	C	E	G♯*	
B♭^{7}	=	B♭(A♯)	D	F	A♭(G♯)*
F^7	=	F	A	C	E*
C^7	=	C	E	G	B♭
G^7	=	G	B	D	F
D^7	=	D	F♯	A	C
A^7	=	A	C♯	E	G
E^7	=	E	G♯	B	D
FM^7	=	F	A	C	E*
CM^7	=	C	E	G	B
D$^{\circ 7}$	=	D	F	G♯	B
C$^{\circ 7}$	=	C	D♯	F♯	A
C♯$^{\circ 7}$	=	C♯	E	G	A♯

If you're making the G-D 'harp, the starred (*) chords noted above would be eliminated and the following chord bars would be needed:

Chord					
A^6/F♯m^7	=	A	C♯	E	F♯
E^6/C♯m^7	=	E	G♯	B	C♯
D$^+$	=	D	F♯	A♯	
B^7	=	B	D♯	F♯	A
F♯^{7}	=	F♯	A♯	C♯	E
GM^7	=	G	B	D	F♯
DM^7	=	D	F♯	A	C♯

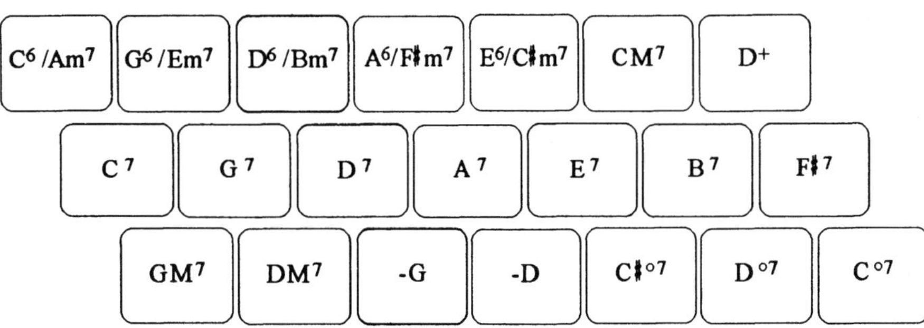

If your autoharp is a 12- or 15-bar, you need to know it can be converted to a 21-bar 'harp. This can be done by ordering a 21-Chord Conversion Kit from Elderly Instruments. (Part # CONVKIT-21. It currently lists for about $81.00.) This kit is not difficult to install.

In the above 'harp, (see previous column), replace -F and -C with -G and -D. Simultaneous barring of the sixth and seventh chords produces major chords of the same name.

For the "Delete-Note" bars, cut pieces of chord bar felt 1/2" long leaving that length on the glue side and trimming to 1/4" on the felt side. After depressing the "naked" bar and marking on the bar-metal the location of each string to be deleted, remove bar from 'harp and center small felt piece exactly on the mark. Test "Delete-Note" bar by depressing the bar and then plucking the "dead" string plus the string on either side to be sure that only the one string is "wiped out." Trim if necessary. Replace chord bars and rename the buttons.

On the F-C 'harp, strings are tuned the same as the standard chromatic 'harp. On the G-D 'harp, strings #1 and #2 should be retuned to G and A respectively.

Making Music On Your Jazz-Style 'Harp

Make a chart of your chord bar arrangement with notations on it as to how to achieve those "extra chords." For the first week or so, while you are training your brain, lay this chart alongside your music. You will be amazed at how smart you are and how soon you can dispense with the chart.

Practice techniques for playing two-button chords and write chord symbols on your music, transposing if necessary.

Use standard notation for major and minor chords, but train your fingers to depress the indicated two bars simultaneously in order to achieve the desired major or minor chord. (Trust me! Your brain is very smart and will "catch on" very quickly!)

Blues and rock and roll: The standard twelve-measure blues progression, which is the basic accompaniment for many blues and rock and roll songs, can be played in any one of four different keys on your Jazz-Style 'Harp by pushing, in succession, four adjacent single chord bar buttons. (Example: C^6, C^6, C^6, C^7, F^7, F^7, C^6, C^6, G^7, F^7, C^6, C^6.) Available keys for this progression are F, C, G, and D.

Major ninth chord substitutes: There are no ninth chords on your Jazz-Style Autoharp, but often substitutes can be made to work. Sometimes the seventh chord of the same letter will "do" in place of the ninth chord. Sometimes a minor seventh will "do." Equivalents are: Gm^7 for E♭M^9, Dm^7 for B♭M^9, Am^7 for FM^9, Em^7 for CM^9, Bm^7 for GM^9, F♯m^7 for DM^9, and C♯m^7 for AM^9.

Enhancing the melody: Enhancing

the melody, when playing an instrumental solo, is highly desirable. This is especially true when playing jazz chords which usually have four notes, three of which tend to "cover up" the melody note. I recommend using a simultaneous thumb strum for the harmony and a "push pluck" for the melody. To accomplish the latter, lay the tip of your finger pick on top of the string. Then push downward (toward the wood), pushing quite hard until the string literally "snaps" off the end of the pick. This will measurably increase the volume of the melody note.

Electronics: Electronics can increase the volume and sustain of your 'harp and enhance the beautiful sound of these great chords. Use a microphone and/or an electronic pickup on your 'harp plugged into an amplifier.

Experiment! While thirty-three chords is a small number compared to the hundreds possible, the variety is wide enough so that when the music calls for an unusual chord, an acceptable substitute can often be found. When all else fails, push a diminished seventh chord bar and pluck a single note. Even if you can't sing it, now you can "swing it" with your Jazz-Style Autoharp! ❖

[1] See "The Ultratonic Autoharp"p.77.

[2] For felting procedure, read "Refelting And Siliconing Chord Bars"p.7.

The Jazz-Style Autoharp
21-Bar Chromatic

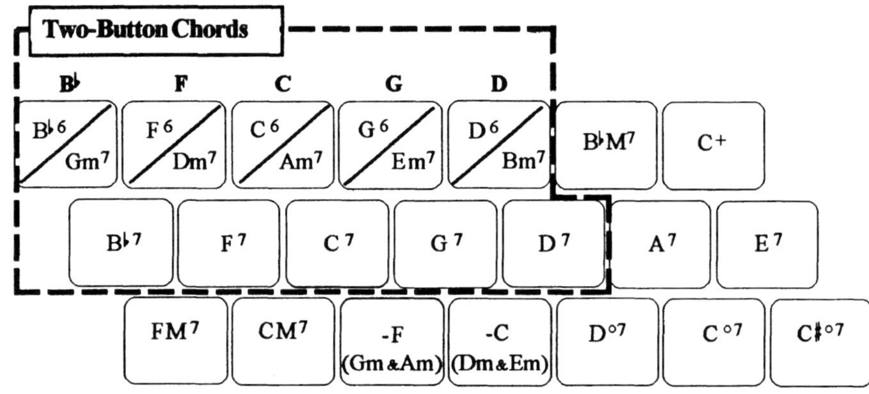

Gm = B♭^{6} + -F
Dm = F^6 + -C
Am = FM^7 + -F
Em = CM^7 + -C

Substitute Ninths

E♭M^9 = B♭^{6}/Gm^7
B♭M^9 = F^6/Dm^7
FM^9 = C^6/Am^7
CM^9 = G^6/Em^7
GM^9 = D^6/Bm^7

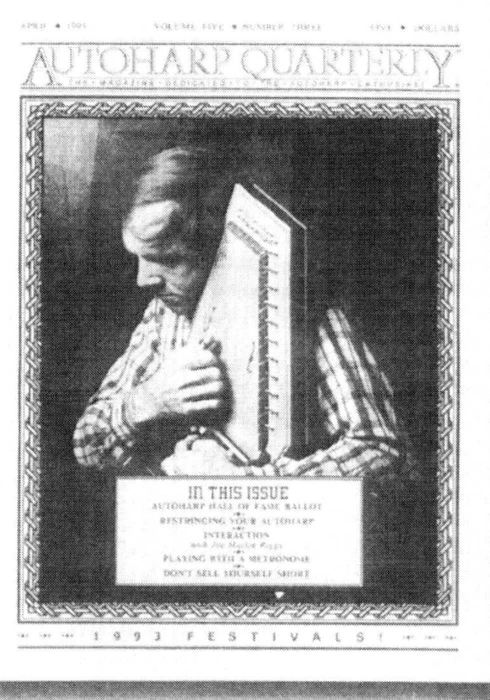

The Ultratonic Autoharp

AQ Volume I, Number 2

THE 15-BAR 30-CHORD ULTRATONIC

Marty Schuman

During the 30 years I've been playing autoharp, I've never, never been totally satisfied. No autoharp ever had all the features or versatility I was looking for. In my experiments to get more bass, range, volume, and chords, I've worked with various tunings, pairings of strings, and squeezing in extra strings and extra-narrow chord bars. I've also been involved in the development of two experimental oversized 'harps, one made of wood, and one of space-age materials.

For the past ten years, I've been playing diatonic autoharp, and again, not content with the standard chords, I developed an additional range of "color chords;" that is, supporting chords around the main key that produce subtle shadings. This opens up the diatonic autoharp to new dimensions.

The usual method for adding more chords to your autoharp is to add more chord bars, which reduces the amount of playing room on the treble strings. And I wanted so many additional "color chords" that I would have run out of playing space altogether.

To get around this problem, I developed a system whereby I double the selection of chords – without adding any additional chord bars to my autoharp.

My harp is tuned to the Key of D, (D, E, F♯, G, A, B, C♯, D), but one can, of course, transfer the principles described here to a diatonic 'harp tuned to other keys.

I use a three-tiered chord system with a cover (sometimes referred to as "C" style) with fifteen chord bars. I have three inches of playing space for the top string.

Thus, with the fourteen chords produced by using one bar alone, plus the sixteen chords possible through combinations, a total of thirty chords are achieved, all surrounding one key.

The arrangement of the bars themselves was carefully worked out to allow for the most rapid movement of the fingers from one combination to another. After getting used to the system, I find that it does not impede my speed or accuracy.

It's amusing to see another 'harper pick up my instrument and try to play a tune. They're baffled at first because they can't get a "straight" chord out of it. But after the system is explained, it usually doesn't take too long to get used to the combinations. After all, we autoharpers have had it kind of easy all these years – with one finger producing a whole chord. Now, by using two or even three fingers, one can greatly expand the selection of chords on the diatonic autoharp.

Please find the chart for combinations of chord bars needed for this setup on the following page:

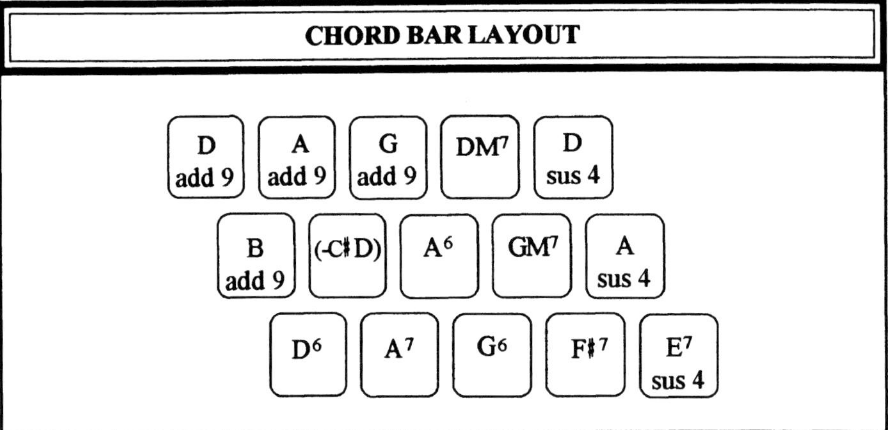

The felts in each chord bar above are cut to allow the following strings to sound:

CHORD BAR	CHORD	CHORD BAR	CHORD
1. D add 9	D F♯ A E	8. A^6	A C♯ E F♯
2. A add 9	A C♯ E B	9. GM^7	G B D F♯
3. G add 9	G B D A	10. A^{sus4}	A D E
4. DM^7	D F♯ A C♯	11. D^6	D F♯ A B
5. D^{sus4}	D G A	12. A^7	A C♯ E G
6. B add 9 (less the 3rd)	B C♯ F♯	13. G^6	G B D E
7. (-C♯D) (A "block chord." Not useful by itself.)	E F♯ G A B	14. F♯^{7}(less the 3rd)	F♯ C E
		15. E^{7sus4}	E A B D

The key to this system is that half of the chords are produced by pressing two or more chord bars at once. The combinations and chords they produce are as follows:

BAR COMBINATION	EQUALS THIS CHORD
1. D^6+ DM^7	D
2. G^6+ GM^7	G
3. A^7 + A^6	A
4. GM^7 +D^6	B^m
5. G^6+(-C♯D)	E^m
6. A^6+ DM^7	F♯ m
7. E^{7sus4} + G^6	E^7 (less the 3rd)
8. D^6+(-C♯D)	B^7 (less the 3rd)
9. E^{7sus4} + (-C♯D)	E^{sus4}
10. D^6 + A^{sus4}	D (less the 3rd)
11. E^{6sus4} + G^6 + (-C♯D)	E (less the 3rd)
12. F♯^{7} + DM^7	F♯ (less the 3rd)
13. G^6 + GM^7+ D^{sus4}	G (less the 3rd)
14. A^7 + A^{sus4}	A (less the 3rd)
15. D^6+ GM^7+(-C♯D)	B (less the 3rd)
16. B add 9 + F♯^{7} + (-C♯D)	C♯ (less the 3rd)

❖

For more information concerning the Ultratonic Autoharp, see: "Expanding The Ultratonic Autoharp" p.81, "Deciphering The Ultratonic Autoharp" p.83, and "The Ultratonic With Floating Pentatonics" p.79.

The Ultratonic With Floating Pentatonics

AQ Volume VI, Number 4

THE IMPROVED ULTRATONIC CHORD SYSTEM

WITH INTEGRATED FLOATING PENTATONICS

Marty Schuman

What kind of babble is this? Actually, it is the descriptive term for a unique chord system for the diatonic autoharp I developed over the years. I first wrote about this system in the January '89 issue of Autoharp Quarterly.[1] *Since that time, I've made a number of improvements that incorporate the following features:*

1. There is an expanded selection of chords to choose – actually thirty-four chords on a 15-bar set-up. Being a diatonic-based arrangement, this one doesn't allow *any* chord. However, one can squeeze out many variations on major chords to enhance one's playing.
2. Although set up as a one-key instrument, some of the extra chords enable one to play, to some extent, in secondary keys.
3. Floating Pentatonics are incorporated into this arrangement. This is a system of playing diatonic tunes off constantly shifting pentatonic scales.[2]

The ultratonic system utilizes a 15-bar, three-tiered chord bar arrangement. The chords are:

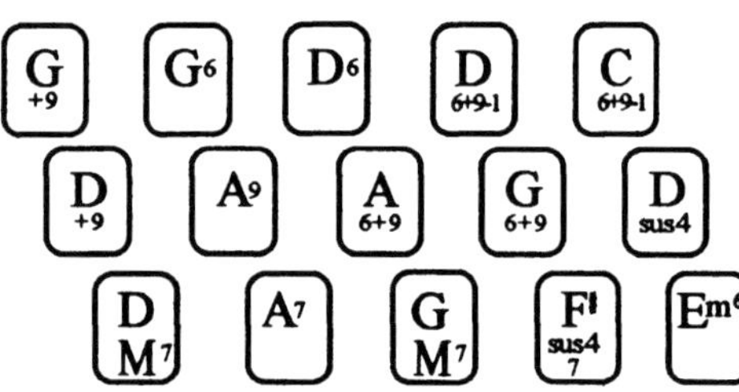

Notice that the A^7 is the only normal chord. However, one can more than double the selection by pressing various *combinations*. It is critical that the proper left-hand fingering is used.

The "home positions" for the left hand are:

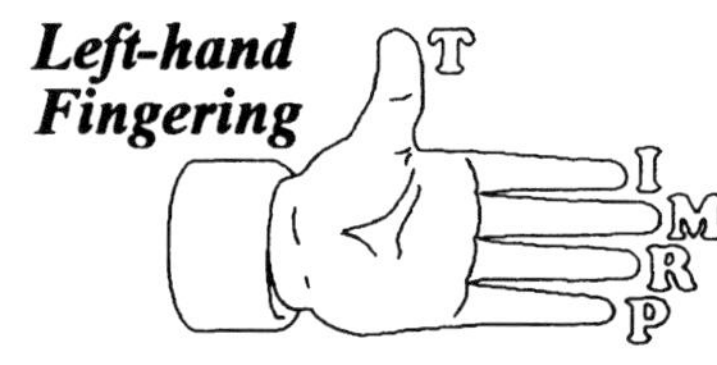

These three chords are the basic major chords for the Key of D.

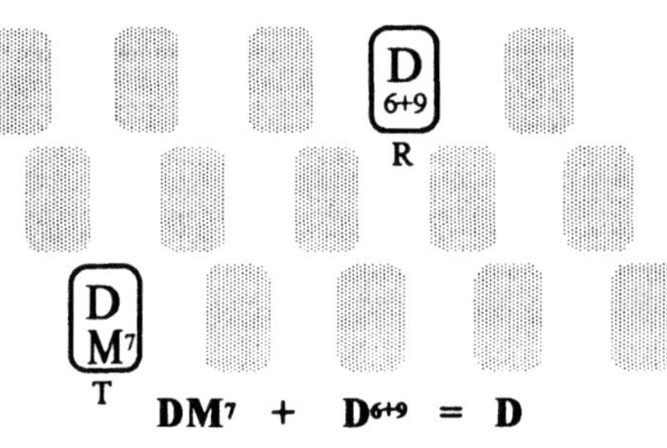

$DM^7 + D^{6+9} = D$

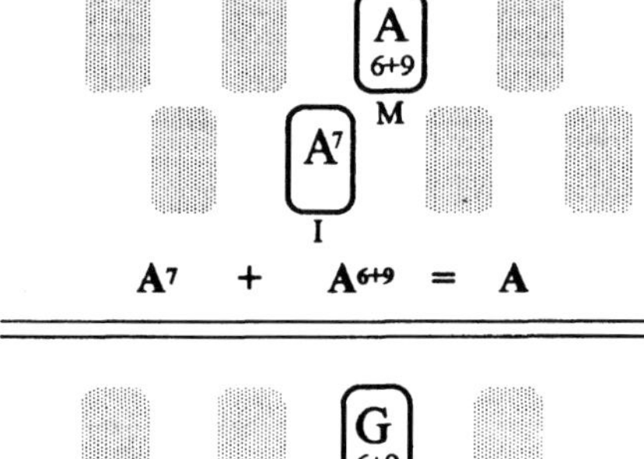

$A^7 + A^{6+9} = A$

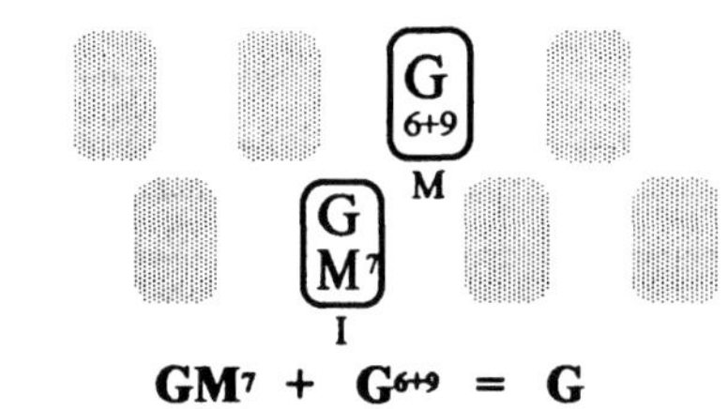

$GM^7 + G^{6+9} = G$

The Fun Begins

With other combinations of chord bars, one can derive the total number of chords available on the instrument.

On the following page find a listing of all the chords available using the ultratonic system. In these schedules, the * indicates there is no C in the D diatonic scale. The two C chords are C substitutes. Also, left-handed fingering for combinations should flow from the home position.

So what use are all these chords? Some can serve as interesting substitutes for straight chords, or as transition chords, or approximations of chords not available. For instance, the added 9th chord is a beautiful substitute for its straight variant. Suspended 4th chords act as transitions, and all chords without the 3rd can serve as modal or minor chords. Many of these chords differ by only a note or two. This enables one to play melody in a more flowing manner.

Although set up as a one-key diatonic 'harp, some of the extra chords enable one to play, to some extent, in secondary keys. For instance, on a D 'harp, not only are the keys of D and Bm present, but one can also play in A, G, and E.

To play in A, use E^{7-3}, E^{-3}, or E^{sus4} as a substitute for E^7.

To play in G, use C^{-1}, or C^{6+9-1} as a substitute for C.

To play in E, use E^{7-3} or E^{-3} as a substitute for E, and B^{-3} as a substitute for B^7.

Sometimes these substitutes work, sometimes not. If you are jamming, other instruments can help fill in the missing notes.

Finally, the three 6+9 chords are actually *pentatonic* scales.

$DM^7 + D^{6+9}$	=	D
$A^7 + A^{6+9}$	=	A
$GM^7 + G^{6+9}$	=	G

By lifting up on the first chord of each combination, one is left with the pentatonic scale to play against. This is the basis for Floating Pentatonics.

Although seemingly complicated, it really isn't. After a while, left-hand fingering becomes second nature. This is not an arrangement everyone might use, but if you feel like exploring a new frontier, this is a perfect way to take the

D CHORDS

CHORDBAR(S)	FINGERING		CHORD	CONSISTING OF
DM^7 + D^{6+9}	(T-R)	=	D	D, F♯, A
D^6	(M)	=	D^6	D, F♯, A, B
DM^7	(T)	=	DM^7	D, F♯, A, C♯
D^{+9}	(T)	=	D^{+9}	D, F♯, A, E
D^{6+9}	(R)	=	D^{6+9}	D, F♯, A, B, E
D^{sus4}	(M)	=	D^{sus4}	D, G, A
DM^7 + D^{6+9} + D^{sus4}	(T-R-P)	=	D^{-3}	D, A
No chord		=	D^{13}	D, E, F♯, G, A, B, C♯

G CHORDS

CHORDBAR(S)	FINGERING		CHORD	CONSISTING OF
GM^7 + G^{6+9}	(I-M)	=	G	G, B, D
G^6	(T)	=	G^6	G, B, D, E
GM^7	(I)	=	GM^7	G, B, D, F♯
G^{+9}	(T)	=	G^{+9}	G, B, D, A
G^{6+9}	(M)	=	G^{6+9}	G, B, D, E, A
GM^7 + G^{6+9} + D^{sus4}	(I-M-R)	=	G^{-3}	G, D

A CHORDS

CHORDBAR(S)	FINGERING		CHORD	CONSISTING OF
A^7 + A^{6+9}	(I-M)	=	A	A, C♯, E
A^7	(I)	=	A^7	A, C♯, E, G
A^9	(T)	=	A^9	A, C♯, E, G, B
A^{6+9}	(M)	=	A^{6+9}	A, C♯, E, B, F♯
A^9 + A^{6+9}	(T-M)	=	A^{+9}	A, C♯, E, B
D^{6+9} + C^{6+9-1}	(R-P)	=	A^{sus4}	A, D, E
A^7 + A^{6+9} + D^{6+9}	(I-M-R)	=	A^{-3}	A, E

E CHORDS

CHORDBAR(S)	FINGERING		CHORD	CONSISTING OF
A^9 + G$_6$	(I-T)	=	E^m	E, G, B
E^{m6}	(P)	=	E^{m6}	E, G, B, C♯
G^6 + D^{6+9}	(T-R)	=	E$^{7-3}$	E, B, D
D^{6+9} + G^6 + A^{6+9}	(T-R-M)	=	E^{-3}	E, B
A^9 + D^{6+9}	(T-R)	=	E^{sus4}	E, A, B

F♯ CHORDS

CHORDBAR(S)	FINGERING		CHORD	CONSISTING OF
DM^7 + A^{6+9}	(T-I)	=	F♯^{m}	F♯, A, C♯
F♯^{7sus4}	(R)	=	F♯^{7sus4}	F♯, B, C♯, D
F♯^{7sus4} + DM^7	(R-T)	=	F♯$^{-3}$	F♯, C♯

B CHORDS

CHORDBAR(S)	FINGERING		CHORD	CONSISTING OF
D^{6+9} + GM^7	(R-I)	=	B^m	B, D, F♯
When playing in B^m use this combination:				
D^6 + GM^7	(T-I)	=	B^m	B, D, F♯
D^{6+9} + F♯^{7sus4}	(T-I)	=	B^{sus4}	B, E, F♯
D^{6+9} + G^{6+9} + F♯^{7sus4}	(T-M-I)	=	B^{-3}	B, F♯

C CHORDS*

CHORDBAR(S)	FINGERING		CHORD	CONSISTING OF
G^6 + A^7	(T-I)	=	C^{-1}	E, G
C^{6+9-1}	(P)	=	C^{6+9-1}	D, E, G, A

TOTAL = THIRTY FOUR CHORDS

plunge. Remember, all the common chords you are used to on a one-key diatonic instrument are still available. The beauty comes with the addition of all the other chords for more interesting music arrangements. ❖

Editor's note: Marty Schuman was an International and a Mountain Laurel Autoharp Champion.

For more information concerning the Ultratonic Autoharp, read "The Ultratonic Autoharp" p.77, "Expanding The Ultratonic Autoharp" p.81, and "Deciphering The Ultratonic Autoharp" p.83.

[1] See "The Ultratonic Autoharp" p.77.
[2] See "Floating Pentatonics" p.51.

Expanding The Ultratonic Autoharp

AQ Volume VIII, Number 2

NEW AGE POSSIBILITIES - EXPANDING THE ULTRATONIC AUTOHARP

Mark Fackeldey

Marty Schuman's Ultratonic system[1] carried to the extreme is a single-key diatonic 'harp on which the open chord (no bars depressed) is the only chord present. To form other chords, there are seven "delete" bars, each one deleting only one tone (and its octaves) from the open chord. This will enable one to play all chords possible in the chosen key.

So, to form a simple triad (three-tone chord such as C or Am), you have to press four delete bars. To form a four-tone chord such as G^7 or Am^7 you have to press three delete bars – and so on. At first, this may seem impossible. In actuality, it can be very simple: (1) the delete bars needed to form a chord are adjacent to each other, (2) the bars and buttons are wide enough to set them up side-by-side with the buttons in just one row, and (3) the bars are arranged in a certain order. A further simplification is made by duplicating three of the delete bars (See a, c, and e bars on illustration.)

The Delete Bar Arrangement

Now, it's time to look at the delete bar arrangement. The "X" indicates the delete bars to use for each chord. You'll see that all the chords listed in the column to the right of the bars from the C chord to the G^9 chord can be achieved by pressing anywhere from four to two adjacent bars. When you get to the G^9 chord, you'll notice the "etc." This means that moving the two delete bar pattern across the bars will produce the rest of the chords in the order shown above the G^9. For example, moving the pattern one bar over will give you an Em^9 – and so on.

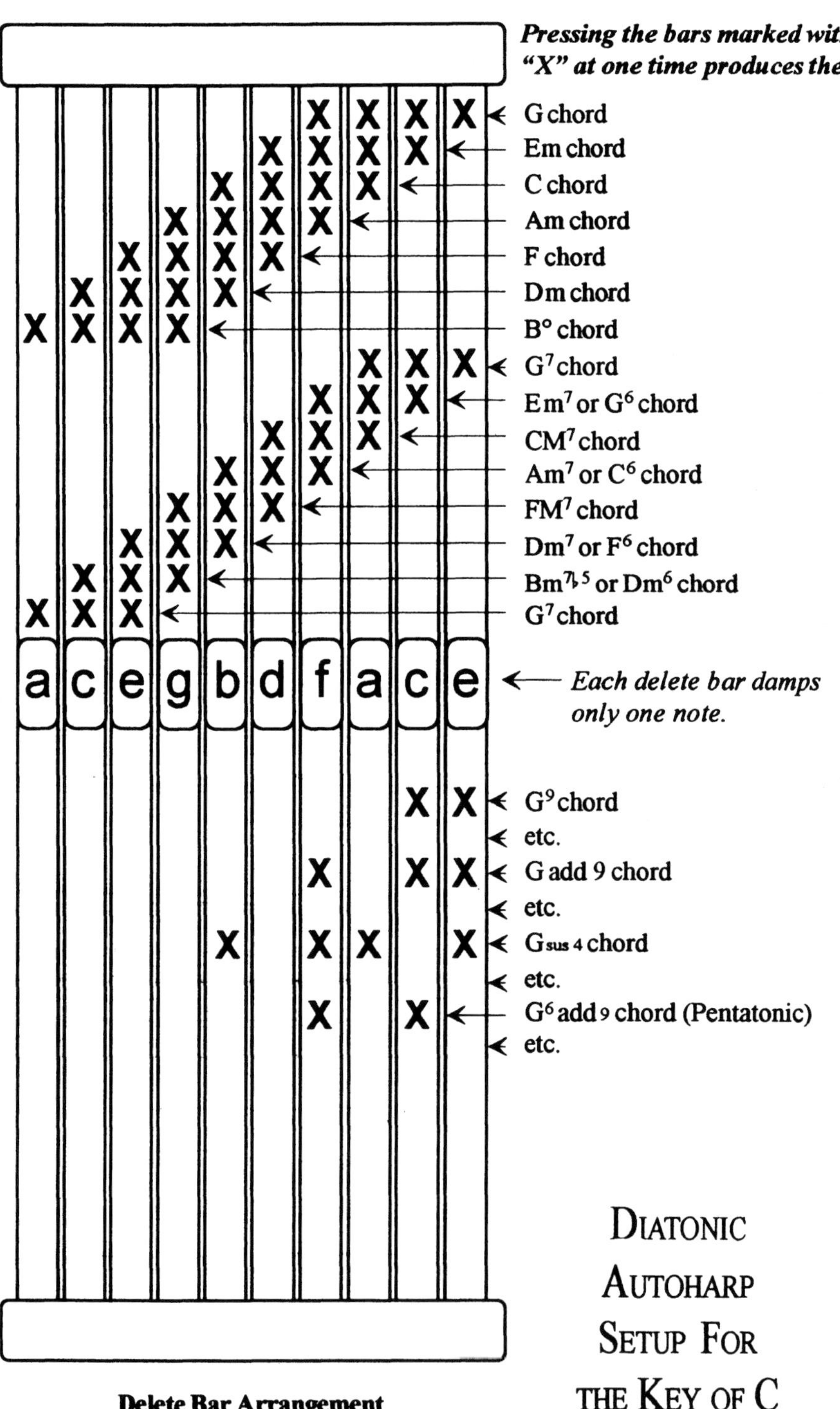

Delete Bar Arrangement

(This order can be reversed if desired)

DIATONIC AUTOHARP SETUP FOR THE KEY OF C

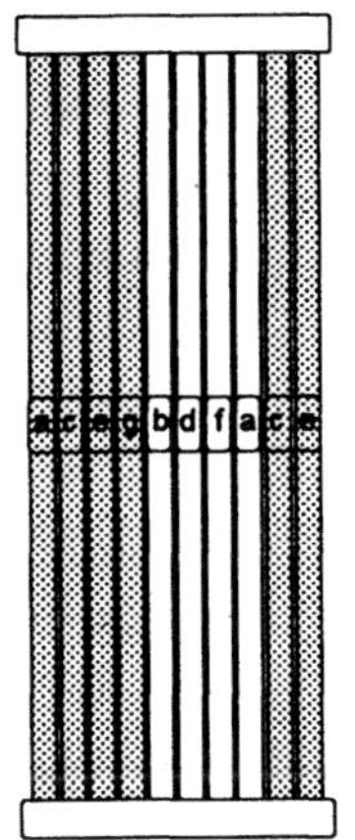

Press these four bars
for the C chord

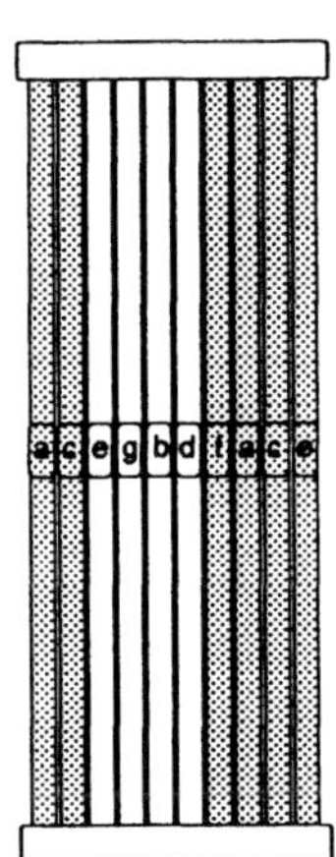

Press these four bars
for the F chord

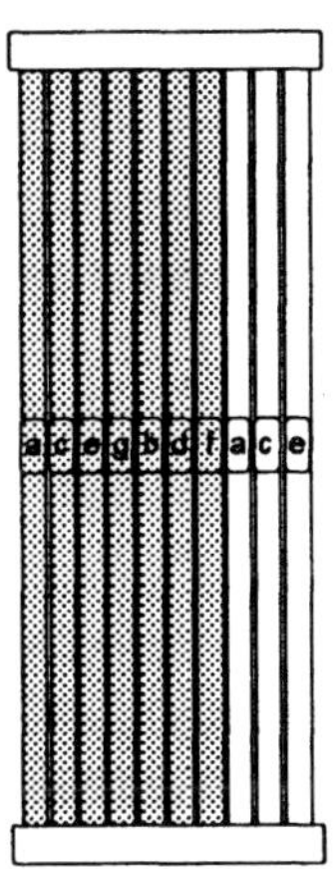

Press these three bars
for the G^7 chord

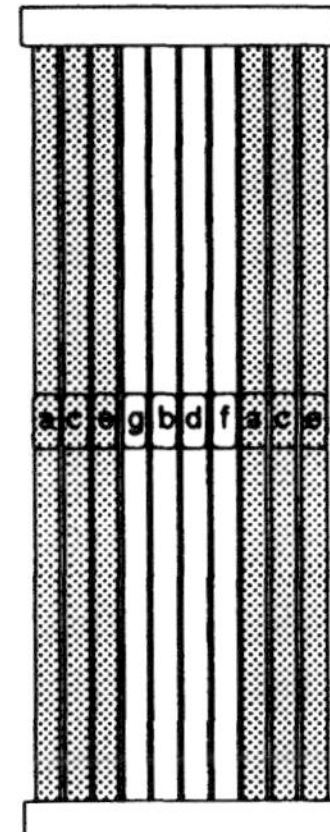

Press these four bars
for the Am chord

As you can see, the "X" pattern for each chord *type* is identical.

This arrangement also makes it easy to remember which chord is which. For example, on each three-tone chord, the name of the chord is the same as the note of the delete bar immediately to the right of the bars being depressed. Therefore, pressing the b, d, f, and a bars produces the C chord, the same as the label on the next bar to the right.

The chords listed from G to G^7 are fairly standard. From G^9 on down, you'll encounter an incredible array of chords with New Age sounds. Remember, each delete bar pattern produces seven chords. Six patterns times seven chords equals 42 chords. All this from just ten bars.

Some Additional Thoughts

The first three delete bars (the repeated a, c, and e) can be eliminated, but it would make the patterns necessary far more complicated. Doable, but not recommended.

The first delete bar (a) can be eliminated if you do not want or need a B° (diminished) chord.

In Summary

Like the original Ultratonic, this setup does not allow very rapid chord changes or single note melody picking. (Of course, through sheer obstinacy, Marty proved me wrong on this point – but, I'm talking about ordinary mortals.) It does make a fine backup rhythm instrument that has *all* the chords for a single key. It also could provide a high bliss factor for you New Age Noodlers. ❖

Editor's note: Mark Fackeldey is an International Autoharp Champion.

[1] See "The Ultratonic Autoharp" p.77.

Deciphering The Ultratonic Autoharp

AQ Volume VIII, Number 2

DECIPHERING THE AWESOME ULTRATONIC 'HARP

Lucille Reilly

Now that I'm "retired" from competition (until the next century, anyway), I can afford the time to explore some areas of autoharp playing which have intrigued me for a while. One area is the late Marty Schuman's ultratonic chording system. His playing continues to captivate me since I first heard him play *Ragtime Annie* at the Walnut Valley Festival in 1991. When my autoharp collection suddenly increased by two in 1995, a 21-chord chromatic 'harp became free to use for ultratonic purposes.

I started with Marty's article, "The Improved Ultratonic Chord System with Integrated Floating Pentatonics."[1] (What a gift he gave us to share its details!) Most of the single chord bar tones are spelled out there, but some more translation is necessary. So allow me, just in case you want to try this and are still scratching your head!

First the key. I picked B♭ Major instead of D for two reasons. First, B♭ was a nice addition to the other diatonic keys I have: A, B, C, D, E, F, and G!

The second reason was based on a trick Bob Lewis showed a few of us at the Walnut Valley Festival in Winfield, Kansas. He held his 1992 Mountain Laurel prize autoharp up in front of his face and sang each tone of the chromatic scale into the sound hole. He felt the 'harp vibrate in his hands the strongest on the tone E. This tone is different for every 'harp, even those built by the same luthier and cut from the same tree. My soon-to-be-converted autoharp happened to vibrate the most on B♭.

In the following chart, I rewrote the chord names in the on-the-'harp order Marty put them in, plus some other information. The chord names (in **boldface** type), while odd, give all the clues to spell each chord in the next row.

Row three shows all the scale tones which *do not* appear in the chord spelling. These tones are "felted out" on the chord bars. From here, I transposed the damped tones to letter names and chord names in B♭ Major.

Chord	**G+9**	**G6**	**D6**	**D6+9**	***Dsus4+2**
Chord spelling	G B D A	G B D E	D F♯ A B	D F♯ A B E	E G A D
Damped tones	C♯ E F♯	A C♯ F♯	E G C♯	G C♯	F♯ B C♯
Chord	**D+9**	**A9**	**A6+9**	**G6+9**	**Dsus4**
Chord spelling	D F♯ A E	A C♯ E G B	A C♯ E F♯ B	G B D E A	D G A
Damped tones	G B	D F♯	D G	C♯ F	E F♯ B C♯
Chord	**D7**	**A7**	**G7**	**F♯sus4 7**	**Em6**
Chord spelling	D F♯ A C♯	A C♯ E G	G B D F♯	F♯ B C♯ E	E G B C♯
Damped tones	E G B	B D F♯	A C♯ E	G A D	F♯ A D

*Marty named this chord "C" 6+9-1. I've changed the name because C♮ is not part of the D Major scale.

Tuning the strings. I referred to my three diatonic autoharps and George Foss' book, *Going Diatonic*, to find out how much range the tuning should span. From everything, my tuning came out like this versus the original chromatic tuning:

Original Chromatic Tuning

F G C D E F F♯ G A A♯ B C C♯ D D♯ E F F♯ G G♯ A A♯ B C C♯ D D♯ E F F♯ G G♯ A A♯ B C

F G B♭ C D E♭ F G A B♭ B♭ C C D D E♭ E♭ F F G G A A B♭ B♭ C C D D E♭ E♭ F F G A B♭

New B♭ Major Tuning

Some strings from the 'harp's original tuning remain unchanged, while the rest are close.

Tuning the new scale was easy with an electronic tuner, as the letter names on the autoharp for the chromatic tuning would become obsolete. I didn't worry about a sweet or just or other kind of tuning because the autoharp would take time to settle into its new string tension.

For the precise placement of felt on each chord bar, I made a schematic of the strings showing the new letter names. I then taped the schematic just above the chord bar cover, removed the cover, and felted the bars.

Once the 'harp was back together, I began pushing buttons and strumming without peeking at Marty's article for his "answers." I wanted to hear the chords for myself in hopes of learning chord button combinations faster.

I found that some chords could be produced with up to four different pairings of buttons! ("What was I getting myself into? And why was there so much repetition?") As I hunted further, I kept wondering: "Why press two or three buttons to get standard chords when I can get them by depressing one button? With room for 21 chord bars on the 'harp, maybe I should rethink the chords and so refelt the bars to one familiar chord per bar? Is this ultratonic setup worth the trouble?" This, of course, made me wonder all the more how Marty came up with this system.

After three days of buttoning and strumming, basking in resonance, and wondering about the meaning of life and music, I overcame my fears (Who, me? Yes!) and decided to clunk through a tune. (One expects considerably more mistakes along the path of learning tunes on this autoharp than would occur on one-chord-per-bar 'harps!)

"O Susanna" gnawed at my mind as a good first tune. And what a surprise it gave! It became a choir whose alto and tenor voices moved *inside* the chords to "bend" the harmony of straight I, IV, and V, all by depressing *single* chord bars! For the first time in my life, I could play cocktail music and the kind of *piano* playing I could never get the hang of!

But the funniest part was the reactions of my musician friends. As they listened in awe to my limited repertoire of three tunes learned in as many days, they said, "Was that a Major-seventh chord?...There was a minor-sixth...Yes, that was a Major-seventh!...What in the world was *that*?"

Can I tell you something? I've had all the same music theory training as these people and *I don't care* what the names of the chords are! (It's actually dangerous to think too hard about what chords one plays on this 'harp!) I play it first by finding the tones in the melody, then by the supporting tone clusters that go with each melody note at that point in the tune. The result: I've never heard an autoharp jingle, shimmer, or laugh so much! Everyone who owns a spare 'harp should make it into an "Ultraharp!" ❖

[1] See "The Ultratonic With Floating Pentatonics" p.79.

Picks

AQ Volume VII, Number 3

TAKE YOUR PICK!

Gregg "Scissorhands" Averett

If I were a finger pick I would be an insecure wreck because few in the musical world are quite so fickle as an autoharp player. Every 'harper secretly harbors a belief that the only thing holding him or her back from musical nirvana is having that perfect set of picks. They would wear as comfortably and securely as the very skin of our fingers and guide on the right strings like homing missiles. The fastest jigs and reels would succumb in a cloud of sixteenth notes. Yes, we all have it in us, if only we had the right picks. So, very little causes nearly the stir in autoharp circles as someone holding up a hand and saying, "What do you think of these?"

I would be willing to bet that every autoharper is a collector of sorts. My own arsenal of attachments for finger and thumb is ever expanding. Part of the ceremony of every festival I attend is meticulously scouring vendor's row for any new developments. Even if I don't particularly like a new pick I'll buy several, just in case I change my mind later. Playing in jams or watching a performer, I always keep an eye peeled for unfamiliar types of picks or tricks of the trade in their use.

Homemade Picks

It wasn't always that way, of course. Early autoharpers didn't have such a smorgasbord of choices. They might have found a celluloid thumb pick or a felt plectrum in the case but, otherwise, they were on their own. Some proved to be quite resourceful. Kilby Snow made his picks out of sheet metal from old, brass car headlights. Using tin snips, a file and some careful bending, he fashioned custom picks to suit his unusual style (He only used a pick on his thumb and forefinger). His son, Jim, does the same today but, automobile styles not being what they were, he uses sheet brass from a ceiling fan housing. Mike Hudak learned the technique from Kilby and used nickel silver stock. Details of his pattern are in the July, '90 *Autoharp Quarterly*.

Autoharp Hall-Of-Famer Pop Stoneman proved equally resourceful. His daughter, Patsy, relates how he would take some of those old-fashioned hair rollers and remove the spiral wire stiffener from them. A little judicious bending to form a loop in the end and, Voila-finger picks! I tried out one Patsy supplied and found it to be very comfortable and secure (The spiral winding extends over the second joint). It was easy to pluck strings accurately but was thinner sounding than conventional picks.

Some notables in the contemporary autoharp community have pursued this personalized path to picking. Joe Marlin Riggs carries on the Kilby Snow tradition with similarly fashioned picks, with some added refinements. They are literally screwed onto his hand and are reminiscent of devices used to elicit confessions from witches. They are also massive enough to exert their own gravitational field! But he gets that characteristic sound that few can emulate.

I've seen Mary Lou Orthey use nickel silver picks George fashioned for her, much like Mike Hudak's. She likes the comfort and security they provide by gripping the second finger joint instead of the fingertip. I found them to be everything she said with, yet, an additional quality – I played louder with them on. This could be especially useful in jam sessions. I believe the reason for the increased volume is the leverage and additional purchase on the string they afford as well as a loss of flexibility in the first joint, which encouraged me to do more pinching than plucking.

Bill Bryant concocted a doubled pick that permits him to strike a string in either direction. Nesting a pair of Dunlop picks to form a top and bottom, he solders the tip and one side, leaving the other side to adjust the size. He uses these to achieve an extremely rapid rhythm filler that has become a signature in his playing style.

Tom Bogardus supplied me with two versions of a metal pick he is marketing. Its most salient feature is that it wraps around the end of the finger allowing, in theory, two-way picking. In its present form I believe the tip is too rounded. When I was first learning to play I experimented with thimbles because they were less prone to getting tangled in the strings. But I soon gave up on them because they just brushed over the strings without getting much sound. A good finger pick needs a sharp end or edge that will draw the string and then release it suddenly and cleanly to produce a satisfactory sound.

Roz Brown has used sitar picks for years. They are a sort of piano wire origami that fits over the finger, gripping at the sides and making a vertical "V" over the tip. It can brush the strings in either direction, although the fit is a bit loose to be really effective this way. This tendency to rotate on the finger detracted from the sound quality and feel of the strings, in my opinion. Also, they can be uncomfortable. It's a little like wearing a mousetrap, with the wire tightly squeezing the sides of your knuckle to keep the pick on. Roz is the only source I know for them (Have you ever gone into a music store and asked for sitar picks?).

Over-The-Counter Picks

Most of us manage with the picks readily available in the marketplace. Actually, there is quite a variety to choose from. The runaway favorite is the old standby, *Dunlop*, in stainless or brass, usually .0225 or .025 gauge. Some people swear by the mellowness of brass. I can't really detect a difference in sound between the two metals but I do feel better, somehow, using the brass. It's not all science, you know! It has a classic look and feel, especially after it's had a chance to tarnish. The tarnish should be left alone, as it improves the grip on the fingertip. The problem with this style of pick, and the many others like them, is that they perch somewhat on the end of the finger and rely on tightness of fit for security. This pressure becomes uncomfortable after extended play. Of most concern to the user is the tendency of the pick to catch an edge on the 'harp string and be launched like a missile from a bowstring. Security is right up there with comfort and playability for any 'harper choosing a pick.

Ernie Ball and *National* make similar metal finger picks except they taper into a little claw-like point. I just never warmed to them like I did the Dunlops, although others have found them just right. (I even found some metal picks that look like ladies' glue-on fingernails. I could never figure out whether they were supposed to go on the top or bottom of my finger.)

ProPick has produced a design in brass, which I favor as the best of this particular style of metal pick. It improves upon the Dunlop by splitting and separating the grip wings, resulting in a more comfortable and secure fit. It's not as foolproof as the Pearse, discussed below, but is an excellent choice if you prefer a more solid feel on the strings, as many do. The business end is virtually the same as a Dunlop, which means the tip is stiffer and heavier than the lighter gauge Pearse.

Mary Lou Orthey showed me a metal pick she said was the type Maybelle Carter used. Sure enough, I could see her wearing one in an old photo close-up. Maybelle suffered from arthritis in her hands in her later years. This pick has cutouts in the wings that bend around to grip the finger, thus relieving pressure on the side of the joint. Another unique feature is that the wings slant back as they curve around to the top of the finger. This produces several desirable effects. The bottom back edge is clear of the first joint, allowing it to flex. The top of the pick extends back just past the joint, giving better leverage against the force that wants to rotate the pick off the fingertip and that digs the back edge into the top of your finger. Third, since it grips higher on the finger than, say, a Dunlop, it doesn't have to fit as tightly to remain secure. This is a very comfortable pick. It's stamped: STEVENS PAT. PEND. I called every store in Atlanta but no one was familiar with that name or knew if they were still in business.

At Galax I ran across a pick called the *John Pearse Hi-Rider*. I don't know John's relationship to Mr. Stevens, Esq., but guess what? The picks are virtually identical! (Should any lawsuits be forthcoming, you didn't hear that from me.) All the above kudos and qualities apply equally to the Hi-Rider picks. They offer excellent feel and control on the strings. The contact portion of the pick is long, straight, and somewhat narrow, with no upward curve at the end. This can, of course, be modified by the purchaser, but I found that such a straight tip extended the reach slightly and yielded a crisp release on the string. It is critical for comfort and proper fit that the grip wings be carefully bent with needle nose pliers and not just squeezed closed, which invariably results in an uncomfortable kink. A very slight coning of the pick can aid the fit. When properly shaped, the picks should fit like a second skin, relying on the wing design rather than a tight grip to remain secure. I bought a bag full and recommend them.

A couple of years ago *Acri* finger picks came on the market. At the time I believed they were the answer to everything I had been wanting in a finger pick. They are heavy gauge brass with wide grip wings that enfold the entire first knuckle. A number of "breathing" holes also aid grip. The wings are cut away sufficiently on the bottom so as not to interfere with bending of the joint and are supportive on the top. The pick end is typical of Dunlop. Careful bending with needle nose pliers is critical but will afford a very comfortable fit. I can say unequivocally that this is the loudest pick for sale anywhere. There is roughly twice the amount of metal on your finger than with a Dunlop and it is stiff and well supported. All of this mass creates inertia to your play that has two noticeable effects. First, as I mentioned, the strings ring loud and long. Second, even in normal pinch-pluck play, I noticed a pronounced ringing, as when patting the strings with metal picks. If this sound is attractive to you, these picks produce it in spades. One not so desirable quality of the picks was a definite loss of feel on the strings, as though I were playing with metal gloves. All of this requires that you evaluate these picks carefully with regard to your style of play.

There are lots of plastic picks around but they're not that popular among 'harpers. They are not very comfortable due to their lack of flexibility and it's hard to find a set that fits all the fingers. Plus, I just never did like the sound of them; too sotto voice and the clacking of the plastic on the strings was irritating. I think most select them to fit very small fingers.

ALaska Piks have been around a while but I've not seen any autoharpers using them. They are difficult to describe but are unique in that they fit on top of the finger like an extension of the fingernail. In fact, some fingernail is required to help secure it in place, as the tip fits under the nail. I thought they afforded exquisite feel on the strings and surprising volume. They would suit someone who does a lot of intricate melody plucking rather than a heavy-duty pincher. Just as with an actual fingernail, these picks afford an opportunity to brush backwards as well as pluck, with some risk to security on the finger.

In fact, in addition to cost, that is their main drawback. The grip wings are somewhat flimsy and it relies on positioning over and under the nail to aid grip. The relatively slack strings of a guitar would not be a problem but the unyielding tension on most autoharp strings would pose a continuing worry. When peace of mind matters, one would most certainly want to secure the picks with adhesive tape or an adhesive spray like Rosinit. It is also likely that vigorous or extended play would create soreness in the tender quick under the nail. Some trimming and fitting is necessary to start with, and continuing nail care is required to keep them usable. Still, for someone who enjoys bare nail picking, as I do, the aLaska pick is an attractive alternative to gelatin or glue-ons.

Marty Schuman turned me on to *Herco*'s nylon finger picks and they are still my personal favorites. They deliver a tone that is mellower than metal but not as muted as plastic, and produce no metallic "ching" or plastic "clack." Being of the fingertip type, they do not interfere with first joint flexibility, allowing easy plucking of a melody line. You can pat with them but not as well as metal, of course. They are quite comfortable. They soften slightly with body heat but are grippy enough that it is not a problem unless they were too loose to start with.

Marty said you could do tricks with boiling water, but I never had trouble finding some to fit me out of the box. They were electric blue until Herco was acquired by Dunlop. The ones I see now are white. An interesting aside is that I saw identical white picks individually packaged and sold in fabric stores as a "Finger Safety Guard" for sewing and quilting. So, if you're ever in a fix and can't find a music store...

Thumb Picks

Thumb picks are another matter of highly personal taste, and choices abound. I've seen very few metal ones that weren't of the homemade variety or some sort of metal/plastic composite. Plastic, celluloid, and nylon seem to be the favorites for commercial manufacture. As with finger picks, there are a growing variety of shapes and designs. There are numbers of what I would call conventional designs. They vary principally in the thickness and type of material.

The large, wide ones, such as *Golden Gate* are the most comfortable and secure. They also have a relatively broad contact area with the strings. I find that these wider, blunter picks can produce an annoying (to me) clacking or "thwip" brushing the strings, and a somewhat subdued tone. They are also clumsy for thumb lead work. Golden Gates are among the pricier selections available.

A line of thumb picks called *Zookies* employs a twist in the tip, available in 10, 20, and 30 degrees, which is evidently intended to bring the tip of the pick into a more perpendicular contact with the string. It looked as if it would work fine for a finger-picking guitarist, but in my trials, the twist was in exactly the wrong direction for an autoharp player and resulted in the pick striking the string with the edge. I lean toward narrower, pointy thumb picks but comfort and security become more problematical.

One pick I prefer among the "conventional" types is a John Pearse design called the *Vintage Thumb Pick*. It fits well down onto the thumb because the tip angles outwards and, fashioned from celluloid, it doesn't soften and loosen from the heat of your hand. The tip is sharp and stiff, which is what I like, and I don't hear any objectionable pick noise.

Another favorite of mine is a clear plastic *Dunlop* offering. It is wider than most (but smaller than a Golden Gate) and tapers to a slightly extended sharp point. It gives a good, clean release on the strings with no pick noise of its own. It's inexpensive and fits securely, though the thick plastic does soften a little. Because of the small, pointed contact surface, it tends to wear quickly and must be filed to shape periodically.

Mike Fenton and Marty Schuman introduced me to the *Kelly Speed Pick*. It is made of yellow, orange, or white nylon, in ascending order of stiffness. The business end is a narrow, flexible tongue that affords great versatility in playing techniques. It is ideally suited for thumb lead, flat-picking and drag notes. While perfect for livelier instrumentals, especially fast fiddle tunes, it can sound harsh and raspy in slow pieces and is probably not the best choice for vocal accompaniment. Additionally, it can be prone to rotating on the thumb or becoming displaced during fast play. I favor rosin spray to secure it, while John Hollandsworth uses the spray and tape.

Of course, I cannot broach the subject of thumb picks without mentioning Drew Smith and his pick of intimidating proportions. He plays thumb lead and uses and markets a plastic thumb pick of his own design and manufacture. I'm not saying just how long it is but I understand, when he's not using it, he carries it in a sheath! He could use it for fondue and never get his knuckles warm. But, if you've heard him play, you know how well it works for his style.

Pick Alterations

Of course, one is not constrained to remain within the constellation of picks as offered out of the manufacturer's box. Some players find some tailoring and modification is necessary to suit their preferences. June Maugery uses a nail clipper to trim down orange Kelly picks. It reduces the harshness and, according to some others who have tried it, improves control. I've heard of some who put little kinks and bends in the tips of metal picks, and also the boiling and reshaping of plastic ones.

Taking a deep breath, I ventured to try my hand at improving upon one of my expensive Golden Gates. Carefully, I trimmed and sanded the broad, blunt tip into a pointed one. Alternating with a stock version, I tried to make sure what I heard was not influenced by what I expected. To be honest, there was less difference in tone than I thought there would be. The round tip was a little mellower; the pointed tip a little brighter. Also, there was little pick noise with either one, though I've heard it from blunt picks in other hands. The most noticeable difference was in the feel of the picks. There was a heavier-felt impact with the strings in the blunt version, and more precision in striking individual strings with the pointed tip.

I tried June's trimming trick on the Kelly pick and found the raspiness of the slapping tongue was definitely reduced. However, I was missing notes when thumb leading because of the shorter tongue length. I'm sure I could compensate with practice but my big hand would still have a problem reaching reliably in the narrow confines of the top strings.

Pick Selection

I find the Dunlop thumb and Herco finger picks suit me as an all-round pick choice, but I don't necessarily stick with one kind of finger or thumb pick for all purposes. I sometimes find that, in working up a tune for a performance, a different pick choice will yield a unique sound quality or facilitate play in some way. Or I may choose to omit picks altogether. In a jam situation, however, one will seldom find the opportunity or need for that kind of fussiness and the old favorites will always come to hand.

The Flying Picks

If the science is in the pick, the art is in the variety of methods intended to ensure that the darn things don't fly off. Some just clamp them on till their fingers turn blue. Others tape them on. A few use tape or other nefarious materials on the inside. Some just stick a pick on every finger to ensure enough will be left to finish the tune. I subscribe to the stick-um theory. When the occasion demands absolute security, I use a spray-on product called Rosinit. It remains sufficiently tacky to remove and replace picks several times and still keep them glued securely to the fingertips. Yet, some vigorous rubbing will remove all trace without the need to wash. I've also heard bowler's rosin products will work. I tried a popular product called Gorilla Snot but found it somewhat greasy and not very tacky.

Picks – Who Needs 'Em?

Lastly, I should mention that, for some, this whole discussion is superfluous. Mark Fackeldey, Adam Miller, Mike Herr, and Skip Beltz are but several who get a marvelous and unique sound using just fingers and nails. The former two will, like as not, be sporting miracle constructs of manicurist's products and super glue – a process much more involved than the mere donning of picks. The bare fingered also run the risk of painful blisters. But the reward is a uniquely haunting tone from the 'harp and wider possibilities for intricate play.

Take Your Pick!

Whatever your personal choice for tickling your 'harp strings may be, I've no doubt that you will continue to harbor an interest in new developments in the world of picks that will help keep your playing fresh, diverse, and entertaining for yourself and others. Keep looking and keep experimenting. You'll discover new possibilities. ❖

Pick Sources

Alaska Pik, ProPick, Herco, Kelly Speed Pick, Dunlop:
Autoharp Quarterly, The Marketplace
PO Box 336
New Manchester, WV 26056-0336
http://www.fmp.com/aq

National, Ernie Ball, Golden Gate, ProPick:
Reid's Instrument Shop
71 W. Main Street
Mechanicsburg, PA 17055
– and acoustic music stores nationwide

John Pearse:
Breezy Ridge Instruments, Ltd
PO Box 295
Center Valley, PA 18034

Dunlop, Herco:
http://www.jimdunlop.com/picks

Kelly Speed Pick:
Fred Kelly
PO Box 532
Grayling, MI 49738

Alaska Pik:
St. Maries, ID

Acri:
http://www.acri@junction.net

Bogardus:
Tom's Musical Supplies
2309 Anderson
Lawrence, KS 66046

Drew Smith Thumbpick:
Great All-American
Autoharp Emporium
529 Ardmore Road,
Ho-Ho-Kus, NJ 07423

Sitar:
Roz Brown
High Echo Lake Productions
PO Box 150518
Lakewood, CO 80215

Learning To Play The Autoharp

AQ Volume VI, Number 1

SOME OBSERVATIONS ON LEARNING

Lindsay Haisley

One of the common complaints of students of any musical discipline is "I'm stuck in a rut." I've been there myself on many occasions. One keeps playing the same tunes, or playing new tunes in the same old style, and after a while it all starts to sound and feel a tad monotonous. I'd like to share with you a few of my observations about the learning process and make some suggestions which may help you move forward if you feel that you're stuck.

First, I ought to say that everyone's "learning curve" in music is not a straight line, but a series of plateaus. This is true for both virtuosi and novices, and is a principle which applies to most forms of learning and growth. We grow (musically, physically, intellectually, etc.) in spurts. After each spurt our brains and bodies take the time to integrate our growth before proceeding to another plateau. Another observation I've made is that frequently the times when we feel the most limited or constrained by being in a rut are the times when we are closest to a breakthrough – the times to be sure that we persevere.

I've been told (and repeated to others more times than I can remember) that every creative discipline has three components – wonder, anger, and technique. Everyone who has fallen in love with music understands wonder, and anyone who has practiced hard to master something difficult understands technique, but anger? Struggling against one's musical limitations is frustrating – and anger is the emotional answer to frustration. Anger is not comfortable and we tend to avoid situations which make us angry. As a result, we often avoid confronting our musical limitations head on, and confront them we must if we want to keep growing musically. The more we feel the beauty of the music we *could* make, the more we throw ourselves against our limits trying to get there. The alternative is to fall back on familiar patterns, stay stuck in a rut and feel vaguely dissatisfied or even bored with our own music.

Here are some suggestions which may help you out of a musical rut. They've worked for me, and for friends and students:

1. Examine just what it is that dissatisfies you about your playing and address some very rational energy to the subject. If, for instance, you find you're only using two or three picking or strumming patterns, listen to the playing of others whose picking or strumming you like, analyze their work, make yourself up some exercises and practice them. Once you've learned some "licks" in this way, try incorporating them into your own style.

2. Practice regularly. When you're trying to make advances in your own style of playing, it's often best to practice alone so that you can feel comfortable doing anything you think is appropriate for your learning. One of the things I keep coming back to in this regard is the way we progress from rational understanding of a technique to its intuitive mastery. This is a fascinating experience which everyone who studied music has had. One learns a new technique move by move, note by note, placing each one in the proper sequence and time with very conscious intent. As we practice the technique in this manner, it becomes easier and more automatic. At some point we stop thinking about it, which frees our brains to start listening to what we are doing with our musical selves – and sometimes quite suddenly, almost as if a switch were thrown in our heads, our musical selves seize upon the technique, take our conscious minds out of the loop, and we're off and playing. For those who have never had the experience, let me tell you that it's a real primal thrill! It's important at this point to come back to the mechanical repetition of pattern from time to time in private practice to keep the new technique well and consciously sharpened.

3. It can be helpful to work hard at mastering something which is totally beyond your abilities, assuming you understand and appreciate the music and the techniques involved. What you will find is that while you may not (and indeed may never) master this particular piece or technique, bits and pieces of the experience you gain in the effort will show up in other things which you play.

4. Playing with others can be really helpful. Other 'harpists will give you ideas for your own playing, while musicians on other instruments may inspire you with tunes, styles or other ways of hearing familiar music.

The important thing *not* to do when you feel frustrated with your musical progress is nothing. Anything positive which you can do to change your practice habits, excite you about new music, sharpen your skills, etc. will help. Refusing to confront the steep portion of one's learning curve is, on the other hand, decidedly nonproductive.

As an aside to this, I frequently hear people say "Well he/she plays so well it just makes me want to quit playing." This unfortunate attitude can be found in people involved in all kinds of creative arts, but is probably encouraged to a greater degree among autoharpists by the emphasis on competitions in the autoharp world. Music in its most fundamental nature is noncompetitive. Baseball is competitive. Chess is competitive. These are games. Music is not a game, it's a creative process, and as such is an expression of each individual's musical feelings. If you come across someone who plays well, you should view it as an opportunity to learn, and to experience something beautiful, rather than a competition which you've already lost. If you experience every musical encounter as a contest you won't enjoy your music very much, although if you become technically proficient you may enjoy winning contests.

This is not to diminish the value of music contests as opportunities for learning. The prospect of winning a new instrument is a mighty fine carrot at the end of a stick, and can incite one to practice diligently (or even frantically) in preparation. However, one's music, like one's child, has a life of its own beyond any agenda which we may have for it, and the real carrot at the end of the stick is the beautiful music which we can make and appreciate and which enriches our lives. A famous musician once said "Music is not just notes, rhythm, and dynamics; music is the presence of possibility." I think that comes pretty close to the ultimate carrot! ❖

OCTOBER ❖ 1994 VOLUME SEVEN ❖ NUMBER ONE FIVE ❖ DOLLARS

AUTOHARP QUARTERLY

THE • MAGAZINE • DEDICATED • TO • THE • AUTOHARP • ENTHUSIAST

IN THIS ISSUE

A STONEMAN FAMILY ALBUM

❖

AUTOHARP'S MEG PETERSON — FOR ALL SEASONS Part One

❖

WHEN IT HURTS TO PLAY

❖

MOUNTAIN LAUREL AUTOHARP GATHERING HIGHLIGHTS

❖

INTERACTION with Tina Louise Barr

❖

PICKER'S PORTRAIT with Willow Skye Robinson

❖

'HARPMONICS — A SOLUTION?

❖ ❖ ❖ ERNEST V. "POP" STONEMAN ❖ ❖ ❖

AQ Volume IX, Number 4

FINDING THE MELODY

Lindsay Haisley

Finding The Melody

You've become tired of taking a back seat to the guitars, banjos, and fiddles when it's time to play a tune. You and your autoharp would love to shine when it's your turn to "Take it!" I'd like to help you to do just that. Follow me through these steps, and you're on your way!

We can define two sets of chords for a piece of music. The first set consists of the chords that go with the music: those which a rhythm guitarist (or autoharpist) would play, we'll call rhythm chords. If you play from sheet music or from a music book, these chords will frequently be written above or below the music line at the rate of about one change every measure or two. The second set of chords is that set which we use to pick out the melody notes on the autoharp. These are the chords which contain the individual notes of the melody and are pressed on the autoharp so that an individual melody note can be plucked while the notes on either side of it are damped out. We'll call these melody chords.

Look at Figure 1. The topmost line of letters represents a C major scale. The topmost line of chord names next to the designation "Common Chords" is the simplest sequence of melody chords we can play which contains the C major scale. In playing a melody on the 'harp we are often changing melody chords with every note.

The interplay between melody chords and rhythm chords can be quite complex. As Figure 1 shows, we have a choice of chords to use as melody chords for any particular note we may play. If one were able to pick out a melody precisely without slopping over to adjacent open strings, it wouldn't matter what chords were used, and the simplest sequence would be adequate for all melodies which stay on the major scale notes. This is frequently neither possible nor desirable, and usually each melody note is accompanied by at least a fragment of the chord used to play it. (It's best to make the melody note the highest note in this chord fragment since our ears tend to identify the melody with the highest note in any group of notes played together.) Thus we need to take care that our melody chords are harmonious with the music as a whole. Arranging a melody for autoharp often presents us with many choices of chord sequences, and there is no "right" sequence to use for a particular song. Some sequences sound better than others. Some sound quite creative. Sometimes there is little or no difference between the choices for a particular note. As a rule of thumb for beginning arrangers, always use the melody chord which coincides with the rhythm chord at that point when there is an opportunity to do so.

You'll find it most useful to start by using the chart below to help you label your music with chords.

So much for theory. Let's proceed to the techniques of melody picking on the 'harp itself. Look at the piece, "Oh, Susanna" on the next page. Start by picking a single note melody. Use your middle finger and dip into the strings and out again. Think of actually pulling the note out of the 'harp. If you use a brush stroke parallel to the 'harp it's difficult to gain the accuracy necessary to play a clean melody. Don't play rhythm with your melody yet. Try to keep the melody line simple and clean, sounding only single notes.

The next step is a pinch using the thumb and middle finger. Aim for an octave pinch, even though all the necessary notes may not be there in the lower octave. Use the same technique, coming into the strings with your hand and pulling out the notes as if you were pulling them away from the face of the 'harp.

The thumb can be difficult to coordinate in picking out melodies. Try picking out the melody just with the thumb using the same picking technique of "pulling away."

Now here's a tricky one. The best autoharp players use this technique to

Figure 1

Melody Chords For The Key Of C Major

Note:	c	d	e	f	g	a	b
Common Chords:	C C^7 F	G G^7	C C^7	F G^7 C C^7	G G^7	F Am	G G^7
Not So Common Chords:	Am F^7	Dm Gm	Em Am	F^7 Dm	Em	Dm	Em
Chords Useful In The Circle Of Fiths:	D^7 B^7	D^7 D	E^7 E	G^7	A^7	A^7 A	E^7 E
Unusual Chords:	B♭			B♭	B^7		B^7

Figure 2

Oh I come from Al - a bam - a with my ban - jo on my knee
C
G7
TAB
etc.

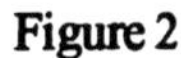

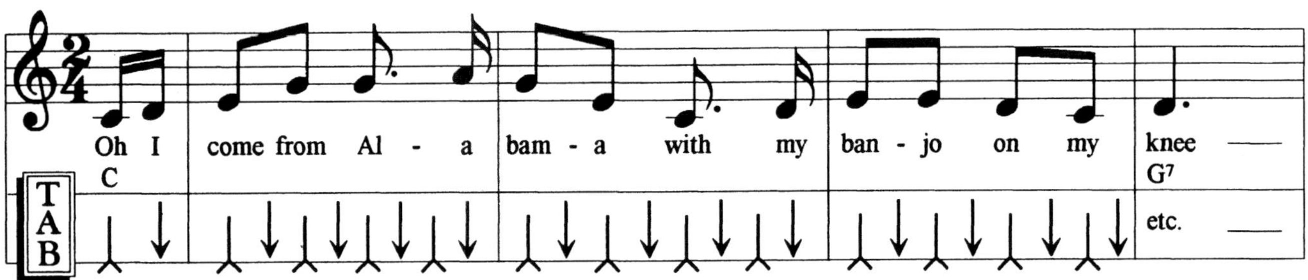

Figure 3

Oh Susanna

Oh I come from Al - a bam - a with my ban - jo on my knee
C G7 C / / F C / / G7 C / G7 C G7
TAB
I'm a goin' to Louis - i - a - na my — true love for to see.
C G7 C / / F C / / G7 C / G7 / C
TAB
Oh, Su - san - ah, oh don't you cry for me, For I
F / / / / C / / / G7 C G7
TAB
come from Al - a - bam - a with my ban - jo on my knee.
C / / G7 C / / G7 C / G7 / C
TAB

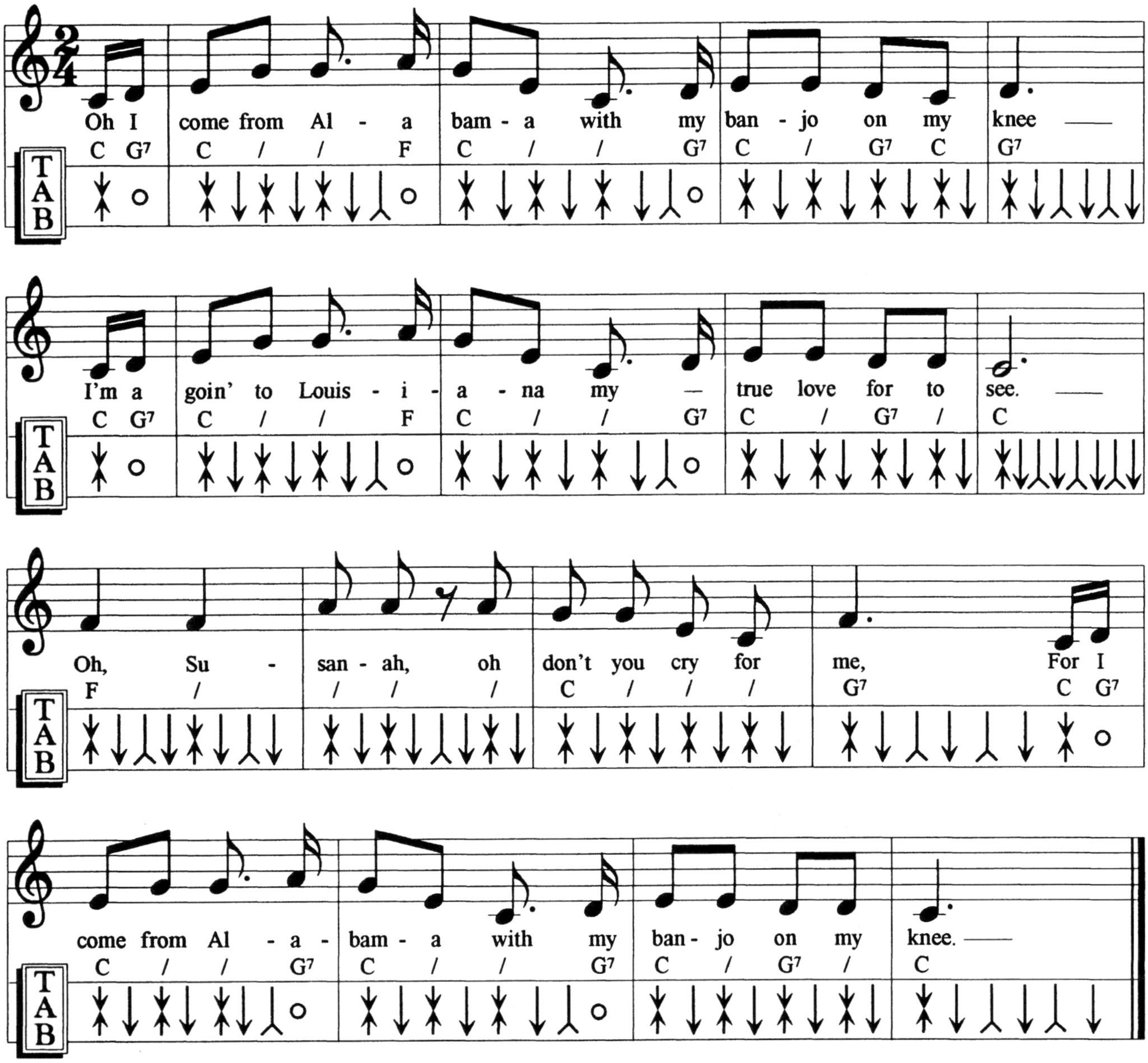

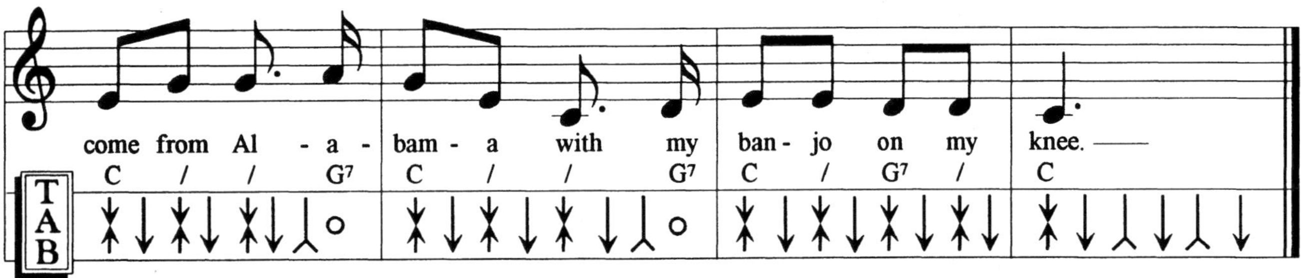

Tablature

= Pinch
= Pluck
= Strum with thumb
= Strum with index

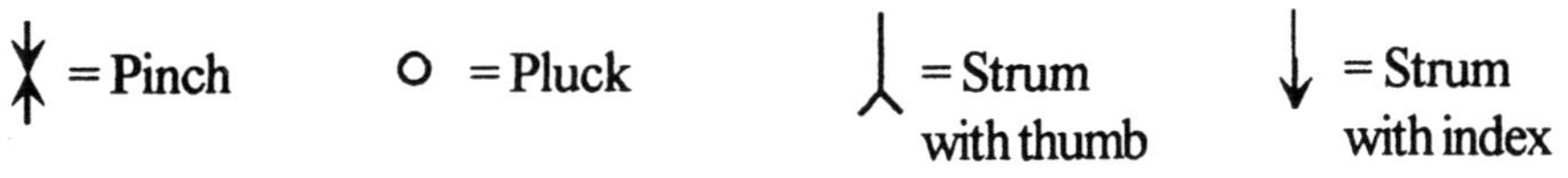

play very fast runs on the 'harp. Pick the melody out with your thumb, but whenever you get to a sixteenth note, play it with your index finger. This means you are playing two or three notes in quick succession, alternating between your thumb and index fingers. Remember to keep your fingers moving on the chord bars at the same speed. If you practice, you can play a whole series of notes this way. This technique is called "cross picking" and is excellent for fiddle tunes and such. Listen to Bonnie Phipps' album, *Autoharpin'*. She is a master of this technique.

A sixteenth note has two flags on its stem:

or

Let's add some rhythm to the thumb melody. Get your finger going back and forth over the strings, so that you're playing "Oh Susanna." (See Figure 2)

The tablature here doesn't tell you much except that your fingers are keeping up a sixteenth note rhythm. Let your thumb and index finger pick out the melody as in the previous exercise. When your thumb or index finger isn't playing a melody note on a particular stroke, let it brush lightly on the strings just above the melody notes. This will add a sense of the rhythm and chords to the piece.

Finally, let your middle finger and thumb pick out the melody notes with an octave pinch (or a wider pinch if you're in the mood for a *big* sound), and let your thumb and index finger brush the strings in between in the sixteenth note rhythm in the last exercise. (See Figure 3) Don't try to pinch on the sixteenth notes in the melody, but let your middle finger carry them alone. This will keep your thumb in an even rhythm.

Start with a simple melody, and work up to speed. If you practice this method, you'll be ready to "Take it away!" when the fiddler nods to you during your next jam. ❖

For a different approach to this subject, see "Playing By Ear" p.94.

Playing By Ear

AQ Volume III, Number 1

RIGHT BRAIN ON, LEFT BRAIN OFF

Alan Mager

Music And Your Brain

The two halves of your brain function in distinctly different ways. The left side of the brain deals with things that have distinct names, defined shapes, and measurable sizes – things that can be dealt with precisely, logically, or mathematically. The right side of the brain deals more with the quality of things – sounds, colors, spatial relationships, feelings – without necessarily assigning names or values to them. In short, the right side of the brain is creative, and the left side is logical.

Playing music is essentially a right brain activity. It is the putting together of a sequence of tones to create a sensation for the listener of pleasure, sadness, confusion, uneasiness, or any of the endless list of other emotions. The names and values of the tones in the music are absolutely irrelevant to the desired result.

Written music was developed so people could pass their musical creations on to others. Of necessity, the process of writing music gives names and values to individual sounds. If you are one of the many people who have learned to play the autoharp or another instrument by using written music, you may have the notion that you can't play by ear. This is because you have transformed music into a left brain activity. To play by ear, you must turn off the left brain and let the sounds, rather than their names and values, guide you.

The process is a lot like learning to drive a car. When you first learned to drive, you and your instructor verbalized (assigned values to) all the actions needed to make the car do what you wanted. "Depress the accelerator." "Shift into second gear." "Turn on your left directional signal." Your instructor said these things to you, and/or you said them to yourself. But once you gained experience, you performed these tasks without expressing them verbally, and you were able to drive without "thinking" about it. Actually, the right brain took over the activity and allowed you to drive better than you ever could if you had continued to let the left brain analyze every move before you let yourself perform it.

You can learn to play music in the same way – by learning to shut off the left brain and letting the right brain do what it does best. You may be surprised to know that you can already play flawlessly by ear. Take a moment and sing or hum "Happy Birthday," or some other familiar song to yourself. Did you make a mistake? Probably not. Did you think of the names or values of the notes as you sang them? Definitely not! You have just played music by ear using your voice as the instrument.

Now let's try to do the same thing with the autoharp. Find a recorded version of a piece of music you'd like to learn. Start with something simple – most folk songs, fiddle tunes, and Carter Family songs fall into this category. First you'll have to play the recorded song over and over until you have it in your head, that is, until you can hum or sing it on your own. Then you'll be ready to transfer the tune to the autoharp. Here are my suggestions for accomplishing this.

Step One
Determine The Rhythm

Push down two or three chord bars that block out all the strings on your instrument. Then strum along with the recorded song as it plays over and over. Almost all music is based on a system of two or three beats (or multiples thereof). Keep strumming along notelessly until you have worked out a nice, comfortable rhythm accompaniment to the song.

Step Two
Determine The Key

As the recording plays over and over, listen for the chord sound at the end of the piece and at the end of sections of the piece (such as the A and B parts of a fiddle tune). Try to match this sound to one of the major chords on your autoharp. Most music in major keys ends on the tonic chord, the chord that has the same name as the key in which the music is played. If you determine, for example, that your song ends on a G Major chord, then the tune is probably in the key of G Major.

The vast majority of folk tunes can be played using only three chords – the major chords based on the first, fourth, and fifth notes of the scale. These chords are often designated by the roman numerals I, IV, and V. Very often the V^7 chord can be used interchangeably with the V chord – it's usually just a matter of personal preference, depending on which sound you like better. The chart below shows the I, IV, and V chords for the most common autoharp keys. (Please excuse this little excursion to the left side of the brain. We won't stay long! You could find the chords you need by matching sounds, but the chart makes it easier. It's really OK to use the left brain for the things it's best at doing. Just be careful that it doesn't try to organize, label, and calculate the whole process.)

KEY	CHORDS		
	I	IV	V (V^7)
E	E	A	B (B^7)
A	A	D	E (E^7)
D	D	G	A (A^7)
G	G	C	D (D^7)
C	C	F	G (G^7)
F	F	B♭	C (C^7)
B♭	B♭	E♭	F (F^7)

Step Three
Work out the chord changes

Position three fingers on the buttons of the chords you'll be using, so you won't have to go hunting for them. Now play along with the recording. Start by using the I chord. Conveniently, the I chord is usually the first as well as the last chord in a piece of music. When you hear a change in the sound of the music, switch to one of the other two chords (IV or V) and try to match the sound on the recording. At first you may have difficulty hearing the changes the instant they occur. What you will more likely notice is, at some point, the chord you're playing sounds wrong. This means a chord change has occurred. Change quickly to one of the other chords and try to match the sound. If you miss a chord change, don't worry, and don't stop the recording. Let it play on through, while you play along as best you can. As you replay the song again and again, you will work out the problem areas one by one.

It may go slowly on the first few songs you try, but keep at it, and you'll soon find that you'll hear the chord changes more easily. Eventually, you'll be able to anticipate changes before they occur. One day, when trying to learn a new song, you'll surprise yourself by not only anticipating the changes, but by knowing which chord will be needed next.

Song lyrics can often be helpful in working out chord patterns and in pinpointing places where changes occur. In "Happy Birthday," for example, the first chord change (to V or V^7), takes place on the first occurrence of the word "you." If you get used to making the chord change on that word, you'll never miss it as long as you sing the song to yourself as you play.

Before going on to the next step, keep playing the tune until you're comfortable with its entire chord pattern. At this point, you will be playing what are called "rhythm chords," which are the minimum chords needed to accompany voice or another instrument that is playing the melody.

Step Four
Find the Melody.

In most folk tunes, the melody notes can all be found in the I, IV, and V (or V^7) chords. While playing along in one of the rhythm chords, you'll frequently have to switch to another chord to get a melody note. The process for working this out is virtually the same as the process for determining rhythm chords. It starts with trial and error, but fortunately the possibilities are very limited. If the note you need isn't in the rhythm chord, there are only two other choices.

As a first experiment in melody playing, take a simple song you already know well and for which you have worked out the rhythm chords. (Songs like "Happy Birthday" or "Twinkle, Twinkle, Little Star" are good choices because their melodies are second nature to you.) Find each melody note and play the tune over and over until the pattern is etched in your brain. Here again, the words to a song can be used as powerful cues to chord changes needed for melody notes.

Remember the pattern you are learning is simply the relationship of the fingers pushing the chord buttons. Don't learn the pattern by assigning chord names or numbers to the buttons as you push them – this tends to force the learning experience back to the left side of the brain.

After working out several songs by tedious trial and error, you should begin to see patterns developing for melody playing. Eventually, you will be able to anticipate the correct chord to use to obtain a specific note.

Finally, it's not magic. It takes lots of practice. But it's possible for everyone to play by ear. Once you've begun to master the basic skills, your musical ability will grow many times faster than it would have by sticking solely to the confining world of written music. ❖

Preparing For An Autoharp Contest

AQ Volume VIII, Number 2

MUSICKING THE AUTOHARP
A CONTESTANT'S POINT OF VIEW

Lucille Reilly

There are no magic formulas for contests. Each one depends on who competes, who judges, the weather... Lucille Reilly, a Champion of both the Mountain Laurel and International Autoharp Contests, gives us some insights and advice which may be helpful, whether you perform or go the extra mile to compete.

Play what you love. It'll certainly come across! And if those pieces have all the technical and imaginative stuff you're known for, so much the better. (More on technique and imagination in a moment.)

Choose tunes that make the autoharp sing. You've discovered you can play "My Melancholy Baby," but now ask yourself: How does it make the 'harp sound? If it sounds tinny or "grovely," hoist a red flag. Go for pieces which play up the autoharp's sweetness and resonance.

Many of my favorite dance tunes on the dulcimer make the autoharp vibrate beyond melodic recognition. (I love sustain, but it does have its limits.) If a massive, multi-tone ring occurs too often and there's no way to break it so the melody can clearly sing over it, I look for other tunes that dance and sing.

Choose tunes that fit the event. Many of us contestants base our tune choices on what we think will catch the judges' ears. It often doesn't work and is usually frustrating. So, for the 1995 International Championship I took a different approach: I asked, "Does this tune *feel like* the Walnut Valley Festival?" (What a question!) I find there is a difference between the "Mountain Laurel Autoharp Gathering sound" and the "Walnut Valley sound." And I've come to realize the judges' only agenda is musical music, not whether one tune is "better" than another.

Play what you play well. It's wise to play tunes in a contest that you've played for a while (meaning anything from a month to a year, depending on your skill level and size of tune cache).

I know about 500 dance tunes on the hammered dulcimer, have noodled with "remodeling" tunes since high school, and have played many contra dances with some wonderfully inventive pianists. Thusly armed (and hammered), I made a daredevil attempt for the 1995 International Championship: I learned a new piece *three weeks* before the contest. (Why? I felt like it!) The only reason I took the risk was because I'd arranged the tune long ago on the dulcimer, making a respectable autoharp arrangement quick to come by.

On the other hand, *one week* before the contest, I discovered yet another dulcimer tune that sounded like a winner. This one I resisted, because there wasn't enough time to become comfortable with its technical demands, even though the arrangement was well in my ear. It became, however, a pleasant diversion from contest pieces that last week, and is now on my performance list.

Years ago I read the biography of a pianist who said that, at least two weeks before his first performance of a work, he finalized all its technical and musical details. It's advice I live by (and you can now see that a two-week cutoff for my new contest tune left one week to complete the arrangement – quite dangerous!). Arranging a tune beyond its basic melody chords takes its own time and can't be rushed. I find that a new tune needs to be in my ear at least two weeks before the arrangement process can begin.

Play for the audience. A contest is also a con*cert*, so consider tunes the audience will enjoy. My two pieces for each round are usually in different keys, and if they're not, I make sure the pace of each is different. How will you know what will appeal to the audience? See the next point!

Play "experienced" tunes. Your contest tunes should be those you've performed elsewhere, preferably for three or four separate audiences. Listen to their responses. If every group swoons over one piece in particular, it could be a winner.

I played my "three-week rush job" for friends and students, and for a church service postlude five days before the contest. It was a close call, but the tune got the "break-in" it needed.

Familiar vs. unknown? While I have been told consistently to play music the judges know, I have just as consistently never done that. Why?

1. Any judge worth his salt better be attentive if I'm doing a good job playing a tune he doesn't know.

2. Every contest is an opportunity to challenge the state of the art, stretching the limits of the instrument, repertoire, and performer.

Familiarity may be more important for songs, but that hasn't been an issue for me as a diatonic 'harpist playing dance music. *Feel* in the dance music I play is the higher priority, followed by melodic and harmonic development.

The art of imagination. Imagination works on three levels. The first, tune choice, is only the beginning. The second, establishing a basic melody-chord progression, is also a beginning stage. Think again if you believe these are enough, then go to the third level: How will you *develop* this novel tune so it sounds even more novel *and* musical?

My dulcimer/piano dance band keeps getting this comment about our music from one of our fans: "It's like you're telling a story." Now that I think of it, all of my autoharp arrangements tell stories, too. Contest rules suggest kudos for a story line as well: In both the Mountain Laurel and International Autoharp contests, 40 points go for arrangement, 20 for playing in tune, and another 20 are designated for dynamics and expression. Because the autoharp either is or is not in tune, you automatically have 20 points in or out of your favor. As for dynamics and expression, to me, these are just two of the many elements of arranging.

There's no real "cookie cutter" approach to the art of arranging that works for sure. Each tune speaks to me a little differently as to where its story line will go. For example, I've found the number of repetitions I ultimately give a tune once I've arranged it varies from one to five. What I *can* tell you is this: I never play through a tune exactly the same way twice. My best arrangements, those that catch the ear and hold on to it beyond the last chord, sometimes fall out of my hands into the 'harp very quickly. But I'm not always that lucky! Most of my arrangements take a week or two to finalize, although some take more time and others take less.

For good tunes whose story line is still forthcoming, I ask along the way: Is the arrangement too short? Too long? Are there too few original ideas? Too many? Does this idea fit here? Or there? Or not at all? I prune and develop, hopefully without overdoing it. The finished product must not sound contrived. (One wonderful jig still resists arranging after several years. This may be because the melody is *too* interesting. Looks like I'll have to continue enjoying that one at home.)

Technique. As you envision your story line, simultaneously focus on the technical details to drive it. Special techniques sound best if they are part of your story line. Avoid sticking them in for the sole purpose of displaying your skills.

Slow each piece down during your practice sessions to get in touch with its fingering. (A metronome can be your best friend here, believe it or not.) Iron out the kinks early on, and let them teach you about fingering for the next tune that comes around. Be sure the melody rings clearly over any filler chords (quiet those filler chords down, too!). And remember to play from your heart at all times. Complete all of this at least two weeks before the performance or contest.

Technical prowess seems to depend on the autoharp you play, too. For my diatonic pick-and-pump style, the right hand is more important than the left. However, the left hand may be more important to playing a chromatic 'harp, (I don't play chromatic 'harp enough to say for sure). Whether you play chromatic or diatonic autoharp, it would be great if your pieces cause the judges to think what a friend of mine exclaimed after he heard one of my contest pieces: "Wait a minute! That isn't possible on an autoharp!"

If I were a judge, a key change wouldn't impress me (the new key often doesn't play differently from the old one), *unless* the chord progression developed further in the new key or the right hand's activity becomes more intricate. An unusual chord here or there would not impress me either (the chord bars are an harmonic *fait accompli*), but an entirely different progression introducing a new kind of harmonic sense could grab my attention.

Play each piece at its natural tempo. A jig played slower than dance tempo, no matter how clean or how many chords are crammed in, wouldn't score high with my ear, but if it dances, oh boy! A waltz played a little slower to allow for lots of passion and melodic frills could also do well. (Admittedly, I've never taken a chance on a slow piece in a contest, and wish they were required for contests, because some beautiful waltzes and such are out there.) If you just play at mach five, be sure the melody remains discernible and rhythmic.

Do something different. Those who reach a contest's final round usually have a different *kind* of sound, regardless of difficulty (and some autoharpists play amazingly simply). The judges do, however, catch on to simplicity in the final round. Can you combine a new sound with dazzling technique, topped off with fun, excitement, passion, etc.?

Play the music first, then the autoharp. The music always starts within the *player*, who conveys it through the autoharp (that goes for fiddle, etc., too). The results are never the same the other way around.

You'll have your best shot at musicality if your fingering is technically up to snuff and if you know what you want each piece to sound and feel like *in your head*. (Loosely translated this means: If you hear blah, you'll play blah!) Sadly, accuracy tends to override musicality in a close race. If I were a judge, I'd excuse a glitch or two if the message behind the music sings and speaks to my soul clearly.

Nerves. They almost never bother me at concerts, but that's because no one judges concerts. To overcome jitters, these last three points may help:

1. There is no luck in this: You say the luck of the draw makes a difference? When I took third place at Winfield in 1994, I was "Contestant Number One" in the preliminaries, and was stunned to be called back for the final round. I learned then it doesn't matter where you are in the lineup if your arrangements and playing are *hot*!

2. Internal drive: In 1995, I did something I've never done before: I didn't play any of my pieces the day of the contest! (I ran through the Mountain Laurel Autoharp Gathering pieces at 10a.m. for a 7p.m. contest.) I reasoned that I never practice up to the last minute before a concert, so why do it at a contest? After a warm-up on technically similar tunes, I put my 'harp down, closed my eyes and *in my mind* "played through" only the two tunes for the preliminary round, instead of all five (including two for the finals plus one in case of a dreaded tie-breaker). If a tune fell apart there, I mentally rehearsed that spot again. (By the way, this is a great way to practice on an airplane trip, a long drive, gardening, etc.)

3. One moment at a time: I prepared in advance to enjoy each note as it occurred, not considering what the judges think, or about winning, because...

The message is all-important. Music has the power to touch the soul in ways that no other art can. Touch souls and you will have won much, for the greatest prize is a supreme compliment thankfully given. ❖

AQ Volume VII, Number 1

WHEN IT HURTS TO PLAY

Catherine W. Britell, M.D.

Medical Complications When Playing The Autoharp

Most autoharp players have experienced discomfort in their shoulders, arms, wrists, or hands at some time, and occasionally are bothered so much by pain in one or both upper extremities that their playing is severely impaired. It seems that holding the 'harp and performing rapid repetitive motions, such as picking/plucking/strumming or quickly depressing successive chord bar buttons, often make preexisting problems more bothersome. Factors important in causing upper extremity pain include mechanical characteristics and support of the instrument, genetic makeup and bone structure, conditioning and strength, positioning and style of playing, and overall stress levels.

Conditions that I have seen in autoharp players and other musicians who perform similar upper extremity movements have included the following:

1. Trapezius muscle spasm
2. Biceps tendinitis
3. Forearm tendinitis
4. Compartment syndrome of the forearm (pronator syndrome)
5. Carpal Tunnel Syndrome (median nerve entrapment at the wrist)
6. De Quervain's Syndrome (tendinitis of the thumb extensors)

What do all these names mean? In the following, I'll explain what each of these conditions is, and review some ways of preventing and treating them.

Figure 1a

Figure 1b

PHOTOGRAPHS BY CATHERINE BRITELL

A slouched posture (1a) while playing causes overwork and spasm of the muscles at the back of the neck and in the upper back. Bringing the head and shoulders into balance (1b) will allow the neck and back muscles to relax and increase playing stamina and comfort.

Trapezius Spasm

This is a spasm of the superficial muscles connecting the shoulder girdle and base of the skull to the backbone, and is generally the place where that back rub feels oh-so-good. This often happens in people who play under stress, who don't have the 'harp supported properly by a strap, and/or who assume awkward neck and shoulder positions when playing. One significant factor in causing trapezius pain is a "slouched" posture – curving the upper part of the spine forward to reach around the 'harp. (Fig. 1a) This tends to make the upper back and neck muscles work much harder than usual to hold up the significant weight of the head. As a result, the muscles have to maintain a hard contraction over a long period of time, thereby not allowing blood to circulate to the muscle adequately and causing a lack of nutrients and oxygen and a build-up of waste products. The result is muscle pain.

By straightening the upper spine, (Fig. 1b) one balances the head. The neck and upper back muscles are then allowed to relax, thereby allowing optimal circulation and maintenance of muscle nutrition and oxygenation. Probably the most important thing one can do to improve the posture and increase comfort of the neck and back muscles is to get a good strap that supports the 'harp in the most comfortable playing position. Some people really like the Slider strap for its uniform support, while others feel that a plain leather or webbing strap is better.

It's also important to avoid bending the head and neck to the side when playing the 'harp (Fig. 2a). This is sometimes a challenge for short people who play the 'harps that are built without a curve toward the treble side. It's often a good idea to stand facing a mirror to check to see that your nose and your umbilicus line up in a straight line (Fig. 2b) while playing, and to carefully adjust your strap to make your head position comfortable.

Another important factor in the development of trapezius spasm is tension while playing. Any time we become nervous or tense, we tend to contract the muscles in our upper back and neck into a hard mass. This may be a primitive protective reflex used by our ancestors to protect the spinal cord and other vital structures while being chased by large carnivorous animals. Since we seldom play the autoharp in the company of lions and tigers these days, this reflex doesn't do us much good. It's a good idea every now and then to shrug your shoulders, take stock of the tension in them, and make a conscious effort to keep them relaxed even while playing the most challenging tunes.

The best way, then, to avoid those upper back and neck pains is to make sure the body and head are well-balanced and that the 'harp is optimally supported, and to "stay loose" even during those fast fiddle tunes. It's better in the long run to use some other excuse to get a back rub.

Figure 2a

Figure 2b

Some players have a tendency to lean over the 'harp and bring the right shoulder up toward the ear; especially when playing something difficult or fast (2a). Keeping the shoulders relaxed and the body in a straight line (2b) will often make the neck and shoulder much more comfortable.

Biceps Tendinitis

The biceps is the large muscle at the front of the upper arm that flexes the elbow (the one that pops up when Popeye eats spinach). Many times, pain and inflammation develop in the tendon where the muscle attaches to the shoulder. This seems particularly to be a problem for people who play hard using thumb lead, but has also plagued some famous finger players. The key here also seems to be support of the instrument. It's very important not to have to keep tension in the biceps for holding the instrument in place while at the same time doing the fine movements of picking or fingering the instrument. This combination seems to invite biceps tendinitis. The cause of tendinitis seems to be ischemia, or a decreased blood supply to the junction of the muscle and tendon. This happens when a muscle is kept under tension without relaxation for a long period of time. That area where the biceps muscle attaches to the tendon is not terribly well-vascularized, and this prolonged contraction causes buildup of carbon dioxide, increased acidity, and leakage of fluid and cells out of the pores of the blood vessels. This process is called "acute inflammation" and leads to soreness and swelling of the area. Then, of course, the swelling and inflammation cause the tendon not to slide in its sheath as well as it should, and there is more pain and more inflammation...a vicious cycle that can be devastating to a committed 'harper. Again, the best prevention of this problem is proper support of the instrument by a strap (or for some individuals on the lap), with the hands and arms entirely free of supporting the instrument. The treatment for biceps tendinitis includes rest, followed by strengthening, and most importantly correcting the mechanics of holding the instrument and playing. Usually the physician will prescribe a potent anti-inflammatory medication for a short time if not contraindicated by any other conditions. Sometimes deep heating with ultrasound hastens the healing process.

Tendinitis Of The Forearm

This is an inflammation of the tendons where the muscles insert into them and where they insert into the bone at the elbow and is most usually seen on the extensor side of the forearm. It is often characterized by a sharp pain just below the elbow when extending the fingers and wrist under stress – a condition called "lateral epicondylitis" or "tennis elbow." The mechanism of injury is similar to that of biceps tendinitis; and instrument support and muscle strength are of major importance here. It seems that in this area, one can actually make the tendon insertions less vulnerable to injury by gradually strengthening the muscles and loading the tendons and tendon insertions. This probably has to do with orientation and cross-linking of the collagen fibers (the chemical building blocks) of the tendons. Rest, possibly a short course of anti-inflammatory medications, and a compulsive strengthening program work very well for this condition. The major problem I have in treating many of my patients is motivation to keep up with the exercise program. If it stops hurting, people tend to stop treating it.

Another thing that can be very useful in preventing tendinitis in the left forearm is maximizing the efficiency of action of the chord bar mechanism. Most mass-produced 'harps have chord bars that sit very high off the strings and require an unnecessarily long excursion of the bar in order to damp the strings. This problem is often compounded by sloppiness in the action and resultant variable angle of depression. In addition, worn or uneven felts require even greater pressure to effectively damp the strings. In the excellent article entitled "Bars – Where the Action Is,"[1] you will learn, step by step, how to make your bars maximally easy to work, no matter what kind of 'harp you play. Taking the steps outlined in that article will not only make your left hand and arm much more comfortable, but also will improve your playing immeasurably.

Figure 3a

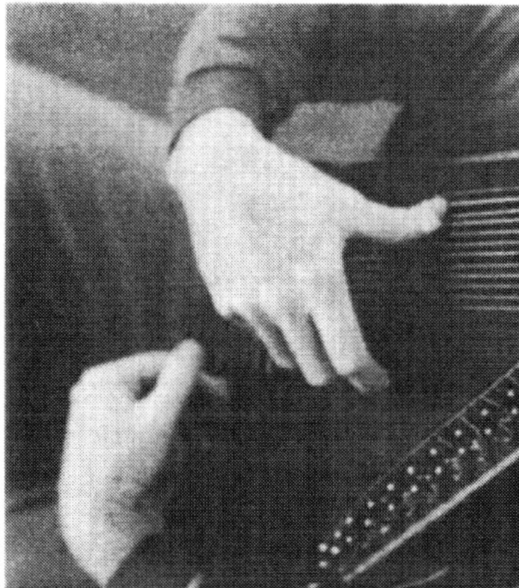

Figure 3b

Excessive flexion of the wrists "reaching back" toward the 'harp (3a) will sometimes aggravate symptoms of carpal tunnel syndrome. Playing with the wrists in a more neutral position (3b) may help prevent numbness and tingling in people who have this problem.

Compartment Syndromes And Pronator Syndrome

As we have seen, overuse of any muscle will cause a decrease in blood supply and nutrients and buildup of waste products. If this is severe, the muscles will swell. Since many muscles reside in firm connective tissue envelopes or "compartments," swelling can cause them to be choked in those compartments, causing pain, further decrease in blood flow, and also pressure on the nerves nearby, which leads to numbness and tingling. There are some muscles that, even though they aren't too tightly enclosed, lie in strategic positions in relation to the nerves, and swelling of them can cause some very uncomfortable nerve compression. One such muscle is the pronator teres (lying across the inside of the forearm just below the elbow). This muscle rotates the wrist and thumb in toward the body and comes into play a great deal when doing thumb lead playing.

Pronator syndrome is particularly common in people who don't play regularly and then go out and jam for an entire weekend. It can often be avoided by practicing regularly and knowing when to stop playing even though you're having a great time. Again, rest followed by slow controlled strengthening is the best way to treat this condition.

Carpal Tunnel Syndrome

Carpal tunnel syndrome (CTS) is an entrapment of the median nerve as it passes through a ligamentous passage in the wrist formed by the wrist bones and the transverse carpal ligament. It is characterized by numbness in the thumb, index, middle, and half of the ring finger, and is often associated with pain in the hand and wrist, sometimes radiating up the forearm. This is a common condition, mostly resulting from the genetically-determined size and shape of the bones and ligaments in the wrist. CTS seldom actually results from playing the autoharp – for the most part, it is a preexisting problem which is aggravated on the left side by flexion of the wrist with added pressure over the left edge of the harp to reach the chord buttons. CTS in the right hand often becomes symptomatic while using the right thumb and fingers in a pinching motion with excessive wrist flexion. The unifying theme here is excessive wrist flexion. This is often caused by keeping the shoulders back while playing and flexing the wrists to reach the chord bars and strings (Fig. 3a) rather than allowing the scapulae (wing-bones) to move forward to bring the arms around the 'harp and allow the wrists to remain in a neutral position (Fig. 3b).

If you have mild CTS, you can probably avoid symptoms by supporting and holding the 'harp properly. In general, hand and wrist splints are not useful, and will tend to alter the mechanics of the hand and wrist so as to significantly interfere with playing and cause discomfort in the shoulder and neck. People who have very severe CTS will probably experience numbness and tingling no matter how they modify their 'harp playing and body mechanics, and will have these same symptoms with many other activities and sometimes even at rest. Often the only thing to do in this case is to have the transverse carpal ligament surgically released by a skilled hand surgeon. This surgery, even when successful, is not completely benign, however. It is important to note that carpal tunnel release will decrease grip strength and if done on the left side will most likely make chording with the thumb difficult if not impossible for a number of months or possibly permanently. This may necessitate a chord bar arrangement that minimizes thumb use. A right carpal tunnel release may also significantly hamper thumb lead playing for some time. Most individuals, however, can expect to be playing as well a year after CTS surgery as they did previously, and hopefully with less discomfort.

De Quervain's Syndrome

This is a common condition, and is a tenosynovitis of the thumb, resulting from a narrowing of the common tendon sheath of the abductor pollicis longus and extensor pollicis brevis muscles. (Whew, that's a mouthful!) These are the muscles that pull the thumb out away from the rest of the hand. What one feels is a severe pain at the base of the thumb either on the right side with strumming or pinching, or less commonly on the left side if you use the thumb aggressively to push the chord buttons.

When De Quervain's Syndrome occurs in the right hand, one should first check the hand position. Hitting the strings with the thumb hyperextended (Fig. 4a) tends to transfer force directly

Figure 4a

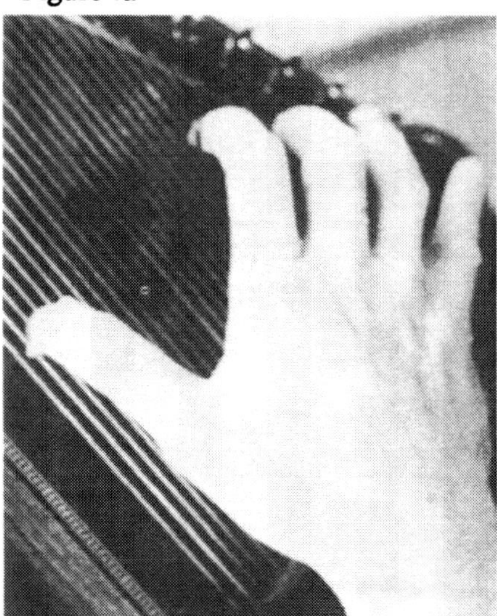

Figure 4b

Hyperextension of the thumb while playing (4a) causes more stress in the thumb joints and tendons than playing with thumb slightly flexed (4b). Additionally, if the entire hand is kept in a relaxed, slightly flexed position (4b), the muscles of the forearm won't have to work nearly as hard, and the forearm tendons will incur less stress.

to the base of the thumb, whereas when one curls the fingers and flexes the thumb slightly (Fig. 4b), the flexor muscles will tend to support and protect the joint. De Quervain's Syndrome may sometimes be alleviated with a change in thumb picks. A pick that stores energy (flexes more) may reduce torque on the joints of the thumb. Also, keeping your strings clean and using Fast Fret string lubricant can sometimes decrease the drag on your thumb pick, thus decreasing trauma to that area.

Rest, anti-inflammatory drugs for a short time if not contraindicated, and strengthening are often recommended for this condition.

General Considerations

There are some simple physical things, then, that one can do to prevent pain while playing. First, make certain your 'harp is supported comfortably in the best position for playing without using your hands or arms – you need those for playing. Second, check your posture and positioning, and see that your back, neck, head, arms, and hands are balanced and relaxed, and in a generally neutral position. Third, make your 'harp as easy to play as possible with clean, slippery strings and optimally functioning chord bars.

It's important, also, to develop a healthy pace of playing. Autoharp playing is a highly demanding athletic activity for the muscles you use, and it's important to warm up adequately. Specifically, it's probably not a good idea to jump into a lightning-fast fiddle tune when you first pick up the 'harp, but rather warm up with a few slow, gentle songs to get those muscles working. Along that line, it's important not to be a "weekend athlete" with the autoharp. If you like to play hard and long on occasion, you need to "keep in shape" by practicing at least 30-45 minutes every other day. If you stay away from playing for more than two consecutive days, you will lose strength and stamina in your muscles and need to build up slowly again. If you simply can't practice on a regular basis, you need to be aware of your own tolerance for playing and fatigue level. This is when you pull out your pennywhistle, mouth harp, or recorder. Use some different muscles for a while.

Tension and stress while playing also need to be minimized. One often becomes stressed when trying to play a tune that is too difficult, too fast, and too early. Lindsay Haisley's article on practice, "Some Observations on Learning,"[2] offers some excellent advice on how to approach the whole issue of practice. Taking seriously the guidelines therein will help prevent "getting in over your head." It also helps to remember that you are doing this for *fun and enjoyment.*

What do you do if you're suffering from pain with playing? If you have addressed the issues outlined above and still hurt, you may need to stop playing altogether for a couple of weeks and learn how to play the pennywhistle. It might be a good idea to see your physician to determine whether anti-inflammatory medications, physical therapy, and an exercise program would be of benefit. Sometimes, anti-inflammatory or pain-relieving agents topically applied to the skin can be quite useful, and this should be explored with your physician. Some physicians recommend steroid injections into the affected area. For most musicians and others using their upper extremities vigorously, I advise strongly against this, because of the tendency of the steroid to weaken the tendon, and make it more vulnerable to rupture – a disastrous complication.

In general, once the pain has subsided, specific exercises to gradually strengthen the affected muscles will be useful in preventing the problem from recurring. ❖

[1] See "Improving The Action Of Chord Bars" p.9.

[2] See "Learning To Play The Autoharp" p.89.

Using Amplification

AQ Volume III, Number 2

PLUG A 'HARP

Lindsay Haisley

Caryl P. Weiss, a singer and songwriter of my acquaintance, recently told me a story that got me thinking. In the midst of the coldest part of an unusually cold East Coast February some years ago, she drove a good distance to play a concert for a folk music society in Maryland. She mounted the stage with her Ovation guitar, the Ovation being a composite of wood and plastic. Upon seeing this, two members of the audience got up and walked out. They'd be darned if they would listen to a folk musician playing a plastic guitar. Caryl, in her inimitable style, gave them a piece of her mind, (the piece in which she keeps the razor blades), and went on with her show. She wasn't about to bring her good Gurion (all wood) guitar out in such weather.

Now I got to thinking, if you think some folks have preconceived ideas about guitars and folk music, by golly, you ought to hear what kind of ideas they have about autoharps and folk music. It's arguable as to whether the autoharp is really a "traditional" instrument at all. With a history of little over 100 years, it's a mere child compared to the violin, the cello, the guitar, the recorder, the banjo, etc. We are the "folk" who are now making the folk tradition that will belong to the instrument three or four hundred years hence.

One of the things I do which causes the traditional folkies a certain amount of angst is to run a wire from my 'harp, in the studio, with a band, or when performing for a sizable audience, and plug into a sound system or amp. I do this for a variety of reasons, not the least of which is that I like the sound I get when I combine the sound of the electric pickup with the acoustic sound received by a microphone. Many modern autoharps, by virtue of their design and construction, are lacking in acoustic "voice," especially in the lower notes. An electric pickup, properly used, can add a richness to the lower notes and an overall fullness which is difficult to obtain simply with a microphone. Some autoharps, such as the Orthey 'harps and the mid-70s 'harps manufactured by Mr. Peterson are somewhat better in this regard. There are still, however, situations in which some sort of amplification is necessary.

But wait, you may say, Maybelle Carter didn't use a pickup! This point is truly made, and it's true also that J. S. Bach didn't use an electronic synthesizer. Bach, in fact, wrote frequently for the pipe organ which is the fluid circuit's equivalent of the electronic synthesizer, and if he'd had one of the latter in his church, I'd lay heavy odds that he would have written music for it as well. What it boils down to is that the real tradition in folk music is an attitude – not a collection of songs, a style of playing, the composition of your instrument, or the path it travels between fingers and ears.

I had an experience in the Ozark Mountains some years ago which brought this home for me. There's a strong music tradition there – visibly and audibly manifested to tourists in many small venues, mountain music concerts, instrument shops, and the like. Much of the music is old-time music – songs derived from the body of music brought in by the original Scots-Irish settlers. However what's really important is the fact that when folks in that part of the country want to get together and have fun – well they don't just buy a six-pack and watch TV! Everyone brings an instrument and they all play music together. One of the most incredible jams I ever took part in was with several people at a small party deep in northern Arkansas. Mark Jones brought his electric bass, Mary and Robert Gillihan brought autoharps, guitars, and their incredible old-time harmonies. I had with me both electric and acoustic, and a couple of other people joined in. Everyone tuned up carefully first and when the music started, we played every kind of song you can imagine – old-time, new-time, Beatles, original, etc. Everyone had a "professional" attitude, (which is to say they put the music first and played from their hearts), even though the setting was strictly "amateur," (which means for the love of it). What more could I have asked? I realized then that the music tradition of the Ozarks was alive and well.

The point of this story, in a roundabout way, is while acoustic instruments may be traditional, electric instruments aren't necessarily antitraditional. This, to some, is a radical point of view. It was more radical in the 1960s, and will be a lot less radical by the year 2050. Then, Chuck Berry will be considered just as much "folk" as Woody Guthrie.

By this point, if I have you convinced, you'll finish the chapter. If you disagree with me, you've probably already skipped to another part of the book. The rest of this discussion is, therefore, for those of you who amplify your 'harps of would like to do so.

There are basically two ways to get sound from an instrument to an amplifier. First, you can use a microphone or a variation thereof. Contact pickups, which fasten to your instrument and depend on the vibration of the wood fall into this class. Second, you can use an electronic pickup such as is used on a conventional electric guitar. This bypasses the effects of the wooden box and turns the vibrations of the strings directly into an electronic signal.

The contact pickup is in common use in what are called electric-acoustic instruments. Many acoustic guitar players who plug their instruments in are using this sort of pickup. Contact pickups can give you something of the sound quality of an acoustic instrument but suffer a couple of drawbacks. First, the sound they produce is very dependent on the placement of the pickup. Frequently these pickups are mounted on the back of an autoharp. Moving the pickup only a few inches can radically alter the sound produced. This is especially true of the so-called piezo-electric pickups such as the old Barcus-Berry pickup. These pickups respond not to the vibrational movement of the wood surface, which is what moves air and makes sound, but to the bending of the wood, which is related to the movement of the wood, but which also has a life (and sound) of its own. The best contact pickups are those which are installed in an instrument at the factory, where extensive research has usually been done to achieve the best possible sound.

Some pickups are actual microphones which "listen" from the inside of the instrument, just as a regular microphone listens from the outside. These can give an exceptionally clear and full sound which some, (but not all), people find very pleasing and close to the natural acoustic sound of the instrument.

Bryan Bowers, whose autoharp sound is incredible, uses a small high-quality lavaliere microphone pinned to his upper left chest. He holds his 'harps high, with the back of the instrument more or less centered over his microphone. This method doesn't leave a wire hanging off one's instrument, which may or may not be and advantage. The wire is attached to the player, which may or may not be a disadvantage.

Both contact pickups and microphones are subject to feedback, an ugly phenomenon which occurs when the volume of a sound system is turned up on a speaker which is too near a microphone. Volume levels just below the feedback point from a contact pickup or a microphone inside an instrument, can make one note or small group of notes stand out way in front of the rest of the instrument's sound. This causes it to make noises not unlike the Autoharp From Hell. Feedback should not be a problem if you're working with a sound technician, (including yourself), who knows the job. However we're all human, and it's rare to find a sound technician who really understands 'harps.

The second kind of autoharp pickup is magnetic, responding solely to the vibration of the strings. Such pickups were used on the Oscar Schmidt E model 'harps, the OSI Lancer, and the accessory pickup from OSI. Such pickups sound very "electric," with the sound quality not unlike that of an electric guitar. This should come as no surprise since the operating principle is the same. The sound tends to be strongest in the middle tones and is weak in the subtle high frequency acoustic nuances which help make an acoustic autoharp sound the way it does. A pure electric pickup will not, however, feed back under normal circumstances. You really have to work at getting it to do so. If you play 'harp with a rock band, the electric pickup is the way to go.

Properly handled, the electric pickup sound can be very pleasing to one's ear, as long as one is not expecting a totally traditional 'harp sound. There are a couple of things one can do to fill out the sound produced by the pickup and make it sound more akin to the Real Thing. First, one can augment it with a front microphone which will pick up lots of the acoustic qualities of the instrument. This is the technique which I prefer. The electric pickup is used to supply some of the tonal elements, (such as the fullness of the low strings on the instrument), lacking from the pure acoustic sound. The rich, full sound which results can be surprisingly beautiful. My Christmas album was done using such a mixture of electric and acoustic sounds. Second, one may use a tone control to calm down the characteristic mid-range of the electric pickup sound. The tool of preference here is called a graphic equalizer – a fancy name for an octave by octave tone control.

Graphic equalizers come in all sizes and price ranges, from cheap to unaffordable. Simple ones for stage work generally run from $75 to $150. Avoid the six- or seven-band units and hold out for a full ten-band equalizer. This is, in my opinion, the minimum for properly equalizing an electric autoharp. Setting the line of linear level controls into a pattern resembling a smile (high on the ends, down in the middle) produces a similar pattern on the faces of listeners, and vice versa.

In spite of the fact that my own opinions show through here, I'll be the first to emphasize that how you deal with amplifying the sound of your instrument is strictly a matter of taste. It's important, however, to be willing to learn about whatever tools modern technology has to offer if they help you communicate your music to your audience. Even the strictest traditional autoharpists find themselves on stage or in a recording studio often times with a sound engineer who knows very little about autoharps. The performing musician must, at times, also be something of a sound engineer. I used to know an acoustic band in Maine, years ago, which detested the fact that they had to use electricity. They bought a cheap PA system, never learned how to use it properly, and were forever fighting with it during their performances – a sorry sight/sound, indeed.

Be alert, (yes, the world needs more lerts!), for other autoharp players using pickups and microphones. Listen to them, quiz them, and learn as much as possible about the sounds you do and don't like, and how those sounds are produced. I, for one, always appreciate it when others come up and ask me intelligent questions of this nature. It gives me the opportunity to be an eager teacher and show off my own bag of toys.

I'm not advocating everyone should use some form of amplification. There are those who still play, by choice, only in totally acoustic settings or prefer to simply stand before a microphone and play. In the final analysis, one must be at peace with the situation in which one finds oneself, and with the sounds of his/her instrument in that situation. The music sounds best that way. ❖

For further information concerning amplification, see "Lapel Microphones" p.104.

Lapel Microphones

AQ Volume VIII, Number 3

THE USE OF LAVALIERE MICS WITH THE AUTOHARP

Lindsay Haisley

The autoharp sounds weird! No, don't shoot me! I didn't say it didn't sound nice, just that it sounds weird. I'm not talking from the point of view of an audient (the singular of "audience"), but from the point of view of a sound technician who is also a performer who cares about the way the instrument sounds when amplified or recorded – a reality in most performances since the invention of the PA system back before most of us were born.

So having stuck my neck out, let me qualify myself a bit. An instrument such as a trombone is easy to amplify. Just stick a microphone at a reasonable distance in front of the bell and you've got it. A guitar is a little more difficult, but still there is a question of where to place a microphone in front of the instrument to get the truest sound.

The autoharp is a horse of a different color in many respects. By nature, it's a quiet instrument compared to most stringed instruments. Its voice comes frequently from both its front and back. What comes off of the front of the instrument is mixed with the sounds of picks (if one uses them) and the sounds of the chord bar action, which varies with the quality and make of the instrument. So where does one put a microphone in order to best reproduce the sound of the instrument? In recording sessions, I have often used a mix of microphones, one in front of the instrument (the pick noises can give a sense of presence to the amplified sound) and one in back, over my left shoulder, so that it picks up something of the back sound of the instrument which often has a smoother quality than the sound from the instrument front. This works well for recording, but is an impractical solution for performing where the freedom to move around stage can be important. For many years, the solution which I adopted was to use a combination of a front microphone and an Oscar Schmidt electronic pickup. The latter can, and in fact must be equalized to produce a pleasing sound, but with this done, a magnetic electronic pickup can produce a rich, full sound with a deep and true bass, something lacking in the acoustic sound of the instrument owing it's geometry and small size.

I'd been listening to Bryan Bowers for many years, and had done guest spots on his shows in the Seattle area and talked to him about my pickup/mic arrangement. "It makes the autoharp sound like an organ," I told him. "I don't want it to sound like an organ, I want it to sound like an autoharp," he replied. Bryan relies heavily on a Sony lavaliere microphone fastened to his chest, It's a good microphone and makes his 'harps sound pretty good too. When I got my first Orthey Instruments autoharp I decided to take advantage of the superior tone and voice of the instrument and see what I could do along the same lines. I was not disappointed.

Lavaliere microphones are generally used for amplifying speech, although they're often used for singers as well. They're made to be hung on a tie or pinned on one's chest or collar and be unobtrusive while still faithfully reproducing vocal sound as would a larger conventional front microphone. While you can buy a cheap lavaliere mic at Radio Shack for $30 or so, one generally gets what one pays for with these little microphones, just as with any other microphone. A good lavaliere microphone will cost in the neighborhood of $250 – in the price range of any quality microphone. The active element in these microphones is usually a small condenser element, meaning that an external power supply is required for the microphone. One usually has the choice of using "phantom power" – provided by the unit into which the microphone is plugged, or a battery power pack which has to be kept supplied with a good battery and worn on one's belt or autoharp strap. Although the battery power pack is less convenient, one can by no means count on all sound systems to provide power to microphones. Although this is becoming more common on modern sound systems, many cheaper systems and many of the good older systems aren't capable of powering a microphone, so the battery system is a sure bet. The output of good lavaliere microphones, like that of all quality microphones, is low impedance, requiring an XLR (3 prong) socket or an adapter to a high impedance socket if required.

These little microphones are generally about the size of a slip-on pencil eraser and come provided with various clips and pins for fastening onto clothing, strap, or whatever is convenient. Because one's lungs constitute a "resonant cavity," such a microphone is generally engineered to compensate for the acoustics of being close to one's chest.

Use of a lavaliere microphone with an autoharp is not difficult, but does require a bit of planning. The microphone needs to be close to the back of the 'harp, but needs to be kept from banging into it as the instrument is moved. As with most microphones, wind screens are available for lavaliere microphones and are often provided as part of the kit with a good microphone. There's generally not much wind between one's chest and one's autoharp, but these screens are made of soft foam which can cushion contact with the back of a 'harp quite nicely. Soft, acoustically transparent foam is also available from good music stores and can be used for the same purpose.

Placement of a lavaliere microphone offers some choices. Some performers prefer to fasten the microphone to his or her chest about four inches below the left shoulder. I have my lavaliere mic (a Shure SM84) clipped to a slit in my strap so that it's always within an inch or two of the back of my instrument, pointed toward it. Lavaliere microphones generally have a "super-cardioid" pattern – most sensitivity in front and very little in back – which gives them good noise and feedback rejection qualities.

The strongest sound from the back of a 'harp is from the middle of the instrument, so the best combination of 'harp and microphone placement generally involves holding one's 'harp fairly high. A little experimentation here will help you find the right combination.

I've been very satisfied with my Shure SM84 microphone, and found it better in many respects than other amplification schemes I've used, although I still like the sound of my electric pickup when combined with a front microphone. A lavaliere mic has the advantage of extreme simplicity – almost too much in some ways, since one has little or no control over volume or has little or no control over volume or tone without stopping to commune with the sound technician during a performance. The sound is *good*, with rich bass and smooth tone over pretty much the full range of the instrument.

If you're interested in trying out a lavaliere microphone, a good music store which deals in musical electronics should be able to help you out. Always try before you buy. Bring your 'harp with a strap and be prepared to put some holes or slits in your strap to try out different placements. Don't settle for second-class quality in your microphone. Consider major brands (Sony, Audio-Technica, Shure, etc.) which are known for quality. Select a battery powered microphone rather than a phantom powered microphone (unless you *always* plan to plug into a sound system which can provide microphone power). I guarantee that you'll like what you and your audiences will hear. ❖

To read about more autoharp amplification, see "Using Amplification" p.102.

Autoharp Appraisal

AQ Volume V, Number 2

YARD SALE FIND – MUSICAL TREASURE OR MUSICAL PLAQUE?

George Orthey

After a two hundred dollar renovation, a ten dollar treasure found in a used furniture store, yard sale, or in Aunt Tillie's attic, may be worth as much as up to five or ten dollars as a musical wall plaque. Even the most skillful do-it-yourselfer will probably spend seventy-five to one hundred dollars for parts to reinstate an old autoharp from total disrepair. Of course, some used 'harps will be in good playable condition, and will, in fact, be a bargain!

So, what do you look for in a used 'harp to find a bargain?

1. Does it have strings – is it tuned up and playable? If not, it definitely falls into the "pig in a poke" category until you string it up. If the joints are obviously disjointed, or if the body is warped, there is no use stringing it without making it structurally sound. If it looks solid, tune it up and let it stand at least a few days. Then continue your evaluation. If the 'harp is just a bit out of tune, tune it up and evaluate it now. Keep in mind that a good 'harp is designed to have its strings pulled up to tension, and stay that way for its entire life, be it one or one hundred years.

2. Are the tuning pins tight? If they turn very easily and drop back out of tune with the slightest touch of the wrench, you have loose pins. This is repairable.[1] If the pins are badly rusted or if the square heads of the pins are all grubbed up from rough wrench usage, you may require pin replacement. They are zither pins, and can be obtained from piano supply houses, or from hammered dulcimer or psaltery makers.

3. **Check out the body of the 'harp.** Is it straight or bowed down along the base (long) edge? A slight bow down less than 1/8 " is normal in many 'harps. This is particularly expected in a ten year old instrument and is more than likely stable as long as no other frame or sound board failure is noted.

Look at that sound board. Is it flat caved in, or bowed up? Again, slight deviation in an older 'harp is likely to be stable and of no consequence. Handcrafted Morgan 'harps have arched sound boards. They are made that way, like a mandolin top.

Check carefully for cracks and frame creep. This may be slight. Just a crack in the finish over the joints is not unusual or dangerous in an older instrument. You may, however, see a gross displacement where the frame pieces join each other, or where the frame joins the top or back. The most common displacement is at the dead pin end. In general, without the aid and advice of an experienced luthier, these body failures should be considered an absolute "no-no" for the average autoharp buyer.

General wear and tear, finish marks, scratches, and other such surface blemishes should not harm the performance of the instrument.

4. Look at the dead pin end of the strings. Check the bridge to see if it is straight. It should not be curved so the mid-portion bows in toward the sound board. This is true of either the ChromAharp bridge or the Oscar Schmidt aluminum anchor or fine tuners. Look straight down on the 'harp. There should not be a curve to this bridge or anchor. Also, with Oscar's anchor bar/fine tuner, be sure the bar is not riding up out of the body of the 'harp. The ride-up, if present, usually goes hand in hand with a curvature of this piece. These problems may be serious, or easily repaired. They should be evaluated by a professional instrument repair person.

One final check for body condition is the flatness of the string bed. Going from bass to treble at the middle of the 'harp , the string bed should be essentially flat. The wound strings at the bass will normally stand slightly above the other strings due to their larger diameter.

Now listen to the sound. If it has all the musical quality of a twig stuck in the spokes of a bicycle wheel, it will make a lovely wall plaque. If it has acceptable sound, you're in business, body-wise.

5. The bar system is the essential mechanics of the autoharp. You can adjust the bar system and make it quiet with relatively little cost.[2] Be sure all the felts are present and in good order. Hold the 'harp up and look through under the bars (between the bars and the strings). Press each bar down. See that each felt is touching its relative string, and that none have deep grooves cut where the strings touch the felts. Also play each chord, listening for notes that shouldn't be there, or notes that should be there, but are not. Discrepancies indicate some repair or possibly a refelting job is in order. Refelting will cost about two dollars a bar for felts of good quality. If you pay someone to refelt your 21-bar 'harp, the cost could be about one hundred dollars.

My general advice to novice buyers is to find an experienced 'harper/teacher who has done basic maintenance and repair to assist you. Or buy only from a reputable dealer who stands behind what he sells.

If you do turn up a treasure for a buck or two, it's worth dragging home and messing about with it. I have a playable 100 year old Dolgeville 'harp bought for 25 cents at a yard sale! Happy treasure hunting! ❖

See "Questions And Answers" p.122 for additonal information on old 'harp repair.

[1] See "Loose Tuning Pins" p.19.

[2] See "Improving The Action Chord Bars" p.9.

Improving The Autoharp: A Panel Discussion

AQ Volume IV, Number 2
IMPROVING THE AUTOHARP
Transcribed by Alan Mager

A panel discussion concerning the improvement of the autoharp was held at the July 1991 Mountain Laurel Autoharp Gathering in Newport, Pennsylvania. The panel was comprised of Bob Taylor, Clapping Trees Instruments; George Orthey, Orthey Instruments; Mark Fackeldey, Autoharpist; Mike McClellan, Luthier and Autoharpist; Jim Thomas and David Rice, Goose Acres; and Mike Seeger, moderator. The following is a transcription of excerpts from this discussion.

Mike Seeger: There is a great deal of room left for experiment and development of the autoharp – to give it a better tone, and to make it more convenient to play.

We felt that players as well as luthiers should be represented on this panel, because the players are the people who are trying to drive the manufacture of the autoharp away from something that just barely holds together to something that sounds really good. Our basic problem is one in having an autoharp that can stand the pressure, but still produce the tone. I think most of you, as makers, will agree. I like the tone of many of the autoharps now, but I'm kind of a dreamer. And I like to think that we can go on even further – not only in tone, but in ways of playing.
Audience Comment: I spoke to Mike McClellan yesterday. He had some suggestions about improving the instrument.
Mike McClellan: Maybe I should give a little history on how I came to the autoharp. When I was a kid, I was down in Virginia, and we had a teacher that played one in class, and on the radio on Saturday. So, I was around autoharps since I was knee-high to a grape, but I didn't own one 'til I went back to Hawaii in '69 and had to teach a class in it. In the interim, I'd learned how to play melody on 'em, and I knew two gentlemen that made experiments on 'em. One was Dave Linely who's famous now for backing up Jackson Brown and doing all sorts of electric stuff. He took a standard 'harp and had a Mexican instrument maker make a bigger body on the back of it, so it had more air inside. That thing sounded wonderful. It gave me an idea that if you got around to owning one, you could do things to it. Then in '63 or '64, I met a guy named Pete Colby. He had a 'harp he made himself with a carved maple back, and that thing was *loud*. To me it had a harsh sound, because I'm from Hawaii, and I like a warm sound. It was, in fact, in Hawaii where I had to teach a class, that I broke down and bought an old autoharp. I took a piece of plywood I found that washed up on the shore – this plywood smelled of diesel oil and salt water. I screwed it to the back with maple supports so that it was a resonator. I got that idea from an article Mike Seeger wrote in *Sing Out!* some time before.
Mike Seeger: I'd tried that in the early '60s, I think.
Mike McClellan: So I didn't forget it, and in '69 or '70, it made that junk old autoharp with strings that were older than I was sound better than the new ones in the store. Of course, some of those strings broke when I tuned it. I just had old, used guitar strings, 'cause I wasn't going to put *new* guitar strings on it. That resonator made it sound better than new ones with new strings.

I kept inheriting parts. I put a 21-chord plastic growth on it, and when the body changed because I went to the mainland with it, it cracked. Finally, it broke so bad I could look inside and see how the old black ones were made, and they were made rather poorly. I figured as an amateur carpenter, I could make one better. Luckily, I found other carpenters with better shops that wanted to get involved in that sort of thing.

What I use now is piano pin-block maple which does not move. It costs as much as a cheap 'harp just to buy a chunk of that wood. I've got a resonator on the back to protect it from breaking. Now this, to me, sounds better. It may not be what I'm looking for, but it's a start. People have told me to turn down the pickup on my autoharp, and I didn't have one. Actually, it sounds better to the listener than it does to me, because the resonator directs the sound outward. Once I made a top out of the leftover maple laminate, and it sounded cold and hard. It sounded like it could penetrate a dance band, but it wasn't a warm sound, which is the sound I like to hear with bluegrass or Hawaiian music. I've been working by myself in California. Nobody cares about autoharp experiments there. We ought to exchange ideas.
Mike Seeger: That's the purpose of this workshop. Perhaps a few ideas from Goose Acres would be good.
David Rice: Well, I think what Mike said at the start is really true. The two variables of structural strength on one side, and acoustic purity on the other side – really, they don't exactly meet. What you do to make it stronger, makes it deader; and what you do to make it sound more alive – more responsive – makes it weaker. So you have to strike some sort of a compromise between structural strength – that ability for the top to stand the compression of 37 strings pulling on it, which amounts to a tremendous amount of force – and making the top free enough to have some sort of quality of sound. Those are the variables that we've all struggled with, and what we've come up with to try to reach a compromise between those two is a method of trying to get the top to be as free as possible. We've abandoned the bracing style that you find in the Oscars – the time-honored crosswise bracing that seems to be tra-

ditional. Piano sound boards are braced that way, It's a traditional bracing scheme for a coniferous wood – most of the tops of our 'harps are spruce. We've sort of gotten away from that pattern. We've managed to get a top that's free. Can you add to that, Jim?

Jim Thomas: We went through several ramifications on the bracing pattern. We're not done – we've got a long way to go yet – but we're making a lot of progress. We seem to be having very good luck structurally, as far as the instruments not coming undone. We've finally learned how to acclimate autoharps to live in the real world, and that's not easy. To get a lot of life and sustain out of the sound – that's the goal we're after. We're about halfway there...maybe a quarter of the way there, and we're still working at it.

This 'harp's front and back are mahogany. We decided to go to mahogany to get the combination of a little more structural strength and maybe a little more sound. The sonority of the mahogany is one of a richer mellower sound as compared to the somewhat brighter, "trebly" sound that you get from other woods, especially spruce. Mahogany in a guitar and in a 'harp gives a rounder, "tubby" kind of sound. We feel we should make 'harps that have different types of tone colors. I think George ought to say some things about the lines he's been working along. He's going down some very clearly defined lines in the way of improvements in the sound and structure.

George Orthey: It's true that different woods produce different voices. I find the most profound variance occurs in the hardwood top, spruce back versus the spruce top, hardwood back instrument. The former has a bright melody line, the latter, a full, rich sound.

I think a significant factor in autoharp progress is, for whatever reason, that the 'harp makers are hermits. They hide in the woodwork. When I began fooling with the 'harp, I was sure I was the only person in the world that did this. We go to about fifteen festivals a year, so I think I speak from experience in this matter. We visit 'harp makers – luthiers who live half an hour away from big festivals – and we never see them there. We are very pleased to see this panel meeting to talk about the autoharp.

If we want to make the autoharp progress, we need to be in a friendly competition with ourselves and every other maker. If you don't try to make a better instrument, forget it. You're doing people a disservice. You're programming to sell them a piece of junk if you don't plan to make something better constantly. That's got to be the underlying drive.

A key difference between us makers and you players, is that you want a full hundred-piece orchestra or at least a Steinway grand autoharp. And we luthiers say, "You know, there's just these hands and those tools. If you want a Steinway grand, you buy and put it in your living room – don't expect me to make you one to carry around."

Mike McClellan: Let me defend that. In '82, I thought I had the ultimate autoharp. I took a picture of it – it was really lovely looking. I figured I had a good product. I was also performing – I was running around the country. In the fall of '82, I did a wedding using that autoharp. An hour after that, as I was driving across the Bay Bridge to Oakland, I heard a crack, and my wonderful autoharp had come apart. My top of the line! The one that I was figuring was what you players really wanted. So I felt I couldn't really go out to shows with a piece of junk. At that point, I was losing so much money that I ended up with a day job, and that's another reason I haven't been going to shows.

Audience Comment: In Missouri at one time we had the world's best zither maker, Franz Schwarzer. When he died and his plant went defunct, all of his plans and archives went to the Missouri State Museum in Jefferson City. I assume that a lot of you perambulate around the countryside. You might want to stop by there and check out just how he built those things. I have one that's 100 years old now. It has the most beautiful sound, and it's absolutely stable. It holds pitch, it's not warped in any which-way. He must have had some very good, sound structural ideas.

Mike Seeger: That's an excellent idea.

We have a person here who made autoharps with Oscar Schmidt for a while – Bob Taylor.

Bob Taylor: In 1977, newly married, I went to Oscar Schmidt as a woodworker and I loved the place. I loved the smell of the lacquer and the woods, and it was wonderful. And a year later, they went into bankruptcy, and that wasn't so wonderful. I had a chance to become a fireman, and I figured, well, I'll be a fireman and that'll pay the bills, and I can build 'harps on the side without any financial pressures. We were at the point of starting a custom shop for Oscar Schmidt when the company was sold. It was bought by a large conglomerate which moved the operation overseas. We moved into our basement and started a company called Clapping Trees Instruments. About a year later, we decided that we were going to have a family, and so I called myself in temporary retirement until my kids are in school.

The way a large factory works is there's sort of a least common denominator attitude. You build each piece so that it can go into any 'harp and you overbuild everything slightly so nothing breaks, and you don't get a lot of returns. There's sort of a bell curve shape, if you want to talk about numbers and quality. Most of the autoharps or any other instrument will fall into this general part, and there'll be a few that are real cream puffs and there'll be a few disasters. What you do with the bell curve and how you take care of your disasters, and even what you do with your cream puffs, is important. Some factories might save all the really good ones and give them to people like Mike Seeger, for instance.

But as a small maker, you can be a lot more selective. You can take woods that go with other woods. You can go up to the edge structurally a little more. I would say that most traditional autoharps could have their frames reduced by about 20 percent, and 80 percent of them would not crack or fall apart. The other 20 percent probably would, because of wood selection, or because of relatively poor joints, compared to what you can do by hand with a lot of care. My love is making custom instruments. I don't have any standard models. I like to talk to the person. I like to build very slowly. I've never completed an instrument in less than a year. There was a time at Oscar Schmidt where we were developing the Centurion and the Festival series. We had a lot of beautiful exotic woods that we experimented with. We also experimented with bracing. But the bottom line always was: If too many instruments came back, stiffen everything up – tighten everything up – make it so it doesn't fall apart. I'm not really condemning this process. It's necessary because of economic realities.

As I said, I really loved working at Oscar Schmidt. They really were very good to me and my ideas. Towards the end, we developed this relationship where I'd come in and sometimes I'd come in on the clock and sometimes I'd come in on my own time and do my own crazy things. So I went through a period of kind of flying-by-the-seat-of-my-pants experimentation, as I'm sure everybody on this panel did, where you just kind of shut your left brain off and just kind of went with it. Most of those things were disasters.

Moving into some general ideas I have about autoharps – there are two things: You look at the body, and you talk about tone and structure. The other half of the autoharp is "the works" – how to get the greatest number of chords in the smallest space, and the best action, and many other contraptions and ideas that everybody has. With regards to the tone and the volume, I think we do have to have a little bit of realism here, as George said. All too often, our autoharps get compared to mandolins and guitars which are bridged instruments where you drive the sound board from the middle with a bridge. You can do that with an autoharp, and I think we all probably tried that at one time or another, too, but it doesn't sound like an autoharp anymore. It sounds like a banjo. You lose all your sustain, and you get a lot of volume. It comes down to a real trade-off between volume and sustain. The way to get both is to build light. Is to have a really strong, resonant frame. You have to think of the frame of the 'harp as the bridge. That's where the energy is delivered. The frame has to radiate the energy into the sound board. In a way, it's like a guitar or a bridged instrument turned inside out. So, when you look at the frame, you have to be thinking not only of structure, but you have to be thinking of how is this going to radiate the sound.

Mike Seeger: We should hear from a really good player. Mark, what would you like to hear in an autoharp?

Mark Fackeldey: What I like is lots of volume and nice, bright sound.

I'd like to go back to this resonator thing. You all probably had the experience of when you hold the 'harp away from the body, you get more fullness of sound and volume, and I think maybe something could be done to capture that. I don't think it would need an entire resonator, but something to keep it off your body. An exception is George's 'harp which gets more volume when I press it against me.

I like nice low action and not much tension to the springs – make them very easy to play – just tap the button and there would be a chord. One way I check the quality of a 'harp is to strum all the strings and then slowly lower the chord bar to see whether all the strings are muted at once, or whether they mute one after the other. I think that maybe if the strings were brought all to the same level, you could improve your action. But I don't see many people filing notches in the bridge or whatever just to accomplish that. But it works. I've tried it, and it does improve your action.

Audience Comment: Would it be possible to change the philosophy of the manufacturing? I see that you're all looking to find a combination of the sustain and volume in one 'harp, but different people have different needs and styles of playing. Some people are primarily string band or bluegrass or solo performers. They might want a 'harp that only has volume. Other people like to play in churches or nursing homes, or like jamming with friends. They might want more sustain. So maybe what we ought to be doing is looking for different types of 'harps, rather than putting all of the combinations of things you can do with the 'harp into one. This is my volume 'harp; this is my sustain 'harp. Which model do you like? Pick the one that's right for you. What do you think?

Mike Seeger: I think that's what these makers are doing, each on his own. The company [Oscar Schmidt] itself is going, just as Bob discussed, in one direction. I think, myself, that it would be nice for the company to go into a premium player's instrument on a sideline, but you can't do that. So, you're talking basically about the makers here, or hand-making.

George Orthey: Some years ago, Glen Peterson asked me to set up a factory operation to make dulcimers. You have to understand what a manufacturer is doing. The Koreans that make the 'harps are probably not getting more than maybe $25 or $30 for a 'harp that you pay $150 to $200 for. How much can you expect them to do even in Korea for 30 bucks? A manufacturer has to have a price structure where the retail price is going to be three to four times what the original price is. That forces them into a position we don't have to put up with. *We* end up, by the time we get done making a 'harp which is a deviant from our standard model, probably working for $2.23 an hour. Business just doesn't operate like that.

Jim Thomas: Gee, I wish I could make that much building 'harps. I do want to say that, at least from the Goose Acres standpoint, we build 'harps in many different combinations of front and back wood. One guy's taste might be in this all-mahogany that I'm holding; another's taste might be in maple and spruce, which is brighter – a little more forward sounding than this all-mahogany, and so forth. We are trying to pay attention to that and without going completely outside the realm of what we call "producibility." We don't mind building a 'harp for 75 cents an hour or whatever it is, but we sure don't want to lose a *lot* of money.

Audience Comment: This is on the subject of sustain versus power. I make clear choices when I pick up an instrument whether I'm going to do instrumental work or sing. If I want to sing, I want more sustain. I don't want that brightness and power. I want the ringing of the strings to carry through to complement the singing. I know the builders seem to try to get the loudest 'harp or get the most power out of what they're dealing with. It's very difficult for me to find or have built for me, an instrument that's really mellow and fine for singing over the instrument. I have some really fine autoharps from George, Goose Acres, Timberline, and some old Centurions that I value very highly. But I would hope to see builders not just go for a middle-of-the-road model, because there's a clear choice between what you would play to sing with and what you'd use for instrumental work. My first Orthey 'harp was an extremely powerful instrument that is always my choice if I'm going to be playing with fiddlers, 'cause they can hear me. I bought it to be able to be heard at a festival and as absolutely the best choice for me, but if

I want to sing, I want an instrument that's much more mellow, much more smooth. I don't want all the power at the same time. You can say that it has sustain and the string will ring for a long time, but how fast does it give you the power and how long does that power last? I don't want it all at one time. So I think the message I would get across is to have a clear separation in models.

Another great concern is that you get a nice sound in the middle; the bass is generally weak, and the high is too shrill. I think you often get that with too much coupling – too low impedance in the higher end of the 'harp. I'd suggest maybe the positioning of the bridges – style of the bridges – is something that needs to be looked at. If the bridge is on the edge of the frame in the middle octave, it doesn't necessarily mean it should be there in the high octave. Maybe it should be angled off a little bit. I find that the high strings are just topping too fast in those kinds of designs.

Mike Seeger: In the last ten minutes of this workshop, are there other areas that should be covered here?

Mark Fackeldey: I have a comment about the weight of the instrument. I would ask you to keep the weight down. Now, I can handle it myself – I play a 50-pound electric bass for a swing band – it pays better than playing the autoharp.

Another way you can reduce the weight is – I love the fine tuners, but they're so heavy. I don't think you need ten pounds of heavy duty steel.

George Orthey: We all complained about the aluminum fine tuners, Mark, 'til they quit making them.

Mark Fackeldey: I loved them. I'm still using them. They work for me. The fine tuners could be reduced in weight, I'm sure, as long as you run them across the bridge.

Mike Seeger: A friend of mine 35 years ago wanted to make an aluminum frame for the autoharp, something like the Steinway that George was talking about; but then we realized that it would flex even more than the wood for its weight, probably. But that is a possibility that could be worked out. How it would work out in the sonority of the instrument, I don't know.

Audience Comment: Why are new autoharps built with such high action?

George Orthey: The chord bars are not fitted 'harp by 'harp. They make sets of parts that go together, and the parts all have to fit, so they have to be set high enough that, given the variance from one instrument to the other, the bars will always work. If you would set the action – build the parts – so they would fit perfectly on one instrument and the next instrument was not identical – had a little bit of bow – the bars would sit on the strings and wouldn't play, which would make you very unhappy. So the way to insure that they will all play, at least a little bit, is to make the action very high.

The difference with any of us that make a handmade 'harp is we put the bars on a particular 'harp, and we make the necessary adjustments to our bars, and the bar holders, and the felts we use, and so on, so that *those* bars fit *that* 'harp. Now, they should be reasonably interchangeable, but still you have to adjust 'harp to 'harp to give just perfect action. And you vary that according to the player. There are some people who play very gently and they want the action a 64th of an inch off the strings. On the other hand, you have somebody that's going to get in there and hit the thing like Marty Schuman or Drew Smith, and some of these guys that are trying to take the strings off.

Let me comment on one other thing, and that is on the business of going to extremes with resonators and other things. Setting aside Marty Schuman and Mark Fackeldey, normal people tend to work back toward the center. I've found the exotic is interesting for a short time, but people, by and large, tend to want a traditional -looking, -feeling, -sounding instrument. These deviances we talk about are limited to the special person who wants that deviance. But across the board, folks tend to come back to say, "I want an *autoharp* autoharp when I look at it and when I hear it."

Mike Seeger: The hour is up. We'll continue this workshop for the rest of the festival, I'm sure – around and about. I think the point is that we should continue to be in communication and evolve the autoharp and our playing based on some of these ideas. Thanks to the panel. ❖

AQ Volume III, Number 2, 3, 4;
Volume IV, Number 1

Building Your Own Autoharp

THE MOUNTAIN LAUREL 'HARP

George Orthey
and Tom Fladmark

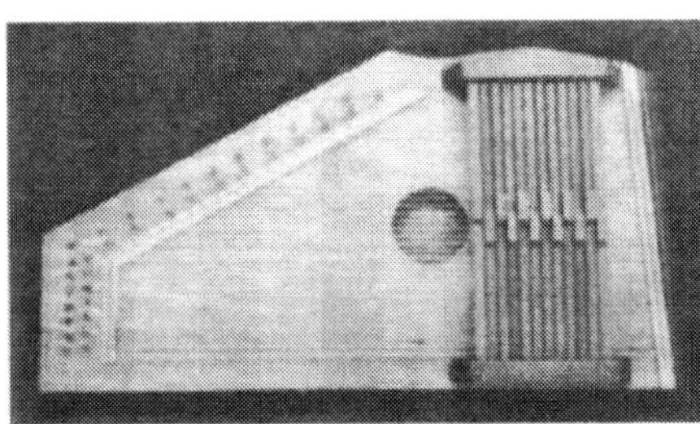

The Mountain Laurel Harp

Made according to these directions, this'harp will have an old-time traditional sound, and will look like an old-time autoharp. Before you begin this venture, please read "The Mountain Laurel Autoharp Eight Years Later" p.119.

Step One: List Of Materials

Machinery Requirements

1. Table saw (radial arm saw)
2. Band saw (can be done by hand with a fine-tooth back saw and jig saw – it's *hard* wood)
3. Drill press (can be done with a hand drill *carefully*)
4. Belt sander (can be done with a disk sander or sanding disk on a hand drill)

Hand Tool Requirements

1. The usual small woodworking shop tools: ruler, square, screw drivers, small hammer, sandpaper, etc.
2. Clamps: 1 bar clamp 24" and 15 - 20 C clamps with at least 3" capacity
3. Assorted drill bits 1/16" to 1/8" at 1/64" intervals. You will need one extra 5/64" bit and one new 3/16" bit.

Wood Requirements and Sources

1. One piece of *flat* (repeating *flat*) 3/4" plywood 12" x 24" *(Source: lumberyard)*
2. Two pieces of solid core 1/4" fir or mahogany marine-type plywood 12" x 24" 3-ply with all three plys of equal thickness. *(Don't* use veneer face plywood with a junk core.) (*Source: boat repair shops; specialty plywood sources may also be available through lumber yards; Harbor Sales Company, 1401 Russell Street, Baltimore, MD 21230 1-(800) 345-1712)*
3. Fine furniture-grade hardwood: One piece at least 8" wide and 2' long planed to 1" thickness. (Hard rock sugar maple or oak is best for this); another piece, 1/2" thick about the same size. *(Source: check Yellow Pages; Craftsmen Wood Service, 1735 Cortland Court, Addison, IL 60101)*
4. One piece of 2 x 4 clear construction-grade pine, spruce, or fir. *(Source: you only need a piece 12" long. Your lumber yard is likely to have a scrap big enough for this.*
5. Somewhere from among your scrap, you need to make a piece 3/4" x 1 1/2" x 12" in the same hardwood you have above.

Other Materials and Sources

1. Tuning wrench; 36 zither tuning pins *(Tuning pin source: piano repair shop or American Piano Supply company, Box 1068 Clifton, NJ 07014; today's autoharp luthiers)*
2. Seventy-two #6 bridge pins and dead pins *(Source: see tuning pin source).* Small nails can be substituted, but aren't as desirable.
3. Three feet of 1/8" brazing rod *(Source: welding shops).*
4. Flat head screws: 3/4" #4, and 1 3/4" #6, four each.
5. One set of Model A autoharp strings and;
6. 12 to 15 10" bar felts and:
7. Model A large diameter springs (get 2 for each bar plus a few extra in case you lose one). *(Source: autoharp dealer/ luthier)*
8. Yellow aliphatic resin glue, like Elmer's Craftsmen Glue or Franklin Titebond Glue. Also silicone glue.
9. One 3/4" wide x 1' long piece of double thickness felt cloth
10. Single-edged razor blade.

Step Two: Making Parts

1. The piece of 3/4" ply is your backing board, and will assist you in keeping the 'harp body flat, straight, and free of clamp marks. Using the Pattern #1, (frame), cut this piece of plywood about 1/2" larger than the 'harp on all sides.

2. The two pieces of solid core marine ply are your soundboard and back. One face of each of these is usually better (free of blemish) than the other. Mark the worse side of each "inside top" and "inside bottom." Mark it right on the piece so you don't make an error later. Draw the full size pattern of the 'harp from Pattern #1, (frame), on the good side of the top. (You may have noted on Pattern #2, the top is 5/8" shorter than the back down at the dead pin end. *For now, however, mark it full size as in Pattern #1.*) Place the back under the top with the good side down so the two faces of these pieces that you marked "inside" are face to face. *Outside the lines,* nail the two pieces together. Be sure the two pieces are exactly even across the bass rail edge:

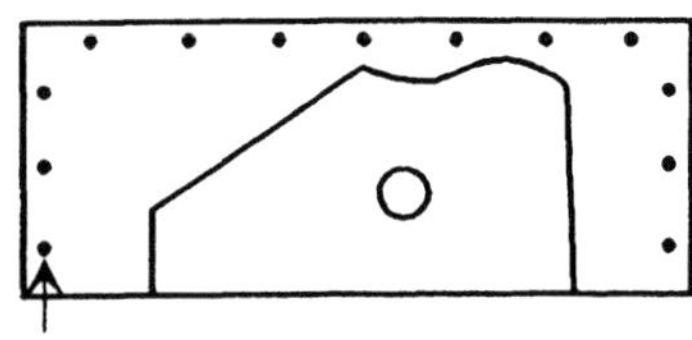

When you cut the top out with your band or jig saw, you will also cut the back to exactly the same size. After they are cut, they will be two separate pieces again, since you put the nails outside the lines as above. The back is done. Lay it aside.

Mark the sound hole on the top (soundboard), and cut it out with a jig saw, saber saw, or hole saw. If you want a different shaped sound hole, let your imagination soar – but don't make it significantly larger or smaller than the round hole on the pattern.

Be creative with the sound hole!

Now mark and cut off 5/8" from the dead pin end of the top (soundboard). (See Pattern #2 – string and pin pattern.) The 5/8" cut from the dead pin end creates a notch in the assembled body 1/4" x 5/8" to accommodate the dead pin bridge and a 1/8" brass string guide rod (see side elevation Pattern #2). The top is finished.

3. Your frame, bar holders, and bridges will be made from the piece of hard maple 8" wide, 2' long. This piece must be cut into strips as follows – (See Pattern #1.): 1" wide, bass rail; 1 3/8" wide, dead pin block; 2" wide, long pin block and top rail; 2 1/2" wide, toe pin block and chord bar holders; 1/2" wide, bridge stock:

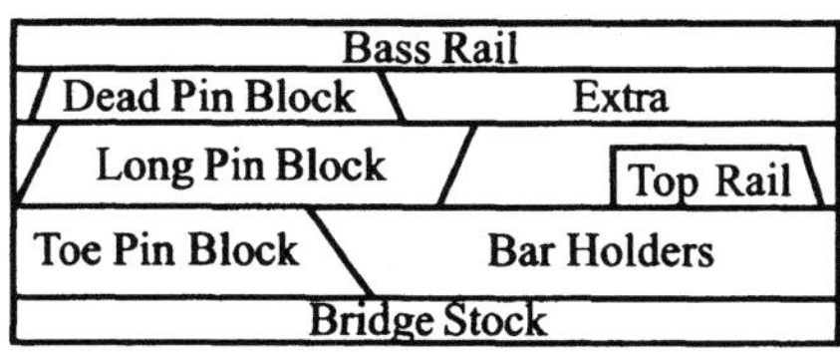

The 8" wide piece allows for 1/8" saw kerfs cutting these strips and will have just a bit to spare. Using a good combination or planer blade will give you clean smooth surfaces for a fine fit without jointing the edges. If your blade cuts rough, do yourself a favor and buy a carbide tipped combination blade for your saw. You'll love it.

Mark the appropriate pattern on each strip. The patterns can be transferred by using tracing paper. Now cut them out, being careful particularly on the end surfaces that will be joined, to keep the cuts straight and square so the frame parts will join nicely.

Set the piece marked bar holders aside for later use.

The piece of 1/2" wide wood for bridge stock is grooved first on each edge:

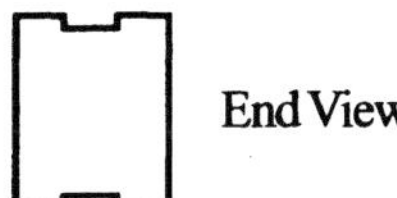

To do this, set the table saw blade so there is 3/16" between the blade and fence. Then lower the blade and place a piece of scrap plywood against the fence and clamp it down to the saw table. Now turn on the saw and bring the blade up through the plywood backing board so it will extend 1/16" above the backing board. Test to be sure it cuts a groove 1/8" wide and 1/16" deep using a piece of scrap. Run the bridge stock through the blade on each edge resulting in a strip as drawn above. Now cut 1/4" off one edge, making a piece 1/4" high and 1/2" wide with a 1/16" deep groove on the one side:

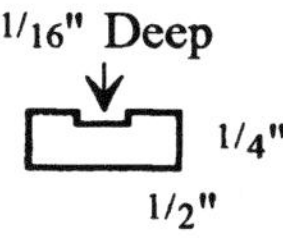

Similarly, cut the remaining piece 1/2" high so it is shaped like this:

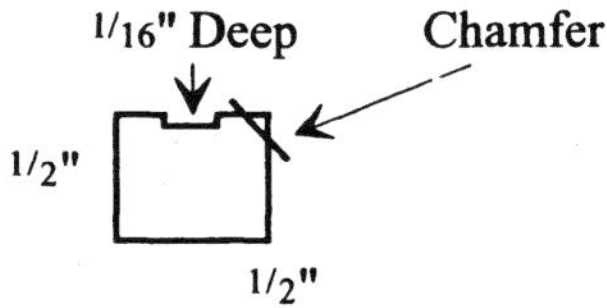

Chamfer the corner of the bridge as illustrated.

So much for that 1" thick piece of maple. Don't forget to save the piece to make the bar holders.

Square one end of the 1/2" thick piece of maple. Cut off a piece exactly 10" long. This will make the chord bar stock.

From the remainder of this 1/2" stock, cut a strip 1 1/8" wide and 3/8" thick. Bevel off the two edges so it has a cross section like this:

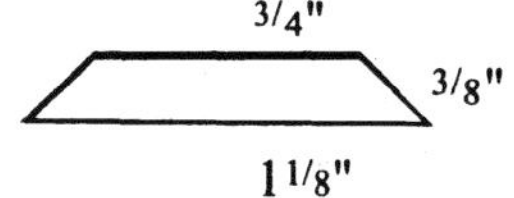

This piece will in effect make the buttons.

Make a line across the bar stock piece 5 1/4" from the end. Be sure the line is square:

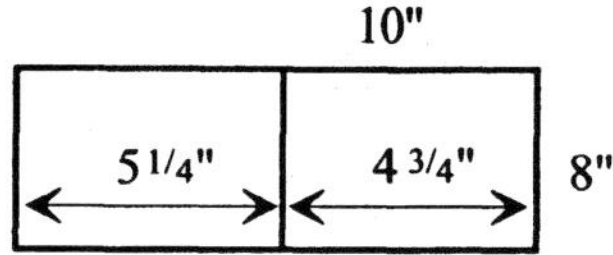

If this piece has any arch to it, put the arched side up, hollow side down. (If the piece is seriously arched, it is unusable for chord bars.)

Cut an 8" piece of the button stock, and glue it across this piece of bar stock adjacent to the line on the 5 1/4" side:

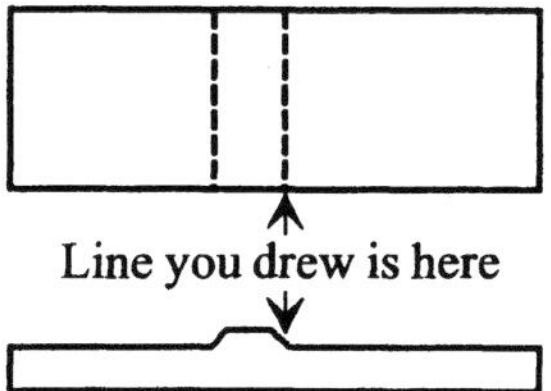

With your table saw, cut 5/16" wide strips off the block, making a series of pieces (chord bars):

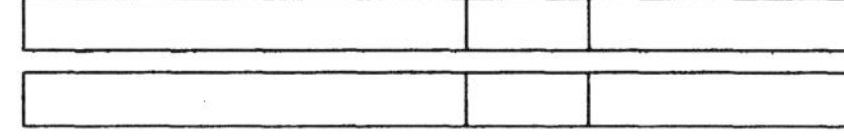

An 8" wide piece should make at least 16 bars. Some spares in case one warps, or – heaven forbid you should grub one up.

The buttons will be all in a row slightly to one side of the center. So if we reverse end for end every other bar, they should look like this:

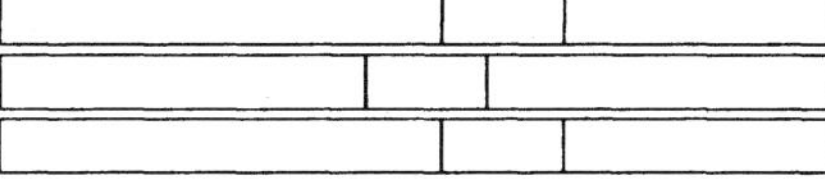

Now you have your chord bar set. Sand off the very sharp corners around the buttons and along the bar. Set them aside to felt and fit later.

4. Drill 5/8" holes in the 12" piece of 1" x 5/8" pine wood as follows:

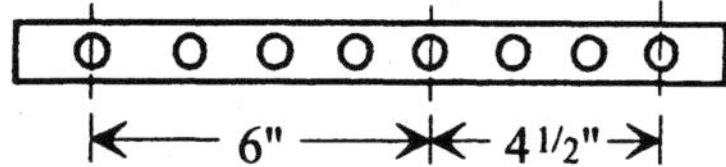

Cut through the holes on the three dotted lines, giving two internal brace pieces. (See Pattern #1.)

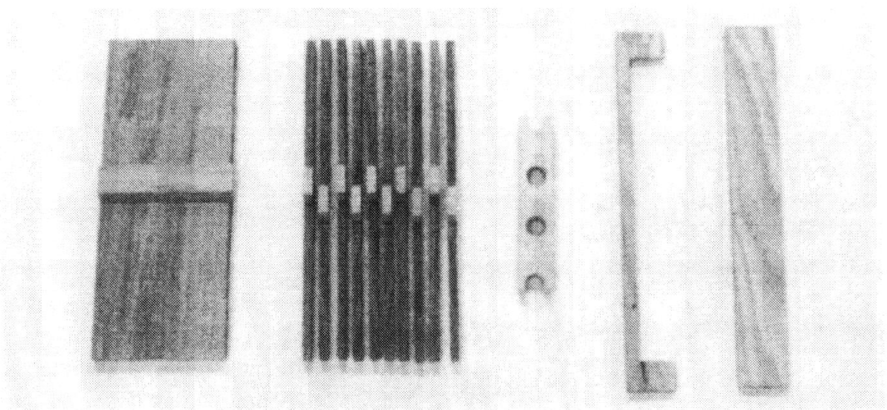

** See the addendum, "The Mountain Laurel Autoharp Eight Years Later" for a different form of bracing, which will give your instrument a fuller sound.*

5. The end cover is made by splitting the piece of 3/4" thick stock into two pieces 5/16" thick. Then cut out one piece like so: (See Pattern #4.)

Then glue them back together so they look like this:

This piece will go on the dead pin end of the 'harp with two screws, one near each end.

Step Three: Bar Holders

The chord bar holders aren't as complicated as they may appear. (See Pattern #4.) Each holder has four pieces; a trapezoid-shaped back, two side pieces which are glued to each end of the trapezoid, and a cap, which is screwed to the top. The channels for the bars are made by cutting small slots into the back piece and inserting cardboard dividers. The drawing shows a 12-bar holder, but you can easily accommodate more or less bars by adding or subtracting 3/8" spaces in the length of the holder.

You should have a piece of frame stock left over that measures 1" thick x 2 1/2" wide and about 16" long. Cut the width of this piece to give you one piece 1 3/16" wide, and one piece 3/4" wide. Saw the 1" thick by 1 3/16" wide piece into two pieces 3/8" thick by 1 3/16". These pieces will make the backs and sides of the bar holder. Cut the 3/4" wide piece to 1/4" thickness. This will make the caps. Make two 1/4" x 3/4" x 5 1/8" pieces. (See Pattern #5.) Remember you'll need your fingers to play your new 'harp, so be very careful when cutting small pieces on the saw!

Mark two pieces 6 3/4" long on one of the 1 3/16" x 3/8" x 16" pieces. Don't cut them apart yet – they're the two bar holder back pieces:

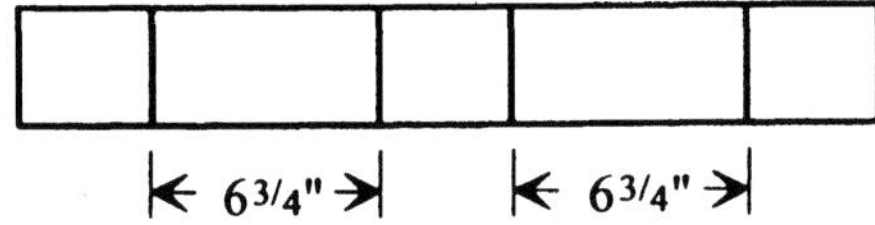

Be sure the lines are square. Now draw a line exactly midway of each piece:

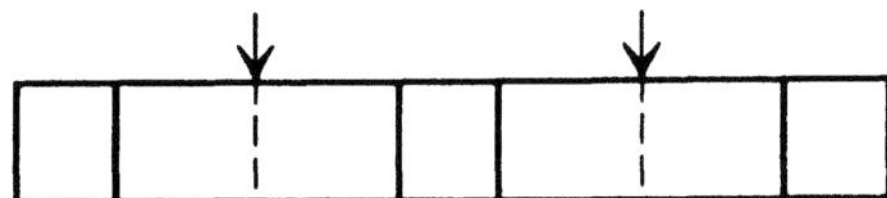

Now add a series of 12 more lines (six on each side of the center line) at exactly 3/8" intervals, all perfectly square:

You now have two sets of 13 lines with 12 equal spaces drawn on your bar holder stock. Look at Pattern #5 again and visualize what you are doing with this piece. Take a hack saw, fret saw, or band saw and cut a slot exactly centered on each of these lines. Cut the slot 1/8" deep. Be sure they go squarely into the wood, not slanted either way:

Right

Wrong

You can now cut the two bar holders to their final length using the first four lines you drew 6 3/4" apart. Cut on the outside of each of these lines so you have two pieces 6 3/4" long with a series of 13 slots centered on one face.

The dividers can be made of any hard cardboard material. One of the best is heavy file folder cover material. It has a highly polished smooth surface, and is quite stiff. Ordinary shirt cardboard sprayed with several coats of lacquer to harden it, then sanded lightly with fine sandpaper also works well.

Cut your cardboard in strips 1/2" wide and slightly less than 1 3/16" long. Carefully put a fine line of glue in the slot and then insert the cardboard piece. Do this in all 13 slots in both bar holder back pieces.

Cut four blocks from your 1 3/16" x 3/8" stock. They should be 1" long and cut perfectly square:

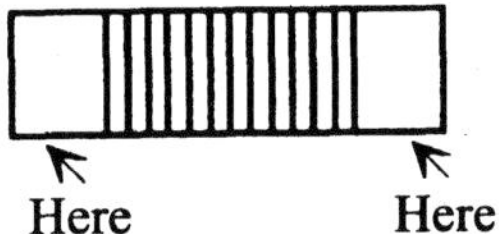

Glue the blocks into position as shown above against the end cardboard divider, and let the piece dry one hour.

Now cut off the ends of the bar holder on a angle so they coincide with the front view – Pattern #5.

Cut a 1/4" wide piece of cardboard 5" long and glue it across the inside face at the lower edge of the bar holder. This is the spring retainer. (See Pattern #5 for exact position.) A small dab of glue at each end and at each divider will secure it in place.

Now we need to drill some holes. Look carefully at Pattern #5. The two long 1 3/4" #6 screws only go in the base portion. They don't go through the cap. They go through the bar holder body into the 'harp body. Drill through the bar holders with a 9/64" drill. Countersink the head of the screw so it is flush with the top of the bar holder. A 7/64" drill will be needed to drill the body of the 'harp later.

Drill the cap as shown on the pattern – a 1/8" hole through the cap, and a 3/32" hole into the bar holder body. Countersink these, also.

Sand sharp corners. Later, after you have put finish on the bar holders, glue a layer of double thick felt material to the underside of the cap using silicone glue.

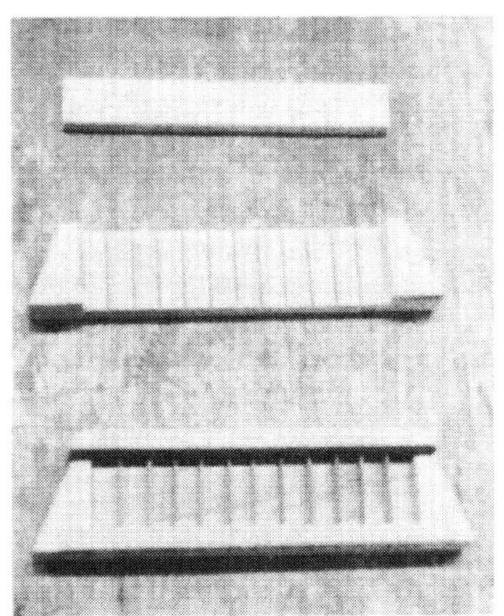

Step Four: 'Harp Body Assembly

Draw Pattern #1 on the inside of the back. If you want to put your own logo or signature in the sound hole location, draw the sound hole, too. This is easily done by aligning the bass rail edge of the pattern with the straight long bass rail edge of the inside of the back. Pin it in place with a push pin. Put one pin in at each line intersection and at each corner of each piece. These pin holes in the inside of the back can then be joined by lines very exactly reproducing the pattern of the frame in every detail. Carefully lay each frame piece and the two back brace pieces in place. Be sure the joints fit perfectly. Discrepancies of less than 1/16" in the width of pieces is trivial. The length of the top and bass rails should be exact.

Take a good old #1 piece of 3/4" plywood and lay a piece of newspaper on it. Lay your 'harp back on top of that so they coincide.

Place the toe pin block in position with glue and clamp it exactly over its pattern position.

Next, place the bass rail in position with glue. Put a bit of glue on the end too, where it joins the toe block. Clamp it lightly at two places and put your long bar clamp long-ways of the bass rail, and draw the bass rail tightly to the toe block. Check to see that you haven't changed the alignment of the bass rail. Then clamp the bass rail in place at each end and apply two clamps equal spaced between the ends. Now remove the long bar clamp.

Put glue on the long pin block and place it in position: (note dotted lines)

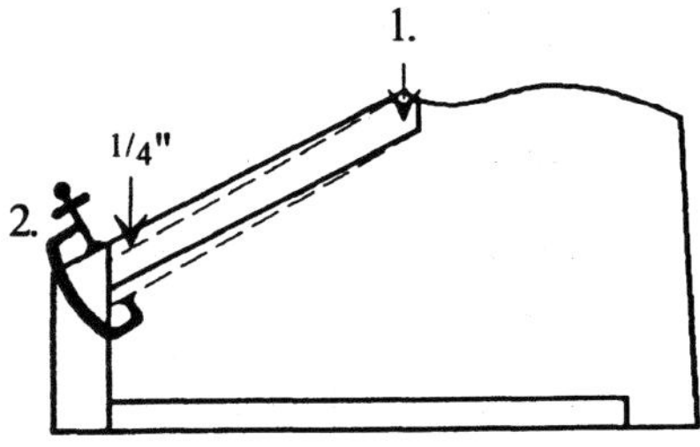

Put a clamp moderately tight at position 1. Then tighten clamp at position 2. This will force the long pin block tightly against the toe block. Be sure the piece is aligned properly with its pattern position. You may want to try a dry run, no glue, of this procedure to be sure you can do it reasonably smoothly and quickly. When it's all glued in place with a good block-to-block joint, clamp it down firmly to the back at each end, and at two places between.

The top rail should now be glued in place. Clamp it lightly. Place the dead pin rail in place without glue. Then put your bar clamp across the 'harp from mid point of the dead pin block to the toe block. When you tighten the clamp, it will draw the top rail firmly against the long pin block. Clamp the top rail firmly and remove the dead pin block immediately.

Now put glue on the dead pin block. Don't forget to put glue between the block and the two rails. Put the dead pin block in place and clamp it lightly near each end. Place the bar clamp across the 'harp again as described above, and draw the joints tight. Tighten the two clamps near the ends of the dead pin block. *Remove the bar clamp now* and then add two more hold-down clamps evenly spaced in the middle of the dead pin block. Leave this mess alone overnight. The directions on the glue say it sets up in a few minutes, and dries hard over night. I say it sets up over night and dries hard in a month. The only exception is when you make a mistake and try to get two pieces apart. You will find it is instant setting, and a team of horses couldn't pull them apart.

If you are going to sign your 'harp, make some smart remarks, or place a label so it can be seen through the sound hole, do it at this time. A light coat of shellac or lacquer over it will preserve it for posterity.

If there's any glue squeezed out between the frame joints, clean it off so you have a smooth, clean, flat top on the frame.

Place the two internal brace pieces in position with glue and weigh them down. They will be stuck in place OK in one-half hour. This can be done any time after you have your main frame pieces in place.

Next, we glue the top on and the thing starts looking like a 'harp. You may have trouble keeping the top from sliding out of position as you clamp it down. You should also keep in mind the top aligns with all edges except the dead pin end. The top is 5/8" short at the dead pin end to accommodate the bridge. To insure good alignment when you clamp it down, drive a 1/2" nail 1/4" into the bass rail, about 1/2" from each end. Then cut them off about 1/8" high. This will leave you two very sharp points sticking up. Put glue on top of the frame, and clamp the top down in position. Clamp the bass rail area first and the two sharp nails will be buried under the top, but will stick into the top insuring it won't move around. Be sure to use a strip of 1/2" thick scrap under the clamps on top of the 'harp, and have your 3/4" backing board behind, so you won't make clamp marks on your new 'harp.

After another eternal overnight wait, take all the clamps, backing board, and stuff off the 'harp body.

Before proceeding, tidy up your 'harp by sanding the edges with a belt or disc sander so everything is smooth and neat. If you fitted the parts well, the amount to be sanded will be minor. If things don't fit well, you now pay the elbow tax. Also be sure to clean out any bead of glue that squeezed out between the top and the dead pin block so there will be a good square, firm seat for your bridge.

Some paste wood filler can be used to correct minor discrepancies on joints or plywood edges.

Caution: when sanding the edges, just clean it up. Don't sand away a lot of frame, thus changing the size and shape of the body!

Step Five: Layout Of Soundboard

Place Pattern #2, which shows the position of all the bridges and tuning pins, on top of your 'harp. The bass rail edge, toe, and long pin block edges should align perfectly – or almost perfectly. Use the bass rail, toe block edges, and corner for alignment. As long as there is under 1/8" discrepancy in alignment at the upper end of the long pin block, you may proceed. If your alignment error is 1/8"-1/4", you can proceed, but will have to move your upper octave tuning pins in, away from the edge of the 'harp. If your error is more than this, you need new lumber, new glasses, and a long vacation.

With the pattern set in this position, place a push pin through the pattern into the 'harp body at the top tuning pin, the bottom tuning pin, and one somewhere near the midpoint in a tuning pin position. These will hold the pattern in position while you mark the remaining tuning pin positions and the tuning pin end bridge position. Use a sharp point (ice pick, awl, or push pin) and punch a hole through the pattern at each tuning pin position. You want a clear mark so you can see it after you have finish on the 'harp. These will mark where you will drill the tuning pin holes. Also mark six points showing the six corners of the two bridge pieces:

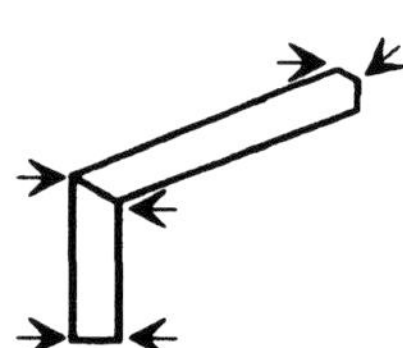

After removing the push pins and the pattern, check to be sure the marks are clean and clear. If any tuning pin marks are not deep enough to avoid being hidden by finish, punch them a bit more. Remember you are going to drill these marks out when you drill for the tuning pins.

Get out the two bridge pieces you made. The 1/2" high bridge goes in the notch along the top at the dead pin end. Cut a piece to fit the full length of this position. Use your 'harp body for the exact pattern and length. Cut it, and clean up the ends and sharp corners with sandpaper. Then glue and clamp it in position. (Look at the Pattern #2 and the side elevation of Pattern #2.)

Using the 1/4" high bridge stock, cut the two pieces necessary to make the tuning pin bridge. These pieces need only be lightly glued in place by placing some weight such as a brick or two on top to hold them in securely in place for an hour or so.

Step Six: Finishing

Finishing is up to you. Any protective finish paint, lacquer, or varnish will work. Decoration is at your discretion. Put finish on your chord bars, chord bar holders, and dead pin end covers as well as the 'harp body. You must sand off the sharp corners and drill the screw holes, (See Pattern #4), before finishing your dead pin end cover.

Step Seven: Pins

The first thing you will need in stringing your autoharp is a stringing square. You make this square with a strip of wood about 1/8" thick and 1 1/2" to 2" wide, 11" long. You'll also need a piece 1/2" x 1" x 6" long:

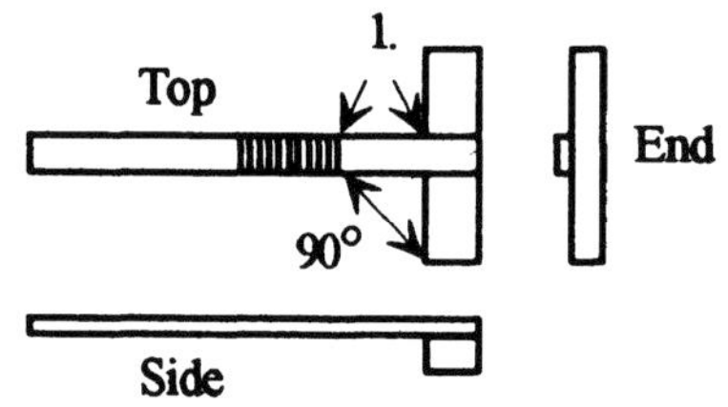

Be sure the pieces are at right angles. Glue and nail the joint with a couple of small nails. You will draw a series of lines across the tongue of the stringing square to coincide with the 36 string positions. The distance (1.) in the above drawing 1 3/16" and each cross line (36 in all) is spaced 1/4" up from the last. Be careful to measure exactly and make the lines across the tongue square with the edge of the tongue. Verify your square by laying it on Pattern #2. The string positions on the square should match those on the pattern:

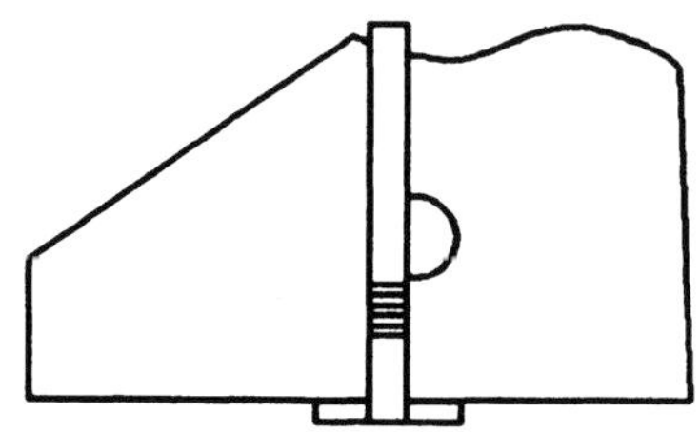

If you lay this square like so on your 'harp, each line denotes a string position. This will then allow you to mark the position of the bridge pins and the small grooves you will make to guide your string position at the tuning pin end bridge and dead pin end bridge respectively. Done properly, it will ensure exact location and spacing of the strings. Always be sure the base of the stringing square is lying flat against the bass rail edge of the autoharp.

At the dead pin end, make a small mark on the bridge corresponding to each string position on your stringing square. Make the marks on the beveled corner of the bridge – like so:

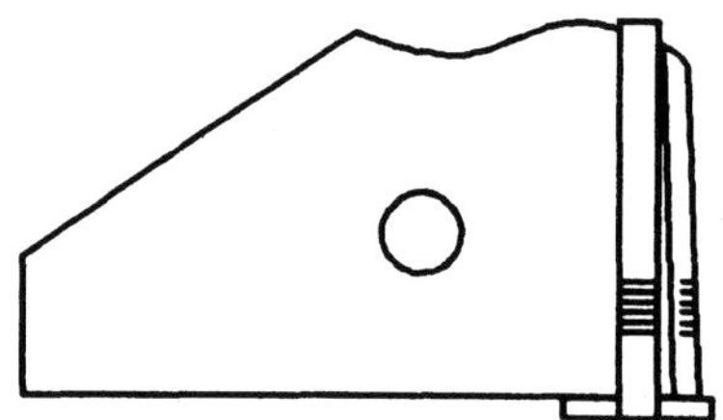

Make a small groove at each of these lines with a triangular or rifling file so when the string comes over the brass bridge rod, it will then lie in this groove and then go down to the dead pin on the end of the 'harp.

To place the dead pins in the dead pin block, (See Pattern #3), scribe two lines 1/2" and 7/8" down from the top of the dead pin block. The pins for the odd numbered strings (1, 3, 5, 7, etc.) will be located on the lower line. Those for the even numbered strings (2, 4, 6, 8, etc.) will be located on the upper line.

These pin positions should be straight down and slightly toward the bass from the 36 grooves you made in the bridge. Look at the pattern, and you will see the strings angle slightly toward the bass. Make a cardboard pattern to coincide with the angle of these strings on the pattern – like so:

Use this to draw a line from the bridge groove to the proper dead pin position as shown on the pattern for each of the 36 strings.

Drill a hole in each of these 36 positions. The pins you will use are the #6 bridge pins. If you can't get these pins, you can make them by using a 6- or 8-penny nail that will fit through the loop in the end of your strings. Be sure to cut the head off the nails and cut them to about 3/4" length before driving them in place.

Since the #6 pins are 5/64", they will fit loosely in a 5/64" drill bit hole. There are two solutions to this. First, if you know a machinist, ask to borrow a drill bit a few thousandths of an inch less than 5/64". If you don't know a machinist, mount a 5/64" bit in your hand drill. Turn on the drill and hold the side of the drill bit against a grind stone. This will slightly reduce the diameter of the drill. Test drill a scrap of wood until you get a hole that you can tap the pin into, hammering gently. Drive the pins in, and your dead pin end is ready.

The tuning pin end bridge must be marked also using the stringing square.

Keep in mind – the string goes alongside the guide pin. The guide pin should be placed just above and alongside the string position:

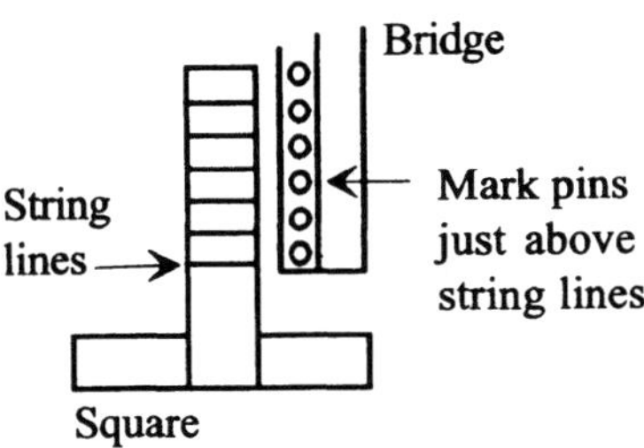

Use the #6 bridge pins here, too. Use the same drill as above. Again, if you can't find #6 bridge pins, finishing nails can be substituted here. Find a size that will drive easily into a 5/64" or 1/16" hole. Use the appropriate size drill bit. If they are too long, cut them to about 3/4" length. Drive these pins in so they extend 1/8" to 3/16" above the bridge.

Bridge rods are made of 1/8" brass rod. The dead pin end requires two pieces 9 1/2" long. The tuning pin bridge needs a piece 15 1/4" long. Cut the two 9 1/2" pieces and round the sharp edges off the ends using a file or grinding wheel. Lay the remainder of your 36" piece of your brass rod along the short base segment of the bridge and mark exactly where the bend should be. (See Pattern #2.) Place the rod in the jaws of a vice so the mark is exactly at the edge of the jaw. While gently pulling on the end of the rod, hammer on it as close as possible to where it extends from the vice. Bend it until the angle coincides with the desired shape as shown on the pattern. Lay this in place on the bridge, mark the treble end of the rod even with the upper end of the bridge. Cut it off, and smooth up both ends of this bridge rod. Put the rods aside.

Now we come to the diamond splitting. I call it "diamond splitting," because if you grub this up, you will start all over again. When drilling the tuning pin holes, use a new sharp 3/16" bit. Take a scrap piece of the same wood you used for the toe block and long pin block, and drill a hole in it with your drill press. Try one of your tuning pins in this hole. See that it drives in tightly and turns firmly with a tuning wrench.

If you must hand drill, have a helper look to see that you are drilling straight down. Be sure you use the stop on your drill so all the holes are 1" deep. If you don't have a stop, put a masking tape collar on your drill bit one inch up from the tip. This is set so it drills 1" deep into your instrument body. The test scrap may not be the same depth as the 'harp, so don't set up on the scrap and then drill the 'harp. The 1" is critical in that a shallow hole may let you bottom out with the tuning pins and split the pin block. If the hole is too deep, you may overheat your drill bit and burn or ream the pin hole.

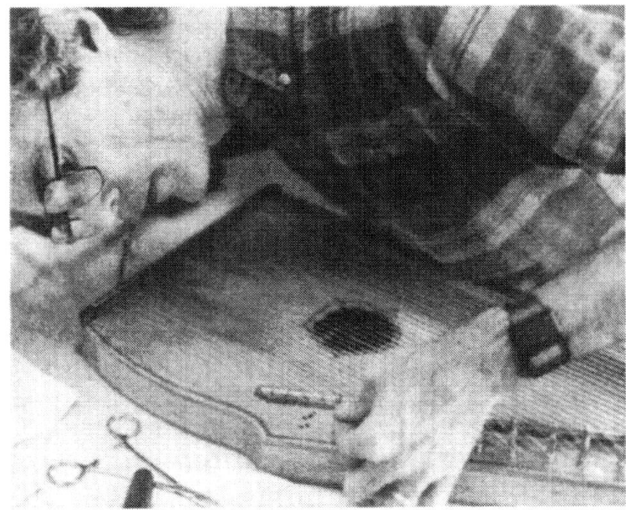

It is also critical that you drill the hole in one easy, clean motion. *DO NOT EVER REENTER THE PIN HOLE WITH THE DRILL!* One motion, one time only. If you make two

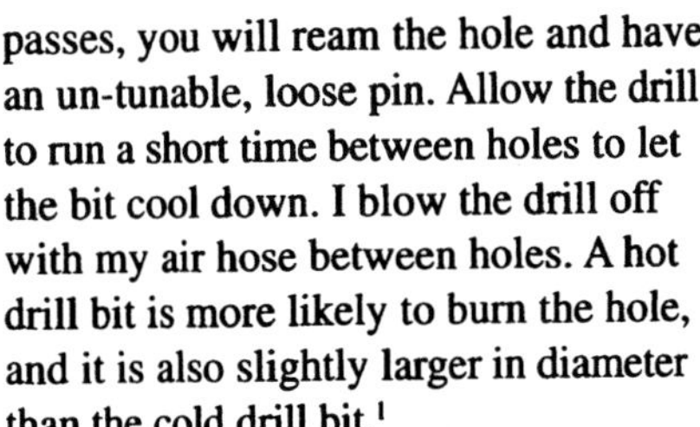

passes, you will ream the hole and have an un-tunable, loose pin. Allow the drill to run a short time between holes to let the bit cool down. I blow the drill off with my air hose between holes. A hot drill bit is more likely to burn the hole, and it is also slightly larger in diameter than the cold drill bit.[1]

Now that that traumatic experience is over, the fun part begins. You are going to teach your new 'harp to sing.

If you wish to mark "alphabet soup" on your tuning pin positions, now is the time to do it. The holes are there, and there are no pins or strings in your way. Small alphabet decals on a black body, or black ink on a natural or light body. A glass writing pen such as Pilot ultrafine point, permanent SC-UF works nicely on lacquer or varnish. If you are handy/arty, acrylic paint and a brush with a fine point works well, also. Mark the strings from bass to treble – F, G, C, D, E, F, F#, G, A, A#, B, C, C#, D, D#, E, F, F#, G, G#, A, A#, B, C, C#, D, D#, E, F, F#, G, G#, A, A#, B, C.

Step Eight: Stringing

Back to your 'harp's first song – get out your Model A string set. Starting with #1F, place the loop end over the dead pin. Have a helper hold it in place there. Lay it up through the groove in the bridge and across the 'harp. Place the tip of the string through the hole in a tuning pin. I prefer to bend a loop in the end of the wire and put the sharp point back into the tuning pin hole. I hate the sharp points sticking fingers and clothes. If the string goes more than 2" beyond the tuning pin, cut off the excess.

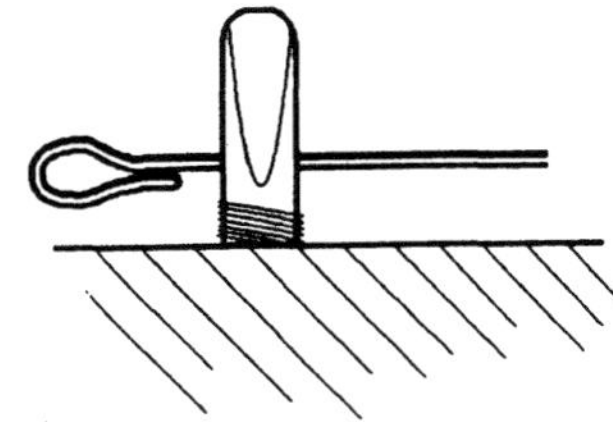

Now find a tuning wrench and wind the pin so the wire forms a smooth coil around the pin below the eyelet. Wind it up until the pin is over the pin hole in the 'harp. Place the end of the pin into the hole and drive it in with a hammer – something a bit heavier than a tack hammer, but less than a log splitter. I use a ball peen hammer. These are made for driving or pounding metal and seem to have the right feel.

Work on a good solid table with a thin firm blanket like an army blanket under the 'harp body. The good firm backing is needed so the pins can be driven smoothly without bouncing the 'harp around too much. The cloth keeps you from ruining the finish on the table and 'harp. After starting the pin, I keep my thumb and finger on each side of the pin as I drive it home. This has two purposes. If you miss the pin, you won't beat up the top of your 'harp, and the pain inflicted on your thumb will greatly increase your accuracy while driving the remaining pins. Drive the pins down to where there is about 1/8" of threads still showing above the soundboard. (A word here – the sound of a ball peen hammer driving a metal pin into a resonant sound box is an unforgettable one. It can bring fear to your heart, and tears to your eyes.)

Check to see that the string is properly positioned at the dead pin end and around its proper guide pin on the bridge. Tighten the tuning pin until the string makes a clear note when plucked. Be sure the lowest winding of string around the tuning pin is close to the face of the soundboard, so the string will stop down hard on the bridge rod like so:

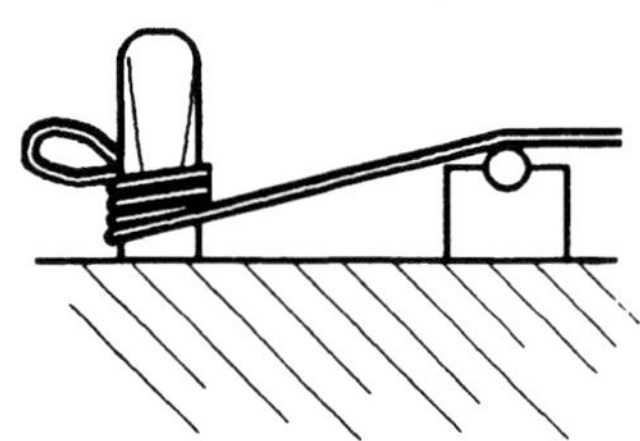

Repeat this 36 times, and you have the 'harp strung.

After this procedure, tune each string up to pitch, and take a very firm thumb pick and strum repeatedly and strongly across all the strings. The noise will be discordant, loud, and awful, but it sets the strings so they will hold tune within a few days.

Step Nine: Installation Of Bars/Holders

The end cover can now be put in place with the hollow side over the dead pins. It should be placed so it is flush with the back of the 'harp. The 'harp frame will need to have pilot holes drilled with a 7/64" drill bit to accommodate the #6 screws.

Chord bars and chord bar holders should be installed now. The chord bar felts have self-sticking adhesive. Carefully remove the backing paper strip and press the felt strip firmly onto the bar. Be sure it is aligned perfectly with the chord bar. If the felts are too long, they should be trimmed of with a sharp razor. Single-edge razor blades work well for cutting felt.

The bar holders will be placed approximately 1/4" below the bass string and 3/8" above the top string.

Place the bass end bar holders in place as shown on Pattern #2, 1/4" below the bass string and 1" from the dead pin bridge. Drill pilot holes through the holder into the 'harp body and attach it in place with the 1 3/4" #6 screws (use a 7/64" drill bit).

Place the treble bar holder in position, but don't drill or put in the screws yet. The bars should be numbered so when fitted to their respective slots, you can be sure to get them back in the same place. I number the bars on the ends, #1-12, left to right. The odd numbered bars will be upper tier, and the even numbered bars, the lower tier. The chords for a standard OSI 12-bar 'harp are:

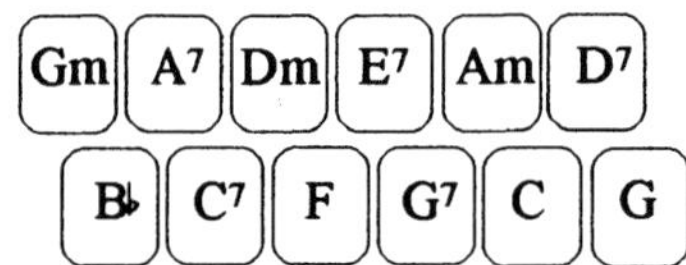

If you wish to put alphabet soup on your bars, now's a good time to do it. Any of the methods mentioned for marking the tuning pins are OK here.

If you have made your bar holders perfectly, every bar will fit perfectly. You may find, however, that some of the bar holder slots are a bit narrower than others, and the bars don't fit freely. If you find this to be true as you fit the bars, just sand a bit off the side of the tight bars until they do fit freely.

With the bars and bar holders in place and the treble holder loosely in place, now put the springs in the bar holder slots and fit all the bars back into the holders. When they all fit smoothly, be sure the treble bar holder is in its exact position so it just touches the dead pin bridges and so it clears the end of the bars by just a "scosh" (a "scosh" being about the thickness of a piece of manila folder). If you make a few 1/4" wide strips of manila folder and put them in between the bar ends and the treble bar holder of several bars, this should position the treble bar holder perfectly.

Drill your pilot holes into the 'harp body and attach it with the other two #6 x 1 3/4" screws. Remove the manila folder shim spacers and the bars should move freely without too much end play. If you have a bar that doesn't move freely, a bit of sanding on the end or side where needed should do the trick.

Step Ten: Felting

Before cutting felts, I always tune the 'harp up again more exactly than the first rough tuning.

Next we cut the felts:

Chord	Notes Played			
Gm	G	A♯	D	
B♭	B♭	D	F	
A^7	A	C♯	E	G
C^7	C	E	G	A♯ *
Dm	D	F	A	
F	F	A	C	
E^7	E	G♯	B	D *
G^7	G	B	D	F
Am	A	C	E	
C	C	E	G	*
D^7	D	F♯	A	C *
G	G	B	D	

* *I do not cut out the low D, G, and C (see above chart) because a third or seventh below or near the tonic of the chord in the bass will sound discordant. Also, I never cut out two adjacent strings in the larger wound bass strings. Thus the low G on the C and C^7 chords is eliminated.*

Place each bar in position and find each note (string) that plays in that chord. Make a small tic mark on the felt immediately above each string that plays in that chord. Your bar will look like this:

Cut out each tic with an inverted V so:

Now as you cut each bar and put it in place, you can strum across to hear the sweet sound of your first chords. About the time I get over to the F chord, I have B♭, C[7], and F – enough to play a few choruses of my favorite three-chord song, "Home on the Range," before I finish the job.

(You will notice the D# does not play on any chord. It only sounds in open chording and drag notes.)

Step Eleven: Enjoy!

After all the chord bars are cut, put the chord bar holder caps on, and Wow! You Are Done! Will wonders never cease! Enjoy!

In October, 1999, the Pennsylvania Cable Network videoed George Orthey in his workshop. This hour-long tape may be helpful to you with this project. Write to: Pennsylvania Cable Network, 401 Fallowfield Road, Camp Hill, Pennsylvania 17011.

[1] If you do end up with some loose pin holes, see "Loose Tuning Pins" p.19.

Autoharp Quarterly

Winter, 1996
Volume Eight, Number Two
Five Dollars

The International Magazine Dedicated to the Autoharp Enthusiast

In This Issue

Oscar Schmidt 1879 – 1975 Part Three by Glen Peterson

New Age Possibilities with the Autoharp

Musicking the Autoharp

Annual Club Directory

Deciphering the Awesome Ultratonic

Kidstock with Bonnie Phipps

Picker's Portrait featuring Ray Sipes

Joseph Marlin Riggs

AQ Volume XI, Number 2
THE MOUNTAIN LAUREL AUTOHARP EIGHT YEARS LATER
George Orthey

The Mountain Laurel Autoharp Eight Years Later

When *Autoharp Quarterly* published the Mountain Laurel 'Harp plans, I had no idea how well these plans would be received, and how many hundreds of instruments would be made using them. Mountain Laurel 'Harps have sprung up not only in this country, but in Europe as well. Many first-time autoharp makers have proudly brought their instruments to me to show their work. I've seen many very well made autoharps solely derived from these plans, and many more with upgraded construction and decoration.

During this time, I've formulated some thoughts concerning improvements on this instrument, which I've discussed with the folks who have contacted me. These thoughts haven't been published, and so I've decided it's time to share them with everyone who has/will be building the Mountain Laurel Autoharp.

Bracing

The one single improvement that does more for the sound of these instruments than any other adjustment is the changing of the internal bracing of this 'harp. The plans call for two braces that go between the sound board and the back of the instrument. These braces should be deleted and replaced by two full-length cross braces. The braces should be in the same position on the sound board as the plans dictate, but extended so they go about 1/4" into the frame. This will, of course, require a small notch be made in the frame to accommodate the tip of the brace. I would use a brace 1/2" wide and 3/4" high, cut down to about 1/8" high near the ends:

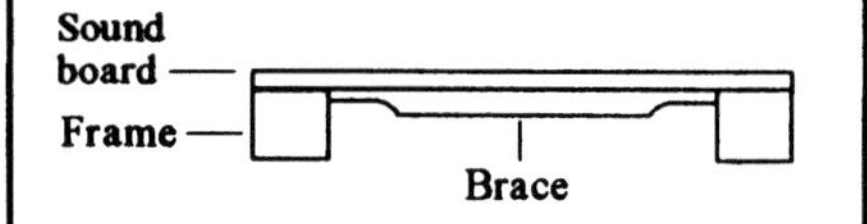

Similarly and slightly offset from the sound board braces, put in two smaller back braces 1/4" wide and 1/2" high. This will allow the top and back of the instrument to vibrate freely, and will enable the instrument to sound fuller and louder.

The Frame

The frame of the instrument is principally a spacer between the top and back, and the butt jointed frame works fine. If you want, though, you can get a piece of laminated piano pin block and cut it to make the section of the frame (see plans) marked "toe pin block, long pin block, and top rail." This must be one continuous piece . So you will have no joints in the pin block section of the frame. This improvement does essentially nothing for the sound of the instrument, but may improve its rigidity and ability to stay in tune.

Appearance

Plywood vs solid wood: Replacing the plywood suggested in the plans with solid wood will substantially improve the appearance of the instrument, if you have quality wood and the equipment to get it to the proper thickness. I suggest about a 1/4" thick sound board, and a 3/16" thick back. In my hands, I have found the Douglas fir marine plywood to produce a sound quality that is quite acceptable with virtually no risk of splitting or warping. With this in mind, go ahead and use good dry spruce or redwood for a sound board, and a hard wood of your choice for the back. (You may find some modest improvement of sound quality using these woods.)

Inlay lines, side facing, and binding strips will all improve the finished appearance of the instrument, but naturally, will do nothing for the sound.

Fine Tuners

Fine tuners can be added simply by deleting the deadpins on the big end of the 'harp and replacing them with a fine tuner bar. If you are using Oscar Schmidt fine tuners, you will need to drill (Very Carefully!) and countersink about nine or ten equally spaced holes through the bar.

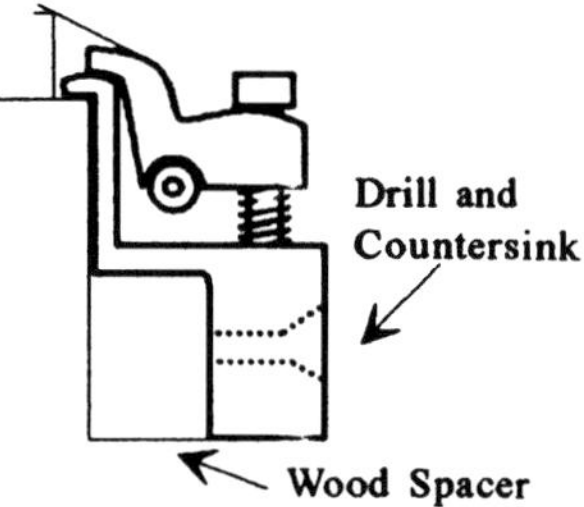

Be sure to drill the holes between the vertical threaded holes. Use a 1/8" drill bit, and attach the fine tuner bar to the end of the 'harp with 1 1/4" flat-head wood screws. You will need to drill a pilot hole into the wood using a 3/32" drill bit. Be sure the bar is attached so the strings will be in the proper position. This is done by using your stringing square. The vertical holes for the fine tuner cap screws should be centered on the string positions. The strings will then naturally come up over the bridge and lie in their proper position.

If you do choose to use the fine tuners, you will need to use Model A special strings which have a ball end rather than a loop end. The standard loop end Model A OSI strings will not work with fine tuners.

If all of these embellishments and improvements are done with care and skill, you may well equal and even exceed your greatest expectations. ❖

Used with permission of Stonehill Productions.

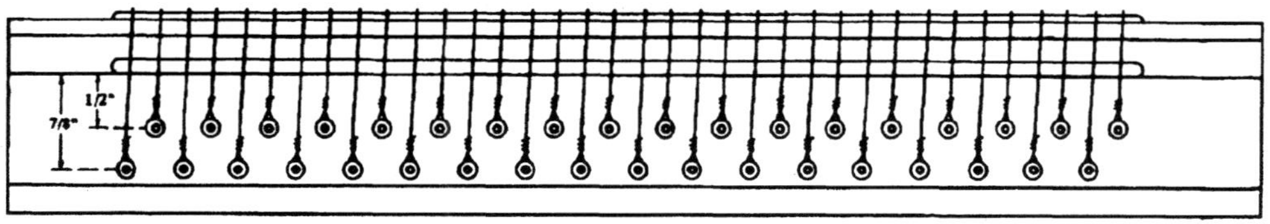

PATTERN # 3
(End Elevation of Pattern # 2)
DEAD PIN BLOCK

1/2"
7/8"

MOUNTAIN LAUREL™ HARP

Plan is reduced. Enlarge 212% for actual size. (Enlargement may cause drawing to distort. Measure carefully.)

PATTERN #2
STRINGS,
TUNING & BRIDGE PINS

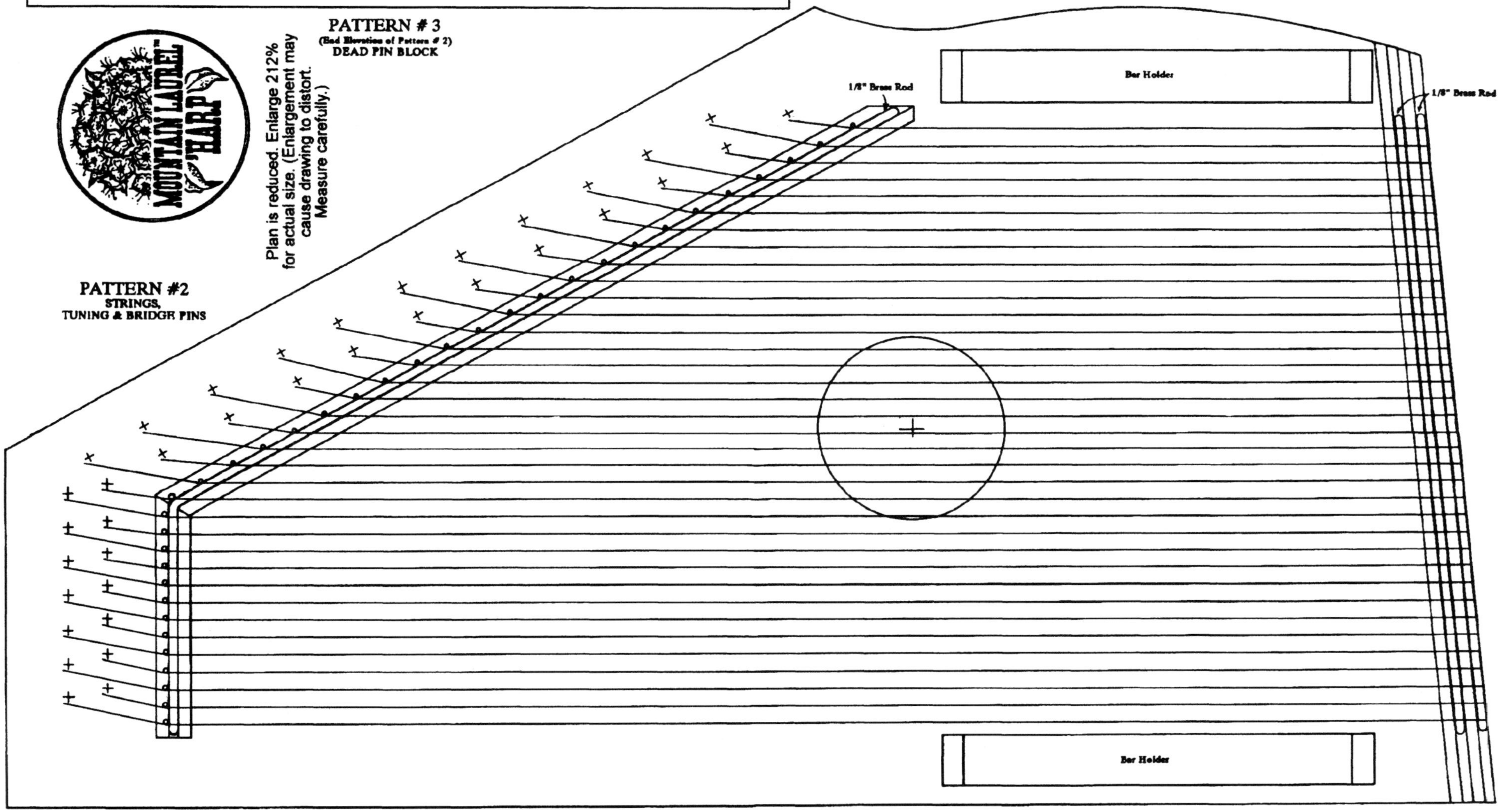

1/8" Brass Rod

Bar Holder

1/8" Brass Rod

Bar Holder

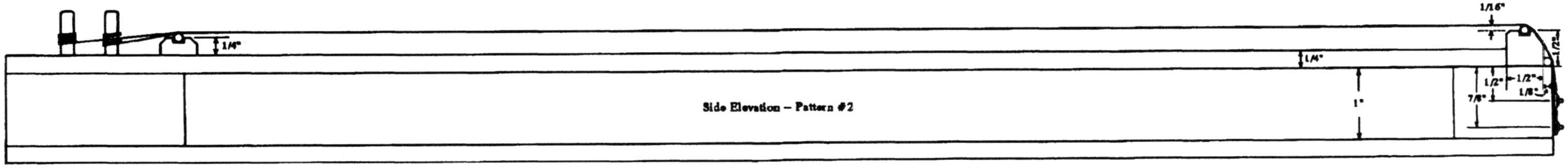

1/4"
1/16"
1/2"
1/4"
1/2"
1/2"
1/8"
7/8"
1"

Side Elevation – Pattern #2

Copyright 1991, Orthey Instruments. All Rights Reserved.

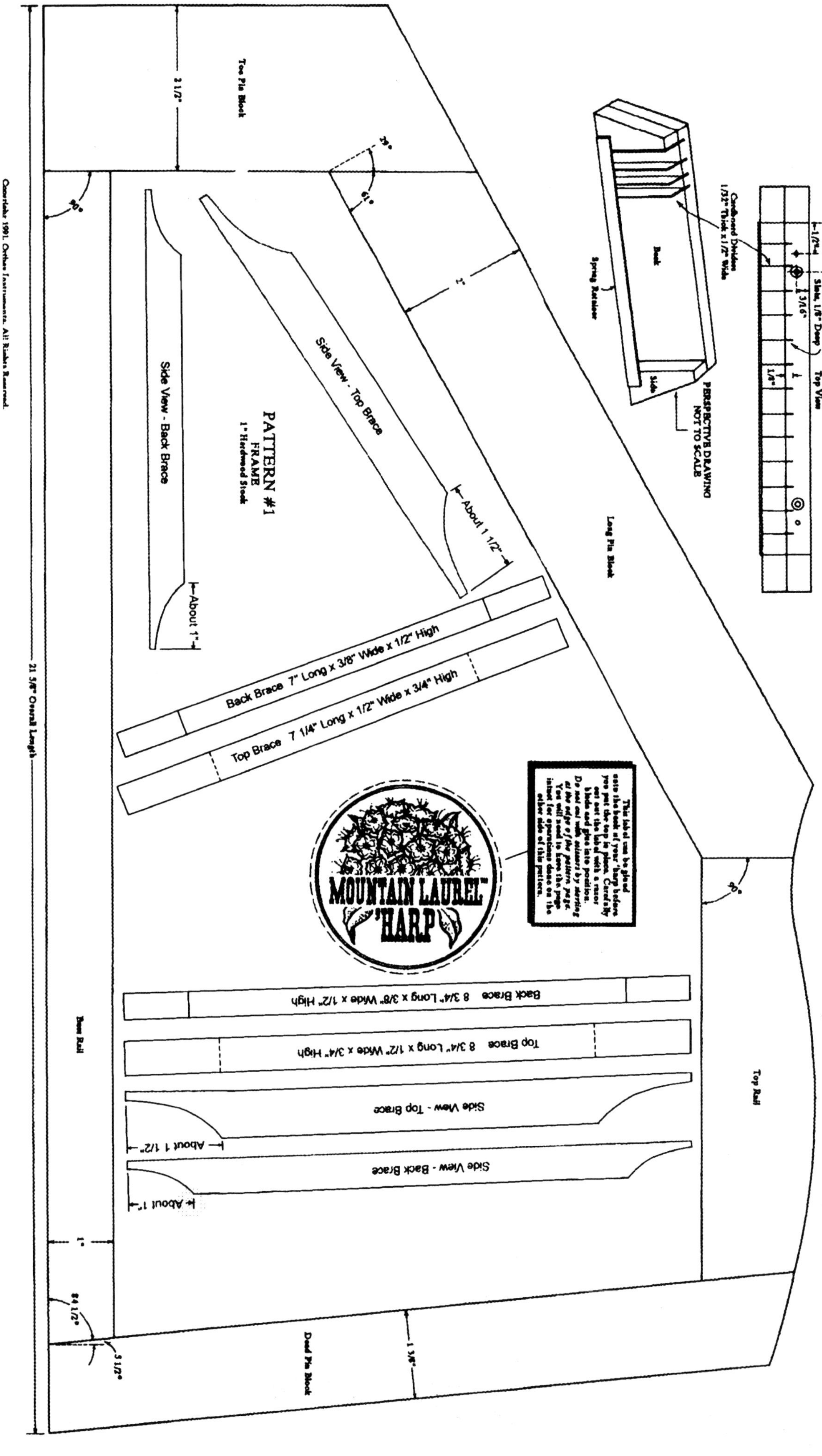

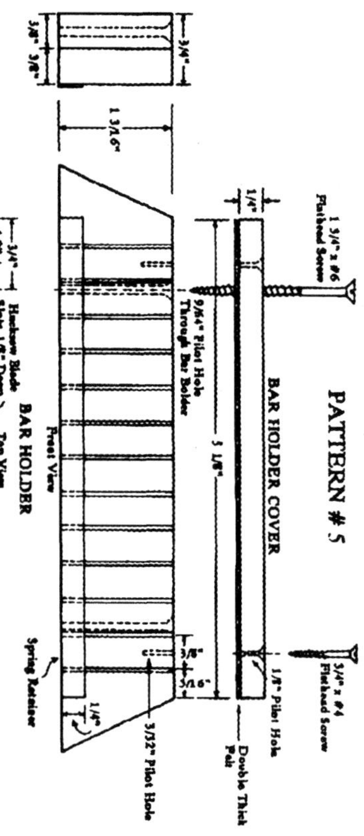

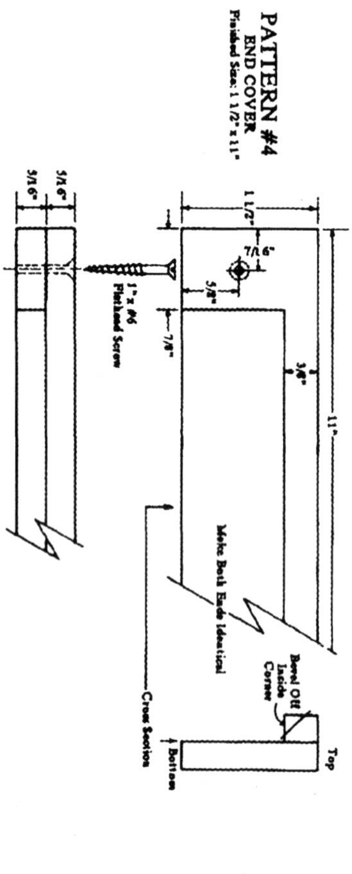

PATTERN # 5

1 3/4" x #6 Flathead Screw

3/4" x #4 Flathead Screw

BAR HOLDER COVER

1/8" Pilot Hole

1/4"

Double Thick Felt

5 1/8"

9/64" Pilot Hole Through Bar Holder

3/4"

1 3/16"

3/8"

5/16"

3/32" Pilot Hole

1/4"

3/8" 3/8"

Front View

Spring Retainer

BAR HOLDER

3/4"

1/2"

Hacksaw Blade Slots, 1/8" Deep

Top View

3/16"

1/8"

Cardboard Dividers 1/32" Thick x 1/2" Wide

PERSPECTIVE DRAWING NOT TO SCALE

Back

Side

Spring Retainer

Plan is reduced. Enlarge 212% for actual size. (Enlargement may cause drawing to distort. Measure carefully.)

PATTERN #4

END COVER

Finished Size: 1 1/2" x 11"

11"

3/8"

1 1/2"

7/16"

5/8"

7/8"

Make Both Ends Identical

Top

Bevel Off Inside Corner

Bottom

Cross Section

1" x #6 Flathead Screw

5/16"

5/16"

Top Rail

90°

Long Pin Block

This label can be glued onto the back of your 'harp before you put the top in place. Carefully cut out the label with a razor blade and glue into position. *Do not cut with scissors by starting at the edge of the pattern page.* You will need to have the page intact for operations done on the other side of this pattern.

MOUNTAIN LAUREL™ 'HARP

Back Brace 8 3/4" Long x 3/8" Wide x 1/2" High

Top Brace 8 3/4" Long x 1/2" Wide x 3/4" High

Side View - Top Brace

Side View - Back Brace

About 1 1/2"

About 1"

1 3/8"

Dead Pin Block

2"

29°

61°

About 1 1/2"

Side View - Top Brace

Back Brace 7" Long x 3/8" Wide x 1/2" High

Top Brace 7 1/4" Long x 1/2" Wide x 3/4" High

PATTERN #1

FRAME

1" Hardwood Stock

Toe Pin Block

2 1/2"

About 1"

Side View - Back Brace

Bass Rail

1"

5 1/2°

84 1/2°

90°

21 5/8" Overall Length

Copyright 1991 Orthey Instruments. All Rights Reserved.

Questions And Answers

AQ Volumes I - IX

George Orthey

These questions and answers are scattered throughout the contents of the first nine years of Autoharp Quarterly.

Bass Tuning

Q. I am baffled by the string tuning of the Oscar Schmidt 21-bar chromatic 'harp. The middle and high octaves contain all of the notes of the chromatic scale, but the low octave omits C♯, D♯, and G♯. Why? Also, why are there two extra low strings, F and G, and why are they F and G instead of some other notes?

A. Keep in mind that the forte of the 'harp is in the middle to upper octave. The melody is played there. The bass is used mainly for fill and harmony. The early 'harps and later 12- and 15-bar 'harps were centered on the keys of F, C, and G. The missing notes are not in those keys. F, C, and G are the tonic notes of those three keys. The tuning was never changed for a 21-bar 'harp. However, I would not recommend a change here, either. This 'harp still centers on the keys of F, C, and G. If the chromatics were added in the bass, something would have to come out above (there are only 36 strings) that would be unacceptable. Some people do drop the F and G off the bass end and start with C, allowing the addition of two other bass chromatics. This is useful particularly if you want to beef up the bass in the keys of D and A. Making a bigger 'harp and adding many extra strings to have a chromatic bass is counterproductive. It gives a lot of rumble for very little return in sound.[1]

More Bass Tuning

Q. On a 21-bar 'harp, I notice some of the chord bars damp notes that are part of the chord: Dm damps the lowest F, D^7 damps the lowest C, Em damps the two lowest Gs, and E^7 damps the lowest D. Why is this? Also, why are these the only chord bars on which this is so?

A. It's true – some notes are left out in the bass. If you have two bass strings next to each other in pitch and proximity, with both sounding in the same chord, they will make an unacceptable rumble and sound out of tune. This is particularly true in the lowest five or six strings. Also the lowest note in a chord should be the tonic of that chord, or a fifth of the tonic. Therefore the Dm plays D as its lowest note, and similarly, D^7, Em, and E^7 play D, E and E respectively as their lowest notes. If you don't believe this, cut them out, save the pieces of felt. Try it. You won't like it. Then glue the felt pieces back in.

Repairing Old 'Harps

Q. I have an old Model A 'harp in need of major repair. What is the best glue for these repairs?

A. In regluing an old "fall-apart" 'harp, I must say if you can get it completely apart, the job is made simpler. The glues I use are handy and effective. Franklin Tite Bond and Elmer's Carpenter's Glue are similar, and in the family commonly called "yellow glue."

By springing joints open with a thin blade putty knife and forcing the glue into joints using a plastic applicator bottle, you can do a good job of getting the glue down into the loose joints. Of course, plan ahead for your clamping procedure so a secure joint is produced. Be sure to use protective pieces between the clamps and the instrument so you don't make a lot of dents in your restored treasure.[2]

Soft Felts

Q. Sometimes I find the sticky layer of new felt bonds well to the bar, but it's soft and doesn't seem to bond well to the felt side of the sticky layer.

A. Using a glue dispenser, put a fine line of Elmer's Glue on the side of the felt where it contacts the sticky edge – close to the bar. You will stabilize this connection, and add a bit of stiffness to the felt. Just put enough pressure on the glue dispenser to drive a bit of the glue into the felt along this base-line of the felt. Don't get glue up on the face of the area that contacts the strings.

After putting the glue into the side of the felt, set the bar down on a flat surface so the felt will be held up against the bar. After it dries overnight, the felt should be considerably more stable and well attached to the bar.

Fine Tuner Fix

Q. Is there anything to keep my fine tuners working smoothly and well?

A. These great fine tuners, like any mechanical device, will work smoother and last longer with a little lubrication. Hey, I said a *little* lube!

I make a mixture of powdered graphite and light machine oil like Three-in-One Oil. The graphite and oil are both available at any good hardware store. Mix about one-fourth graphite powder with three-fourth oil. (They used to make oil called Lockease that's already mixed.) Anyway, with this, you get a residual layer of graphite that lasts even after the oil is dry and gone. Just dip the thread end of each screw 1/4" into the graphite/oil mixture. Then put the screw on a paper towel and let the oil drain off. A thin layer of graphite will remain in the threads – just enough to lubricate without dripping out anywhere else. I follow this procedure every time I install fine tuners, and every time I restring a 'harp.

Diminished 7th Chords

Q. I'm interested in changing three chords to diminished 7th chords. What information is needed to accomplish this?

A. You'll need three felts, and will have to "get rid" of three chords on your present 'harp layout. Refelt those three bars.[3] Then start with any note, (middle C or above), and count that note as #1. Mark it on your felt. Skip two notes on the *chromatic* scale and mark the next one – etc. Match the notes below middle C to the notes you have already marked above that point. Cut out the notes you have marked on the felt.[4]

The Three Diminished 7th Chords
Cdim⁷ = C D♯ F♯ A C D♯ F♯ A etc.
C♯dim⁷= C♯ E G A♯ C♯ E G A♯ etc.
Ddim⁷ = D F G♯ B D F G♯ B etc.

"V" Cuts On Felts

Q. I've noticed in some of your articles you make "V" cuts on the chord bar felts rather than the normal square cuts. Why do you do that?

A. I find that by cutting an inverted V notch, leaving a bit of backing and felt in place at the bottom of the V, gives the felt good stability and also makes it easier to strip it off the bar when refelting.

New Felt Paper

Q. How can I get the paper off the back of new bar felts without pulling some of the glue off?

A. If you start from the middle of the strip, it's easier. Bend the felt backwards (paper side under), then tease a small area of paper loose from the middle of the strip.

Chromatic VS. Diatonic Decision

Q. I'm thinking about getting a new autoharp. Should I buy a chromatic or a diatonic? I really don't understand the difference between the two.

A. You've asked a question that could bring on a volume of fact, fiction, and opinions. My answer will be oriented mainly to the novice 'harp player.

In simple terms, a chromatic autoharp gives you a panoramic view of music. It sees and plays a wide range of keys. A diatonic gives you a telescopic view of music. It plays a few keys with more clarity and brilliance, but is limited in its scope of chords and keys which may be played. The most common diatonic 'harps are in one, two, or three keys. If you have more keys, you approach a requirement for a chromatic scale to accommodate the chords you'll need.

If you need a multiple key diatonic, the keys you select must be immediately adjacent to each other in the circle of fifths:

Circle Of Fifths

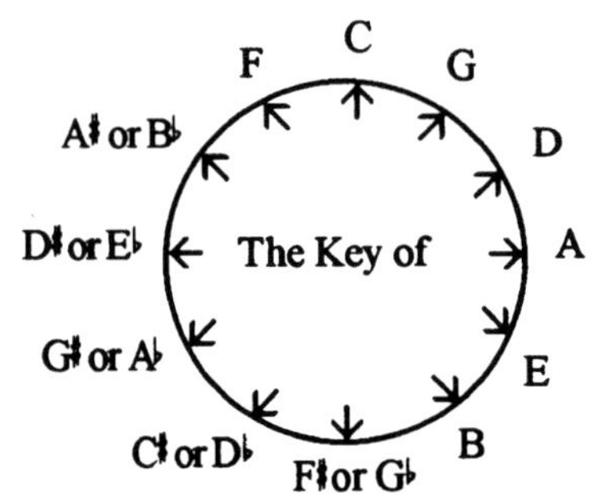

You can have a G-D-A 'harp. (Note: the Keys of G, D, and A are next to each other on the chart above.) Each of those keys differs from the next by only one note. On the other hand, you can't have an F-E 'harp, because they differ by five notes, and would therefore require a chromatic scale.

A diatonic C scale is limited to the "do, re, mi" notes. It has no accidentals (sharps or flats). Because you have 36 strings on your instrument and only the diatonic scale, you can tune that 'harp by pairing many strings. The sound effect is similar to a 12-string as compared to the sound of a 6-string guitar – a louder, clearer, more singing sound. The major chords on a single key diatonic autoharp will play 16-21 strings. The same chords on a chromatic will play 10-13 strings.

The other major factor of the diatonic 'harp is the ability to play "open notes" (notes played without depressing a chord bar). This allows you to play a speed level for fastest fiddle tunes with greater accuracy, since many of the notes (strings) are paired.

With this simplified explanation of a diatonic versus chromatic 'harp in your mind, let's go back to your question – which type of instrument you should buy.

Think about the kind of music you play. Do you enjoy singing/playing gospel music? It's often in the keys of B♭ and F. Old-time music is most often played in the keys of G, D, and A. If you enjoy both kinds of music, you should buy a chromatic instrument. If, on the other hand, you belong to a dulcimer club and play mostly in the keys of D and G, (cool it, dulcimer players!), then you might want a diatonic D-A 'harp.

If you say "We play almost everything in G, D, and A except one song in G♯," I'd advise you to forget that song and go with a G-D-A 'harp.

If you do a lot of jamming around a campfire and don't stick to a few keys, you'll either need a good chromatic 'harp or a lot of patience and a great enjoyment for listening.

Remember when deciding how many chords you would put on your diatonic instrument, you must, if you want to play "open noting" (diatonic style), count a lock bar for every key on your 'harp. That would mean, if it were to be a 3-key instrument, you must figure on 3 lock bars – these will each take up one chord bar space!

If you're contemplating buying a custom-built instrument and already have a chromatic 'harp, I'd suggest buying a good chromatic instrument and converting your older 'harp to a diatonic one. If you buy a custom diatonic and keep your older 'harp the way it is set up now as a chromatic, you will find the newer one will so outperform your older instrument for sound and playability, you'll end up with a 'harp that sounds great, but is limited in common usefulness. And you'll have a 'harp that should be your work horse that sounds mediocre.

With all this in mind, sit down and think about what you do – what you need to expand your horizons. And talk to some chromatic and diatonic players. Then make your decision.[5] ❖

[1] See "Strings – Their Ideal Sizes and Lengths"p.31.

[2] See "Autoharp Appraisal" p.106.

[3] See "Refelting And Siliconing Chord Bars" p.7.

[4] For a complete explanation of diminished 7th chords, see "Explanation And Use Of Diminished 7th Chords"p.49.

[5] For a road test to give you the feel of playing a diatonic autoharp, see "A Diatonic Tryout"p.65.

Oscar Schmidt

AQ VolumeIII, Number 3
THE TRUE HISTORY OF THE AUTOHARP
Ivan Stiles

The True History Of The Autoharp

The Autoharp –
"An American instrument of American invention."
(19th century advertising slogan)

For years, we have read that Charles F. Zimmermann of Philadelphia, Pennsylvania invented what we call the autoharp. America would certainly have something to be proud of – if, in fact, it were true.

Over two years ago, I had a conversation with Mark Fackeldey (1988 International Autoharp Champion) during which he asked me, "What's this I read about the autoharp not being invented by Zimmermann?" This more than piqued my curiosity. Mark went on to say that the 1988 edition of the *Encyclopaedia Britannica* listed the inventor of the autoharp as C. A. Gütter.

Was it Zimmermann, or was it Gütter? To understand fully what transpired in the early days of the autoharp, we first have to look at exactly what Zimmermann patented. On the next page are patent drawings of Zimmermann's and Gütter's instruments. The first thing we see is that Zimmermann's instrument bears little resemblance to what we call an autoharp. This fact seems to have been either ignored or glossed over by autoharp historians. Aside from the obvious difference in the shape of the instrument, the mechanism used to damp the strings is significantly different from the autoharp as we know it. Instead of depressing the chord bar vertically to damp the strings, the bar on the Zimmermann instrument is pulled horizontally by a "trigger." The felts extend down from the bar and go in between the strings. The strings are damped by pulling sideways. It is interesting to note that this method would have made the multiple-chord bar impossible. (On a multiple-chord bar, certain felts were moved laterally to a different position by a lever which allowed one bar to function for more than one chord.)

Another difference is the incorporation of a flageolet bar. This bar is in the center of the chord bar arrangement and over the exact center of each string. When this bar was utilized with another chord bar, the result was a rise in pitch of the chosen chord to one octave higher.

The following are the first two paragraphs of Zimmermann's patent. It is clear, upon reading the patent, that Zimmermann has never claimed to have invented a new instrument, but rather "...certain new and useful Improvements in Harps..." These improvements are clearly referred to as "...the appliances constituting my invention..." Zimmermann also refers to "... a harp with my improvements shown as applied thereto." Again, this is a reference to his improvements, not a new instrument.

Charles F. Zimmermann plays his autoharp. No example of this instrument has ever been discovered.

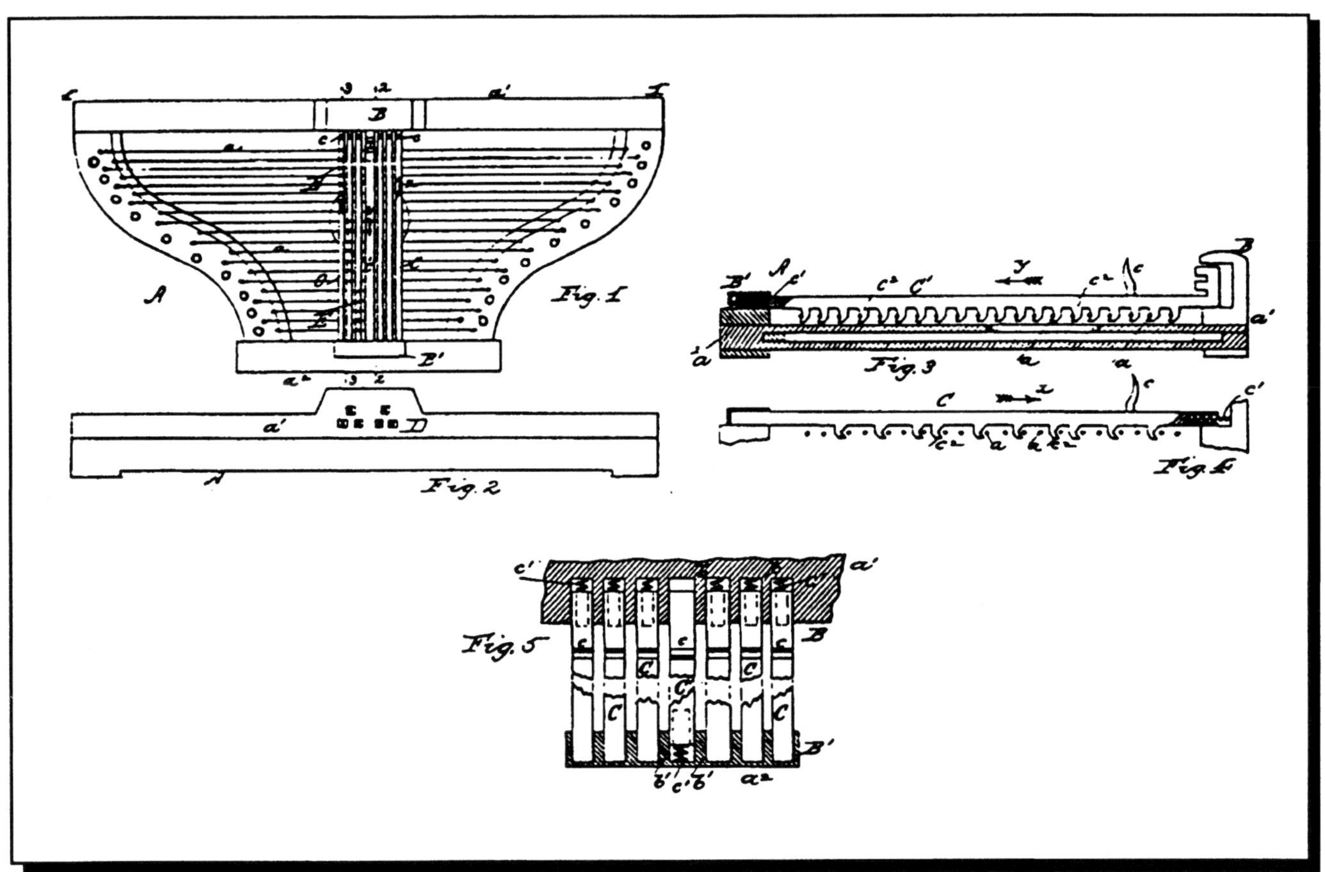

Drawings accompanying Zimmermann's patent for "new and useful Improvements in Harps." No model was supplied with the application for this patent.

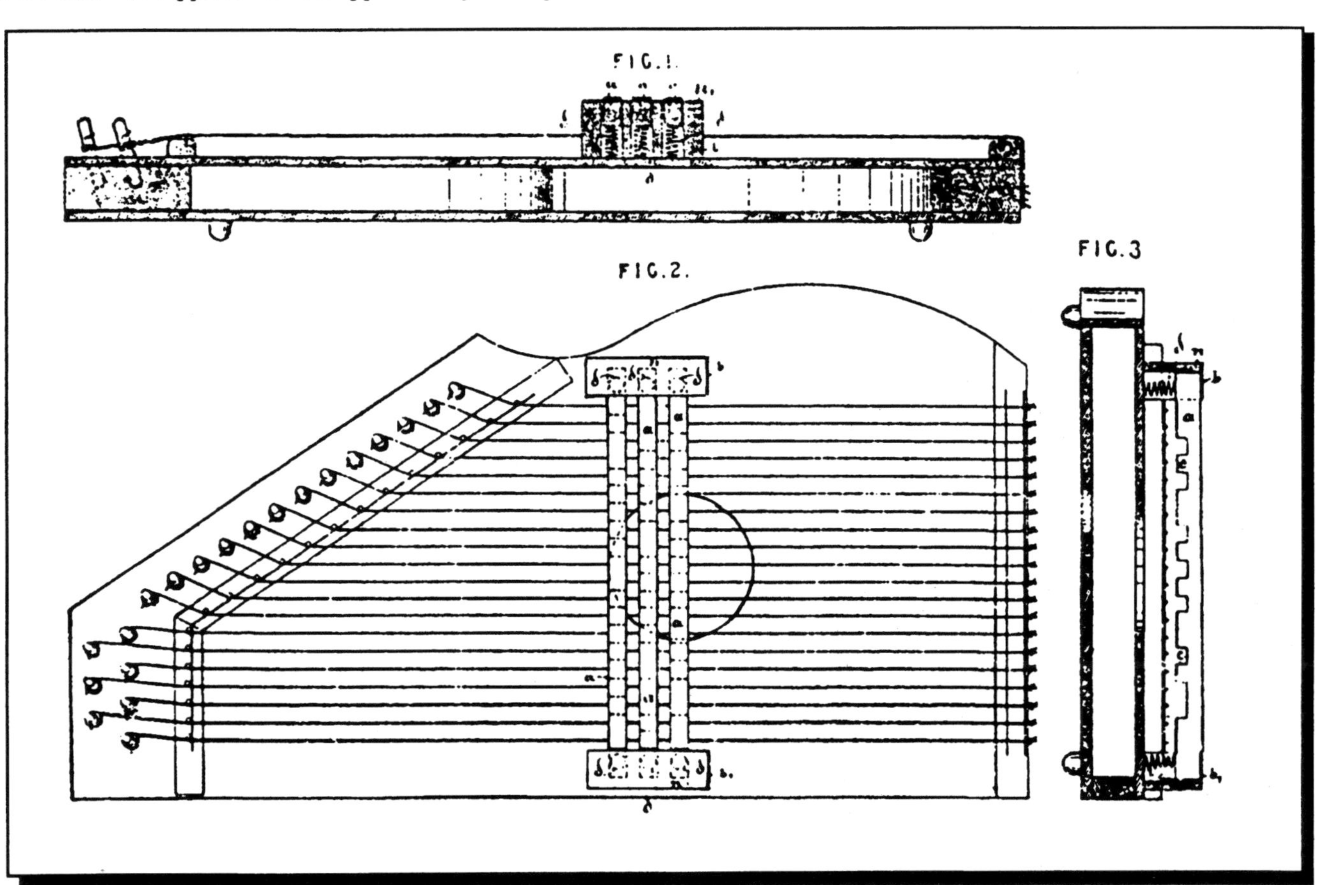

Drawings of Gütter's chord zither. This is clearly the instrument we know as the autoharp. These drawings were communicated to Herbert & Co., Patent Agents in England in 1884.

To all whom it may concern:

Be it known that I, Charles F. Zimmermann, a citizen of the United States, resident of the city and county of Philadelphia, in the State of Pennsylvania, have invented certain new and useful Improvements in Harps, of which the following is a specification, reference being had to the accompanying drawings, wherein – Figure 1 is a plan of a harp with my improvements shown as applied thereto. Fig 2 is an elevation on line 1-1, Fig. 1: Fig. 3 is an enlarged vertical section on line 2-2, Fig. 1. Fig. 4 is a similar view on line 3-3, Fig. 1; and Fig. 5 is a broken plan, partly in section, of the appliances constituting my invention, and shown as drawn to an enlarged scale.

Zimmermann makes one more reference to his invention when he states in another paragraph of his patent, "Such appliances I call 'trigger-bars,' and they are arranged transversely with the strings of the harp. A harp so provided has the size of a zither, and which I term an 'autoharp,' and the manner in which the instrument is played is entirely new." At this point, Zimmermann has very clearly established the concept that any harp outfitted with his invention would constitute an autoharp. To date, no such instrument has ever been uncovered. It can be assumed that at least one instrument was built since we have a photograph of Zimmermann playing it. However, it probably was built after the patent was received since he did not submit a model of his invention when application was made for the patent.

Next, we'll look at Gütter's instrument. The drawing shown is from a British patent which had been "Communicated from abroad by J. M. Grob, of Leipzig, and K. A. Gütter, of Markneukirchen, both in the German Empire." There is no reason to describe this instrument since it is obviously the instrument we call an autoharp today. One can see that it is identical in shape and function to the instrument that Zimmermann produced and called the "autoharp."

According to A. Doyle Moore, the autoharp was not manufactured in Philadelphia until 1885. ("The Autoharp: Its Origin and Development from a Popular to a Folk Instrument," *New York Folklore Quarterly*, Vol. 19, No. 4, December 1963.) This occurred approximately one year after Gütter's British patent was published.

What this all really boils down to is that Zimmermann never produced what he patented and he never patented what he produced. Instead he manufactured Gütter's instrument and called it an "autoharp." He also put his patent number on the instrument – a patent issued for "new and useful Improvements." Had he, in fact, employed his chord bar improvements, then we could give credit to Zimmermann for a new way of playing a harp. However, what we are playing today is actually Gütter's Chord- zither, or "Volkszither," and not Zimmermann's "autoharp."

Tracking down the true inventor of what we call the autoharp was not an easy process. After my first conversation with Mark Fackeldey, I checked out many books which all gave credit to Zimmermann. I then discovered a reference to Gütter in *Grove's Encyclopedia of Musical Instruments*. It listed only his name and where he lived (Markneukirchen, Germany). Further research led me to the Philadelphia Free Library and the Curtis Institute in Philadelphia; the Stearns Collection of the University of Michigan at Ann Arbor; the East German Embassy in Washington, D.C.; the Lincoln Center Library and the Goethe House Library in New York City; numerous museums and libraries in Germany including the Musikinstrumenten Museum der Musikstadt-Markneukirchen; the German Patent Office; and the C. Robert Hopf Company, the only remaining factory still producing autoharps in Germany. One very educational day was spent in the foreign patent section of the United States Patent Office. It was there that the Gütter drawing surfaced. The research was greatly expedited by the efforts of supervisor Bernard Hamilton. Helpful personnel like Mr. Hamilton make every penny of tax money that goes to the Patent Office worthwhile. The Musikinstrumenten-Museum der Musikstadt Markneukirchen also supplied a wealth of information through its museum assistant, Th Kunze.

What did we discover about Gütter? Christian August Gütter was born on July 22, 1823 and died on September 21, 1900. Also, despite what the reference books say, his name was actually Karl, not Christian. He lived his life in Markneukirchen, Germany and had nine children. (Three of those children emigrated to the United States.) Some sources list Gütter as a violin maker and others say that he was a guitar maker. Regardless, it is safe to say that he was the man who gave us the instrument we enjoy today.

In 1883, Gütter sold the rights to the chorded zither to Herman Lindemann from Klingenthal, near Markneukirchen. Lindemann's company traded in all types of musical instruments. Lindemann must have been quite irritated that others were manufacturing an instrument for which he owned the patent. In a monthly journal of 1890, he published the following statement:

Warning:

I warn hereby especially not to buy or sell the recently sold instruments under the name of Chord- zither or Autoharp that are in the mar ket as imitations of my patent "Volkszither." I sued through the district attorney against the manufacturer C. F. Thierfeld against patent rights. Everyone of those individuals should be brought to court who sells these imitations in the stores.

H. Lindemann
The Only Manufacturer of
the Patented and Privileged
"Volkszither"

One question still persists. Why didn't Zimmermann produce the improvements he invented? The answer to this may never be known. Zimmermann had a long history of failed business ventures and perhaps his new design gave him problems when he went to manufacture it. Zimmermann's patent notes that no model was supplied with the drawings. Perhaps he felt that Gütter's design was easier to manufacture than his. It's difficult to reconstruct a history that is shrouded in mystery, but one thing can be postulated: Zimmermann probably learned about the chorded zither during a return trip to Germany where he saw the instrument that was perfect for employing his tone-numbering system which he had patented in 1871.

Many questions regarding the history of Gütter's instrument will also have to go unanswered. According to Messrs. Hopf of the C. Robert Hopf Company in Germany, "Perhaps our father and certainly our grandfather could have given you some information about the 'Volkszither' patent rights and the like but, unfortunately, neither a family chronicle nor other material still exists. We suppose that such documents got lost during or shortly after World War II. And under the socialist system in the former GDR, nobody took an interest in the history of a private firm – just the opposite. Our firm, C. Robert Hopf was nationalized in 1972 and became part of the combined works 'VEB Musikinstrumentenbau Markneukirchen' like Messrs. Rauner which was liquidated as a zither producing firm later on."

Even though we know that Zimmermann did not invent the chord zither, he certainly was responsible for popularizing the instrument in the United States. However, now that the true history of the autoharp is known, it is important to give credit to Karl August Gütter, the real inventor of the instrument we know as the autoharp. ❖

Autoharp Quarterly®

Spring, 1997
Volume Nine, Number Three
Five Dollars

The International Magazine Dedicated to the Autoharp Enthusiast

In This Issue

Improvisation
by Scott Tichenor

Annual Events Guide

Helen Carter Jones
by Ronnie Williams

Les Gustafson-Zook – Long Time Traveler
by John Arthur

Interaction
with Julie Davis

It's Springtime... Felt & String Tips
by Dr. George Orthey

Battlefields, Campgrounds, and the Home Front – Songs of the Civil War
by Alice Ann Whitehall

Erratic Luthier Learns to Read
by Ray Sipes

Mother Maybelle Carter

Oscar Schmidt-International, Incorporated 1879 - 1975

AQ Volume VII, Number 4; Volume VIII, Numbers 1, 2, 3, 4

OSCAR SCHMIDT
1879 - 1975

Glen R. Peterson

This series of articles has been taken directly from transcripts written by the late Glen Peterson and presented to us by Meg Peterson, to document the history of the Autoharp during the Oscar Schmidt – Peterson Era.

The Petersons fought long and valiantly to maintain the name of our instrument as a trademark of the Schmidt company, so in deference to them, we shall print the word, "Autoharp," as Glen wrote it. However, due to their great accomplishments in the expansion in the use of, and improvements in the manufacture of this instrument, "autoharp" is now a part of the English language – a word of common usage. This fact of legitimacy – to be placed among the instruments of the English language – the world – is in truth a giant leap forward for our instrument, and a tremendous and forever tribute to the work of Glen and Meg Peterson.

I have composed this series of articles from separate reports written by Mr. Peterson in 1975. These reports have been copied and interlaced with each other, allowing the articles to follow a chronological order as much as is possible. Early historical discrepancies concerinig the origin of the instrument are due solely to the fact that the true history of the autoharp was not uncovered until 1991.

The words which are in italics, as in this paragraph, are transcribed from a multi-paged unnamed manuscript. The words in normal type, *are copied from a report entitled "Oscar Schmidt-International, Inc. 1879-1975."*

We *thank Meg Peterson for giving us her permission to print this unpublished history written by her late husband, Glen R. Peterson.*

Mary Lou Orthey

Has it ever occurred to you that nobody - not Zimmermann, Dolge, Oscar, Finney, or myself - all people who made a 'success' of the Autoharp was a musical virtuoso? Does Henry Ford drive in the Indianapolis 500? His engines are there. He isn't. He plays a different role. So do we. I once pointed out to Bill Ludwig (owner of Ludwig Drum Co.) that musicians create nothing other than music. And that it is innovators such as him (and me) who dream up the new musical products that permit the musicians to pick up their part of the ball and run with it. He was modestly amazed at the concept.

Think of modern rock music. It was Don Randall and Lee Fender, the guys out there in California who dreamed up the electric solid-body guitar, who really got it going. Without them there would have been no Beatles or a rock generation. To be sure, someone else might have come along and done it - but the fact is that they did it then. To analyze the history of rock music, you must first take into consideration the people who made it possible. And why they did it.

- Glen R. Peterson

Oscar Schmidt was born in the Kingdom of Saxony in the mid nineteenth century. As a youth, he was apprenticed as a bookbinder. When he completed his apprenticeship he went into that business and failed. Under Saxonian laws of the time, this meant that he had not studied properly as an apprentice. He was required to go back and start all over again.

He decided instead to emigrate to the United States. He wound up in the publishing business. This somehow led to the music publishing business which in turn led to opening a rather extensive chain of music schools along the east coast which he supplied with his music.

Apparently this led him into making the instruments his students were using in the schools. When Schmidt died in October of 1929, he was perhaps the largest, certainly one of the largest makers of musical instruments in the world. He died in Karlsbad, Czechoslovakia, on his 76th round trip to Europe where he had four factories. He had three more factories in the U.S. He was involved in literally everything musical except what the industry calls "keyboard" – pianos and organs.

One month after his death came the stock market crash of 1929 and not too long after that the German inflation and the U.S. depression. His estate and his musical empire shrunk down to one leased factory in Jersey City and in 1936 the company was reorganized under the present name. Everything except what the author calls multi-stringed musical instruments (zithers, Autoharps, psalteries, etc.) was sold off. The Harmony Company of Chicago, this country's largest guitar manufacturer, still sells the Stella and Sovereign guitars – former Oscar Schmidt products.

The Autoharp, which today represents the largest portion of Oscar Schmidt sales volume, was not originally a Schmidt product. It was invented in 1883 by a man named Zimmermann from Danzig, which was then part of Prussia. He made them in Philadelphia for five years and then went under. Alfred Dolge, after whom the town of

Dolgeville, N.Y. is named, (he named it), took over the Autoharp and the history books say he parlayed it into "America's most popular musical instrument." Dolge also finally went under, the Autoharp passed to the Phonoharp Company of Boston, Mass., and then Schmidt merged Phonoharp.

With Phonoharp, the Schmidt organization also acquired Mr. Harold Finney, a man who managed the company until his death in 1963. He also owned slightly less than one-third of the stock in Oscar Schmidt-International. This stock today is owned by his widow, Mrs. Lucretia Finney who resides in Cornwall, NY.

Under the terms of his will, Oscar Schmidt's stock (65%) was held in trust for his son Walter, with his widow to receive the income from it. His widow survived until 1958 at which time his stock passed to his son Walter.

Approximately 30 days after this, Walter Schmidt died and the stock passed to his sister, Elsa Schmidt.

In 1963, when Harold Finney died, Elsa Schmidt asked Glen Peterson (her nephew) to run the company for her. He agreed contingent upon an agreement that he would acquire all her common stock. That was arranged and today the 65% is held by Glen Peterson and his family.

The next turning point in the history of the Autoharp came in February 1963 when Elsa Schmidt, one of Oscar Schmidt's daughters and owner of more than two thirds of the company's stock called her nephew Glen Peterson with a panicked announcement – "Mr. Finney is in an oxygen tent. What do I do. Help Me."

Peterson, who had spent a career as a city manager, nonprofit foundation executive, and political campaign manager (but who at the moment was involved in drilling oil and gas wells in West Virginia) was not enthusiastic about helping his aunt. But family is family, she was a woman alone, and he reluctantly agreed to "mind the store" while Finney recovered.

Glen Peterson came into the music industry with absolutely zero experience in it. He had never, since his childhood, ever even set foot in the Schmidt factory. His background was in government, politics and politically-related public relations. In these areas he had an outstanding track record.

But Finney did not recover and about a week later died. Peterson agreed to stick with his aunt, put the books in order, and suggested that she try to sell the company. She did not want to sell it. She begged him to run it and keep it in the family. He told her "I'll run it only if I own it" and Elsa agreed to a deal whereby (for tax reasons) over a period of a few years she would turn over her stock to him and his family.

This photo, made in the Schmidt office at 87 Ferry Street, Jersey City, sometime in the Thirties, shows at left Harold G. Finney, General Manager of Oscar Schmidt-International, Inc; and at right, Walter Schmidt, the only son of Oscar Schmidt.

There is one other stockholder in the company. He is Mr. Fred Reiniger, a retired former director of public relations for the New York Stock Exchange. He owns approximately 3%, a gift from his stepmother who was another of Oscar Schmidt's three daughters. He is completely inactive in the company and lives in retirement in Ocean County, NJ.

During this period, which spanned perhaps two months, Peterson had come to realize that while it was an obviously decrepit operation, it had nowhere to go but up and that it had good potential.

Peterson's misgivings about the company derived from more than the fact that he had never before run a manufacturing operation. For example, he found an office with no electric typewriters, the letterhead hadn't changed in about 50 years, there was only one phone line (which was frequently tied up by employees placing bets with their bookmakers). The company had been running a boiler plate advertisement in a trade magazine and hadn't changed the copy in 20 years, and the woman who packed the accessory envelopes for the harps worked under a 20 watt light bulb so the company could save money. He was used to much classier operations. Perhaps his first change in the company was to go out and personally buy that packer a 100 watt bulb.

(At this point, I will switch to the first person:)

In 1963, I took over a company that was unbelievably decrepit and antiquated. Literally everything about it was over the hill. It occupied two separated floors of a former Schmidt loft building in Jersey City. The woodworking shop (the guts of the operation) was in a sub basement, heated by one 3" steam pipe, and it was not unusual to see workmen wearing overcoats and galoshes to keep their feet dry from the water that came in over the window sills.

Final assembly, finishing, and shipping were on the third floor with everything going up and down one freight elevator which was used in common with two other companies in the building.

The most sophisticated piece of machinery in the operation was a drum sander. Next in order were drill presses. Everything else was done by hand tools.

He was also shocked when he inquired why the words "Manufacturer's Advertising Corporation" were painted on the front door window. He learned that it was a phony company used as a collection agency to dun money from poor farmers down in the Appalachians who had bought zithers or ukelins on the installment plan from one of the three traveling salesmen still involved with the company. He promptly had the words razor-bladed off the door, fired the salesmen, and not long after that abolished the ukelin.

Peterson also began to read the letters of complaint coming into the company – complaints about warping, twisting, panels delaminating, split panels, chord bars that stuck in the holders or rubbed against each other, almost everything. The first production change he ever made came about because he took a harp home and put it on his dining room table. His five children played with it. Then he found massive scratches in the table. Why scratches? Because, he learned, the nails used to put on the feet on the bottom of the harp were given only one swat with a hammer and often protruded. So the first big change was to order that the nails be countersunk. He was warned by the old timers that this would take more time and "raise production costs." He was astounded by such a response and ordered it done anyhow. That mentality on the part of company employees told him he had a big job ahead.

The factory manager, Henry Ruckner, was a man in his fifties who had worked for various Oscar Schmidt companies since he was 12 years old. Peterson once asked him what the model number system was all about. Why the fractions such as on the 2³/₄? What did 73 relate to? He didn't know and said the system was so old nobody knew. Or cared.

Approximately 90% of the output of the company was in the Model 73 Autoharp which came off the line and was put into master cartons. When orders were received a shipping label was attached and the shipment made. This sounds efficient except for the fact that identical instruments were sold by Sears Roebuck, Montgomery Ward, and all music retail stores – and Sears and Wards had them priced below wholesale! Naturally, most retail stores refused to carry the instrument for fear of selling one at list, only to have the customer find out that he/she could have bought it at Sears for less than half the price. This is what I call decrepit marketing, and one doesn't have to spend a lifetime growing up in the music industry to recognize that. Off the record I advised both Sears and Wards (who bought 39% of our output) that they would either have to raise their catalog prices to sensible levels or I would drastically raise my prices to them. They complied.

Oscar Schmidt, he found, had been basically a zither company until rather recently. As late as 1955 zither sales exceeded Autoharp sales. He found old records going back to 1925 when the company made 41,175 total instruments – of which only 1,838 were Autoharps. Most importantly, he learned that Autoharp sales had grown over the years despite, in a sense, any effort on the part of the company. Music educators across the nation had begun to find them useful in elementary classrooms. Aside from Sears and Wards, the company's three biggest customers were direct mail school musical instrument suppliers.

He also designed the "piano key scale label" after Peterson discovered that the old paper one was still keyed to the Zimmermann dream of a new scoring system. But, worse yet, the notes did not line up correctly under the strings because years earlier the printing plate had become distorted and the company never bothered to change it.

Moreover, it was an absolutely archaic manufacturing operation. All of the equipment was outdated and inefficient. The glue used to make the bodies, for example, was nothing but flour and water, despite the fact that much better adhesives were available at almost the same cost.

Not only did the Model 73 Autoharp represent 90% of the company's sales; it had not had one design or materials improvement (except for the replacement of a couple of wooden parts with plastic parts) since its design in 1883. It was a truly lousy and undependable music instrument whose only virtue, from the company's point of view, was that it could be made by a hammer, saw, and drill press by what can only be gently categorized as sub-unskilled minimum wage labor. The volume of complaints and customer returns was so high that at one point (before we redesigned it) Sears advised me that their returns to some control stores were running as high as 40%. Previous management's system for responding to complaints is commonly known as the circular file. Mr. Finney wintered in Florida, and the company was managed by a bookkeeper and the plant manager, a man who had begun his career with the Schmidt organization at the age of 12.

The company had rerun the same institutional ad in our major trade magazine for 20 straight years. The letterhead was designed in 1936 when the company was reorganized. The most sophisticated piece of office equipment was a hand crank adding machine. We had one incoming line.

How can a company like this survive? The Thirties, World War II, and the late Forties were undoubtedly tough and nothing is known about the company's history. Mr. Finney was a non-degreed accountant who kept all company's records only as long as required by the IRS. In the early Fifties the concept of music education in the early grades began evolving, principally at Columbia University. The pioneers in this field latched on to the Autoharp as an instrument that any classroom teacher could quickly and easily learn to play, which needed no musical knowledge or training, and which could therefore be used by the unmusical teacher to accompany the children singing.

There was happily nothing else to equal it for this rudimentary function. Ideally, according to the educators, every classroom should have a piano. But that simply isn't feasible. The schools don't have the money and the teachers don't know who to play them. The only other practical alternative was the Autoharp.

Sales, therefore, grew without any extensive effort on the part of the company as the concept of elementary music education took hold all over the nation.

So the company was profitable, despite the quality of its product and its general style. Unfortunately, over the years the company had paid out a minimum of 85% of its profits in dividends so practically nothing was left for upgrading the plant and the operations. The company had been milked dry by elderly people who were naturally not thinking ten and twenty years ahead. It was profitable because it felt it had a monopoly (which it did) and could tell the customers to go jump – which it also did.

The most unbelievable illustration of this attitude was forced on me when I was told by a music educator that there was something wrong with what we call the scale label, a printed part with a musical scale on it which lines up under the strings on the instrument and tells the player which string is what note. When I checked I learned that the man was correct. Our scale was wrong. I also learned that the error had been known by the company for a long time, that the company had knowingly shipped tens of thousands of incorrect instruments, and that the correction had not been made because this would require the expenditure of $7.00 for a new printing plate!

Equally shocking to Peterson were the manufacturing facilities and also some things he soon learned about the materials used in the harp's construction. Saws which cut up the frame parts and chord bars could not be held to tight tolerances because they were so antiquated. Much of the machinery was still driven by overhead belts. The antique sanding machine used to smooth the panels could not be trusted and could not use fine grain paper. (The company's solution for that was to use a heavy varnish finish which covered up the defects.) The sides were sanded on a "spindle" sander which guaranteed that scratches would be left on the sides. The bottoms were painted a dull flat black – to save money. The woodworking shop itself was in a subbasement that leaked and when it rained heavily water came in and the employees made harp bodies standing in their galoshes or boots. And the basswood panels, which came all the way from southern Minnesota, were stored in this damp humid environment.

Ruckner recognized many of these deficiencies and fired one idea after the other at Peterson for improving things. Peterson picked up the ball and the changes and improvements accelerated. The sander was rebuilt, the varnish was changed to lacquer, the "music rack" was eliminated when Peterson surveyed customers and found that nobody used it – because it wasn't suitable for holding a music book.

He found that the tuning pins, which were made for Schmidt by the company that made pins for most of the U.S. piano manufacturing industry, were raw steel and prone to rust very rapidly in various high humidity areas of the nation. He promptly ordered them finished nickel-plated.

Literally dozens of changes were made in all aspects of the company's operations and the harp itself. Between late 1964 and 1968 when the first "B" models were made there was hardly a month went by that some significant change in harp design, construction, or quality didn't take place. Many of them, such as plating the tuning pins, or tightening up frame tolerances, or using better adhesives, went unnoticed by the consumer.

Perhaps the first major change visible to the consumer was the introduction of the styrene 15 and 12 bar holders. The old 12 chord holder was bakelite – a material too heavy, too brittle, and incapable of being molded to tight tolerances. The old 15 chord holder was made of wood and fiberboard – a slow and expensive system which resulted in many unfilled orders because they couldn't be made fast enough. Peterson had an expensive new mold made and, without fanfare, began using the improved holders.

The next big change was the elimination of the sound-hole. This was one of Ruckner's ideas. He was very familiar with how frequently the basswood panels cracked – sometimes even while on the production line before they were boxed. And Peterson had stacks of letters from bewildered (and angry) consumers. Because such cracks are not repairable Schmidt had to make good on the guarantees. Ruckner, without revealing to Peterson what he was doing, contrived to have "listener tests" made using professional musicians, the company's tuning personnel, and mere laymen listening to Autoharps with and without the sound-hole. His reasoning was that because of all the internal bracing in the harp the hollow "sound box" was too small to be meaningful and the hole served no useful purpose – it was mainly a tradition.

The unwitting listeners uniformly supported Ruckner. They chose the harps without the holes and termed them "sweeter" and "less twangy." That was all Peterson had to hear – and the new harps, without the holes, were immediately put on stream. These [sound-hole] harps had braces that were glued to both the top and the bottom of the harp. They were very near the sound-hole, making the air cavity inside the harp very small and virtually ineffective. The braces also prevented the top of the harp (the sound board) from vibrating independently of the back. Consequently, the sound-hole did very little to increase the volume of the instrument, and it caused the most problems regarding cracking and warping. By eliminating the hole, the harp had fewer production problems, fewer consumer complaints, and since the harp was still hollow-bodied, not solid, it retained its sound qualities. They were not to be reintroduced until Peterson found ways of eliminating the basswood panels and much of the internal bracing.

Peterson was aided in all these changes by two key people – both of whom made dramatic contributions to all the harps in the future. One was Joseph DiPisa, an experienced industrial production manager whom Peterson hired as general manager. He found many ingenious ways to build better harps, and do it at lower costs to offset the costs of the quality improvements. Peterson was constantly introducing – such as the molded end pin cover (for which expensive molds had to be built) which replaced the ugly plastic extrusion used previously, and which itself merely replaced a wooden molding. The economic trade off in that case was that the old extrusions had to be sawed off, mounting holes had to be drilled, and then they had to be painted. The more expensive molded parts weren't really very much more expensive. The sawing, drilling, and painting operations were all eliminated. And the harp was a better and more saleable product.

The most significant contributions to upgrading the Autoharp were brought about by Robert McKay of Bronx, NY. Peterson turned to this old friend of his, an artist, when he needed help to redesign the logo on the "A" model harps and also the archaic and useless "scale label" at the big end of the instrument. McKay created the piano keyboard scale label. He also, early on, redesigned the instruction book given away with each instrument.

Once I had my feet on the ground, once I had learned something of my new vocational environment, I began improving both the product and the company. I brought in brighter people. I killed small volume items and added new models which I thought would be more popular and profitable. I began exhibiting at educational conventions. I generally upgraded the whole operation.

Even as he made one improvement after the other to the standard black harps, Peterson came to believe that there was a demand for a better sounding and better looking harp that would appeal both to the traditionalists and to the new "folk music" fans. In just a few short months he had sought out and had come to know such popular performers of the day as Maybelle Carter, Mike Seeger, Cecil Null, and Tom Morgan. He turned to them for their preferences in such a new instrument. They were delighted to help – and also welcomed the opportunity to finally be able to talk with someone at the factory who would listen to their accumulated complaints.

In 1966, I put us into the publishing business. We put out two books on how to play the Autoharp and three song books. In the last eight years, we have sold approximately 250,000 of these books very profitably. We went into this because, strange as it seems, until that time there were no detailed instructions on how to play the Autoharp available anywhere. These books have been extremely important to the company's economic health and to its image in the industry. They have been copied but never equalled.

Cecil Null, in addition to his assistance in developing the Appalachian, made another, and undoubtedly more enduring contribution. It was he who finally triggered an interest in the Autoharp for Meg Peterson, Glen's wife. A classical violinist, she was completely negative about the Autoharp. From her perspective a poorly made thing which wouldn't stay in tune, that could play only a few chords and sold through Sears for about thirty dollars couldn't even be called a legitimate musical instrument. A guest in the Peterson home, and later as a frequent visitor when he was working for Peterson, Cecil Null taught Meg how to hold the harp up against her chest, how to pick melody, and how to expand the versatility of the harp. He was proud that his own LP was selling, and Cecil showed Meg that the Autoharp was a much more "legitimate" musical instrument that she had ever imagined.

At that time, as a reluctant favor to her husband, Meg was trying to write "The Many Ways to Play the Autoharp." Peterson had recognized that one of the main things holding back Autoharp sales was that there were no instruction or song books available for the people who bought them. A few skimpy things were available, but they were all aimed at school teachers, and none of them even hinted at playing "Appalachian Style." She wasn't really very happy about the whole project. Meg's book wasn't coming along very rapidly. Cecil Null, in a sense, became the catalyst. He triggered her musical curiosity.

Meg's major problem had been to develop a scoring system for picking melody and other strokes and strums normally used on the harp. With input from her husband, Null, and McKay (who plays piano), a system was finally devised that enabled her to finish Volume One and then go right to work on Volume Two. (Since their publication, the "Many Ways" books have probably sold more than 300,000 copies, that they were very profitable for the company, and that it was publishing profits from these books and later the "Parade" series that enabled the company to survive the recessions of the 1970s.)

McKay provided the painting of the Autoharp for the cover of Volume One and did all the graphics for both volumes. Meg sought out Mike Seeger, Maybelle Carter, and John Sebastian, among many other players, to expand her knowledge of the instrument. She had been won over by the Autoharp's charms and has since written or arranged more than 25 publications for the Autoharp.

While Meg continues writing and arranging for the Autoharp, she also keeps very busy with Autoharp instructional workshops across the United States and Canada.

Peterson wasn't satisfied with his improvements (of the Autoharp) and began to design a better-sounding and better-looking instrument. Realizing that much of the growing interest in the instrument was from traditional musicians and the new "folk music" fans, he consulted with the popular performers of the day – Maybelle Carter, Mike Seeger, Cecil Null, and Tom Morgan. They told him what they would like to see in the Autoharp, and by the end of 1963, the first Appalachian model harp was ready for the market. This harp did have a sound hole, but the braces inside were spaced farther apart to give a larger air cavity for increased volume. The Appalachian model also had 15 chords. The three new chords were not diminished seventh chords on the 15-chord Golden Autoharps, however. They were E, A, and D major, chords which are frequently used in traditional and folk-style music.

All of Peterson's advisors asked for a spruce top rather than the basswood. They felt that this would enhance the sound. Peterson located the company which was the major maker of piano sound boards in the United States and made arrangements to have them make the top panels for the new Appalachians.

Actually, the manufacturer was delighted to get the work because it enabled him to use the "wasted" corners which were sawed off the sound boards to conform to the grand piano shape. The closed grain spruce was the finest in the world.

Because the spruce was much more dependable than the basswood, it enabled Peterson to design a sound hole into the Appalachian, and to enlarge the sound box internally. Very few splitting problems were encountered.

The major problem with the original Appalachians was that, because the chord bars were wood, and the new rectangular buttons were now standard (McKay assisted in their design), the buttons would sometimes fall off because the correct adhesive had not yet been found. As a matter of fact, it never was found, which is what gave impetus to the later development of aluminum/plastic chord bars to which the button could be chemically bonded.

The molds for the new chord bar holders were now available and so it was possible to put 15 chords on the Appalachian, to move the holders farther down on the body, and still leave a reasonable amount of space for playing "Appalachian Style." (To the advisors, the problem of playing space above the chord bars was probably equally as important as the spruce top, and the new styrene holders made that possible.) Cecil Null, by then working at the factory, assembled the first test models and finally found the correct location for the holders.

The advisors recommended using E, A, and D major chords rather than the diminished seventh chords, which were standard on the regular 15-chord models. Peterson, who is a great believer in taking advice from people who know more about a subject than he does, put these chords into production.

My decisions were good ones and for a couple of years we made much more money on substantially increased sales. In 1965 and 1966 the federal government poured into the school systems a staggering amount of money. Likewise into the poverty programs. (In 1974, the New York City Schools still had an inventory of un-issued Autoharps purchased by federal grants in 1966!) Some of this found its way to us and our orders went out through the roof. We became heavily back ordered and there was no immediate way out of the trap because: 1. The design of the product was such that it did not lend itself to rapid increases in output. For example, all of our top and bottom resonant panels were made by one mill in Iowa, there was no other mill I could find anywhere which would cut this particular veneer, and this mill was both unwilling and incapable of increasing its output. Our plant was not big enough to accommodate more people, even if I had been able to get more materials. Everything went in and out of one tiny loading dock, we were sharing one elevator, and we were on a narrow one-way residential street in Jersey City. On repeated occasions, truckers either delivering or picking up refused to wait in a lengthy line and left – often with materials we desperately needed.

By late 1965, Peterson was in a trap. Autoharp sales were zooming, and he couldn't fill the orders. The folk music boom was part of it, but Washington and the Great Society programs were also throwing money at the schools and the schools, in turn, were throwing some of it into buying Autoharps. Plus the fact that the company was now making a much better harp. The basswood mill, the tuning pin supplier, the string supplier – nobody could keep up with the orders Peterson was placing with them.

Lockheed and similar companies have a great appeal when they are heavily back ordered. To me, however, our back order position was a giant threat hanging over our heads. An Autoharp isn't all that difficult to make, I reasoned. Unless I whip this back order situation it will occur to someone else in the industry (probably in Germany where they already make a variation of the instrument and where zither know-how is well established) that they can pick up a substantial part of the market with little effort because Schmidt simply can't fill all the orders it has. The musical instrument industry is a tight little family and there are few secrets kept for very long.

Worse yet, it became obvious that the Jersey City factory was incapable of coping with this demand, Peterson subcontracted to have bodies built in Vermont and in Virginia – anything to relieve the pressure on the factory and increase production. When he took over in 1963, orders were about 20,000 harps a year. By late 1965, they were coming in at a rate of over 60,000 a year. Every customer was demanding more, more, more. But Schmidt couldn't produce this.

One answer was obvious. Schmidt had to have a better factory, and in early 1966, Peterson bought a modern plant of twice the size in Union, New Jersey. The Jersey City days, 65 years of Schmidt family involvement in that city, were ended.

Accordingly, at the first opportunity, I moved the plant from Jersey City to Union, New Jersey. This was in the summer of 1966. DiPisa laid out the new factory and moved the machinery – every thing based on the goal of making at least 100,000 harps a year. He installed new, modern paint spray booths, conveyor lines, modern equipment.

For minimum front end money we obtained a good industrial building with both a first and second mortgage. This has proven to be a good investment.

Then, one day John Sebastian of the "Lovin' Spoonful" came to Peterson with an "electronic" Autoharp built for him by some craftsman in New York City. It was a horror. There were three holes cut into the bottom of the body to permit the placement of three contact pickups attached to the underside of the basswood panel. The body was terribly warped. It was not much for a musical instrument. Sebastian realized this and asked whether we, as the original makers, couldn't do better.

Peterson, who knew from his children that the "Spoonful" were at or near the top of a lot of charts, saw this as a golden opportunity. Thus began an orgy of product development and improvement such as the company had never seen.

The new home of Oscar Schmidt-International, Inc. on Garden State Road, Union, New Jersey. The modern 22,500 square foot building was purchased in July 1966

McKay went back to his drawing board to design the all-electronic Autoharp. Peterson decreed that it had to be a solid body all-electric instrument. He also dreamed up the idea, later to be the Cutlass model, of a split channel harp with separate tone and volume controls for the lower bass strings and the higher treble strings so that each side of the harp could be played through separate amplifiers, at varying levels and tone qualities, from different sides of an auditorium – all controllable by the artist. Peterson also told Sebastian that the new harp would have wound magnetic pickups ála Fender guitars, not contact microphones.

What started out as an apparently simple project became very complex. Where do you hook the strings on the bottom, knowing that the current system is nothing more than zither-making going back hundreds of years? How do you keep it consistently in tune, keep the tuning pins from enlarging their holes so that it will never stay in tune? How do you put a brilliant lacquered finish on cheap basswood? How do you build an instrument that, instead of 15 chords really cries out for at least 21 chords? Where do you put the electronics? The design dilemmas were almost endless.

Peterson hired more talent for the effort – all very bright people, their purpose to build the ultimate Autoharp. And he reached deeply into the resources of his raw materials suppliers. Tapping their laboratories and scientists to assist him in doing what had never been done before. Tom Kole, for example, who was later to become Peterson's right-hand man, was a salesman for an aluminum supplier. He was extremely helpful in developing the new chord bars and the extrusion which became known as the "string anchor."

These people worked day and night. Peterson set up a charge account at a nearby motel which also had a good restaurant. Anyone on the team was authorized to eat there, sleep there, and charge it to Oscar. Eighteen hour days and nights were the norm.

The string anchor, for example, had been a major headache. McKay's lovely body design would not permit the old system, wrapping the strings around the end of the instrument and hooking them on to little pins. For six months the team struggled with the problem of how to anchor them on top of the body. Dozens of ideas were tried, models made, and they all failed. Peterson finally conceptualized the successful design on a paper napkin at luncheon one day in that restaurant... Kole confirmed that it could indeed be extruded. With minor variations, it is still in use.

McKay and DiPisa worked more or less harmoniously trying to fit design concepts into production feasibility. McKay would design it, DiPisa would say it can't be made. McKay would go back and redesign.

But the team of Autoharp up-graders didn't work alone. Peterson, through his industry contacts, had enlisted the resources of the Baldwin Piano Company and it was their research people who, for example, suggested using a laminated maple pin block (as in their pianos) and said that it made sense to use vertical rather than slanted tuning pins. Peterson was elated when Baldwin told him that vertical pins would be OK. Vertical pins had become an obsession with him. Why? Because the stringing operation was the biggest headache in the company. It took at least six months for a trainee to master the tricky technique, standing all day in front of a drill press with a slanted bed. Employee turnover was at least 500% a year. Every April, Peterson would have to recruit and begin training ten new stringers to be sure that, when the big demand hit in September and October, he would have, of the original ten, even one proficient stringer still working.

Peterson mandated the new design had to be "stringable" by a person comfortably sitting down and trainable in less than one day. Only a customized homemade machine, using pneumatics, could possibly accomplish that. They knew it could not be done with slanted pins. DiPisa finally designed such a machine. They are still in use and work beautifully. But this is the real reason why the pins have been vertical since 1968 – and one of the major reasons the old "A" models were abolished. They could not be made on the new machinery.

DiPisa made the other big breakthrough when he located a company in Ohio which could build a machine, a giant drill press, which would drill all the tuning pin holes and bridge pin holes – 72 holes in total – in one shot and every hole would be perfect. No longer would a woman stand at a drill press doing them one by one, and, when she was in a hurry, some of them became burned by the heat of the drill and could never hold a tuning pin tightly. This machine, called a Zagar, was the reason why later model harps stayed in tune so much better than any harp ever made. The Zagar cost a lot of money, but it took only 15 seconds to make 72 perfect holes. The previous system took five minutes and resulted in undependable holes.

Peterson also learned through his investigations, that contrary to traditional beliefs, spruce was not the most resonant wood. The Armour Institute at Illinois Tech had determined that hard maple was provably a more resonant wood for use in musical instruments. It was this study which finally led Peterson away from basswood and spruce panels to maple panels. This finally solved the problem of sound hole splitting and cracking. This offended many traditionalists, who were wedded to spruce, but Peterson had the facts on his side and he acted in spite of them. His goal was a better instrument for the mass market.

The team, under Peterson's guidance, then bored in on the problems of a 21-chord holder. Everything was tried, up to and including foam rubber springs to provide a soft touch and eliminate chord bar noise. He also mandated that the whole chord system be contained under a plastic cover and that the bars be movable from one position to another. His target was ultimately a hinged cover which would permit the player to either move the chords, or to change chords, quickly and easily. He never succeeded in that, but that was the goal. Again, McKay designed the cover and participated in designing the new buttons.

The original Cutlasses were all literally hand made prototypes. The first one went to John Sebastian as a gift for being the genesis of this burst of creativity. But they didn't work perfectly and legend has it that one day aboard a chartered plane, Sebastian, trying to get it working properly, grew so frustrated with what he called the "Blue Pig" that he furiously hurled it the length of the cabin and smashed it.

The Cutlass and also the one-pickup Lancer version of the solid body harp were months late in getting into volume production because a very famous musi-

cal electronics company with which Peterson had contracted to produce the pickups failed again and again to make deliveries – and much of what they did finally ship was rejected for quality control reasons. Peterson cancelled the contract and went searching for a better supplier. He finally found one, but the "launching" of the Cutlass and Lancer had been severely crippled, all the expensive publicity was wasted because eager buyers could not find them in the music stores, and the scale of Summit Musical Instruments, (the company Peterson had set up to market these instruments) had to be severely cut back.

In some ways it was a blessing for Autoharps players and fans. Peterson realized that Schmidt now knew enough about building a good harp, that much of what had been learned and developed could be used for an acoustic model to finally obsolete the "A" model.

McKay went right to work on designing the shape and styling of the new "B" model. Peterson went back to the drawing board, and DiPisa struggled with the new machinery and tooling that would be required. Out of this came the one piece pin block (which solved the problem of tuning pins being placed in a glue joint as on the "A" models), the rugged tongue-in-groove frame, the rounded edges (which were intended to solve spray painting problems), and the general shape – which was intended ultimately to permit placing microelectronic components in cavities below the string anchor to create an even better "small" electronic instrument.

We were no sooner in the Union, New Jersey building and operating than we were hit by another flood of orders. This forced us on to overtime in the middle of the summer. But, despite the new building, because of the inherent design of the instrument, it wasn't possible to increase production sufficiently. We also subcontracted some body assembly, but even this was insufficient.

A few words about the significance of the back orders. Approximately one third of our sales went to the major chain store catalog operations, another third went to specialized educational supply companies selling direct mail to elementary schools, and the final third went to wholesalers and a part of that last third also eventually wound up as sales by local dealers to schools. The extreme shortage of Autoharps was therefore well known in educational circles. This makes teachers very angry because when they make up orders in the spring, place them in the summer, they expect the instruments to be on hand when they return to school in September so they can begin the programs they planned in the spring. If they are forced to revise all their lesson plans and wait, perhaps till the following February or even longer for their instruments, they become hostile toward the marketing company they sent the order to, and toward the manufacturer who is always blamed by the marketer for the problem. Autoharps are not like TVs. If the brand of TV you want is out of stock, you can switch to another and still be satisfied. There is only one Autoharp, there is no substitute, and when the teachers can't get them, a giant problem has been created.

Compounding the back order problem was my decision in late 1966 to re-engineer and design the whole product line. (We were no longer just making one basic model. I had developed the "Appalachian" which is by now a fixture on the musical scene and played by many big-name country and western people, and also an educator model which I developed in collaboration with the major textbook publishers and which is now approximately 50% of our Autoharp sales.)

My instincts told me that we were going to get competition, that it would come from Germany, and that it would be better than our instrument. And less expensive.

We did redesign. We then had to retool the plant at substantial expense. We had to retrain our people, at a considerable loss in production efficiency. For a time, we ran both old models and new models simultaneously as we tried to phase in and debug the new model and its production system. Supervisors who could not or would not adjust to the new ways of doing things had to be replaced. Suppliers had to be changed. The whole company was turned upside down and inside out. It was difficult and expensive.

Peterson turned on the pressure to get the "B" model done, and history says that he was lucky he did. The month that the "B" model was announced in 1968 there also burst on the market – the ChromAharp, a Japanese-made version of the "A" model. Its importer was one of Schmidt's biggest school catalog supply companies. Prices were substantially below the Autoharp (this was prior to President Nixon's devaluation of the dollar), and ChromAharp advertising claimed that it... "stays in tune up to 60% longer..." The Oscar Schmidt Autoharp was in big trouble and Peterson knew it. His first step was litigation, charging the importer with violation of seven Schmidt patents, unfair trade practices, and a host of other charges. Schmidt also launched an advertising counterattack in both educational and trade publications. And Peterson cranked up the pressure to get the "B" models out into the market place.

We introduced the new models in February of 1968, about 14 months after we began the project. In the same month, one of my biggest school supply customers, Rhythm Band, Inc., Fort Worth, Texas, filed trademark applications for an instrument called the ChromAharp. They launched this instrument in April, 1968. I was wrong about one thing. My inevitable competition didn't come from Germany. It came from Japan and it came from one of my best customers, an aggressive outfit that had born the brunt of the back order grief and decided to capitalize on it.

On the other hand I was right about one vitally important thing. It was a better instrument than the ones we had been making. It was our basic design but better construction, better finishing, and much more attractive. However, it was not a better instrument than our all-new models and it was this that saved us from being wiped out. Had we not redesigned, had we not retooled, had we not made the investment, there would be no Oscar Schmidt-International today.

As it was, the Texas company (known and hereafter referred to as RBI) moved onto the market ruthlessly.

We had to go into the federal courts in Texas to put a stop to an extremely vicious advertising campaign. They not only went into the educational market via RBI but also into the conventional retail market via our wholesale customers. And they went in with prices roughly 20% lower than ours. Our sales declined but there is no way of knowing how much RBI took from us because there is no way of determining the total market. Conceivably all they took was our decrease in sales. On the other hand, if total national demand was up again in '69 and '70, they took our decrease plus the additional demand.

More than that. Another of our biggest customers, Peripole, Inc., a competitor of RBI (at that time these two companies plus a third company known as Lyons Band Instruments in Chicago, controlled at least 90% of the market for elementary musical instruments, a fact we have determined from repeated surveys among educators) began having extreme financial hard times – and was into us for approximately $20,000. I refused to ship any more instruments.

The upshot is – we lost another big customer for Autoharps, and Peripole began selling the Japanese version. It cost us in sales volume and it cost us in cash. Our legal expenses equalled our recovery from them. This company was finally forced into reorganization, changed its name, fled from Brooklyn to New Jersey, and I believe is known to be in a precarious financial condition. They have been unable to fund a new catalog since 1968.

Ultimately, the importers of the ChromAharp agreed to cease violating Schmidt patents and desist from the tone of their advertising campaign. Schmidt knew that this all had cost a mountain of money in legal fees, but they did not know what damage had been done to sales. They saw that sales were now "plateauing," going neither up nor down. But they also knew that the federal government had cut back drastically on funds for elementary education, the nation was in a "recession," and sales through the Sears catalog were not encouraging. One of the encouraging facts was that Sears tested ChromAharps and decided to stick with the Schmidt Autoharp.

During the 1968-70 period, Schmidt continued to make both the new "B" models for the educational and music store trade, and the old "A" models for the major chain stores. And by now, each of the major chains had its own version.

Another big breakthrough occurred with the development of laminated maple resonant panels which Peterson, guided by his promotional spirit, felt deserved a new name – "Acoustiwood." The original maple panels were five veneers of rock maple all aligned along the same axis. Because a rash of sound hole splits developed the panels were changed to slightly skew each alternate veneer – a solution which worked and did not inhibit the superior tonal and resonant qualities of maple. Basswood had been a chronic headache for Schmidt. There was only one mill in the country which would cut it to Schmidt's specifications – and Peterson happily converted everything to maple. That included the Appalachians of that and recent years. The maple was augmented by a very thin top veneer of spruce to maintain the image of the instrument.

Traditionalist pleaded with Peterson to continue making the "original" Appalachian, but he was satisfied that it was an inherently inferior instrument so the "B" styling was adopted for the Appalachian. Peterson probably committed the ultimate crime among traditionalists by introducing an electronic version in 1970. These bursts of creativity – a new factory, new designs, more personnel, new machinery, a big inventory buildup – took a toll on Schmidt's healthy financial condition. The plateaued sales and the legal fees involved in fighting the ChromAharp made matters even worse.

Summarized, by 1970 the loss of sales to the Japanese competition, the cost of moving, redesigning and retooling, the costs of litigation, the costs of advertising and public relations counter efforts, and especially our inability to raise prices in the face of low-ball Japanese prices, put Oscar Schmidt in a difficult and money-losing financial position. I had done all the right things. I had even cut off dividends back in 1965 in order to put money back into the company. But events beyond our control were the order of the day.

In the spring of 1970, our bank (First Jersey National) asked us to go elsewhere for our credit line. They did not shut us off. They just reduced us to an inoperable level of credit. Management spent the spring and summer of 1970 looking for a new credit line. This was the summer of Lockheed, Penn Central, brokerage back office disasters, and new stock market lows. It is my understanding that our bank was also having several internal problems that year.

Management was unable to find a new line, and in August advised the bank that they either open up the line again or sell us out. Fortunately the bank did not take the latter course. We did however agree to continue our search for a new line.

In the spring of 1970 another significant event occurred. The state of Idaho, on behalf of all of its school districts, extended a bid invitation for 600 Oscar Schmidt Autoharps, or equal. I was not aware of this. Such bid invitations are sent to sales companies, not to manufacturers. When the bids were opened, not one single company had had our Autoharps. The business went to RBI. I called the Lyons Company in Chicago and asked them why they had not bid. They told me that they had "gotten out of the bidding business because there wasn't enough profit in it." I asked why they hadn't so advised me, and they replied that they were sorry.

It was at that point that I decided that extreme steps would have to be taken to recover our educational market and, for all practical purposes, to even survive as a musical instrument manufacturing company.

Schmidt had two basic dilemmas; it had a bigger factory than it needed, and it was a one-product company. If something drastic wasn't done, and promptly, there would be no more Autoharps, no more Oscar Schmidt-International.

This was the genesis of the Music Education Group. We had looked at all sorts of product diversification – furniture, toys, OEM woodworking jobs, guitars, and many other things. None of them, for one or more overriding reasons was sensible and promising of financial turnaround.

One key diversification move we had made was taking over the sales of a line of recorders (small wooden flutes) made in Israel. The man who introduced them to this country, a young Israeli, had built sales to the point where he could no longer cope with the ware housing, shipping, and marketing problems. We took over the whole operation and paid him a fixed annual sum for the use of his trade name. These instruments were and are sold to the same wholesale customers who buy our Autoharps so our actual additional costs amounted only to some catalogs and some factory floor space which we had in excess. This immediately added about $100,000 of profitable volume to our sales, and we needed it badly.

As an aside, printed below are statements made by the Petersons in pub-

lished interviews over their Oscar Schmidt years. The following statements pertain to the years 1964 –1971.

"By 1964 an entire new line of Autoharps was under way. The familiar scroll logo that had appeared on the harps since 1951 was replaced with a more modern trapezoid-shaped design. Rectangular buttons were put on the wooden bars. A 15-chord molded plastic chord bar holder was made which brought the 15-chord model's price down into direct competition with the 12-chord model. The old extruded plastic end pin cover was replaced with a molded plastic cover with rounded edges.

A "standard" model 15-chord harp had the three diminished seventh chords, and in 1965 another 15-chord harp with D, E♭, and F7 chords was introduced. With the Appalachian 15-chord harp, there were now three 15-chord models on the market, and their popularity soon surpassed the 12-chord model. The five-chord model was dropped in 1964. With the exception of the Appalachian model, the harps still were without sound-holes, and a new "keyboard" type of music scale was added beneath the strings at the lower end of the harp.

When the new models went on the market, special models were developed for the mail-order catalogs of Sears Roebuck and Montgomery Ward. Up until 1965 the harps in the catalogs were identical to those in music stores. After that year, however, their harps would be made especially for them. In 1964-65 Sears also had an exclusive "Electroharp" made by Oscar Schmidt, which was the forerunner of the electric Autoharps.

Also in 1964, the Guitaro was introduced. Designed by Peterson and Henry Ruckner, there were two models. One had a sound hole on the back side of the instrument and a resonator attached. The other had the sound hole in the front and no resonator. The resonator model was eventually dropped in the early 70s. The original patent for the Guitaro, filed on June 17, 1963 (issued March 1, 1966), was the first of numerous patents to be issued to the company through 1971. A Guitaro instruction book was published in 1964."

"The first new item to come out of the Union factory was a new chord bar. The old wood bars were easily warped, resulting in poor contact with the strings. The new bar was made of extruded aluminum with styrene tops. The rectangular buttons could now be chemically fused to the plastic top instead of glued. The new bars were immediately put onto the Autoharps. (Patent #3,401,586 filed August 8, 1967, and issued September 17, 1968.)

The Many Ways to Play the Autoharp *instructional books were introduced shortly after the move to Union. The new factory seemed to provide a good environment for creativity and product development. The popularity of the Lovin' Spoonful turned Peterson's thoughts to designing a good solid-body electric instrument which could be used in rock music."*

The Electroharp that had been made for Sears Roebuck Company had a microphone for amplification, creating problems with noise from chord bars. A magnetic pickup was clearly in order and experiments began.

The most significant change ever to be made in the physical design of the Autoharp came in mid-1967 with the first "B-model" harps. An ad in the September 1967 issue of Music Educators Journal *proudly announced that the Autoharp had "been completely redesigned." There were four major changes in the B-model Autoharps: 1) The pin block was laminated maple originally 4-ply, but later increased to 8-ply; 2) The strings no longer went around the end of the Autoharp to hook over the end pins. A slotted aluminum string anchor was fitted into a special groove routed into the lower frame of the harp; 3) The upper soundboard bridge was replaced by individual guide posts (bridge pins) for each string; 4) The tuning pins no longer slanted backwards at an angle, but were perpendicular to the soundboard. A new machine accurately drilled all 72 holes for the tuning pins and guide posts at the same time... efficiently and precisely.*

The new B-model harps came in the same four styles as the previous A-model harps: 12-chord, two types of 15-chord standard models, and the 15-chord "Appalachian" model. Only the Appalachian model had a sound-hole.

Special A-model harps were still produced for Sears and Wards. In 1968 Sears started using their own "Silvertone" brand logo on the harps. In 1972 Sears began to offer the B-model harps in their general catalogs, and no more A-model harps were made. Wards also used their own "Airline " brand on their special A-model harps during this period. Special blackbody B-model harps were made for J. C. Penny, and Autoharps were also offered in the Spiegel catalog.

During 1967-68 the solid-body electric models were developed and ready for the consumer market. On January 25, 1967, Summit Musical Instruments was incorporated. A brochure explained the purpose of the new company:

"Instruments like these, and a market potential that big, called for the formation of a new marketing organization. Summit Musical Instruments is it. Summit will market these Autoharps exclusively through musical instrument retailers. They will not be sold through any other outlets. Our goal is to build a dealer organization composed of wide awake hustlers who see the potential in these instruments and then go out and get fat selling them."

Patent number 3,499,357 (filed July 21, 1967, and issued March 10, 1970) shows the Cutlass model with two pickups: one bass and one treble. Both the Cutlass and the single pickup Lancer were 21-chord models. They were the first to be introduced with the new interchangeable chord bars and plastic chord bar cover. The less-popular and more expensive Cutlass model was dropped in the early seventies.

Two other patents were applied for and successfully granted: One was the logical follow-up to the new electric Autoharps, and another was for a specially designed styrofoam carrying case. Both the pickup accessory and the styrofoam case appear in the 1969 brochure for the new "BH" model Autoharps. For all practical purposes, the BH models were simply B-models which now had sound-holes in them. The sound-hole breakthrough was attributed to the discovery of the trademarked "Acousti-wood," which one can only assume comes from "Acousti-trees" and is naturally suited for the making of "Acousti-instruments." This hard maple made it possible to completely eliminate the internal structural braces. The air cavity was thus enlarged to its maximum, and the sound-

board and back could oscillate separately. The Appalachian, of course, already had a sound-hole, but the soundboard was changed from spruce to maple and the interior braces removed. The first acoustic/electric instrument was offered as an option for the Appalachian 15-chord BH model, bringing the Autoharp line to five models.

Advertisements were not as frequent after 1969, the feeling of the company being that they weren't effective, and most promotion efforts were done by direct mail from that time until 1978. Much of the company's energy in the early seventies was spent in dealing with the newly introduced ChromAharp. The ChromAharp was a Japanese import was distributed in the United States by Rhythm Band, Inc. at prices substantially below the Schmidt Autoharp. The ChromAharp was the first serious competitor to the Autoharp brand and had an immediate effect on Autoharp sales, particularly in the large educational market.

Peterson's response was to diversify the product line and to do that by going into direct competition with his ChromAharp tormentors. A new company would enter the school marketing field – and Schmidt would build many of its products.

On January 12, 1971, another corporation was formed, Music Education Group, more commonly known by its acronym, MEG. McKay designed the logo and laid out the catalog, and MEG in a very few months became a power in the school marketing business. MEG Autoharps were identical to all others. The only difference was they had a MEG logo rather than the regular Schmidt logo. Many of these MEG harps found their way into the recreational music market when school teachers sold them to friends, or bought them for friends at a school discount through the MEG catalog.

MEG was formed to diversify "Oscar" and make full use of the factory. "Oscar" made most of the products for MEG, but MEG was a separate company aimed directly at music educators. It carried a full line of school musical instruments, including the ever-popular classroom Autoharp. MEG permitted Schmidt to experiment with various models to test market reaction. A 21-chord model, not then available to regular music stores, was introduced. Also an electronic version of this instrument was introduced. These were basically "B" models with the 21-chord system and Peterson termed them "C" models. The 15-chord model with three diminished chords was dropped from the line because there was very little demand for it. Perhaps most importantly, in 1973 Schmidt introduced the "Attache" Autoharp. Peterson thought he saw a market for a "backwards" Autoharp (with the player depressing the chords with their left hand and stroking with their right hands without crossing the hands), built into its own molded plastic case. He knew that countless repairs to harps resulted from people buying an expensive instrument and then transporting it in a cheap cardboard case, or even in the original corrugated shipping carton. The Attache would solve those problems. McKay again added his talents and handmade the first Attache. Later, the Attache was made available to the general retail trade and a 21-chord model was developed.

Company records indicate that by 1978 more than half of all Autoharp sales were 21-chord models. Peterson's reasoning (going back to 1963), and he is not a musician, was that the more flexibility the Autoharp had, the more he would sell. This was why he abolished the 5-chord harp, why he invested heavily in the 15-chord harp, and later bet the chips on the 21-chord harp.

Perhaps more importantly, taking over a line of recorders also made the task of putting us into the educational sales business much easier. We already could supply Autoharps which are a big part of the market. We could now supply recorders, which, while they are not a big market item in the elementary schools, are never the less a must if you are going to offer a complete product line. To go without recorders would be like running a super market where you could by food but couldn't buy a box of laundry soap.

To round out the essential product line, we had to internally develop the capability of making school-type tone bar instruments – commonly called xylophones. They are pictured in the Music Education Group catalog. The remainder of the products necessary for such a sales effort could be obtained at the necessary prices from conventional sources.

Accordingly, we began developing these xylophones. One might raise the question of the wisdom of "doing it yourself" and suggest that the fast and inexpensive way would be to buy them from someone else. The reality is that there is no company anywhere in the world which makes these particular bells other than our two competitors, RBI and Peripole. RBIs are made in Japan, and Peripoles are partially subcontracted because they have neither the competence nor the manufacturing capability of producing them. It may not sound credible, but if we had to have bells (which we did) we had to make them ourselves.

It, again, may sound incredible, but all of the bell sets were designed in one summer by my teenage daughter, and the teenage son of a neighbor. They drew specs and then reduced the specs to a manufacturing process which permits us to make such tone bars better, faster, and cheaper than anyone else in the world.

Musical instrument dealers had been unable to compete because they were unable and unwilling to stock the approximately 1,000 separate items required to service this market. My MEG plan offered them a central national inventory, drop shipment to the schools, and billing to the dealer by MEG. It also offered them ready made know-how in the elementary market, an area in which even the educational music store was and is woefully weak because the mail order companies had effectively kept them out of it. They knew how to sell horns and violins; but they didn't know how to sell flutophones and resonator bells.

My MEG plan shifted the cost of catalog preparation, plus mail distribution, plus the capital requirements for carrying school credit from MEG to the participating dealer. Schools are not fast players and this latter aspect was crucial to the success of the venture.

Thus, with a minimum cash investment, with the use of the Oscar Schmidt credit line, and with the good wishes and help of almost the entire music industry, the MEG operation was launched and is now a provable success – not only in its basic goal of saving Oscar Schmidt – but in its conventional function as a business.

Dealers were very carefully chosen. There are less than 100 of them. In Georgia, Ken Stanton Music owns school music in Georgia. Our dealer in Minnesota has a free incoming WATTS line for educators. Our one dealer in South Carolina owns educational music in that state. Our dealer in Columbus, Ohio, is national president of NAMM.

MEG dealers also include: C. H. Duncan, our dealer for the western portion of North Carolina, is president of the National Association of School Music Dealers. Not all of our dealers can be presidents, but they are certainly a first-class group of retailers.

Harps marketed by MEG had the MEG logo on the soundboard, but otherwise they were the same instrument as the standard Autoharps. Two new models were introduced in 1971: the acoustic 21-chord and an acoustic/electric 21-chord. The bodies of the 21-chord acoustic harps were the same as the standard BH models, but due to the unique chord bar assembly, these new harps were called "C" models.

The 15-chord model with the three diminished seventh chords was dropped from the line, and around 1972-73, MEG introduced the first Attache model designed for the teacher to play on top of the desk. It was a 15-chord model, also with the MEG logo. Also in 1973 production was begun on their own brand of Orff instruments. In 1975, MEG Autoharps were renamed the "Educator" models. A 21-chord Attache model was finally offered to the general public that year, and the Appalachian model was changed from a 15-chord model to a 21-chord model. By 1978, the 21-chord models would account for more than 50% of the new Autoharp sales.

In 1977, Schmidt continued to diversify its products. Dulcimers were added to the line, and in the June 1977 issue of "Musical Merchandise Review" Schmidt announced the new "Redondo" guitars. Reflecting on the original Schmidt corporation's selling its guitar business to the Harmony Company, the announcement continues with, "Now history has sort of come full circle. In March 1977, we acquired much of the fine guitar making machinery owned by Harmony, and moved it to our plant in New Jersey. Our affiliate company, Omniguitar, is now in production on a full-line of the most beautiful, most saleable, economy guitars ever made in the U.S.A.."

In three years MEG sales went from nothing to $387,000 in 1974. When the dealer markup of 42% is added this means we have made a penetration of more that $550,000 in the elementary market. This may not seem like a very big sum, but in this market it is. Moreover we are punishing our competition, not just taking expansion and growth business away from them. We beat the theme of "Keep your money in your own home state," – and it has worked very nicely everywhere except in Texas.

Equally important, we have cut the Japanese imitation Autoharp down to manageable proportions. They are no longer beating us on bids, and their invasion of the retail store market has been aborted. The wholesaler who was heading it up and handling national distribution is now back on our customer list. At the 1975 music industry trade show in July there was not one single Japanese imitation displayed by any of the exhibiting wholesalers.

Ludwig, again, is the other U. S. company called the Orff Company. There are no others in the United States, and in the whole world there are only three other significant companies: in England there is "Premier;" in Germany there is "Studio 49," (the originators of these instruments and the dominant force in them); and "Sonor," a company affiliated with the Hohner organization of harmonica fame.

Back to the MEG Game Plan. To reach the elementary music market, one must somehow reach 60,000 schools, 4,000 colleges, and an unknown number of miscellaneous musical personnel. (The national music educators organization refuses to make its membership lists available.) This must be done with a catalog offering a complete array of instruments, accessories, and publications used in the schools.

To direct mail all these schools, to pay the postage, prepare and print a competitive catalog, to have an opening inventory of product, to have a trained staff ready to go, was financially impossible either for Oscar Schmidt (assuming Oscar would own MEG) or to me personally, assuming I owned it.

Form follows function, but form also sometimes follows necessity as well. My solution to the dilemma was to franchise the concept to a select group of music retailers across the country who were already heavy in band instrument sales, to charge them for the catalogs and mailing, and to give them a territorial exclusive so they would have a sufficiently large furrow to plow to make money. These dealers had traditionally been unable to compete against RBI, Peripole, and Lyons, all three of which were well known to music educators and who sold direct mail at discounted prices.

A basic element of the MEG Game Plan was to use Oscar Schmidt as a manufacturing base whenever possible and thereby diversify it and insulate it to the maximum possible extent against the ups and downs, (both real and anticipated) in the Autoharp market.

That goal has been achieved. Oscar Schmidt today is either first or second in the nation in the manufacture of tone bar type instruments for educational purposes. There is no number three. The other company is the Kitching Division of Ludwig Industries in Chicago, the world's largest drum manufacturer. The competence and techniques developed in making small inexpensive school xylophones has led us into being an OEM manufacturer for the Slingerland Company (Number two in drums), into marching band bell lyres, and into being the only other company in the U.S. making what are known as Orff instruments.

MEG was not enough to solve Schmidt's financial problems. More diversification, more intense use of the factory, were required. So Schmidt developed and began marketing its own line of Orff instruments, for use in elementary education. All other lines were imported from Europe and Peterson reasoned Schmidt could make them just as well, and less expensively. His vision today seems to have been accurate. Schmidt is a major factor in the Orff market.

This was still not enough production or diversification to satisfy Peterson. In 1977 Schmidt bought the assets of the Codé Corporation, a minor guitar maker in Jersey City which had been originally started back in the 20s by ambitious ex-employees of the old Schmidt empire. In 1977, Schmidt bought at auction most of the significant production machinery of the Harmony Guitar Company in Chicago. Harmony, which later became the biggest guitar maker in the nation, started up with the remnants of Oscar Schmidt's guitar business. The legendary "Stella" and "Sovereign" guitars were originally Oscar Schmidt guitars. Millions of American children learned guitar on

Stellas. As Peterson announced in trade journals in June 1977, "... history has now come sort of full circle."

Peterson moved all the Harmony and Codé machinery into the Union plant and launched a company he called Omniguitar. His announced goals were to carve out a portion of the low priced guitar market in the U.S.A. with instruments made in this country. (Meg Peterson: "He also started making high quality dulcimers and thumb pianos. But he never charged enough to cover the high labor costs of these beautiful instruments.")

Then another opportunity struck. Peterson learned that through quick and decisive action he could buy, out of bankruptcy, a company in Holland known as "C.F. Martin/Netherlands," a company authorized by the legendary U.S. guitar maker in Nazereth, PA to make its instruments and use its name worldwide. Within 18 hours, Peterson flew to Holland and after two weeks of negotiation with Dutch banks and the Dutch government, obtained an option to buy what was probably the most sophisticated guitar factory in the world.

He returned home, ecstatic. He now had it all together. Add Autoharps to Orff instruments to dulcimers to economy guitars to professional guitars, and the company was invulnerable. (Meg: "All he needed to do was to raise $500,000 in three months.")

But he was wrong about the company's vulnerability. He returned to find that, for a number of reasons, many of them attributable to his lack of attention to the nitty-gritty of financial detail, he was now seriously financially overextended. He became a rerun of Alfred Dolge. History was repeating itself.

In the spring of 1978, Peterson took OSI into a voluntary Chapter XI bankruptcy – protecting it from its creditors and permitting it to operate under tight governmental controls.

A receiver was appointed and production carefully regulated until a suitable buyer could be found. Peterson continued as President and "debtor in possession," producing harps, but with all other products except Orff either severely restricted or eliminated. In October of that year, the company, Oscar Schmidt International was purchased by the owners of Fretted Industries, Inc., Northbrook, Illinois, owned by Rudolf Schlacher and Richard Johnstone.

Epilog by Meg Peterson
July 1996

We were dumb-struck! How could this have happened? We went into bankruptcy with a building worth $500,000, and $500,000 in receivables. When we returned from Holland, we discovered that a disgruntled employee, our comptroller, had squirreled away $75,000 worth of checks made out to the federal government for withholding taxes. He had lied to Glen about covering this important obligation. The signed checks were found in his desk. Of course, nobody messes with the federal government, and they promptly put a lien on our building. The bank shut off our line of credit, so we couldn't fill our outstanding orders. The money had run out. It was a sad day at OSI. We limped along for a couple of weeks, trying to generate enough business from inventory to pay the government, but it didn't work. Exhausted and discouraged beyond belief, we had lost.

Glen's tenure at Oscar Schmidt was marked by constant struggle and constant challenge. This is how he looked at it. He was excited about taking the lowly Autoharp – an obscure, almost extinct instrument – and designing it into a quality instrument that can proudly take its place in the lexicon of American musical history. He was its potential, first in music education, and next as a popular expression of a human being's desire to make music. Music for everyone, he used to say, whether simple strumming or melody picking. It didn't matter. It makes people happy. It creates fellowship. It gives them a chance to participate in music at whatever level they choose. But he knew that it would never be accepted widely until it could stay in tune, stand up under difficult conditions and produce a mellow, pleasing sound. The old black instruments warped and pulled apart. Their strings rusted and their twangy sound was at times unbearable.

Glen's efforts to improve the instrument were tireless. Once I went into the plant to locate a racket that threatened to bring down the building. "What's going on?" I shouted over the din. There were Glen and Joe DiPisa slamming Autoharp bodies on the cement floor to see how long it would take to break them. All they managed to do was chip the plastic chord bar holders. "Have you any idea what kids can do to a musical instrument in the classroom?" he asked. "Nothing like that, I hope," was my reply.

Yes, Glen wanted quality and durability. He made sure the frames were solidly built! He was also a patriot, and he wanted these instruments made in the United States. He felt that the strings and wood were better here than in other countries. The metal wouldn't rust; the wood wouldn't crack. And Americans would have jobs. This was the kind of man he was. Ask anybody. Glen believed in self reliance. He believed in solving a problem. And he would never cheat on quality. I think he would be overjoyed to see the beautiful offshoots of his Autoharps made by skilled craftsmen and luthiers across this land. It would have been worth all the struggle to keep this instrument alive and well and living in the United States.

Glen was a man with a dream. He thought big, sometimes too big. He lost the battle, but he won the war. The Autoharp is here to stay! ❖
